Psychophysiology

Psychophysiology
Human Behavior and Physiological Response

John L. Andreassi
Department of Psychology
Baruch College
City University of New York

New York   Oxford
Oxford University Press
1980

Copyright © 1980 by Oxford University Press, Inc.

Library of Congress Cataloging in Publication Data

Andreassi, John L
 Psychophysiology.

 Bibliography: p.
 Includes index.
 1. Psychology, Physiological. 2. Human behavior.
I. Title
QP360.A53 152 78-31655
ISBN 0-19-502581-4
ISBN 0-19-502582-2 pbk.
Since this page cannot accommodate all the
copyright notices, the pages at the end of this book
constitute an extension of the copyright page.

Printed in the United States of America

For my wife,
Gina,
and our children,
John, Jeanine, and Cristina

Preface

The material for this book was originally gathered and organized for a course which I introduced at New York University's School of Engineering and Science. Since that time, the material has been presented several times to psychology majors on an undergraduate level and to students on both undergraduate and graduate levels at NYU and Baruch College of the City University of New York. The objectives of the course were to provide students with elementary information regarding the anatomy and physiology of various body systems, methods of recording electrical activity of these systems, and ways in which these measures have been correlated with various aspects of human behavior and performance. These are also the objectives of this book.

Concepts in the field and applications of physiological measures in practical situations are presented to provide a conceptual framework for this research area and to illustrate the use of these measures in real life. A separate chapter is devoted to the rapidly developing area of biofeedback applications. Psychology students, students in other life sciences, and biomedical engineering students should find useful basic information in this presentation. The beginning researcher and interested professional were also kept in mind as the text was being written.

This book reflects my own research interests in the form of relatively extensive coverage of event-related brain potentials and behavior. Very helpful encouragement and research support for studies under the general heading of "Evoked Cortical Potentials and Information Processing" have been provided to me by the Physiology branch, Office of Naval Research, over the past several years. Dr. Donald P. Woodward, project officer for ONR, has patiently read and made valuable comments on a preliminary draft of the entire manuscript. Mr. Joseph A. Gallichio and Ms. Nancy E. Young also read and commented upon the entire first draft from the student's point of view. In addition, Ms. Young assisted in organizing the bibliographic materials and Ms Janice Coburn helped in preparing the subject index.

A number of individuals graciously agreed to read and comment upon the first draft of one or more chapters. To these persons I am greatly indebted because they provided important insights into areas with which I was not thoroughly familiar, suggested additional references, and in general helped to improve the presentation of material. These individuals are: Dr. Joseph Arezzo, Albert Einstein College of Medicine; Dr. Jackson Beatty, University of California at Los Angeles; Dr. Robert H. Browner, New York Medical College; Dr. Robert G. Eason, University of North Carolina at Greensboro; Dr. Arthur Gaynor, Montefiore Hospital and Albert Einstein College of Medicine; Dr. James H. Geer, State University of New York at Stony Brook; Dr. John D. Gould, IBM, Thomas J. Watson Research Center; Dr. Rafael Klorman, University of Rochester; Dr. Susan J. Middaugh, Medical University of South Carolina; Dr. Walter Ritter, Lehman College, City University of New York and Albert Einstein College of Medicine; Dr. Stover H. Snook, Liberty Mutual Insurance Co.; Dr. Walter W. Surwillo, University of Louisville School of Medicine; Dr. Joseph J. Tecce, Tuffts University School of Medicine and Boston State Hospital; Professor Bernard Tursky, State University of New York at Stony Brook; and Dr. Robert C. Wilcott, Case Western Reserve University. I am also indebted to Bob Wilcott for introducing me to psychophysiology. Any conclusions in this book, and any shortcomings that remain, are solely my responsibility and cannot be attributed to any organization or person.

Others who deserve special thanks are my parents, Agnes and Croce, and siblings George, Eugene, and Matilda for their faith in me, Mr. William Halpin and Mr. Marcus Boggs of Oxford University Press for their faith in the project, Ms. Nancy Amy of Oxford for her editorial assistance, Ms. Joyce Hyman for her typing of the entire manuscript from initial to final draft, and my wife Gina and children John, Jeanine, and Cristina who provided emotional support and numerous refreshing moments during the many hours devoted to working on this book.

New York
September 1979

J.L.A.

Contents

1. Introduction to Psychophysiology   3
2. The Brain and Measurement of Its Activity   13
3. The EEG and Behavior: Motor and Mental Activities   35
4. The EEG and Behavior: Sensation, Attention, Perception, Conditioning, and Sleep   48
5. Event-related Brain Potentials and Behavior: Measurement, Motor Activity, Hemispheric Asymmetries, and Sleep   70
6. Event-related Brain Potentials and Behavior: Mental Activities and Sensory, Attentional, and Perceptual Functions   92
7. Event-related Slow Brain Potentials and Behavior   122
8. Muscle Activity and Behavior   144
9. Electrodermal Activity and Behavior   173
10. Pupillary Response, Eye Movements, and Behavior   199
11. Heart Activity and Behavior   227
12. Blood Pressure, Blood Volume, and Behavior   262
13. Applications of Physiological Measures to Practical Problems   281
14. Biofeedback Applications to Clinical Problems   303
15. Concepts in Psychophysiology   327

Appendix I—Environmental Influences on Physiological Responses   355
Appendix II—EEG Recording System   387
Appendix III—Laboratory Safety   389
References   393
Index   462

Psychophysiology

Introduction to Psychophysiology

The field of psychophysiology is concerned with the measurement of physiological responses as they relate to behavior. The behavioral situations that may be studied range from basic emotional responses (anger) to higher cognitive processes (thinking). In fact, the student will find that in this text the word "behavior" is used broadly to encompass a variety of human activities such as learning, problem solving, sensing, perceiving, attending, and motor acts. The physiological responses might include brain, heart, and muscle activity, among others. Thus in psychophysiology, we may be interested in heart rate changes that occur in response to unexpected stimuli or in brain activity patterns recorded while an individual solves a problem. Speed of response and related muscle activity may also be a topic of study, as well as eye movement patterns when a person searches for a specific target among other visual stimuli.

The underlying premise in the conduct of these kinds of studies is that the information obtained will enable us to better understand the relations and interactions between physiological responses and behavior. Ultimately, this understanding will allow the development of conceptualizations regarding physiology-behavior relationships, an endeavor that is examined in the final chapter of this book. At this point it would be instructive to take a brief look at the historical development of psychophysiology.

Historical Development of Psychophysiology

The rationale for the psychophysiological approach stems from a desire to know more about ongoing behavior which is not discernible through mere observation. Just as a blood sample tells a physician something about the physical condition of an apparently healthy patient, a sampling of heart rate may tell the psychophysiologist something about the emotional state of an outwardly calm individual.

How did this desire to know more about body-behavior relationships develop? Records of when man first asked about psychophysiological relationships do not exist. It is reasonable to assume however, that very early man must have wondered about the source of his thoughts and other mental activities. There is evidence that Stone Age cavemen associated distressing thoughts or evil spirits with the inside of the head, because trephined[1] skulls have been found among the remains of cave dwellers (Coleman, 1976). Trephining was sometimes performed in medieval times to allow evil spirits to escape from inside the heads of tormented or deranged individuals.

One of the earliest recorded expressions of a relationship between a body organ (brain) and mental events is found in the writings of Hippocrates, the father of medicine (Penfield & Roberts, 1959). About 500 B.C., Hippocrates wrote that the brain is the organ by which we experience sights, sounds, thoughts, joy, laughter, sorrow, and pain. He wrote further that the brain is our interpreter of conscious experience. Plato, who lived four centuries B.C., also believed that mental activities were localized in the brain. He and other Greek philosophers of his time were concerned with the body-mind problem or the relationship between physiological activities and mental events. Aristotle, who lived three centuries B.C., taught that the seat of mental functions was in the heart. The Roman physician Galen, who lived in the second century A.D., supported the idea that the mind is located in the brain. Galen's position was widely accepted

---

[1] A trephine refers to an opening in the skull which, at one time, was made by chipping away one small area of the skull.

through the Middle Ages without much refinement. It was not until the 19th century that the experimental investigations of Flourens clearly related different brain areas with various animal behaviors, such as visual perception and voluntary movement (Boring, 1950).

Thus, early philosophers and later physiologists devoted thought and experimentation to understanding the physiological bases of behavior. French physiologists of the 19th century held that the brain is the center for perception, intelligence, and judgment but that emotions are generated by the internal organs (Boring, 1950). In the late 19th century, this idea influenced what is now known as the James-Lange concept of emotional behavior. This concept holds that an emotional state is experienced because of the internal events, such as increased heart rate and muscle activity, produced by a provocative stimulus. Thus, according to the James-Lange theory, if we encounter a frightening event, we feel afraid because we run; we do not run because we are afraid! The perception of danger occurs first, then escape behavior, and finally the feeling of fear. This concept was opposed by the Cannon-Bard theory of the 1930s, which proposed that an emotional state resulted from the influence of lower brain centers (hypothalamus and thalamus) upon higher ones (cortex) rather than from impulses produced by internal organs. Thus, danger is perceived, fear is experienced, and we flee the threatening situation.

Concepts that have implications for understanding the physiological correlates of emotional behavior and for integrating data in the field of psychophysiology are presented in the last chapter of this book. It is clear, however, that throughout recorded history, the brain has been a focal point in attempts by physicians, philosophers, physiologists, and psychologists to understand behavior.

Contemporary Psychophysiology

In the last 15 years, there has been a tremendous growth in the number of research studies in which physiological measures, as well as behavioral ones, have been taken in the course of studying human activities and performance. That this particular field has been growing rapidly is evidenced by the increasing number of publications in the area, as well as by the increasing number of universities that offer courses and training in psychophysiology (see Feuerstein & Schwartz, 1977; Johnson & May, 1973).

Applications of Psychophysiology

There is currently a growing trend toward applying psychophysiological techniques and information to practical problems. No single area illustrates this widespread interest in applications of psychophysiology as does the discipline known as biofeedback. In recent years, biofeedback training (BFT) has been applied to a wide variety of human ailments ranging from tension headaches to asthma. There is, in fact, suggestive evidence that the provision of feedback (information) about muscle activity in the throat and facial areas may help in treating the common speech disorder known as stuttering. Because of the large number of biofeedback studies completed in recent years, as well as the potential importance of this field, a separate chapter has been devoted to this area (see chapter 14).

Chapter 13 presents examples of psychophysiological applications ranging from the controversial procedure of lie detection to the study of behavioral disorders. An important and very recent psychophysiological application involves the use of event-related brain potentials to study sensory capacities. For example, vision and hearing tests of young infants have been accomplished with this physiological measure.

Psychophysiology and Physiological Psychology

You may ask how psychophysiology differs from the discipline known traditionally as physiological psychology, and the answer is that it is mainly in the approach and subject matter of the two areas. To summarize and paraphrase some distinctions made by Sternbach (1966): *Psychophysiologists* typically take several surface measures simultaneously; do not make permanent changes in the organism; use stimuli that are designed to influence mental, emotional, or motor behavior; and the investigators are not necessarily psychologists. The *physiological psychologist,* on the other hand, often uses animals other than humans as subjects, takes measures through chronically implanted electrodes, may make permanent changes in the organism through lesions or ablations in some physiological system, and usually has had major training as a behavioral scientist.

Importance of Brain Measures

In this text, psychophysiological studies that relate brain activity to behavior will play a prominent part in the overall presentation. This is because the brain is the central organ of behavior. Without it we would not be able to think, move, create, or perform any of the complex functions that we associate with human endeavors. However, other physiological measures such as heart and muscle activity provide important insights into behavior which may not be directly available through the study of brain activity. For example, regular increments in muscle potentials have been associated with increased rewards for efficient performance in a motor task. Such continuous close relations between brain activity and incentive increases have not, as yet, been reported.

Another reason for the prominent position given to brain measures in this text is the surge of this type of research over the past 15 years. Much of this has been the result of the application of computer technology to the study of brain processes, enabling scientists to obtain a number of new measures, particularly event-related brain potentials (ERPs). This latter measure enables the study of brain responses to specific stimuli. Various brain measures and related research are presented in chapters 3 through 7.

Physiological Measures in Relation to the Nervous System

The measures taken by psychophysiologists may include one or more of the following: the electroencephalogram (EEG), the event-related brain potential (ERP), the electromyogram (EMG, a measure of muscle activity), pupillography (measures of changes in pupil size), electroculography (EOG, a measure of eye movement), electrodermal activity (changes in sweat gland activity), heart activity, blood volume, and blood pressure. Some other measures obtained by psychophysiologists, but not treated extensively in this text, include respiration, oxygen consumption, salivation, and skin temperature.

The average scientist in this field normally focuses on one or several of these physiological measures, but usually not all of them, at any one time. An example of multiple physiological measurements and how some people may view the scientist in this field is illustrated in Figure 1-1.

The physiological measures outlined above are all under the control of the nervous system. The nervous system is highly integrated, but for the sake of convenience, we can list the various

Figure 1-1. How some people view the psychophysiologist at work.

"NOW I WANT YOU TO RELAX COMPLETELY!"

measures as being primarily controlled by one or another subdivision of this system. First, a brief diagrammatic summary of the nervous system is in order. As can be seen in Figure 1-2, it may be divided into two main branches, the central nervous system (CNS) and peripheral nervous system. The CNS includes the brain and spinal cord. The peripheral nervous system refers to nervous tissue outside the brain and spinal cord, including the cranial and spinal nerves. The peripheral nervous system is further divided into the somatic system, concerned with muscular activities, and the autonomic nervous system (ANS), which controls visceral structures (glands and organs of the body). Finally, the ANS is subdivided into the parasympathetic nervous system (PNS), the innervation mechanisms of which are dominant when the individual is at rest, and the sympathetic nervous system (SNS), which is dominant in situations requiring mobilization of energy. The PNS can be thought of as a system of rest and repair, while the SNS is a system of energy mobilization and work. The schematic drawing in Figure 1-2 is imperfect, since there are parts of the ANS that are in and under the control of the CNS, for example, the hypothalamus and medulla of the brain are important in the control of ANS functions.

The assignment of physiological measures to the nervous system and its subdivisions from the point of view of general control of function would lead to the organization shown in Table 1-1.

Many of the responses of interest are controlled by the ANS, and this is a very important system for the field of psychophysiology. The student interested in obtaining more information about the anatomy and physiology of the ANS can consult such texts as those of Pick (1970) and Gardner (1975).

Aims and Organization of this Book

The primary aim of this text is to illustrate the kinds of questions being asked by researchers, the studies they are conducting, and the conclusions that are being drawn or that seem justified at this time. Conclusions are provided at the end of each major section of each chapter. In some cases, specific conclu-

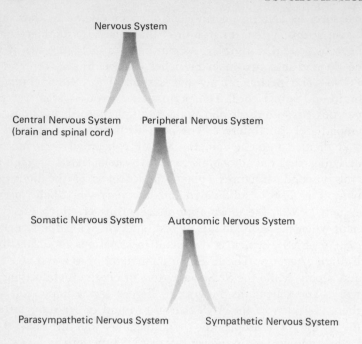

Figure 1-2. Schematic drawing of nervous system showing its major divisions.

sions are reached, while in others, no definite conclusions are formulated, indicating either that more work is required to clear up an issue or that a stalemate exists. The existence of a stalemate may mean that a satisfactory conclusion may never be reached with the approaches currently being employed to provide answers.

Secondary aims of this book are to provide elementary information regarding the anatomy and physiology of the various body systems under discussion and an outline of how the activity is measured. The purpose of this information is to provide basic information about how to obtain physiological measures. The student who requires more detailed information about anatomy and physiology and recording techniques can refer to specialized texts on these subjects. For example, *Gray's Anatomy*

Table 1-1 Nervous System Mechanisms in the Control of Physiological Responses

Central Nervous System	Somatic System	Autonomic Nervous System
EEG (ongoing activity)	EMG	Heart rate (PNS, SNS)
Event-related potentials	EOG	Blood pressure (PNS, SNS)
		Electrodermal activity (SNS only)
		Pupil response (PNS, SNS)
		Blood volume (PNS, SNS)

(1977), *Basic Human Physiology* (Guyton, 1977), and *Manual of Psychophysiological Methods* (Venables & Martin, 1967) may be consulted.

Chapters 2 through 7 focus mainly on the brain and the relations between measures of its activity and behavior. Chapters 8 through 12 treat the psychophysiology of body systems peripheral to the brain. They include, in order, the muscles, sweat glands, eyes, heart, and blood vessels. Chapters 13 and 14 are concerned with applications of psychophysiology, while chapter 15 covers concepts in the field. This organization emphasizes the brain as the central organ of behavior, with activity in the peripheral systems reflecting the outflow of brain influence. This is not to minimize the role played by these peripheral systems in psychophysiology, since it is known that (1) feedback of their activity can influence brain activity, and (2) peripheral measures often contribute information about body-behavior relationships that measures of brain activity do not.

Once the student has obtained some knowledge of body systems, measuring techniques, and representative studies in the field, he or she will be ready to appreciate the theoretical issues that characterize the field of psychophysiology. Although the organization of the text reflects the view that concepts should follow empirical data, individual instructors may prefer to cover the conceptual material at some earlier point. This could have the advantage of alerting the student to issues in the field and how one or another study either supports or refutes a particular view.

Other instructors may prefer to present the material dealing with peripheral body systems prior to that which covers brain activity. A feature of this text is that the coverage of the various body systems is such that each is self-contained. Hence, the individual instructor may choose any particular chapter sequence he or she wishes without losing the flavor of the book.

Information regarding environmental influences on various physiological responses appears in Appendix I. These factors include external (e.g., temperature, air) and internal (e.g., drugs and hormones) influences. While some of the environmental studies may not be strictly psychophysiological, in that they fail to use a behavioral measure, environmental factors must be considered because of their possible interaction with both behavioral and physiological measures. It should be noted that research with humans is emphasized in this book. Animal research has been, and continues to be, crucial to the development of psychophysiology. However, a comprehensive treatment of animal studies requires a separate book.

2

The Brain and Measurement of Its Activity

This chapter focuses primarily on the source and nature of the brain's electrical activity and how it is measured. Included is a brief presentation of some neuroanatomy and neurophysiology necessary to understand the activity being measured. The material presented here forms the background for understanding the physiological basis of the EEG and the evoked cortical potentials discussed in subsequent chapters.

Source of the Brain's Electrical Activity

Electrical activity of the brain is produced by billions of brain cells, called *neurons*. Activity is never absent in the healthy living brain. Neurons are always active: when we are asleep or awake, active or passive, during meditation or hypnosis. The entire nervous system is dependent on neurons for its activity. These cells are the functional units of the brain and spinal cord.

Although there is general agreement among scientists that neurons are the source of brain electrical activity, the exact nature of their contribution is an area of contention. For example, Noback and Demarest (1975) propose that the EEG is produced by electrical activity at synapses (where brain cells transmit information) and by electrical activity within brain cells. They suggest further that recordings made from the scalp reflect the algebraic summation of excitatory and inhibitory activities that occur in underlying brain tissue. That is, some brain cells produce excitation and some reduce the level of activity; the resultant is the record called the EEG.

Elul (1972) makes a strong argument for the position that the EEG is a resultant of activity within nerve cells in the cerebral cortex. He indicates that analyses of correlations between gross EEGs (recorded from many cells) and the activity of individual nerve cells suggest that gross activity is due to the synchronized firing of a relatively small number of cerebral neurons. Thus, according to Elul, the EEG is produced through the intermittent synchronization of cortical neurons, with different neurons becoming synchronized in successive instants. This implies that the EEG represents a series of bursts of aggregate neuron activity, with each burst being the synchronized activity of different groups of cortical neurons. According to Elul, these bursts of activity are what we see in the EEG recording. He also points out that subcortical areas such as the thalamus have an influence over the EEG, since it is known that the thalamus plays a role in the production of at least one type of spontaneous activity, that is, sleep spindles. He suggests, however, that other subcortical centers may also contribute to EEG rhythms. Let us now briefly examine the structures that produce the brain's electrical activity.

The Neuron

Neurons consist of a cell body, dendrites, and a single axon. There are approximately 10 billion neurons in the nervous system. The cell body contains the nucleus which controls cellular activity. The dendrites are extensions that come off the cell body and transmit impulses to the cell. As many as 75 to 80 dendrites may be present on a motor cell, while sensory neurons may only have a single dendrite. Dendrites are short relative to axons. The single axon comes off the cell body and transmits information away from the cell body to other neurons. Axons sometimes reach a length of several feet. Diagrams of a neuron within the CNS and a motor neuron located in both the CNS and peripheral nervous system are shown in Figure 2-1.

Neurons can be multipolar, bipolar, or unipolar. Multipolar neurons have many dendrites coming off the cell body. The motor neuron illustrated in Figure 2-1 is an example of a multipolar

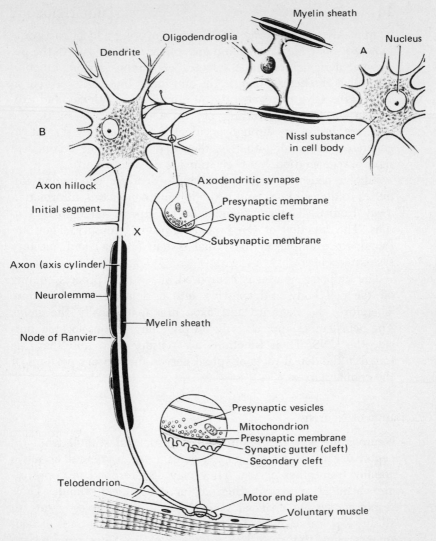

Myelin sheath

Oligodendroglia

Dendrite

Nucleus

A

B

Nissl substance
in cell body

Axon hillock

Axodendritic synapse

Initial segment

Presynaptic membrane

Synaptic cleft

X

Subsynaptic membrane

Axon (axis cylinder)

Neurolemma

Myelin sheath

Node of Ranvier

Presynaptic vesicles

Mitochondrion

Presynaptic membrane

Synaptic gutter (cleft)

Secondary cleft

Telodendrion

Motor end plate

Voluntary muscle

Figure 2-1. (A) A neuron located within the central nervous system. (B) A lower motor neuron located in both the central and peripheral nervous systems. This synapses with a voluntary muscle cell to form a motor end plate. The hiatus in the nerve at X represents the border between the central nervous system above and the peripheral nervous system below.

15

neuron. Also shown is the neurilemma covering which exists only in neurons outside of the brain and spinal cord, that is, in the peripheral nervous system. A concept of nervous system function holds that the neurilemma is the substance that allows a neuron *outside* the CNS to regenerate by providing a pathway and protection for the regenerating neuron. Once neurons inside the CNS are destroyed, through accident or disease, they do not regenerate functionally; that is, they may show some anatomical signs of regeneration, but their function does not return.

Bipolar neurons consist of a single dendrite conducting impulses to the cell body and a single axon conducting information away from it. The neurilemma never appears on bipolar neurons. The function of the bipolar neuron is sensory. They are found, for example, in the visual system (retina) and auditory system (cochlea).

The unipolar neuron is composed of a single process coming off the cell body and splitting into a dendrite and an axon. Therefore, the dendrite and axon are anatomically the same. The neurilemma appears only on unipolar neurons located outside the CNS. Their functions are sensory only, and they are found in the dorsal roots of spinal nerves and sensory portions of the cranial nerves.

Excitation of Neurons

Neurons are effectively stimulated by natural stimuli from receptor organs (e.g., in the eyes or ears) or by neural impulses coming from other nerves. They may also respond to appropriate chemical, electrical, thermal, or mechanical stimuli. Their responsiveness to artificial stimuli has enabled investigators to study electrical activity of single neurons or small groups of neurons through tiny recording microelectrodes. Since neurons are rather small, their size ranging from 4 to 100 μm (micrometers, or millionths of a meter), the electrodes for recording from single cells must be only a few micrometers in diameter to enable insertion into these cells. In experimental work, electric current has often been used because of its convenience, accuracy of quantification, and the fact that it does not damage the neuron at appropriate levels of stimulation. To produce an impulse from a neuron, a stimulus must be of a certain strength and duration.

The stimulus strength just capable of producing a neuron response is termed the threshold intensity and is usually given in terms of voltage. A stimulus must be applied for a certain period of time before it will produce a neuronal impulse. Thus, a strong stimulus will not have to be applied as long as a weak one to elicit a neuronal response. The strength of this minimal level stimulus required to produce a response is called the threshold or rheobase. The excitability of neurons can be determined by ascertaining the *chronaxy* or the minimum length of time it takes an electric current two times the rheobase value to create an impulse (Gardner, 1975).

A neuron must receive a certain minimal level of stimulation or it will not fire at all. Upon adequate stimulation, it will fire with its maximum strength. This has been termed the "all-or-none principle" of neuronal firing. Once the stimulus triggers the firing of a neuron, the electrical impulse continues along the entire length of the axon and possibly to the dendrites of another neuron. Transmission to another neuron takes place across a small juncture called a synapse. The terminal portion of an axon and the dendrites of another neuron do not touch. Transmission across the synapse is accomplished by chemical mediators. Figure 2-2 shows a schematic drawing of several types of synapses.

The speed of electrical impulse conduction along a neuron depends on axon diameter. Large-diameter axons transmit impulses at higher speeds. A rough estimate of transmission speed can be made for mammalian neurons that contain myelin. The diameter is multiplied by a constant of 6 to give approximate conduction speed in meters per second. Thus, for an axon 20 μm in diameter, conduction velocity is about 120 m/sec (Gardner, 1975). Myelin is a whitish material composed of protein and fat which appears on some axons in the nervous system. It is the myelin that causes masses of axons to appear as "white matter" of the brain, as compared to the masses of cell bodies that comprise the "gray matter."

Neuron Potentials

Although the neuronal impulse can be measured in terms of changes in electrical activity, it is actually produced by physiochemical activity which occurs when the neuron is stimulated.

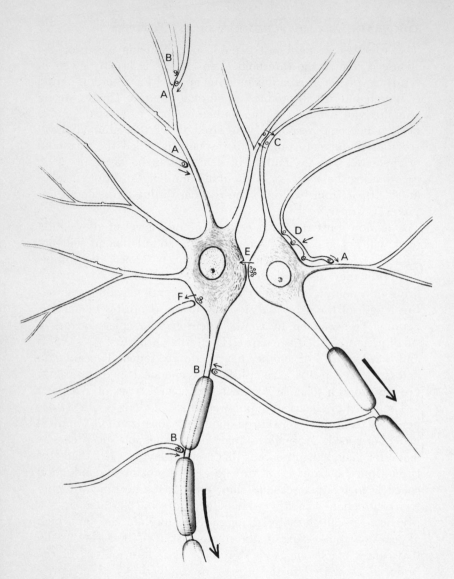

Figure 2-2. Several types of synapses: (A) axodendritic synapses; (B) axonaxonic synapse; (C) reciprocal dendrodendritic synapses; (D) en passant axosomatic synapses; (E) somatosomatic synapse; (F) somato-axonic synapse.

To understand how this physiochemical activity occurs, a brief explanation of the chemicals existing inside and outside the neuron and their relation to various potential states of the neuron will be given.

There is usually what is termed a *resting potential* difference on the two sides of the cell membrane, such that the inside of the cell is negative relative to the outside. This occurs because the inside of the cell has higher concentrations of potassium ions and the outside of the cell has more sodium ions. When a stimulus of sufficient strength and duration comes along, it causes physiochemical changes to take place in which the cell membrane becomes permeable, allowing the sodium to enter at a high rate and the potassium to move outside the cell, thus causing a reversal of the resting potential along the entire length of the axon. This reversal of resting potential is called a *wave of depolarization*. When depolarization occurs, the inside of the membrane registers a potential of about +30 mV, a change of 100 mV from the resting potential of approximately −70 mV. After depolarization has occurred along the axon, the neuron returns to its original resting state. The exchange of positive and negative ions produces a potential difference between the active and inactive areas of the neuron, and a current flows between the two regions. The mechanism by which sodium is returned to the outside of the cell and potassium to the inside has been termed the "sodium-potassium pump." The precise nature of how this pump works is not known (Gardner, 1975).

The Action Potential of the Neuron

The action potential of the neuron is made up of three components: the spike potential, the negative afterpotential, and the positive afterpotential. The spike potential is the large, sharply rising part of the action potential represented in Figure 2-3. Note that the action potential may excite or inhibit activity in the postsynaptic neuron. The spike potential represents the period during which depolarization takes place. The spike potential lasts only .5 to 1.0 msec (thousandths of a second). The excitability of the neuron, in terms of its ability to respond to another stimulus, is greatly reduced during the spike period. In

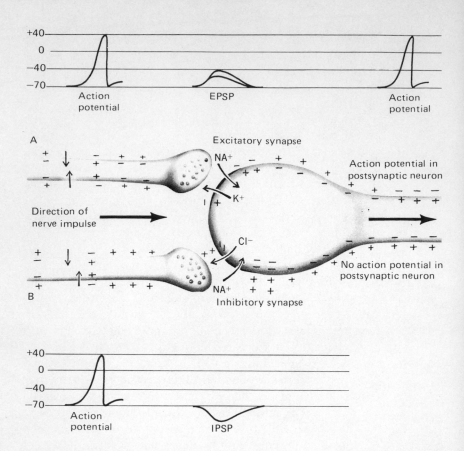

Figure 2-3. Sequences in (A) excitatory and (B) inhibitory transmission from presynaptic neurons (left) and across synapses to postsynaptic neuron (right). (A) the action potential conducted along the presynaptic axon to an excitatory synapse produces an EPSP, which in turn can contribute to the generation of an action potential in the postsynaptic neuron. (B) The action potential conducted along the presynaptic axon to an inhibitory synapse produces an IPSP, which in turn suppresses the generation of an action potential in the postsynaptic neuron.

20

fact, during the absolute refractory period, lasting about .5 msec, no stimulus will produce another neuron response. The relative refractory period of the spike is the period during which only a stimulus of much greater intensity than normal will produce another firing of the neuron. The relative refractory period lasts about .5 msec. An absolute refractory period of .5 to 1 msec would limit the response of an individual neuron to about 1,000 or 2,000 times a second.

The next phase of the action potential is the negative afterpotential, which lasts from 5 to 15 msec and is lower in magnitude than the spike potential. The excitability of the neuron is "supernormal" during the negative afterpotential. This means that a stimulus of lower intensity than normal will be sufficient to cause another neuron response. Some scientists have hypothesized that this occurs because more than the usual number of sodium ions are still inside the neuron, causing it to be more excitable than normal.

The last portion of the action potential is the positive afterpotential, which lasts for about 50 to 80 msec. However, the neuron is in a "subnormal" phase during the positive afterpotential, meaning that it will take a stronger than normal stimulus to produce another spike potential during this period. One notion is that the sodium pump has pushed too much sodium outside, resulting in a lower than usual number of sodium ions inside the cell and, therefore, a lower excitability. After about 80 to 100 msec, the normal excitability of the neuron returns.

The action potential is an example of neuronal activity that occurs in response to specific adequate stimulation. Another, more common neural activity is the graded potential, which occurs primarily in the cell bodies and dendrites of the neurons. These are continuous potentials, and they also occur in neurons in situations when stimuli are subthreshold or not intense enough to produce a spike potential.

Now that we have reviewed some aspects of electrical activity changes in neurons, it would be instructive to examine the organization of large masses of neurons in the human brain. This description of brain areas will prove useful in understanding the brain measure studies discussed in chapters 3 through 7. For example, when the patterning of EEG responses occurs during the performance of a task a proper interpretation requires knowledge about the brain areas contributing to this patterning.

Gross Brain Anatomy

The average weight of the adult human brain is about 1,400 g (3 lb.). The brain may be divided into three main portions for convenience of description: the cerebrum, the cerebellum, and the brain stem. The cerebrum, or cerebral hemispheres, occupies much of the external surface of the brain. The two hemispheres, right and left, contain virtually identical structures. The cerebellum overlies the posterior aspect of the brain stem. The brain stem is the portion that remains after removal of the cerebral hemispheres and the cerebellum and is the structure upon which the cerebellum rests (see Figure 2-4).

The surface of the cerebrum has many convolutions. The raised portions of these convolutions are called gyri (gyrus) and the grooved portions are termed sulci (sulcus) or fissures. The cerebellum is also convoluted, and the raised portions are called folia. There are slight differences in the shape and location of the gyri and sulci in the cerebrum of individual brains, but they are still useful in localizing various brain areas. For example, the fissure of Rolando (also called the central sulcus) travels down from the top of the brain toward the sides in both hemispheres to the lateral sulcus. It conveniently serves as a dividing line between what is termed the precentral cortex (motor functions) and the postcentral cortex (body sensory functions), as shown in the lateral view of the cortex in Figure 2-5. The numbers in Figure 2-5 are from the system of functional localization of Brodmann. The other drawing in Figure 2-5 illustrates the division of the cerebral cortex into four lobes: the frontal, parietal, occipital, and temporal. Note that the fissure of Sylvius (also called the lateral sulcus) separates the temporal lobe from the frontal and parietal lobes.

The medial aspect is what would be seen if the brain were cut in half, from front to back (called a midsagittal section). The medial aspect is presented in Figure 2-6. Note that if we examine the head area from outside to inside, we first see the scalp

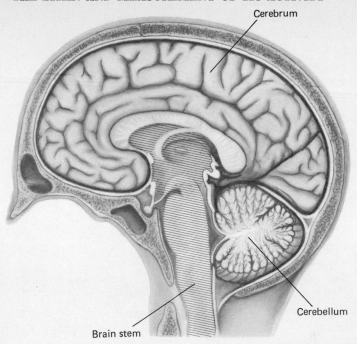

Figure 2-4. Diagram showing three divisions of the brain: brain stem, cerebellum, and cerebrum. The brain stem is illustrated as the shaded portion of the diagram.

and then the skull bone. Immediately below the skull is the dura mater, which is a tough, elastic membrane covering the brain. Below the dura is the arachnoid tissue. The pia mater is a very thin, soft membrane below the arachnoid that covers the brain and follows the gyri and sulci very closely. In the subarachnoid space is located the cerebrospinal fluid, which is believed to supply nourishment to the brain as well as providing a protective envelope of liquid for the brain and spinal cord. The subarachnoid space communicates with the ventricular system of the brain.

There are four ventricles in the brain: two lateral ventricles (one in each cerebral hemisphere), a third ventricle located between each thalamus, and a fourth ventricle connected to the

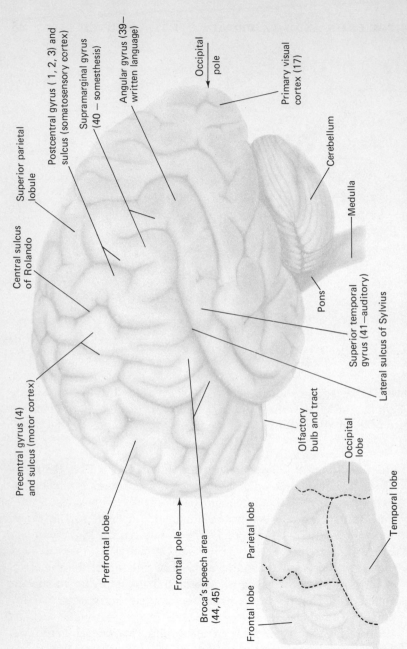

Figure 2-5. Lateral surface of the brain. Numbers refer to Brodmann's areas.

Central sulcus of Rolando

Superior parietal lobule

Postcentral gyrus (1, 2, 3) and sulcus (somatosensory cortex)

Supramarginal gyrus (40 — somesthesis)

Angular gyrus (39— written language)

Occipital pole

Primary visual cortex (17)

Cerebellum

Medulla

Superior temporal gyrus (41—auditory)

Pons

Lateral sulcus of Sylvius

Precentral gyrus (4) and sulcus (motor cortex)

Prefrontal lobe

Frontal pole

Broca's speech area (44, 45)

Olfactory bulb and tract

Frontal lobe

Parietal lobe

Occipital lobe

Temporal lobe

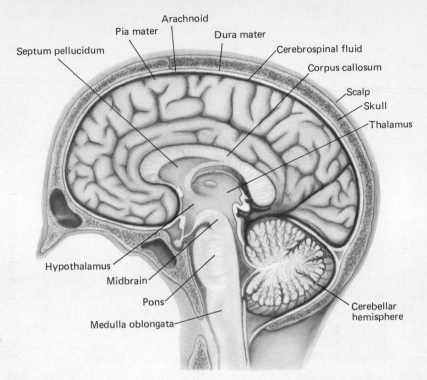

Figure 2-6. Median sagittal section of the brain and part of the head.

third by a narrow channel (cerebral aqueduct). The ventricles are spaces through which the cerebrospinal fluid circulates in and around the brain.

Projections from Thalamus to Cortex

One subcortical area, the thalamus (brain stem; see Figure 2-6), will be singled out for a brief elaboration, since it has important functions as a relay station for sensory and motor input to the cortex. The thalamus contains many important nuclei such as the ventral nuclei, posteroventral nucleus, lateroventral nucleus, medial and lateral geniculate bodies, pulvinar, and reticular nucleus. The reticular nucleus (reticular formation) has a role in influencing both general and specific cortical activity and functions. This reticular formation has been referred to as the ascending reticular activating system (ARAS) and has important implications for behavior.

Another structure of special interest is the corpus callosum, a thick band of fibers that connects the left and right hemispheres of the brain. The corpus callosum allows the transfer of sensory and other information between the cerebral hemispheres.

This basic information about neuron and brain structures will allow you to better understand the material that follows in chapters on the EEG and event-related brain potentials.

The Electroencephalogram

The electroencephalogram (EEG) or "brain wave" was described in rabbits and monkeys by Richard Caton in 1875. In 1902, Hans Berger began his work on brain waves with dogs, and in 1920, he started to study human EEGs. In 1929, he published his findings in which he identified two basic types of brain wave activity for humans, which he termed alpha and beta. Later investigators identified other types of brain waves and continued using the Greek alphabet labels, calling them delta, theta, kappa, lambda, and mu waves. The most reliable of these later-identified waves, in terms of consistency of occurrence, has been the delta wave, although it has been found possible to condition theta waves (Beatty et al., 1973; Brown, 1974). The characteristics of some of these waves are described below and depicted in Figure 2-7.[1]

Alpha Waves

The alpha is a rhythmic wave that occurs at a rate of 8 to 13 times a second [cycles per second (cps) or hertz (Hz)] at a magnitude of about 20 to 60 μV (millionths of a volt). Alpha waves can be produced by almost anyone sitting quietly in a re-

[1] In addition to these waves, there are the "K complexes" and "sleep spindles" of the sleeping EEG (see Figure 4-1 and Table 4-1). The sleeping EEG is discussed in chapter 4.

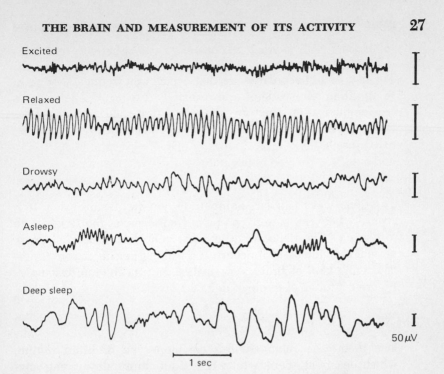

Excited

Relaxed

Drowsy

Asleep

Deep sleep

50 μV

1 sec

Figure 2-7. Electroencephalographic records during excitement, relaxation, and varying degrees of sleep. In the fourth strip, runs of 14/sec rhythm, superimposed on slow waves, are termed "sleep spindles." Notice that excitement is characterized by a rapid frequency and small amplitude and that varying degrees of sleep are marked by increasing irregularity and by the appearance of slow waves.

laxed position and with eyes closed. (Some persons do have difficulty in producing alpha waves.) As soon as the individual becomes involved in any mental or physical activity, the alpha wave generally becomes reduced in amplitude or disappears. For example, a person may be sitting in a chair, relaxed or not thinking of anything in particular, and at least some alpha waves will be in evidence. If the person is asked to spell a word, the alpha will change to a higher frequency and lower amplitude wave called beta. Alpha is illustrated by the second wave from the top in Figure 2-7, labeled "relaxed."

Beta Waves

The beta is an irregular wave that occurs at a frequency of 14 to
30 cps at an amplitude of approximately 2 to 20 μV. Beta waves
are common when a person is involved in mental or physical activity and is illustrated by the topmost tracing in Figure 2-7 (labeled "excited").

Delta Waves

The delta wave is a large-amplitude, low-frequency wave. It is
typically between .5 and 3.5 cps in frequency, in the range of 20
to 200 μV. The delta wave appears only during deep sleep in
normal individuals. If it occurs in a waking person, it could indicate some kind of brain abnormality. See the bottom tracing in
Figure 2-7 for an example of delta activity.

Theta Waves

The theta is a relatively less common type of brain rhythm
which occurs at about 4 to 7 Hz, at an amplitude ranging any-
where from 20 to 100 μV. It has been reported to occur more frequently in the spontaneous EEG recordings of children than in
adults. Walter (1953) found it to occur during states of displeas-
ure, pleasure, and drowsiness in young adults, while Maulsby
(1971) reported amplitudes of 100 μV in babies experiencing
"pleasurable" events (e.g., drinking from a bottle or being fon-
dled by their mother).

Kappa Waves

Kennedy et al. (1948) discovered waves of about 10 Hz which
appear to be associated with thinking. They reported that it occurred in about 30% of their subjects.

Lambda Waves

Lambda waves were discovered in humans by Evans (1952) and
Y. Gastaut (1951). They have been recorded from over the visual cortex and are considered to be a type of visual response re-

sulting from a shifting image of some objects in a person's visual field. They are triangular in shape, range from 20 to 50 μV, and last about 150 to 250 msec in response to stimulation.

Mu Waves

The mu rhythm (described by H. Gastaut, 1952) has sharp peaks and rounded negative portions. It appears in the normal EEG of about 7% of the population and can be recorded from over the fissure of Rolando. The frequency is usually 9 to 11 Hz. A recent study of Koshino and Niedermeyer (1976) found that it was enhanced by scanning a patterned stimulus and not suppressed, as has usually been reported. These latter researchers found that 182 of 2,284 persons sampled (8.1%) showed evidence of the mu rhythm.

Measurement of the EEG

The various kinds of brain waves can be measured by means of electrodes attached to the scalp. This is the most common technique used by researchers studying brain activity. It must be pointed out that the amplitude of the EEG as measured from the scalp is much lower than if it were measured from the surface of the cortex (the electrocorticogram), because the electrical activity must pass through the dura mater, the cerebrospinal fluid, the skull bone and the skin of the scalp before it reaches the scalp electrode. This greatly reduces its amplitude. The electrocorticogram is measured in millivolts, while the EEG is in microvolts, showing the disparity in magnitudes. Since the difficulty and hazards of penetrating the skull are great, the electrocorticogram is rarely recorded, even in clinical cases. Since the EEG signal is so small at the scalp, the electronic circuitry for measuring it must be very sensitive.

Electrode Location (Monopolar)

To measure EEG, one may use either a monopolar or bipolar recording technique. The monopolar method is described in this section, and the bipolar is discussed in a later section. A mono-polar technique involves placing one so-called, active electrode in good contact with the skin over an area of interest, for example, the occipital (visual) cortex. Another electrode, termed the reference lead is placed on a relatively inactive area,[2] such as the earlobe or tip of the nose. Since any reference electrode on the head is not completely inactive, some investigators prefer to place them on other parts of the body, for example, the back or chest. These may be difficult to use, since they could pick up muscle activity if the subject is not completely relaxed.

The diagram shown in Figure 2-8 illustrates some commonly used scalp locations in EEG research. The locations are based on a portion of the International EEG nomenclature (Jasper, 1958). It is called the "10-20 System" because the various locations are either 10% or 20% of the distance between standard points for measurement. For example, in obtaining the location designated O_z, a centimeter measurement is taken between the nasion (bridge of nose) and inion (a projection of bone at the back of the head found over the occipital area; also known as the oc-cipital protuberance). Then 10% of this distance is measured (to-ward the nasion), and the electrode is placed at this spot. The tape measure must pass straight along the midline between nasion and inion, through those points labeled with a z (indicating mid-line). This area is designated O_z and is over the occipital cortex. Those labeled P, F, and T are over parietal, frontal and tempo-ral areas, respectively. The C locations are central areas, with C_z as the center of both the anterior-posterior (front-back) and coronal (side to side) planes. The location labeled F_p is the frontal pole and is 10% of the nasion-inion distance. The F_z, C_z, and P_z locations are each 20% of the nasion-inion distance back, starting from F_p. The locations along the coronal plane are based on the distance measured between the midpoints of the two ears taken through C_z. The sites labeled F_{p1} and O_1 are 10% from F_p and O_z, respectively. The other locations along this anterior-posterior line are 20% of the distance apart from each other. This side view is illustrated in Figure 2-9. Note that the locations on

[2] Relatively inactive with respect to the amount of brain electrical activity that can be recorded from that location.

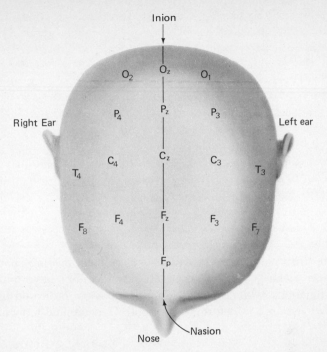

Figure 2-8. Top view of scalp locations used by researchers studying relations between brain activity and performance. The locations are the active, or EEG-producing, areas. The reference area may be the earlobes, singly or in combination, or the nose. The numbering system is a portion of that used in the International EEG 10-20 system. The nasion refers to the bridge of the nose, while the inion is the occipital protuberance.

the left side of the head are indicated by odd numbers. This system of electrode location has enabled different investigators to communicate the sites in their EEG studies in a standard way. The method also has the advantage of being based on each subject's own head size. Anatomical studies carried out when the numbering system was first presented (Jasper, 1958) indicated that the locations do approximate the areas that they are claimed to be over, for example, occipital, parietal, frontal, or temporal lobes.

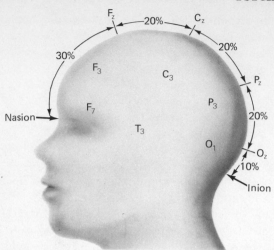

Figure 2-9. In this diagram the 10-20 system locations are shown for the left side of the head. Note that left side locations have odd-numbered designations, while the right side locations are indicated by even numbers. (F, frontal; C, central; P, parietal; O, occipital; T, temporal.)

Electrode Attachment

The electronics of the recording equipment enable a comparison of the activity measured from over the cortical area of interest with that at the reference electrode, and the difference is the written EEG record. The electrodes should be small (6 to 8 mm in diameter) and easy to attach. The scalp area should be prepared by rubbing it with a cleansing material (alcohol or acetone on a cotton ball works well) until the skin shows a slight pink tinge. Then a standard electrode paste (a conducting agent) is carefully rubbed into the skin of the scalp until it permeates the pores. The electrode can be held firmly in place with an elastic headband or a variety of other devices available commercially. The reference lead can be a convenient clip electrode which merely is attached to the earlobe or nose after the area has been cleansed of any oils or dead skin by rubbing with alcohol. Electrode paste is also used when attaching the reference lead. The resistance between the active and reference leads can be measured by ohm (Ω) meters[3] conveniently built into most good recording devices. It should read less than 5000 Ω. If it does, you know that your electrodes are making good contact. A ground electrode[4] may be placed on the other earlobe, on the mastoid area behind the ear, or on the wrist.

Even with a good contact through careful electrode attachments, artifacts can be seen in the EEG record if subjects move about excessively or tense up the muscles of their forehead or jaw or blink their eyes. Subjects must be cautioned against producing this type of EEG artifact. Other unwanted signals, such as heart activity or skin potential responses, would be considered artifacts if they appeared in the EEG record.

Silver cup electrodes are commonly used for active leads, while flat silver electrodes held in a clip are convenient reference electrodes. Some investigators use gold electrodes, solder pellets, or a cellulose sponge permeated with the conducting material and held in place by an elastic headband.

Electrode Placement (Bipolar)

When using a bipolar recording technique, two active electrodes are placed over cortical areas of interest. Bipolar leads record the difference or algebraic sum of the electrical potentials beneath the two regions at every instant. Some researchers prefer bipolar recording because it avoids some of the problems of selecting an inactive reference area inherent in monopolar recording. However, bipolar recordings have the disadvantage of producing a record of combined activity at two locations. For clinical purposes, that is, the recording of EEG to detect brain abnormalities, the interpretation of EEG records usually requires the comparison of data obtained from symmetrically placed electrodes (e.g., from two electrodes on the right frontal area compared with two on the left frontal area). The presence or absence of symmetry in the two tracings may be of clinical significance. Bipolar leads may also be used in research applications other than clinical. When clinical evaluation requires the appli-

[3] See Appendix II (EEG Measuring Systems).
[4] See Appendix III (Laboratory Safety).

cation of arrays of electrodes all over the scalp, then needle electrodes may be used. The needle electrodes are placed under the skin of the scalp and thus meet with very little skin resistance. They are not as comfortable for the person as are the skin surface electrodes, but in a situation where an EEG technician must place 20 or 30 electrodes on the scalp, they save quite a bit of time. The characteristics of a good EEG recording system are outlined in Appendix II. Laboratory safety procedures are presented in Appendix III.

Now that we have considered briefly the anatomy and physiology of our most complex organ, and one way of recording its activity, we are ready for a description of experimental studies. Chapter 3 will introduce you to studies of EEG and behavior.

The EEG and Behavior:
Motor and Mental Activities

This chapter examines the literature regarding the relationship between brain waves and behavior, that is, changes that occur in the EEG while individuals engage in various mental and physical activities. A consideration of environmental factors that may affect the EEG is presented in Appendix I. In this chapter, changes in EEG that occur with different kinds of motor activities are discussed first, and then we consider the question of whether intelligence can be predicted from EEG patterns. Spatial abilities and right-left hemispheric asymmetries as related to EEG measures are discussed in later sections of this chapter.

Motor Performance and the EEG

This section first examines the relationships between EEG recordings and simple motor reaction time. Then, under the subheading of Visuomotor Performance, we consider EEGs measured simultaneously with more complex motor performance, requiring continuous eye and hand coordination.

Reaction Time

In their classic book *Experimental Psychology*, Woodworth and Schlosberg (1954) note that reaction time (RT) which is also referred to as response latency, includes the time it takes for a sense organ to react to some stimulus, brain processing time, nerve time (to carry impulses to and from the brain), and muscle time (the time for muscles to contract and move some external object). One of the most common RT experiments involves one stimulus and one response (simple RT). For example, a light comes on and a subject is requested to press a response key as soon as he sees the light. The interval consumed between the light coming on and the response being made is timed to the nearest thousandth of a second and constitutes the RT.

Some investigators have related speed of reaction to EEG activation (Lansing et al., 1959). The term *EEG activation* refers to the desynchronization or blocking of the alpha wave which usually occurs at occipital locations when an individual responds to visual stimuli. Lansing and his colleagues recorded RTs to a visual stimulus in nine normal persons and found that RTs were significantly faster when alpha block occurred before the visual stimulus was presented. The alpha block was produced by warning signals presented shortly before the stimulus. They interpreted both the faster RT and the alpha block in terms of an alerted state produced through action of the ascending reticular activation system (ARAS). More recent studies have indicated that the alpha blocking and faster RTs may not be related to each other but instead may be independently related to the warning signal that produces a preparatory set to react (Leavitt, 1968; Thompson & Botwinick, 1966). Leavitt (1968) has rejected the concept that faster reactions were caused by a unitary arousal system such as the ARAS and suggests instead that several neural processes underlie the relation between the point in time at which the warning signal occurs and the speed of reaction. He noted in his study that when a warning signal appeared 500 msec before the stimulus, the quickest RTs occurred along with maximal alpha desynchronization. At different foreperiods of 200, 1,500, and 4,000 msec, however, the degree of alpha desynchronization was not related to speed of reaction. There were times, in fact, when RT was similar whether the percentage of alpha desynchronization was 0% or 56%.

Thompson and Botwinick (1968) measured the RTs and EEGs of 26 persons between the ages of 62 and 87 years and compared these measures to those of a group between 19 and 35 years. The average age in the older group was 77, while in the younger group it was 23. They found reliable differences in the RTs of the two groups, the older group being slower, but no difference appeared between the groups in the EEG measure used, that is, the decrease in EEG amplitude from rest period to the stimulus-presentation period.

In a series of developmental studies, Surwillo (1968, 1971a, 1971b, 1973, 1974) has found relationships between speed of response and *period* of the EEG. Period of the EEG is defined by the total number of waves recorded in the interval of time between the stimulus and the response. The average duration (period) of these waves was obtained by dividing the number of waves into the length of the interval. Surwillo's (1968) rationale for using the EEG period is based on the premise that behavior and CNS activity occur at the same time and, therefore, should be examined at identical moments. He reported that RTs became slower and more variable in old age and interpreted this as due to brain processes which can be measured by period of the EEG. In his 1971 study, Surwillo measured EEG period and correlated this with RT of 110 boys ranging in age from approximately 4 years to 17 years. One task used was disjunctive RT in which the subject had to decide whether or not to respond to two auditory stimuli, according to a predetermined criterion. The other task used was simple RT to an auditory stimulus. Decreases in the frequency of the EEG were associated with slower RTs.

The time it took to make a movement to a sound, as well as simple auditory RT, was measured along with EEG period by Surwillo (1974). The movement time (MT) was the time it took the subject to leave a contact and touch a target 28 cm away with his preferred hand. The subjects were 17 boys between the ages of 8.5 and 17.2 years. Both RT and MT decreased with age. The RT was found to be faster when EEG period was shorter, thus confirming the results of Surwillo's earlier studies. MT was not related to EEG period, however, which indicated to Surwillo that frequency of the EEG could not account for motor information-handling processes. In addition, there was no relation between MT and RT, indicating that the two activities represent different types of motor processes, that is, that speed of response and the more gross speed of movement are relatively independent activities.

It should be noted that the positive results for the relationship

between RT and EEG obtained by Surwillo have been obtained
with the use of EEG period as the measure of CNS activity. The
negative findings (Leavitt, 1968; Thompson & Botwinick, 1966,
1968) used degree of alpha desynchronization, for example, a
50% decrease in the amplitude of the alpha rhythm for more
than 200 msec (Leavitt, 1968). In fact, when Surwillo (1972)
used a measure similar to alpha desynchronization, namely
blocking latency of the EEG (the time it took EEG to drop
in amplitude when stimulation occurred), he found no relationship between the EEG and reaction time. Thus, while degree of
alpha desynchronization may not be related to RT, other measures such as EEG period, EEG half waves (Surwillo, 1975), and
average alpha frequency (Creutzfeldt et al., 1976) appear to be
related to RT. The relationship perhaps may be due to more efficient stimulus processing (sense organ time, brain time, and
muscle time) when the CNS shows more activity than when it is
relatively quiescent.

Visuomotor Performance

A study of EEG during motor activity was conducted by Khrizman (1973). The EEGs of 12 two- and three-year-old children
were measured during rest and while they performed two kinds
of motor activity. EEG was recorded from frontal, motor, parietal, temporal and occipital electrode placements. The motor
tasks were finger-tapping and arranging checkers in a row by alternating their colors. The EEG activity between the various
cortical areas was correlated. In the tapping task, the motor cortex showed the highest frequency and amplitude correlations
with the lower parietal regions, while the checker arrangement
task produced the highest correlations between the motor and
frontal areas. The high motor-frontal correlations might be interpreted in terms of coordination of motor and cognitive
(checker arrangement) activities often believed to be related
to functioning of the frontal lobes. The high parietal-motor correlation (tapping test) suggests coordination between two brain
areas for a simple motor task, perhaps involving a lower level of
cognitive activity.

Busk and Galbraith (1975) analyzed EEGs from over four

areas of the brain while 15 male subjects performed three motor tasks. The EEG was recorded from over the visual cortex (O_z), left and right motor areas (C_3 and C_4), and premotor cortex (F_z). The EEG measure used was C, or weighted average coherence, which is a measure of similarity between two brain areas. The $\bar{C}$ value between motor and premotor areas (F_z and C_3; F_z and C_4) showed a decrease following practice, while visual-premotor (O_z and F_z) coupling was not altered. The authors suggest the possibility that visual input to the premotor area remains stable during visuomotor learning (pursuit rotor), while the premotor-motor interactions decrease. This is a provocative finding, since it may suggest lessening of required cooperation between two cortical motor areas when motor performance improves, but a continued requirement for coordination between two cortical areas differing in function, that is, the premotor and visual areas.

In summary, demonstrations of relationships between EEG and RT seem to depend on the method of measuring EEG. In particular, Surwillo's technique of measuring EEG period during the stimulus-response interval has been successful, while the use of alpha desynchronization as a measure has produced equivocal results. A tendency toward coordination of the amount and areas of cortical activity, depending on the difficulty and type of motor task, represents a provocative finding and deserves additional research attention.

EEG and Mental Activity

In this section, we consider some recent research bearing on the controversial question regarding the relationship between EEG and intelligence, the intriguing findings with respect to EEG related to verbal and spatial performance, and some reports of EEG, hypnosis, and imagery.

EEG and Intelligence

After many years of research, the question of the relationship between EEG and intelligence (usually measured by intelligence

test performance) is still controversial. The literature on this
question was reviewed by Lindsley (1944) and covered studies
conducted in the 1930s and early 1940s. At the time of his review, Lindsley concluded that most of the studies indicated no
relationship between EEG and intelligence. An updated review
of the literature was accomplished by Ellingson (1956) covering
the years between 1944 and 1956, and he also concluded that the
available evidence did not establish a relation between EEG and
intellectual performance. Vogel and Broverman (1964) argued
that although no significant relationships had been found between EEG and intelligence for normal adults, such a relationship had been shown for children, mentally retarded persons,
geriatric patients, and brain-damaged patients. Ellingson (1966)
reviewed the Vogel and Broverman conclusions and reported
that the evidence for children and mentally retarded individuals
was contradictory and inconclusive; in addition, with regard to
geriatric and brain-injured patients, he noted that EEG abnormality and decreased intellectual capacity are both effects or or-
ganic brain disorder. That is, the EEG does not reflect intelligence but instead reflects decreased CNS functioning in the
brain-damaged and geriatric patients. Shagass (1972) pointed
out that the positive findings that appeared in the past involved
relatively small samples of subjects, while studies using large
samples (several hundred subjects) failed to show such relationships. Thus, it appears that the bulk of evidence to the late
1960s indicated a stalemate regarding the relation between EEG
and intelligence. Let us examine a few of the more recent
research efforts to see whether there are any changes in this
situation.

Surwillo (1971a) has criticized some of the positive findings
with respect to EEG and intelligence on the basis that studies
either did not control for age of the subjects or that the EEG
was, in most instances, recorded when the subject was "resting"
and not engaged in the task that was the measure of intelligence.
One such task is the digit span of the Wechsler Intelligence
Scale for Children (WISC), which tests ability to hold information in short-term mental storage. In digit span, lists of digits are
presented, and the subject is asked to repeat them exactly or in
a reverse order. Seventy-nine normal boys ranging in age from

4½ years to 17 years were subjects for Surwillo (1971a). The EEG period was used as the EEG measure and was based on tracings recorded from occipital and parietal leads during the interval when digits of the longest lists recalled were presented. Correlations between digit span length and EEG frequency were in the expected direction, that is a greater span, or capacity for short-term storage of information, was related to higher EEG frequencies. However, this relationship resulted from the age of the subjects, since when age was held constant, through a technique known as partial correlation, the relationship disappeared. Surwillo concluded that there was no evidence that digit span and EEG frequency recorded during acquisition of digit lists were related in normal children.

In another approach, Surwillo (1971b) recorded EEGs from over the parietal and occipital cortex while subjects performed the digit span (backwards) test. The EEG period was examined from O_1–P_3 (left hemisphere) and O_2–P_4 (right hemisphere) and compared (left and right homologous area) and was also examined across hemispheres as O_1–O_2 and P_3–P_4 (transverse derivations). When longer lists were processed, the EEG periods from right and left hemispheres (homologous) were more alike (synchronous) than when shorter lists were processed. In addition, subjects who were capable of processing longer lists of digits showed more synchrony between EEG of the two hemispheres than subjects who did not do as well. Thus, Surwillo seems to have support for the hypothesis that when increased EEG synchrony between the hemispheres occurs, a greater amount of information is being processed.

Giannitrapani (1969) reported that a frequency asymmetry score correlated significantly with Verbal, Performance, and Total IQ scores in the Wechsler Adult Intelligence Scale (WAIS). He measured average EEG frequencies during mental multiplication and correlated these with intelligence test performance (WAIS). A relationship was found between EEG frequency and full-scale IQ scores, since higher frequencies went with higher IQ. This was especially true for EEG frequency from left hemisphere (parietal) derivations. Griesel (1973) investigated the relationship between EEG frequency and period and several tests of intellectual ability. The tests measured mental alertness

(numerical, verbal, and reasoning ability), information processing, and ability to think analytically (Gottschaldt Figures Test).
The results indicated no relationship between the intelligence
test scores and the EEG frequency or period measures.

Maxwell et al. (1974) evaluated the EEG spectra (analysis
based on amplitudes of various EEG frequencies) of 150 children (mean age of 7 years) for whom they had intelligence test
scores. The children were divided into two groups, below average and above average in reading. The EEG analysis resulted in
the conclusion that the poor readers used larger portions of their
brain than the good readers, that is, they exerted more physiological effort to less effect. To test the hypothesis that EEG spectrum analysis would differ for poor and good readers, two new
groups of subjects were tested. The subjects were 52 good readers and 52 poor readers, all of whom were 14 years of age. EEG
spectrum analysis for the two groups confirmed that power generated by the poor readers was greater for all EEG frequencies
measured than that of the good readers. (The EEG spectral
analysis examines the amplitude of the EEG at various frequencies.) They suggested that more neurons are used by the less
proficient individual in a cognitive task, resulting in the larger
EEG amplitudes observed. One might ask whether this finding
can be related to that of Busk and Galbraith (1975), namely that
greater amounts of EEG synchrony occurred between cortical
areas in the performance of a difficult tracking task as compared
to an easy one (reading could be regarded as a difficult task for
the poor readers). Also, Surwillo (1971b) noted more EEG synchrony between the two hemispheres when subjects were processing longer, more difficult lists of numbers.

In summary, it seems that the several recent studies reviewed
do not resolve the impasse regarding the relationship between
EEG and intelligence. One promising approach may involve the
comparison of EEG activity from both right and left hemispheres and noting the relationship of the two hemispheres to
intellectual performance. This approach resulted in two of
the positive findings reported (Giannitrapani, 1969; Surwillo,
1971b). Perhaps new methods of analysis may lead to more positive results in the future, but the bulk of evidence for the relationship between EEG and intelligence is negative at this time.

It should also be noted that the amount of EEG research in this area seems to be decreasing, perhaps because of the interest generated recently in relating the averaged evoked cortical potential to intelligence, a development that will be discussed in a subsequent chapter.

A final note concerns the caution advanced by Satterfield and associates (1974) that EEG abnormalities may not be a good criterion for the placement of children in special education programs. When they compared the WISC scores of 22 hyperactive young boys, considered to have abnormal EEGs, with those of 63 hyperactive boys with normal EEGs, they found that the boys with abnormal patterns scored significantly higher (WISC full-scale scores of 106 compared to a mean of 98). This finding would seem to justify their cautionary note.

EEG Related to Verbal and Spatial Performance
(Including Hemispheric EEG Asymmetries)

This section reviews information concerning the EEG and mental activity involving the use of words, numbers, language (including musical information), and spatial visualization. It has long been known that EEG activity becomes desynchronized, that is, higher in frequency and lower in amplitude, with the onset of mental activity (Ellingson, 1956). Giannitrapani (1966) investigated the nature of EEG changes during mental activity for several scalp areas corresponding to left and right frontal, temporal, parietal, and occipital areas. The mean EEG frequencies of 20 normal subjects were computed for resting and for mental multiplication (a consecutive series of multiplication problems that would take subjects more than 5 seconds to solve, e.g., 3×5, 7×9, 12×8, etc.). An increase in average EEG frequency was observed at all areas, especially for the frontal and left temporal. In addition, faster EEG activity was recorded from the left as compared to the right hemisphere for the frontal and temporal leads during both resting and mental activity. Giannitrapani suggested that the differential hemispheric activity may have been related to the fact that most of the subjects were right-handed. No interhemispheric differences were found for parietal and occipital areas.

A demonstration of the amount of alpha (8 to 13 cps) and beta (14 to 30 Hz) activity produced during rest and during verbal activity was performed by Andreassi (1973). The EEG was recorded from left and right occipital areas from eight subjects under two conditions: Condition A—resting, in which subjects were asked to "close your eyes and relax as though going to sleep" (p. 905); and Condition B—working, in which they were asked to close their eyes and make as many words as possible in 40 sec, using the letters in the word "engineering" or in the word "recover." A significantly greater amount of beta activity was recorded from both hemispheres during the mental verbal activity. There was no difference between the left and right occipital hemispheres with respect to amounts of alpha and beta activity under both resting and working conditions, a finding similar to that of Giannitrapani for those locations.

Hemispheric asymmetry of EEG patterns was studied while subjects performed either verbal or spatial tasks (Galin & Ornstein, 1972). The results showed that right hemispheric involvement was greater in the spatial task and left hemispheric participation was dominant during the verbal activities. This finding of Galin and Ornstein was confirmed and extended by McKee et al. (1973). They found that lower amplitude EEG activity was present (more involvement) in recordings from the right hemisphere when persons performed a musical task (detecting a theme in an unfamiliar Bach concerto). When a linguistic task was used, lower amplitude EEGs were observed from left hemisphere recordings.

EEG was recorded from the left hemisphere of 32 male college students during the presentation of words (Warren & Harris, 1975). The subjects were asked to recall the words 2 minutes later. Those words associated with an immediate reduction in alpha activity (from the 2-second period preceding to the 2-second period following word presentation) were recalled better than words not associated with alpha reduction. Warren et al. (1976) followed up this study with recordings from both left and right hemispheres and the use of words known to produce emotional arousal (e.g., corpse) or a neutral reaction (e.g., vapor). Thirty-six right-handed male college students participated. One group of 18 students received instructions to visualize the words by construction of a visual image of the object or idea represented by the words (both arousal and neutral). Another group of 18 were instructed to silently construct sentences using the words. Thus, one group was visualizing, a process that should activate the right hemisphere more than the left, and the other group was verbalizing, which should have involved the left hemisphere to a greater extent. The results confirmed these expectations. However, immediately after word presentation, alpha reductions were seen in both hemispheres, interpreted by the authors as being due to a brief automatic activation of both hemispheres with stimulus onset. The asymmetries showed up shortly after this immediate change and reflected the active stimulus processing according to the instructions given.

Nonmusically trained subjects showed a significantly greater activation of the right hemisphere during whistling the melody of a song versus speaking the lyrics of the song, as compared to musically trained persons (Davidson & Schwartz, 1977). Basically, this indicates that the musically trained subject listened to the melody analytically, thus making it a left hemisphere task rather than a right hemisphere function. The authors suggest that long-term training in a cognitive skill, such as reading and playing music, may be accompanied by permanent changes in brain activity.

In summary, it would seem that recent evidence strongly supports the contention that the type of mental activity differentially affects the two hemispheres of the brain, as indicated by EEG measures. The consensus seems to be that the right hemisphere is involved to a greater extent than the left in the performance of spatial and musical tasks, while semantic, verbal, and mathematical tasks primarily involve the left hemisphere. Exceptions may arise, as in the case of musically trained individuals in whom the analytic information processing of music may transform music listening into a left hemisphere activity.

EEG, Hypnosis, and Imagery

For many years it had been thought that hypnosis was some type of sleep. Most contemporary evidence, however, favors the view that hypnosis is actually a modification of the waking state, with all the EEG characteristics indicative of such a state. The question of the relationship between EEG and hypnotic susceptibility has been investigated by a number of researchers. For example, London et al. (1968) reported greater amounts of alpha activity among subjects who scored high on a test of hypnotic susceptibility. Galbraith et al. (1970) examined this question further in a study of 59 volunteer subjects. Scores on the Harvard Group Hypnotic Susceptibility Scale (HGS) and EEG from frontal, parietal, occipital, and temporal leads were recorded. The findings supported the previous ones regarding a relationship between EEG and hypnotic susceptibility, that is, subjects with high HGS scores produced more alpha activity than those whose low scores, especially under an "eyes-open" condition. Galbraith and his collaborators suggest that the common factor between hypnotic susceptibility and the high alpha amplitude with eyes open is "attention." Subjects with high HGS scores may be better able to attend to hypnotic suggestions among competing stimuli, thereby shutting out distracting stimuli of various kinds. Morgan et al. (1974) also found that persons highly susceptible to hypnosis produced more alpha activity during task performance and hypnosis than those who were less susceptible.

A Vividness of Imagery scale was given to 71 undergraduates to assess degree of visual, auditory, and kinesthetic imagery (Gale et al., 1972). Then, while EEG was recorded from the occipital area, subjects responded to instructions designed to produce minimal imagery, passive elicited imagery, voluntary elicited imagery, and autonomous voluntary imagery. The minimal imagery condition involved relaxing with eyes open or closed. In the passive elicited imagery task, 10 high-imagery words (e.g., acrobat) and 10 low-imagery words (e.g., answer) were presented, and subjects were instructed to "see if the words suggest mental pictures." The elicited imagery task required subjects to move a circle and a triangle around in their minds. Imagining the activities of a family (father, mother, and two small children) on a beach over a 2-min period constituted the autonomous imagery task. The most clear-cut result was the decrease in alpha activity during all the imagery tasks except the minimal imagery one. The EEG of weak and vivid imagers was differentiated by alpha frequency under the eyes-open condition;

that is, it was significantly higher for the vivid imagers as compared to weak imagers.

In a recent study of physiological changes during meditation, Elson et al. (1977) matched a group of 11 meditators with 11 nonmeditating control subjects. The EEGs of both groups were measured over a 40-min period during which the control subjects were instructed to remain "wakefully relaxed" for 40 min, while the others meditated for the same amount of time. The meditators remained in a relatively stable state of alpha and theta EEG activity, and none fell asleep. On the other hand, six of the controls fell asleep during the experiment as indicated by K-complexes and spindles in their EEG records. The results indicate that meditation produces a physiological effect different from that produced in nonmeditating controls who try to relax with eyes closed for the same length of time.

The recording of EEG during hypnosis, meditation, and imagery is a relatively new type of endeavor. One interesting finding concerns the greater amount of alpha activity produced by highly hypnotizable persons compared to low hypnotizables under a variety of conditions. This high degree of alpha has been related to attentive ability by at least one investigative team (Galbraith et al., 1970). The evidence reviewed with respect to imagery is less clear but suggests that EEG activity changes according to type of mental productions, regardless of whether these are produced by imposed or naturally occurring mental events. EEG evidence also seems to establish meditation as a state different from hypnosis, autosuggestion, or sleep.

The next chapter covers EEG measures taken under different conditions of sensory stimulation, attention, and perception. Conditioning of the EEG and its patterning in a variety of sleep studies are also presented in chapter 4.

The EEG and Behavior: Sensation, Attention, Perception, Conditioning, and Sleep

This chapter discusses various human processes and their relation to EEG activity. The sections concerned with sensory, attentional, and perceptual problems are followed by a brief treatment of EEG during different kinds of conditioning. The EEG and its relation to sleep includes discussions on dreaming, depth of sleep, effects of presleep work on sleeping EEG, sleep learning, and sleep deprivation effects.

Sensation, Attention, Perception, and the EEG

In the context of this chapter, perception will be considered to involve the active processing (making meaning) of sensory data. Thus, it is proposed that the detection of a stimulus and attending to it precede perceptual integration by the individual. In this interpretation the processes of sensation, attention, and perception are viewed as being functionally linked. The purpose of the resulting integration is to allow the perceived material to be used in some cognitive activity (e.g., decision making, problem solving, or thinking). In this section the assignment of EEG research into one of these categories is based on whether a given study is primarily concerned with stimuli, attentional processes, or perceptual-integrative functions. The separation is artificial, and the close interactive influence among sensation, attention, and perception must be emphasized.

Sensation and the EEG

Stimulus Complexity

The effects of stimulus complexity upon desynchronization of the EEG alpha wave was the topic of an investigation by Berlyne and McDonnell (1965). They hypothesized that more complex and incongruous visual stimulus patterns would produce longer lasting desynchronization of alpha activity, for example, that more complex stimuli, presented while subjects were in alpha, would result in a longer lasting disappearance of alpha than less complex stimuli. Based on EEG recordings of 88 male subjects, their hypothesis was confirmed. The more complex or incongruous patterns produced 500-msec longer desynchronizations than the simple patterns. The result was interpreted to be consonant with those that indicate that aspects of the external environment such as novelty, surprise, and complexity of stimuli can induce heightened drive or arousal.

This intriguing notion that stimulus complexity can affect arousal level of an observer (as measured by duration of EEG desynchronization) was examined by Christie et al. (1972). They criticized the Berlyne and McDonnell experiment on the basis that no measure of the subject's reaction to the stimuli was taken, that is, the experimenters themselves judged whether a stimulus was complex or simple. Another criticism was that EEG desynchronization was a relatively crude measure. Christie et al. (1972) set out to correct these shortcomings by obtaining subjective ratings of complexity and by measuring EEG amplitude in detail over a frequency range of 2 to 20 Hz. Displays presented to the subjects had differing numbers of items (2, 4, 8, 16, or 32) which corresponded to subjective complexity. The alpha activity decreased as the number of items increased. Thus the level of complexity (as judged by subjects) did affect the amount of EEG alpha, confirming the earlier results of Berlyne and McDonnell. Christie et al. (1972) pointed out the encouraging sign that different measures of EEG used in studies of complexity yielded similar results.

Stimulus Aftereffects

The effects of fixating a rotating spiral on alpha activity and the time required for alpha to return after eye closure were measured by Claridge and Herrington (1963). They found a relation between the reported duration of this visual aftereffect and the time it took alpha to return (longer duration, longer time to return). Longer durations or aftereffects were also related to lower alpha indices. They concluded that subjects who showed more and longer desynchronization were affected by the aftereffect to a greater degree. This result is related to those of Ali (1972), who found differential effects of red and blue lights on the amplitude and amount of EEG alpha recovery in the post-stimulation period. That is, blue light favored earlier alpha recovery than did red light. On the basis of this result, he predicted that the longer duration and greater alpha attenuation associated with the red stimulus would lead to a longer estimate of its duration by subjects than would a blue light. This prediction was tested in another experiment (Ali, 1973). The stimuli, either red or blue lights, were presented to 40 subjects while EEG was measured from the occipital area. The subject was asked to look at the light as soon as it appeared and to keep looking until it was turned off. The prediction regarding time estimation was confirmed, since subjects made a mean estimate of 58.52 seconds for the red light and 47.50 seconds for the blue light. Greater EEG response was again found for red as compared to blue. Ali expressed the view that the duration of the cortical response, as measured by alpha activity, affects the organism's perception of the duration of the stimulus. As for the differential effect of the red and blue lights, Ali suggests several possibilities: (1) red light is more effective in central (foveal) vision, while blue is more effective in peripheral vision; (2) red may elicit greater attention; (3) red has autonomic arousal effects, but blue light has soothing effects. The differential effects of red and blue light could cause the variation in alpha EEG, which in turn might affect time estimation. Thus the brief review suggests that stimuli have aftereffects with respect to EEG activity. The possibility that red light has greater effects on foveal receptors than blue light remains to be investigated.

Attention and the EEG

A good working definition of attention is one offered by Tecce (1972, p. 100). Attention is defined as a hypothetical process of an organism which facilitates the selection of relevant stimuli from the environment (internal or external) to the exclusion of other stimuli and results in a response to the relevant stimuli. Tecce emphasized that the process of attention has steering functions, a point previously made in definitions proposed by Berlyne (1970) and Hebb (1958). Thus, attention is seen as an active, directional process that continues up until, and perhaps after, a response to the stimulus is made.

Attention was a lively topic of psychology in the early 1900s, but research and interest in the area declined with the rise of behaviorism, since this school of psychology tended to reject the study of attention on the grounds that it was "mentalistic." It was not until relatively recently (1960s and 1970s) that interest in problems of attention has been revived, partly because of attempts to find neurophysiological bases of attention and related phenomena, such as the orienting response. Recent books (Estes, 1976; Kahneman, 1973; Mostofsky, 1970) attest to this renewed interest.

Vigilance and Signal Detection. A bridge between early studies of attention and modern investigations was constructed by studies of vigilance in the 1940s and 1950s. The term "vigilance" was used by Mackworth (1950) and others to describe the situation in which an individual had to respond to randomly occurring and infrequent signals over an extended period of time. The original reason for studying vigilance performance was a very practical one, since it was noted that detection efficiency of World War II radar operators dropped off drastically in a short period of time. In fact, the Mackworth studies indicated a serious drop within the first 15 to 30 minutes of performance. The study of vigilance decrement has implications for other practical situations. For example, monitoring of relatively monotonous stimuli for long time durations occurs in assembly line inspection, as well as in the long-term vehicular control of truck drivers, airline pilots, and train operators. Some of the more recent studies relating brain activity to signal detection and fluctuations of attention with monotonous stimulation are presented in this chapter and in chapter 6 on cortical evoked potentials.

Beatty et al. (1974) hypothesized that learned regulation of theta activity (3 to 7 Hz) would affect detection performance in a prolonged monitoring task. They proposed that learned suppression of the occipital theta rhythm would maintain efficient detection, while increased theta activity would lead to a greater than normal decrement in performance of a monitoring task. The EEGs of 19 undergraduates were recorded from over the left occipital and parietal cortex. Twelve of the individuals were trained to suppress theta and seven to increase the amount of EEG activity in the theta band. The poorest detection performance was that of the group which produced theta during monitoring a radar simulator, in whom vigilance performance dropped continuously over the 2-hour period. Conversely, the best monitoring performance was shown by the group that was taught to suppress theta activity. In fact, an improvement in detection was observed for the theta-suppressed group in the last segment of the experiment, a period during which the theta-augmented group showed its worst performance. The authors suggest that the theta rhythm may be associated with arousal processes that determine monitoring efficiency under monotonous conditions. This result would have implications for improving the performance of persons who are involved in long-term monitoring activities, such as the inspectors, drivers, and radar operators mentioned previously.

In a paper submitted to a NATO Symposium on Vigilance, Gale (1977) makes a strong argument for the use of EEG in the study and prediction of signal detection performance. One of his own findings was that greater amounts of theta activity occurred in persons performing more poorly. This agrees with results of Beatty et al. (1974) in which theta enhancement was found to be related to poor detection performance.

The findings regarding EEG and attention are not numerous, but those that exist are interesting. The question of how and why theta production influences signal detection requires more study.

Perception and the EEG

Perception of the Vertical and the Effect of Arousal. The Rod and Frame Test (RFT), as described by Witkin, measures ability of subjects to judge the verticality of a luminous rod in a darkened room. To test the hypothesis that arousal, as defined by alpha blocking, would improve RFT performance, Hayes and Venables (1970) recorded EEG alpha in 21 subjects while they performed this task. To manipulate level of arousal, noise levels of 112 to 120 decibels (db) were presented over earphones whenever EEG alpha exceeded 80% of the person's maximum alpha. Performance did not improve in the noise versus no noise conditions, but neither did the percentage of alpha differ in the two conditions. The authors concluded that previous reports of improvement in the RFT may have been due to some factor other than arousal by meaningless noise.

Perceptual Structuring. In an interesting approach to studying the role of perceptual processes as reflected in the EEG, Giannitrapani (1971) measured EEGs of 32 eleven- to thirteen-year-old males under eight conditions. Measurements were made from 16 areas over frontal, parietal, occipital, and temporal locations during (1) awake resting, (2) listening to white noise, (3) listening to a portion of Tchaikovsky's "Marche Miniature," (4) listening to a segment of Mark Twain's *Tom Sawyer,* (5) silently performing mental arithmetic, (6) looking at a poster (7) looking through diffusing goggles, and (8) awake resting. The amount of high beta activity (21 to 33 Hz) increased when subjects were required to structure the stimuli. For example, listening to a portion of *Tom Sawyer* required structuring in that the verbal material is perceived by organizing sounds into words and words into a context; therefore, high beta activity increased under this condition. Conversely, the music condition shows a minimal beta effect, since it was probably already structured for the subjects used. Beta activity disappeared when the stimulus acquired the necessary structure.

Object Recognition and Discrimination. The EEG was analyzed during the preparatory stages and during recognition of objects by Zhirmunskaya et al. (1975). They presented 174 objects to 15 subjects by means of a tachistoscope. The exposure time was gradually increased from subthreshold values until the subject could name the object. The EEG was recorded from leads within each hemisphere (longitudinal placement) and from leads at similar areas of the two hemispheres (transverse placement). They reported greater degrees of EEG desynchronization (low voltage, fast activity) during recognition of objects than during simple mobilization of the subject's attention. The authors expressed the view that the EEG desynchronization is caused by the influence of subcortical brain structures upon cortical neurons.

The difficulty of an auditory discrimination task was varied as occipital EEG of 19 college students was measured (Wang et al., 1975). As difficulty of discrimination increased, the subjects made more errors and produced less alpha activity. This result supports the notion that more difficult discriminations demand greater mental effort with a resulting increase in the amount of alpha desynchronization.

In summary, complexity of stimuli, visual aftereffects, and stimulus color appear to be factors in producing changes in EEG activity. Modern studies of attention often come under the heading of vigilance or signal detection. The utilization of such approaches along with EEG measurements seems to be a fruitful one. For example, the production of theta activity has been related to inferior vigilance performance. Perhaps it may someday be possible to predict and control levels of attention and alertness by providing EEG-related feedback measures, as suggested by Mulholland (1974). Other studies have indicated that perceptual structuring and recognition and discrimination of stimuli appear to be accompanied by EEG changes in the direction of faster activity.

Conditioning of the EEG

Classical Conditioning of the EEG

Shagass (1972) reviewed a number of studies which indicated that classical conditioning of EEG responses could be produced; that is, after pairing of conditioned and unconditioned stimuli, changes in EEG patterns were observed at various recording sites on the scalp with presentations of the conditioned stimulus. Shagass believes that conditioning may play an important role in determining an individual's EEG pattern and might indicate that certain more or less permanent EEG characteristics, for example, the alpha index, may be affected by conditioning.

Operant Conditioning of the EEG

There do not appear to be many recent reports in the area of classical conditioning of the EEG with awake humans. On the other hand, there are many reports of operant conditioning of the EEG, where the presentation of a stimulus or a reward is contingent upon the production of a particular EEG pattern by the subject. A number of the operant conditioning studies may be placed under the heading of biofeedback training (BFT). For our purposes, an arbitrary distinction will be made between those studies showing operant conditioning of some physiological activity and those using BFT in an attempt to produce a beneficial effect, for example, to alleviate some human ailment such as tension headache. Thus, some EEG operant conditioning studies not expressly done in a BFT clinical context are reviewed in this section, while a more extensive review of BFT directed at alleviating specific ailments is reserved for a later chapter.

Dr. J. Kamiya has been one of the pioneers in demonstrating that human subjects can exert operant control over their EEG activity (Kamiya, 1969). The control of EEG alpha activity and the mental state associated with such production was investigated by Nowlis and Kamiya (1970). The EEGs of 26 persons were recorded from occipital, central, and frontal areas of the scalp. A tone was presented whenever the individual produced rhythmic activity in the 8 to 13 Hz range that measured at least 20 μV. The subjects were given trials in which they were asked to produce as much alpha as possible and others in which they tried to suppress alpha. The results showed that they were able to exert differential control over alpha production. Postsession questioning regarding how they exerted the control led to such responses as "relaxation," "letting go," "floating," "feeling of pleasure," and "security" being associated with alpha production. The alpha-suppressed condition was associated with "being alert and vigilant," "tension," and "agitation." Some individuals reported that they did not know how they achieved the result. Brown (1970) was able to demonstrate similar effects in a situation where subjects enhanced the amount of alpha activity signaled by a blue light. They were also asked to describe the feeling states associated with keeping the blue light on. Persons who "lost all awareness" or "drifted" or "floated" tended to have greater amounts of alpha activity. The technique used included "relaxation" or concentration on mental imagery. The question arises as to whether the achievement of the feeling states alone can be sufficient to produce alpha activity without the use of some external signaling device (sounds or lights). Beatty (1972) showed that it was possible for individuals to control alpha activity equally well if they were given feedback when it occurred (a tone) or if they were instructed about the nature of alpha and beta activity and the feeling states associated with them. If given neither type of information, alpha regulation did not occur. Beatty and Kornfeld (1972) ruled out the possibility that changes in heart or breathing activity were responsible for EEG changes in the operant conditioning paradigm. They trained 14 subjects to operantly control alpha and beta frequency while heart rate and respiration were measured. No significant changes were found in heart or breathing activity during conditioning of the EEG.

The training of theta activity was demonstrated by the ability of 12 subjects to suppress the 3 to 7 Hz band of EEG activity upon instruction to do so and by the ability of 7 others to increase the amount of such activity (Beatty, et al., 1974). The number of positive results relating to EEG control in a BFT context is impressive. However, there are some possible problems in the conduct of operant EEG conditioning procedures, as indicated in the next section.

Expectancies and Noncontingent Stimuli

Two recent studies indicate that researchers must be careful in their experimental design to eliminate or reduce the possibility of expectancy effects in the operant control of EEG (Clarke et al., 1976; Valle & Levine, 1975). In the Valle and Levine study, subjects who were led to believe that they enhanced alpha were actually able to control alpha better than those who believed they suppressed alpha. In the Clarke study, both "experimenters" and subjects were naive and the biasing effects of the experimenters' expectations were found to influence EEG alpha measures in the direction of the expectation.

Another possible problem is reported on by Fath et al. (1976). They monitored alpha EEG activity of 17 subjects who were divided into three groups: (1) feedback (auditory clicks) contingent upon production of alpha, (2) noncontingent clicks; and (3) no clicks. The noncontingent group produced the greater amount of alpha, with the contingent group second and the control group third with respect to amount of alpha activity. They make the point that noncontingent control groups should be used in operant conditioning of alpha; otherwise the alpha increases could be attributed to stimulus-elicited behavior, that is, the randomly occurring or noncontingent stimuli. If replicable, this finding would also have important implications for operant conditioning of other physiological responses as well as EEG pattern.

Eberlin and Mulholland (1976) performed an interesting experiment in which they controlled for intermittent, noncontingent stimulation in a novel way. They recorded EEG from left and right parietal-occipital electrode placements. Presentation of a visual stimulus was contingent on the production of alpha in one hemisphere only; if the other hemisphere produced alpha, no control over the stimulus occurred. Thus, in this second hemisphere, when stimulation occurred, it would be noncontingent; that is, it had nothing to do with the type of brain activity being produced. The results showed that EEG changes were due to the contingency between EEG and stimulation, not merely to the effects of noncontingent intermittent visual stimulation.

Thus, it would appear from the several studies reviewed here that control of alpha activity does occur. In a recent review, Johnson (1977) concluded that unmediated operant control of alpha activity has not been demonstrated. In other words, the person may not be learning to produce alpha per se, but may be influencing the amount of alpha through learning something else, such as the ability to ignore distracting stimuli. However, the study by Eberlin and Mulholland (1976) strengthens the possibility of operant control, since it would be difficult to explain why mediators would affect one brain hemisphere and not the other.

Sleep and the EEG

There has been a substantial amount of effort devoted to the study of EEG patterns during sleep, despite the fact that sleep studies are not at all easy to carry out. They may require that subjects sleep in a laboratory on one or more nights while EEG is recorded, and they require a considerable amount of effort and patience on the part of experimenters. The justification for this effort is that sleep is such an important biological activity and that it also has implications for human performance, behavior, and well-being.

The Nature of Sleep EEG

Why should researchers be interested in a state that appears to occur at such a low behavioral level? The answer is that there is actually much "behavior" going on during sleep, and investigators have been tackling such problems as levels of mental activity during sleep, depth of sleep and capacity to respond, dreaming behavior, sleep learning, effects of work schedule and exercise on sleep EEG, and effects of sleep deprivation on EEG and performance. Behavioral studies on the depth of sleep were carried out in the 1800s and often involved the question of how loud or strong a stimulus had to be in order to wake a person from sleep. It was not until the 1930s, however, when EEG measuring devices became widely available, that researchers were able to examine brain activity during sleep. Figure 4-1 presents EEG wave forms that distinguish sleep from waking. Sleep has been classified into four stages by Dement and Kleitman (1957a). The top tracing in Figure 4-1 illustrates the regular, cyclical alpha activity of the waking state. The second line from the top illustrates Stage 1 sleep, characterized by low-voltage

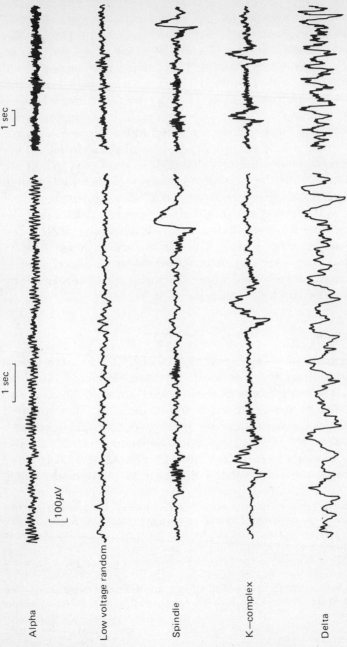

Figure 4.1. EEG wave forms distinguishing sleep from waking. The same patterns are shown at two recording speeds: on the left, a conventional rate of 25 mm/sec; and on the right, a rate of 10 mm/sec, widely used in sleep research.

random EEG activity. Stage 2 is shown in the third tracing and indicates an irregular EEG pattern with 12 to 14 Hz spindles every few seconds. Stage 3 sleep is depicted in the fourth line and is characterized by alternate fast activity, low-voltage waves, and large, slow waves (delta). The large wave with faster frequencies superimposed on it (line 4) was first described by Loomis et al. (1938) as the "K-complex." The K-complex is not associated with Stage 3 sleep per se but instead appears to occur spontaneously during the spindling phase of sleep. In fact, it occurs most commonly in Stage 2 sleep. It is considered to indicate arousal similar to the orienting response[1] of the waking state (Snyder & Scott, 1972). Dement and Kleitman quantified Stage 3 sleep as containing 10% to 50% delta activity (delta being defined as those waves of at least 100 μV amplitude, with a frequency of less than 2 Hz). The last line shows Stage 4 sleep, defined as containing more than 50% delta waves. Another commonly used sleep classification scheme is that developed by Rechtschaffen and Kales and is shown in Table 4-1.

EEG and Dreaming

The discovery that rapid eye movements (REM) were associated with dreaming was made by Aserinsky and Kleitman (1953). The eye movements they noticed varied in direction and amplitude and were 1 second or less in duration. They reported that persons awakened during REM periods could remember their dreams 75% of the time, while they could remember dreams in only 7% of the non-REM (NREM) awakenings.[2] This study was classic in that it initiated the scientific study of dreaming.

---

[1] The orienting response was a term introduced by Pavlov (1927) to describe reactions of animals to novel stimuli, a response which interfered with the conditioning process. One component of the orienting response is a change in EEG activity toward increased arousal, that is, faster and lower amplitude activity (Sokolov, 1963). The orienting response, as a concept, is discussed more fully in the final chapter of this book.

[2] Rechtschaffen (1973) has pointed out that subsequent investigations, which used less strict criteria for dreaming, have revealed that dreaming occurs fairly commonly in NREM sleep, but the contents are not as vivid or detailed as those associated with REM awakenings. Foulkes (1962) reported that 74% of NREM awakenings produced recall of mental activity and 54% resulted in accounts that could be defined as dreams.

Table 4-1   Classification of Sleep EEG

Stage W (waking)	Alpha activity and/or low-voltage, mixed frequency EEG
Stage 1	Low-voltage, mixed-frequency EEG with much 2–7 Hz activity (no rapid eye movements, REM)
Stage 2	Presence of sleep spindles (12–14 Hz) and/or K-complexes (high-voltage, negative-positive spikes) on background of low-voltage, mixed-frequency EEG
Stage 3	20% to 50% of epoch with high-amplitude delta waves (2 Hz or less)
Stage 4	Delta waves in more than 50% of epoch[a]
Stage REM	Low-voltage, mixed-frequency EEG activity and episodic rapid eye movements
Stage NREM	Stages 1, 2, 3, and 4 combined, i.e., those stages with no rapid eye movements

Note. From *A Manual of Standardized Terminology, Techniques and Scoring Systems for Sleep Stages of Human Subjects* by A. Rechtschaffen and A. Kales (Eds.). Washington, D.C.: U.S. Public Health Service, U.S. Government Printing Office, 1968.

[a] Measurement epochs are 20-30 seconds.

Researchers interested in the psychophysiology of dreaming now knew fairly precisely when dreaming occurred and could obtain reports of dreams and correlate these with various experimental manipulations and physiological responses. Later estimates of the percentage of times that dreams could be vividly recalled after awakening subjects from REM sleep vary from about 60% to 95% (Snyder & Scott, 1972). Some areas explored with the REM technique include: (1) changes in dream content over the night, (2) dream content among patients with differential psychiatric diagnoses, (3) effects of drugs on dream content, and (4) effects of presleep stimulation on dreaming.

Depth of Sleep and Capacity to Respond

Cyclical variations in EEG patterns occurring throughout the night were noted by Dement and Kleitman (1957a) and indicated a progression from light (Stage 1) to deep (Stage 4) sleep and back to light sleep again. The cycle from Stage 1 back to Stage 1 again takes approximately 90 to 100 minutes. After the first and second cycles, the deeper stages of sleep (3 and 4) rarely occur, that is, sleep becomes progressively lighter as the end of the sleep period approaches. This cyclical pattern of EEG activity throughout a night's sleep has been observed in many subjects. Studies have shown that the capacity of a sleeping individual to respond to stimuli depends on a number of factors, including the stage of EEG sleep, stimulus intensity, and significance of stimuli (Snyder & Scott, 1972). For example, Dement and Kleitman (1957a) found that louder sounds were required to wake subjects when they were in REM sleep as compared to onset of Stage 1 sleep. Williams et al. (1964) suggested that this might stem from the person's involvement in the content of some dream being experienced during REM sleep.

Actual awakening would be considered a behavioral measure of capacity to respond during sleep, while changes in EEG pattern, for example, desynchronization, would be physiological indicants. EEG desynchronization (increases in total number of waves) was used by Levere et al. (1973, 1974) to study effects of auditory stimuli upon arousal from sleep. The stimuli were found to be more physiologically arousing during a slow-wave delta-type EEG activity than during fast-wave activity. The higher intensity stimuli were more capable of producing behavioral arousal from sleep.

The effect of meaningfulness of stimuli upon arousal from sleep has been demonstrated by a number of researchers. For example, Oswald et al. (1960) reported that a subject's name produced more EEG and behavioral responses during sleep than did the name presented backwards, that is, keeping the stimuli the same but the meaning different. The EEG response was the K-complex. Williams et al. (1966) reported that the probability of responding during sleep to an auditory stimulus was increased when failure to respond resulted in punishment. The required response was closing a switch within 4 seconds, and the aversive stimulus was a fire alarm about 100 db above threshold. They suggested that these findings indicate the operation of "higher" nervous functions during some stages of sleep. Correct responses were greatest in Stage 1 sleep and decreased progressively to

Stage 4 sleep. Meaningful stimuli produced quicker awakening from sleep than nonmeaningful stimuli in a more recent investigation (Langford et al., 1974). Criteria for wakening were both behavioral (sleeper's acknowledgment of waking) and physiological (onset of alpha rhythm).

Dreaming and REM Sleep

In general, findings suggest that in REM periods, as well as in other stages of sleep, the individual is psychologically active, that is, the sleeper is occupied with inner mental events, and responses to external events may depend on whether they are significant compared to ongoing inner events (Snyder & Scott, 1972). This theory was reinforced by findings such as those of Levere et al. (1976) regarding the hypothesized intrusion into sleep of stimuli related to reward consistency. Variations in REM duration have been related to estimates of dream duration by Dement and Kleitman (1957b). Subjects were awakened after 5 or 15 minutes of REM sleep and were able to estimate dream duration in 92 of 111 cases.

The occurrence of "positive occipital sharp transients of sleep" (POSTS) was observed in the records of six normal subjects by Vignaendra (1974). The POSTS were described as having a rate of 5 Hz and an amplitude of from 20 to 75 μV. The POSTS occurred frequently during all stages of NREM sleep, especially Stages 2 and 3. The author suggests the interesting possibility that the POSTS represent the "playback" of visual information, obtained during the day, during NREM sleep. Supposedly, this playback enables the sorting, analyzing, and compressing of novel and relevant data for long-term memory storage, while rejecting redundant or irrelevant information. If this were true, it would represent a high level of psychological processing during the sleep state, a possibility that must be confirmed by further experimentation.

Learning During Sleep

The practical implications of being able to learn during sleep are considerable. But the question of whether sleep learning really occurs is still a controversial one, as indicated in a recent review of sleep learning research by Aarons (1976). A very basic question is whether people are really asleep when materials are being presented. In a study which used EEG criteria for sleep, Simon and Emmons (1956) tested subjects before and after sleep with 96 information items. The answers were given during sleep. Sleep was defined as the absence of alpha activity for at least 30 seconds before and for 10 seconds after answers were given to ensure that the act of giving the answer did not waken the individual. The number of correct answers before and after sleep showed no evidence of learning.

More recent studies, however, suggest that the EEG criteria set up by Simon may have been too restrictive. Studies by Williams et al. (1966), Langford et al. (1974), and Levere et al. (1976) indicated that an operant response can be performed during sleep and that meaningful materials were successful in arousing persons from sleep. These indicated at least some rudimentary information processing during sleep.

A study by Firth (1973) suggests that habituation of the EEG response, a very simple form of learning, can take place during sleep. Firth used auditory stimuli presented at either three regular intervals (10 to 30 seconds) or three irregular intervals (8 to 36 seconds). The number of K-complexes (sleeping analog of the "orienting response") decreased with the number of repetitive, irrelevant stimuli. The greatest habituation occurred for the 10-second, regular interstimulus interval. Firth suggested that earlier attempts to find habituation in sleep may have failed because stimulus intervals were too long. However, in a carefully conducted study by Johnson et al. (1975) which, in one part, duplicated the 10-second, regular interstimulus interval used by Firth, no evidence of the EEG K-complex was found. They analyzed the K-complex during Stage 2 sleep and found that, in fact, the percentage of subjects giving K-complexes increased over trials, probably reflecting arousal within Stage 2 sleep with repeated tone presentations. On the other hand, more encouraging results are presented for the EEG K-complex by McDonald et al. (1975). They report that a conditioned discrimination, learned during a waking condition, was carried over into Stage 2 sleep as indicated by K-complex responses to the conditioned stimulus (tones of either 200 or 2000 Hz). The authors propose that these results may indicate that information stored in long-term memory (processed during waking) remains available for processing during sleep and that information from long-term memory is most available in Stage 2 and less so in Stage 4 sleep. This is somewhat similar to results showing EEG responses to meaningful stimuli, since in McDonald's study the conditioned stimuli attained meaning during the waking state. The studies reviewed thus far indicate that a response to a simple, meaningful stimulus may take place during sleep, but none show learning of verbal materials.

In a detailed review of sleep learning studies, Aarons (1976) analyzed 11 studies that monitored EEG and sleep in procedures designed to estimate learning of verbal materials during sleep. These studies took place between the years of 1956 and 1974 (including Simon & Emmons' 1956 study reviewed earlier) and used various criteria for sleep stages, different kinds of verbal materials, and different tests of retention. Aarons concluded that *some* learning was evident in all but one study. Learning of small amounts of material was shown more often for the less rigorous recognition tests than for recall tests. The consistently small amount of learning observed led Aarons to agree with the conclusion that sleep learning of verbal materials is possible but not practical. An examination of Aaron's data indicates that in 7 of the 10 studies showing some learning, the learning was associated with fast-wave sleep or alpha activity. It would appear that the minimal amount of sleep learning observed occurred in lighter stages of sleep. Another possibility is that the act of presenting the verbal materials may have served to keep subjects in lighter stages of sleep. For example, Lehman and Koukkou (1974) found that presentations of verbal materials during sleep caused EEG activation of varying duration. Successful learning was related to higher and longer EEG activations after the presentation of the material.

In summary, it would appear that some simple information processing can take place during sleep, especially with respect to meaningful materials. The information processed seems to extend to verbal materials. Whether the amount of verbal material retained would ever justify the extensive use of sleep learning procedures and devices on a large scale would have to be decided on the basis of practicality and possible detrimental effects stemming from the loss of restful sleep over long periods of time.

Effects of Work Schedule and Exercise on Sleep EEG

The daytime sleep EEGs of 10 hospital corpsmen, working an 11 p.m. to 7 a.m. shift, were recorded by Kripke et al. (1970). The daytime EEG sleep patterns were similar to those previously reported for young adults: Waking (W) = 2%, Stage 1 = 7%, Stage 2 = 46%, Stage 3 = 12%, Stage 4 = 13%, and REM sleep = 20%. However, REM sleep tended to occur early and was frequently interrupted, and Stages 1 and 3 occurred later than usually recorded in nighttime sleep. The authors interpreted these changes in terms of biological effects produced by inversion of the sleep-wakefulness cycle.

The day and night sleep of 12 nursing students was found to differ with respect to both duration and pattern (Bryden & Holdstock, 1973). They fell asleep sooner during day sleep periods, but slept shorter amounts of time (6.6 hours vs. 7.2 hours). In addition, they showed an increased amount of Stage 1 sleep and a decrease in slow-wave sleep during daytime as compared to nighttime sleep. As in Kripke's study, REM sleep of the student nurses occurred sooner during day sleep periods.

The effects of exercise on sleep EEGs of eight healthy males were examined by Horne and Porter (1975). Afternoon exercise (85 minutes on a bicycle ergometer with a 15-minute break at the halfway mark) resulted in increased slow-wave sleep during the first half of the night. The same amount of morning exercise produced no changes in sleep EEGs. The authors interpret the results as reflecting the role of slow-wave sleep in recovery from work done later in the day. Recovery from work done earlier presumably takes place during the rest of the day. Browman and Tepas (1976) had nine young males engage in either progressive relaxation, light exercise, or a monotonous task (vigilance) on three separate nights, immediately prior to measurement of sleep EEGs. The three different presleep activities (approximately 45 minutes each) did not differentially affect sleep EEG patterns during the 7.5-hour sleep period. The subjects fell asleep faster after the relaxation condition, while the exercise condition kept them awake for the longest period of time.

The studies reviewed in this section seem to suggest that subjects need to adapt to the laboratory sleep situation, that daytime sleep differs from nighttime sleep, and that the effects of exercise and presleep activities may depend on the time of day and amount of work involved. Questions regarding effects of day versus night sleep and presleep activities on the sleeping EEG pattern need to be investigated further.

Effects of Sleep Deprivation on EEG and Performance

Naitoh (1975) distinguished between three types of sleep deprivation studies using human subjects: (1) total sleep deprivation, in which the person is kept awake throughout one or more entire sleep periods; (2) partial sleep deprivation, which involves loss of a portion of the regular sleep period; and (3) differential sleep stage deprivation, where certain sleep stages are selectively prevented from occurring, usually by arousing the person when the EEG records show signs of the particular stage to be deprived.

A systematic review of sleep loss effects on performance was conducted by Woodward and Nelson (1974). They noted that the types of activities most likely to suffer impairment were those that involved quick reactions, short-term memory, reasoning, decision making, and attention. The amount of sleep loss required to produce deficits in performance ranged from 24 hours for monotonous, routine tasks to 48 hours for cognitive tasks, such as decision making.

Naitoh (1975) warns traditional psychologists to consider the possible subtle effects of sleep loss on performance of subjects in their various experiments. Williams and Williams (1966) studied the recovery period sleep EEGs of 16 army men after total sleep deprivation. The sleep loss took place over a period of 64 hours (loss of two complete sleep periods). The EEGs during recovery from sleep loss showed an increase in slow-wave sleep during the first night. The subjects showed impaired short-term memory as a result of sleep deprivation. Lubin et al. (1974) also found impaired short-term memory during total sleep deprivation.

A long-term study of partial sleep deprivation was conducted by Webb and Agnew (1974). The subjects had sleep EEGs measured one night a week, over a 60-day period, while on a schedule of 5½ hours of sleep per night. Performance on a variety of tests (vigilance, addition, word memory, grip strength, and psychological mood) was also measured once a week. Initially, the amount of Stage 4 sleep increased, but this returned to normal levels by the fifth week. The amount of REM stage sleep decreased by 25% during the course of the experiment. Performance on only one test (vigilance) decreased with continued sleep restriction. The authors concluded that a chronic loss of sleep of about 2½ hours a night is not likely to result in major behavioral consequences.

Moses et al. (1975) selectively deprived subjects of either Stage 4 or REM sleep in two separate experiments. In the first experiment, they examined effects of REM deprivation or Stage 4 sleep deprivation after two nights of total sleep loss, while in the second experiment, effects of total sleep loss were examined after three nights of REM or Stage 4 deprivation. The number of arousals required to keep subjects from entering Stage 4 was significantly greater after sleep loss (Experiment 1) than it was in Experiment 2. The number and patterns of arousals indicate that the two nights of wakefulness increased the tendency to obtain Stage 4 sleep but not REM sleep. They interpret the results as supporting the hypothesis from previous studies that Stage 4 has priority over REM sleep in terms of recovery from sleep loss.

In an interesting study entitled "An Extreme Case of Healthy Insomnia," Meddis et al. (1973) described the case of a 70-year-old woman (Miss M.) who slept less than 1 hour each night. She rarely experienced fatigue, and this had been her sleep schedule since childhood days. In one experiment she remained awake for 56 consecutive hours and then only slept for 99 minutes while her EEGs were recorded. This sleep period was divided into the following stages: 37 minutes of REM sleep, 13 minutes of Stage 2, 31 minutes of Stage 3, and 18 minutes of Stage 4 sleep. In a second investigation, she slept in the laboratory on five consecutive nights, during which she averaged 67 minutes of sleep per night, without any behavioral signs of sleep deprivation. During the five nights, she spent 51% of the time in Stage 2 sleep, 23% in Stage 3, 9% in Stage 4, and 17% in REM sleep. With the exception of the absence of Stage 1 sleep, this pattern is not much different from that reported for healthy young adults (Kripke et al., 1970). This unusual woman spent much of her waking time engaged in activities which she enjoyed, such as writing and painting. She could not understand why other people slept for such long periods and wasted so much time!

In summary, it has been shown that sleep loss can affect short-term memory in normal persons. The amount of slow-wave sleep increases immediately after sleep deprivation. Results from a study of long-term partial sleep deprivation do not indicate serious consequences for performance. Selective deprivation of various sleep stages indicates the apparently greater importance of Stage 4 versus REM sleep. Rare individuals show no detrimental effects of very little sleep on either performance or sleeping EEG pattern. Perhaps in "healthy insomnia" the restorative functions attributed to sleep occur more quickly. Individuals such as Miss M. may be at some extreme point of a normal distribution of sleep time requirements. Conceivably, there are individuals at the other extreme who require 12 or more hours of sleep for normal functioning.

Research in the area of brain psychophysiology has been given impetus by electronic developments that enable the measurement of evoked brain potentials from the scalp. This development and associated studies of brain psychophysiology are discussed in the next three chapters.

Event-related Brain Potentials and Behavior: Measurement, Motor Activity, Hemispheric Asymmetrics, and Sleep

A great deal of research has been devoted to studying the relationship between evoked cortical potentials, or event-related brain potentials (ERPs), and human performance. Most of the work has been conducted over the past 15 years and is continuing at a high rate. The ERP has been found to be dependent on both physical and psychological characteristics of stimuli, although in some instances, ERPs are independent of specific stimuli. For example, brain responses have been reported to occur at the precise time that stimuli were expected but not actually presented (Sutton et al., 1967).

Vaughan (1969) proposed the term "event-related potentials" to refer to a variety of brain responses that show stable time relationships to actual or anticipated stimuli. Those ERPs were classified by Vaughan as (1) sensory evoked potentials, (2) motor potentials, (3) long-latency potentials, and (4) steady potential shifts (SPS).

The *sensory evoked potentials* include those produced by visual, auditory, somatosensory, and olfactory stimuli. Examples of ERPs are shown in Figure 5-1. They are based on the composite averaged potentials of eight individuals. The various negative and positive waves (components) of these ERPs can be seen in the illustration. *Motor potentials* (MP) refer to potentials that precede and accompany voluntary movement. Vaughan observed that the amplitude of the MP varies with the strength and speed of muscle contraction.

The *long-latency potentials* refer to those positive or negative

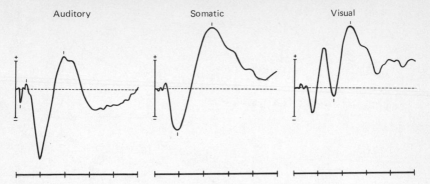

Auditory   Somatic   Visual

Figure 5-1.   Averaged evoked responses obtained from eight adult subjects. Each tracing is the computer average of 4800 individual responses. Calibration 10 μV, 100 msec/division (negative down).

components of the ERP that occur at 250 to 550 msec. They reflect subjective responses to expected or unexpected stimuli, including the orienting response (see Ritter et al., 1968). This is especially true for a positive component occurring at about 300 msec, termed P300, which was originally discovered by Sutton et al. (1965).

One example of a *steady potential shift* (SPS) is the contingent negative variation (CNV) first described by Walter et al. (1964). The CNV may be observed when a subject is told that he or she must respond to an event some time after a warning signal is given. For example, a warning tone (S1) may be given, and approximately 1 second later light flashes (S2) occur, at which time the subject must press a button. The CNV occurs between S1 and S2. Another SPS is the readiness potential (RP) of Kornhuber and Deecke (1965)[1] which builds up just before the onset of voluntary movement. Examples of the CNV, motor potential, and readiness potential are given in Figure 5-2. The long-latency potentials and SPS will be discussed further in chapter 7.

At the other extreme of long-latency potentials are the very early "far field" potentials. These were originally discovered in

[1] Originally called "Bereitschaftspotential" by Kornhuber and Deecke (1965), a term still used by many investigators.

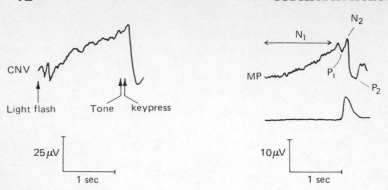

Figure 5-2. Examples of CNV, motor potential, and *Bereitschafts-potential* (readiness potential). On the left is CNV. ($n = 6$ trials) recorded from vertex (C_z) to right mastoid. Relative negativity at the vertex is upward. On the right (upper trace) is a motor potential ($n = 400$ responses) associated with dorsiflection of the right wrist and recorded from the left Rolandic area 4 cm from midline to a linked ear reference. The lower trace on the right is the summation of the rectified EMG resulting from muscle contraction. The slow negative component "N_1" is the readiness potential.

humans by Jewett et al. (1970), who demonstrated that several auditory ERPs of very short latencies (2 to 7 msec) could be recorded from the vertex after presentations of stimuli. These low-amplitude responses (0.5 to 1.5 μV) were attributed to electrical activity in various brain stem structures. Their existence has subsequently been confirmed by many other investigators. They are termed "far field," since they can be recorded from scalp electrodes (e.g., C_z) that are some distance from the source of the activity (brain stem). These brain stem potentials will be discussed again in chapter 13 "Applications of Physiological Measures."

Origin of ERPs

The specific brain areas involved in the generation of various kinds and components of ERPs are currently being sought by a number of researchers. Knowledge of these sources is important to the understanding of how brain areas participate in certain mental processes and in the application of ERP findings to practical clinical situations (Beck, 1975; Ritter, in press). The methods by which these sources are determined involve recording activity from subcortical and cortical areas of animal and human subjects. In addition, the use of multiple electrode placements on the scalp surface provides information about primary sources for various ERPs. This latter approach, in which detailed records of activity obtained at various scalp areas are carefully mapped out under various stimulus conditions, is termed topographical analysis. These approaches have indicated the brain sources of a number of specific ERP components. Several examples of these will be presented here.

There is evidence that early auditory evoked potential components (0 to 8 msec) recorded from the scalp in humans are produced at the brain stem (Jewett & Williston, 1971). Further, components of this response appear to be generated by specific structures in the auditory system. For example, a positive component occurring at about 3 msec after stimulation has been related to activity at the cochlear nucleus (Picton et al., 1974; also see wave II of Figure 13-1). Components of the somatosensory evoked potential have also been related to specific brain areas. For example, a negative wave occurring at 55 msec appears to be generated in the postcentral gyrus (Goff et al., 1978). Recordings made from the cortical surface of humans indicate that most sensory ERP components (auditory, visual, and somatosensory) seem to originate in or near the primary cortical sensory areas (Goff et al., 1978).

As implied earlier, the long-latency potentials are strongly influenced by subjective factors (e.g., task-relevant information). Scalp recordings of late potentials indicate maximal response from over frontal cortical areas, with a secondary focus at the parietal areas (Squires et al., 1975; Courchesne et al., 1975).

Motor potentials recorded in humans with the onset of voluntary movements indicate origins in the precentral cortex at the hemisphere opposite to the moving limb (Vaughan et al., 1968). The MP has also been found maximal from the precentral cortex of monkeys trained to make wrist extension movements (Arezzo & Vaughan, 1975).

One type of SPS, the CNV, has been found maximal over the

central cortex and less pronounced at frontal areas (Cohen, 1969). This finding has been confirmed by Simson et al. (in press), who found the later segment of the CNV to be localized primarily over the central cortex. The findings thus far suggest the central cortex as the primary CNV generator, with relatively little activity in frontal areas. McCallum et al. (1976) also recorded CNVs from areas of the human brain stem and midbrain.

Another type of SPS, the readiness potential, has been recorded from areas of brain stem and midbrain in human patients by McCallum et al. (1976). They reported that these slow potentials had distributions throughout the brain stem and midbrain. Deecke (1976) observed that the scalp-recorded RP is pronounced over parietal areas and nonexistent at frontal sites.

In summary, there are data that link certain sensory evoked potentials and motor potentials to activity in or near subcortical and cortical sensory and motor areas. Results from human and animal studies have implicated contralateral precentral cortical areas in the production of MPs associated with voluntary movements. Scalp recordings of long-latency potentials, CNVs, and RPs indicate maximal response at frontal, central, and parietal areas, respectively. The continued use of topographical approaches and the development of appropriate animal research are essential to further progress in identifying the brain areas responsible for generating various ERPs.

Method for Obtaining ERPs

As was pointed out previously, ERPs are derived from the EEG. Therefore, before one can obtain these potentials, the EEG must be recorded, as discussed in chapter 2. That is, the system of placing electrodes is the same, as well as the location designations, according to the "10-20 International System." If a researcher is interested in obtaining visual ERPs, he or she might place recording electrodes at O_1 and O_2, corresponding to locations over the left and right occipital areas. The researcher may also wish to place electrodes over other brain areas, such as parietal, temporal, and frontal, to determine how responses from these areas may vary with the kind of visual stimulus (its shape or color or its meaning, e.g., pure sounds or words).

Normally, when the EEG is recorded in a relaxed person and a visual stimulus is presented, some gross activity change, such as alpha desynchronization may be seen. The ERP will not usually be discernible in the EEG recording because it is much smaller than background EEG activity. Therefore, the evoked potential must be extracted from the EEG by using an averaging technique in which EEG samples are taken at the instant each successive visual stimulus is presented. The EEG samples are fed into a digital computer which sums the individual evoked potentials to successive flashes of light, for example. Thus the system is set up so that the presentation of a stimulus will produce sampling by a computer over a preset period of time, perhaps 500 msec. It should be emphasized, therefore, that ERPs are usually averages of a number of brain responses. There are instances where an ERP may be produced by one or a few presentations of a stimulus. For example, in a study by Cooper et al. (1977), ERPs were obtained to a single stimulus; and it is common to obtain the CNV with as few as 6 to 12 stimuli.

A basic premise in obtaining averaged ERPs is that the changes in brain activity are time-locked to some event, while the background EEG activity stays approximately the same. For example, suppose a single ERP is 5 μV and the background EEG activity is 20 μV. It is assumed that the evoked potential will increase as a function of N samples (e.g., $N = 100$), while the background EEG will increase as a function of $\sqrt{N}$. This can be expressed mathematically as

$$\frac{\text{Evoked potential amplitude } (N)}{\text{EEG amplitude } (\sqrt{N})} = \frac{5 \ \mu\text{V} \ (100)}{20 \ \mu\text{V} \ (10)} = \frac{500}{200} = 2.50$$

Thus the 2.50 figure represents an ERP that will be larger than the background activity. Usually, an averaged ERP that is twice the background EEG amplitude will be easily recognized. This ratio may be increased by increasing the number of samples.

Figure 5-3 shows a schematic drawing of the basic elements required to obtain a visual ERP (VEP). Depicted are a light source, a subject with appropriate electrode attachments, a physiological recorder, a computer of average transients, and an X-Y plotter. If the light intensity is high, the visual ERP may be obtained with the eyes closed.

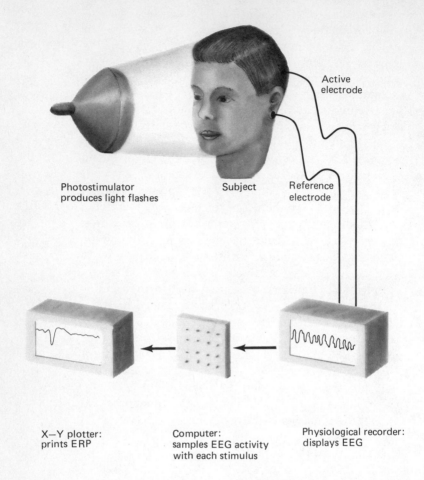

Active
electrode

Photostimulator
produces light flashes

Subject

Reference
electrode

X—Y plotter:
prints ERP

Computer:
samples EEG activity
with each stimulus

Physiological recorder:
displays EEG

Figure 5-3. Schematic drawing of recording situation to obtain a visual ERP. A stimulus source (light flashes), electrodes, physiological recorder, digital computer, and X-Y plotter are shown in the sequence from initiation of the stimulus to the printout of the ERP. Additional equipment might be a tape system to store brain activity and an oscilloscope for additional on-line monitoring of the EEG.

Quantification of ERPs

There are a number of ways to designate and measure amplitudes and latencies of the various positive and negative waves of the ERP. The two visual ERPs shown in Figure 5-4 were each produced by 100 flashes of light presented to the same person. Negative components are labeled N and positive components, P.[2] Notice that there are two positive and two negative waves or components clearly visible in this ERP. The N1 component was considered to be the first negative dip in the tracing which occurred 50 msec after presentation of the stimulus. The amplitude of the N1 component was measured as the vertical distance from "baseline" (initial horizontal portion of the X-Y plot) to the trough of this first depression. The P1 component was measured as the vertical distance from N1 to the peak of the first positive component, while N2 was measured as the vertical distance from the peak of P1 to the trough of the second major depression, and so on for P2. The latencies (or time after stimulus presentation) were measured to the midpoints of each positive and negative peak. If the "peak" is flat and appears more as a plateau, the midpoint of the plateau is taken as the latency measurement. The amplitude (in microvolts) and latencies (in milliseconds) of the larger of the two visual ERPs in Figure 5-4 (Condition A) were obtained according to these criteria. The amplitude measurements of each component are not strictly independent, that is, the amplitude of P1 will depend on the degree of negativity of N1, and so on. Therefore, it is more accurate to refer to N1-P1 amplitude or N2-P2 amplitude when giving magnitudes of response.

Vaughan (1969) suggested a flexible system for indicating polarity and latency of various ERP components. For example, a negative component at 150 msec would be labeled N150, while a positive wave at 200 msec would be designated P200.

The equipment for obtaining a P300 is identical to that used for sensory ERPs. However, the sample time after stimulus presentation should be extended to at least 1000 msec. To demonstrate P300, a subject might be requested to detect an occasional

[2] Some investigators designate the downward-going component as positive (P) and the upward one as negative (N).

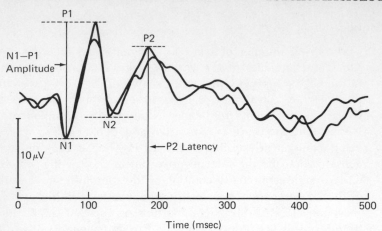

Figure 5-4. Method for measuring amplitudes and latencies of ERP components. The amplitude of the N1-P1 component (larger of the two traces) is 17.2 μV, based on the calibrated 10 μV signal. The P2 latency is 190 msec. Each of these two ERPs was based on averaged responses to 100 light flashes, on two different occasions. Negativity is downward. (From author's unpublished data.)

odd stimulus (e.g., a soft tone) interspersed in a series of relatively loud tones. When ERPs to soft and loud tones are summed, odd stimuli will produce a larger positive wave in the ERP than will frequent stimuli at approximately 300 msec after presentation.

The typical method for obtaining CNV involves the presentation of a warning stimulus (S1), followed within a fixed time period by a second stimulus (S2) to which the subject responds. The S1 may be a light, S2 may be a tone, and the response might be a key press. The interval between S1-S2 might be 1.5 seconds (see Figure 5-2). The CNV is maximally recorded with a scalp lead at C_z (vertex) referred to leads either on the earlobes or on the mastoid process (behind the ear). An important consideration in the measurement of CNV is the time constant (TC)[3] used. Cooper (1976) recommends, as a rule of thumb,

[3] The TC is the time for the amplitude of a wave to fall from 100% to 37% of its input value (Geddes, 1967). The TC should be long with respect to the physiological event being recorded.

that the TC should be at least three times the S1-S2 interval. Cooper mentions that use of too short a time constant results in a CNV that falls below baseline after the response is made. Tecce[4] recommends a TC of 8 seconds. The CNV may be obtained by averaging responses to between 6 and 12 combinations of S1 and S2 (Tecce, 1972). Electrical potentials produced by eye movements and blinks are possible sources of contamination in ERPs, especially the CNV. The measurement of these eye potentials and exclusion of contaminated trials produces satisfactory results.

The readiness potential can be produced in situations that require subjects to make voluntary movements at regular intervals. The recording electrode may be placed at C_z, and brain activity is sampled for several seconds prior to the movement until shortly after the motion is completed. A typical RP between 10 and 15 μV in amplitude may be obtained by taking 32 to 64 samples of brain activity with a time constant of 5 seconds (e.g., see Becker et al., 1976). Now that a variety of ERPs have been described, we shall see how they are related to human activities.

ERPs and Behavior

There have been many studies of ERP correlates of motor performance, perception, attention, higher cognitive functions (including language, meaning, and decision processes), intelligence, and stimulus complexity. Because of the abundance of studies, arbitrary criteria have been used to make the task of presenting even a selective review more manageable. One of these criteria was to limit coverage of areas that have already been extensively treated. For example, books by Callaway (1975), Regan (1972), and Shagass (1972b) emphasize individual differences, neurological factors, and clinical aspects, respectively, with regard to the ERP. Extensive review articles of the contingent negative variation and selective attention have been written by Tecce (1972) and Näätänen (1975). Second, we have selected only those articles that are representative of findings in a particular area. A third criterion involved the exclusion of animal ERP studies. However, the importance of animal investigations to

[4] J. J. Tecce, personal communication, August 26, 1977.

psychophysiology in general, and ERP work in particular, is acknowledged as being crucial to the development of the field.

The research material on ERPs has been divided into three chapters. This chapter covers ERP correlates of motor performance, hemispheric asymmetries, and ERPs during sleep. Chapter 6 is devoted to a treatment of mental activities and ERPs and sensory, attentional, and perceptual functions. Chapter 7 considers the long-latency potentials and steady potential shifts and their relation to behavior and performance.

ERPs and Motor Performance

Reaction Time

The time it takes to respond to an external stimulus is a function of many factors, including the intensity of the stimulus. Studies have shown that response time of the visual system decreases as stimulus intensity increases, whether the measure of time is purely physiological or behavioral. For example, Vaughan and Hull (1965) found that latencies of VEP components decreased with stimulus intensity. Further, Vaughan et al. (1966) reported that RT, as well as VEP component latencies, decreased as a function of increasing stimulus intensity. Thus, quick reactions were related to shorter VEP latencies.

Donchin and Lindsley (1966) measured RT to a flash of light, using a warning click and a variable foreperiod (from 1.0 to 2.5 second). They found that VEP amplitude and RT were definitely related, with faster RTs associated with larger VEP amplitudes. Telling the subjects how quickly they responded tended to shorten RT and increase VEP amplitude. Morrell and Morrell (1966) also measured visual RT and VEP, the latter being recorded at occipital and central locations. Their results agree with those of Donchin and Lindsley in that increased amplitudes of both positive and negative VEP components were associated with faster RTs. They suggested that factors such as selective attention and fluctuations in alertness are possible determinants of the relationship between RT and VEP amplitude.

Karlin et al. (1971) extended the relationship found between averaged evoked potential (AEP) amplitude and RT to auditory stimuli. They measured ERPs during simple and choice RT tasks and found larger auditory ERP amplitudes to be associated with faster RTs. In one choice RT condition, stimuli that did not require a motor response resulted in a higher late positive component (P300) than stimuli that did require a response. Thus, it could not be said that the enhancement of late positive components was due to effects of motor potentials.

Morris (1971) measured both VEP and RT to light flashes. He found significantly larger VEP amplitudes to be associated with faster RTs. The studies reviewed thus far seem to indicate that there is a relationship between the CNS response to a stimulus and speed of reaction. The relationship has variously been explained in terms of increased reactivity of the nervous system, arousal, or attentiveness. Karlin et al. (1971) suggested that the enhancement of the P300 component found in their study might be related to "effort, or the degree of a subject's self mobilization" (p. 135), and they proposed that holding back a response, in a context where responses are required to be made quickly, may require effort.

Ritter et al. (1972) measured ERPs to auditory stimuli while subjects engaged in simple RT and an auditory discrimination task (responding to changes in pitch). They found that the P200 component did not vary much in latency under the different conditions. However, P300 latencies were longer (100 to 200 msec) when subjects were required to make auditory (pitch) discriminations. Reaction times were also longer when discriminations were required. Further, P300 latencies and RT were longer with difficult discriminations than with relatively easy ones. The P300 component was largest at P_z, smaller at C_z, and smallest at O_z. Thus the P300 component was related to both discrimination difficulty and response speed.

The effects of bisensory stimulation on RT and the ERP were investigated by Andreassi and Greco (1975). Bisensory stimulation refers to the simultaneous, or near simultaneous, stimulation of two sensory systems (e.g., visual and auditory). Since it has long been known that RT to auditory stimuli is faster than to visual presentations, these investigators presented the visual stimuli prior to auditory stimuli. The time difference was determined in two ways: (1) the first, called $\triangle$ RT, used a temporal offset equal to the difference between each subject's RT to light and sound; (2) the second, called $\triangle$ N2, set the offset to equal the average latency difference of the N2 component to light and sound. The ERPs were measured from O_z and C_z under conditions of light alone, sound alone, light-sound offset by $\triangle$ RT, and light-sound, offset by $\triangle$ N2. All conditions of bisensory stimulation resulted in faster RTs than did unisensory stimulation. In addition, bisensory stimulation produced larger amplitude ERPs than did auditory or visual stimulation alone. Andreassi and Greco proposed that the results indicated the occurrence of facilitative sensory interaction in the nervous system, since bisensory stimulation resulted in faster RTs. They hypothesized that a possible site for this sensory interaction is the ascending reticular formation, since it is known that this subcortical structure has a role in coordinating sensory input and attentional mechanisms (Samuels, 1959; Scheibel & Scheibel, 1967) and has diffuse projections to the cortex.

In summary, some studies suggest that faster RTs are associated with higher amplitude ERPs. Others indicate the relation between latencies of certain ERP components and response speed. The ERP amplitude RT relationship could be a reflection of greater attention and CNS arousal when RTs are fast.

Motor Activity and the ERP

Vaughan et al. (1968) found that the MP accompanying voluntary movements was maximal over the Rolandic cortex (see Figure 5-5). Figure 5-5 shows data from Vaughan et al. (1968) in which MPs recorded from different scalp locations of one subject are illustrated for movements of the right foot. The points of maximal MP amplitude for foot, hand, and tongue movements are related to those brain areas known to produce these movements.

The effects of muscular activity upon the VEP have been studied by several investigators. Eason et al. (1964) measured VEPs to flashes of light while subjects maintained a 25-lb. force on a hand grip. The muscular work increased the amplitude of VEPs to light flashes. Andreassi et al. (1970) measured visual ERPs and motor ERPs from O_2 and C_3 while subjects maintained a dynamometer grip equivalent to one-eighth of their maximal

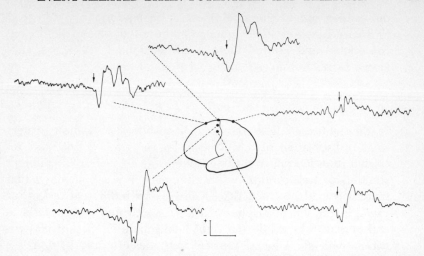

Figure 5-5. MPs associated with dorsiflexion of the right foot. Sum of 400 contractions. Calibration 500 msec, 2.5 μV.

squeeze. The major findings were that VEP was greater in magnitude with muscle tension than with a visual stimulus alone and that the MP was also enhanced under conditions of dual stimulation as compared to squeezing only. Landau and Buchsbaum (1973) used four light intensities and two tasks (relaxation and mental arithmetic) over several days to test effects of holding 10 lb. of weight on ERPs of male and female subjects. Their recordings were made from the vertex (C_z). They noted two effects: (1) an overall decrease in ERP across days when subjects held the weights, and (2) an increase in ERP amplitude under the weight condition, as compared to relaxation, on the third day of testing. They concluded that both arousal and attentional factors interact with muscle activity to influence the visual ERP. Thus the Landau and Buchsbaum study agrees with earlier ones to a limited extent.

Investigators of motor activity as related to the ERP seem to have been limited to very simple responses such as required in RT and induced muscle tension. The muscle tension studies, in general, appear to support the notion that impulses from two senses can interact to influence ERPs recorded at the cortex. For example, input from visual and proprioceptive (muscle) impulses may sum at the level of the reticular formation and lead to enlargement of ERPs under conditions of dual stimulation. Attentional and arousal factors may also be involved, as suggested by several investigators.

Hemispheric Asymmetries in ERPs

In the context of ERP research, hemispheric asymmetry refers to the observation of a difference in the evoked potential recorded from left and right hemispheres as a function of different stimulus or task conditions. In chapter 3 it was concluded that there was evidence for EEG asymmetry with different tasks. For example, the left hemisphere EEG was activated with numerical and verbal tasks, while the right hemisphere EEG showed activation with spatial and musical activities. In this section, we shall consider evidence regarding ERP asymmetries under the following categories of stimuli and tasks: visual, auditory, and cognitive.

Asymmetries with Visual Stimulation

If the eyes are fixated straight ahead, the locus of retinal stimulation varies with the position of a stimulus in the visual field. For example, if you look straight ahead while driving a car, the object you focus on will stimulate receptors in the foveal area of the retina, while objects off to the side will produce peripheral stimulation. A number of studies by Eason and his colleagues have indicated a relationship between locus of retinal stimulation and visual ERPs. For example, Eason et al. (1967) recorded from over left and right hemispheres and found that the occipital area receiving primary projections from the retinal area stimulated produced larger amplitude VEPs than did the other lobe. The right lobe is primary when stimuli appear in the left visual field, and the left is primary for stimuli in the right visual field.[5] Eason et al. (1967) also reported asymmetries based on

[5] This is because the temporal retina (outside half) of the right eye and nasal (toward nose) retina of the left eye are primarily stimulated by objects in the left visual field. Both of these retinal areas project visual impulses to the right hemisphere. The opposite occurs for stimuli in the right visual field.

whether a subject was right-handed or left-handed. That is, the VEP recorded from over the right lobe of left-handed subjects was greater than that from the left hemisphere. Right-handed subjects did not show this difference. Thus, these investigators concluded that the difference in amplitude between the two lobes was related to handedness.

Eason and White (1967) reported that VEPs from the right occipital area were greater in amplitude to flashes imposed on the temporal retina of the right eye than to flashes presented to the nasal retina of the same eye. They pointed out that this probably occurred because the right occipital cortex does not receive projections from the nasal retina of the right eye. Eason and Dudley (1971) stimulated three retinal areas (fovea, 20 degrees from fovea, and 40 degrees from fovea) of the right eye with light flashes varying in size from 0.14 to 20.63 degrees of visual angle, centered at the three sites. The VEPs, measured from over the right hemisphere, indicated that latencies varied directly with distance from the fovea, that is, as the stimulus was moved from the fovea, the latencies became longer. The initial deflection of the VEP increased in amplitude with stimulus size at all retinal locations.

Andreassi et al. (1975) examined VEP in two separate experiments as a function of stimulus location. In Experiment 1, three stimulus locations were used: a .67 degree diameter stimulus at the center of the visual field, at 2.67 degrees to the left, and at 2.67 degrees to the right. Stimuli presented in the left visual field resulted in shorter VEP latencies at the right occipital area than at the left, while for stimuli presented in the right visual field, the opposite occurred. In Experiment 2, the same .67-degree stimulus was presented in seven different locations, ranging from center to 4 degrees of visual angle in the left and right fields. The same VEP latency asymmetries were obtained. In addition, there was a trend toward a decrease of VEP amplitude with increasing distance of stimulation from the fovea. The postulated explanation for the VEP latency asymmetries observed was in terms of the angle at which the visual stimuli entered the retinas of the two eyes from the various locations. For example, under conditions of right visual field stimulation, the stimulus impinges most directly on the temporal retina of the left eye and the nasal retina of the right eye (areas that have projections to the left lobe), resulting in shorter latencies for VEPs recorded from over the left occipital hemisphere. The delayed VEP, recorded from over the right lobe in this instance, may be due to the cross-over of visual system impulses from the left lobe via the corpus callosum and other cerebral commissures. Thus the time taken to cross the commissures explains the latency differences observed at the primary and secondary lobes.

There is also evidence that the visual presentation of verbal materials results in hemispheric asymmetries. For example, Buchsbaum and Fedio (1969) reported greater VEP differences to words and nonsense patterns for the left occipital hemisphere than for the right hemisphere. Similar findings were obtained by Buchsbaum and Fedio (1970) when they compared VEPs to very common three-letter words and nonsense stimuli composed of random dot patterns. Both experiments by Buchsbaum and Fedio were conducted with right-handed subjects (i.e., persons who had a very high probability of left hemisphere dominance with respect to speech functions).

Davis and Wada (1974) measured visual and auditory ERPs in 12 normal (left-sided speech-dominant) persons and in 10 epileptics (5 right and 5 left speech-dominant). The visual stimuli (light flashes) produced ERPs of similar form in the non-speech-dominant hemisphere, while auditory stimuli (clicks) produced similar ERPs in the speech-dominant hemisphere. Davis and Wada hypothesized that the speech-dominant hemisphere possesses superior auditory perception capabilities, while visual perception is more of a nondominant hemisphere function. Although these asymmetries are related to speech dominance, they may be more fundamental than speech processing, since they do not require verbal stimuli. These are provocative suggestions and certainly deserve continued research effort.

Asymmetries with Auditory Stimulation

Butler et al. (1969) recorded auditory ERPs from over the right hemisphere only under conditions of monaural and binaural stimulation. A 1000-Hz tone was presented at intensities ranging from 20 to 100 db. They found that when the monaural stimulus was delivered to the left ear, the right hemisphere derived ERP components showed consistently shorter latencies than when the monaural stimulus was presented to the right ear (when the tone was in the range of 50 to 100 db). That is, auditory ERP latencies were shorter for contralateral (opposite side) than for ipsilateral (same side) stimulation. They explained this finding in terms of the more direct route to the cortex offered by contralateral auditory pathways as compared to ipsilateral projections. But this explanation is unlikely because ipsilateral and contralateral pathways are equally complex. They also noted that contralateral stimulation produced larger ERP amplitudes than did stimulation of the ear on the same side of the head.

Andreassi et al. (1975) examined auditory ERPs recorded from over both left (C_3) and right (C_4) hemispheres during monaural and binaural stimulation. The stimulus used was white noise at a level of 80 db. They found that auditory stimulation produced larger amplitude ERPs in the contralateral hemispheres as compared to the ipsilateral. This agrees with the findings of Butler et al. (1969). However, Andreassi et al. found no difference in ERP latencies from contralateral and ipsilateral hemispheres. The amplitude results were interpreted as providing further evidence for the predominance of the contralateral pathways of the auditory system. It is known that each ear has more neuronal connections to the hemisphere on the opposite side than to the auditory cortex on the same side.

One might expect that simultaneous stimulation of left and right ears with verbal stimuli would lead to superior detection performance by the right ear, since dominant pathways from the right ear lead to the left hemisphere, which controls language function in most people. This has been found to be the case in a number of studies in which the two ears were presented with similar stimuli (Kimura, 1961, 1967). Shorter ERP latencies for contralateral auditory stimulation were reported by Majkowski et al. (1971). Higher amplitude contralateral responses with auditory stimuli have also been observed by Price et al. (1966) and by Vaughan and Ritter (1970).

Peters and Mendel (1974) determined effects of monaural and binaural stimulation (40-db clicks) on the early components of the ERP, that is, components with latencies of less than 50 msec. No contralateral-ipsilateral differences were found. Possible reasons for this given by the authors included a suggestion of different underlying neural mechanisms for early versus late ERP components and the use of a low level of stimulation (40 db). It will be recalled that Butler et al. (1969) found evidence for laterality in late ERP components only with stimuli of 50 db or greater in intensity.

The effects of more complex stimuli on the ERP, such as speech stimuli and word meaning, are discussed in chapter 6. With regard to asymmetry, however, it may be noted that Morrell and Salamy (1971) found ERP amplitudes recorded from over the left hemisphere to be larger than those from the right in response to speech stimuli. Asymmetries have also been reported for linguistic information (Wood et al., 1971), speech versus mechanical sound-effect stimuli (Matsumiya et al., 1972), contextual meaning of words (Brown et al., 1973), and verb and noun meanings of ambiguous words (Teyler et al., 1973). However, Grabow and Elliott (1974), who required their 14 subjects to make either simple speech sounds (e.g., ba) or words (e.g., kangaroo) found no evidence for hemispheric asymmetries during verbalization. A similar finding has been reported by Galambos et al. (1975).

Asymmetries and Cognitive Functions

Rhodes et al. (1969) reported that bright children produced right hemisphere visual ERPs that were larger than their left-sided ERPs. This contrasted with dull children who had no hemispheric amplitude asymmetries. A similar finding was obtained by Richlin et al. (1971), who found larger right hemisphere visual ERPs in children of normal intelligence but the reverse effect with retarded children. Galin and Ellis (1975) recorded visual ERPs from over left and right hemispheres while subjects performed verbal and spatial tasks. The ERP asymmetry obtained reflected hemispheric specialization for these tasks. They caution that studies of ERP lateral asymmetries should carefully control the cognitive mode of participating individuals, since this can be a source of variability.

In summary, a number of studies have indicated a relationship between location of stimuli in the visual field and hemispheric asymmetries in the VEP. These findings have been related to the projections of the temporal retinas to the same-sided (ipsilateral) cortex and of the nasal retinas to the contralateral visual cortex. VEP asymmetries have also been reported for verbal versus nonsense visual stimuli (i.e., the speech-dominant hemisphere produces larger responses to verbal material).

Hemispheric asymmetries (both latency and amplitude) have been reported as a function of ear stimulation. The shorter latency and higher amplitude responses from the contralateral hemispheres have been interpreted as consistent with the known contralateral predominance in the pathways of the auditory system. AEP asymmetries for speech and language materials have been reported by some investigators and not by others. However, there appears to be more evidence for the positive findings.

There is some evidence to indicate that ERP asymmetries may be related to intelligence and cognitive functioning. These remain to be confirmed by future research.

The ERP and Sleep

The classification of sleep into distinct stages on the basis of brain wave activity was discussed in chapter 4 (see Table 4-1). These distinctions have enabled investigators to present sensory stimuli to persons in different sleep stages in order to study ERPs as a function of sleep stage. Shagass (1972b) summarized findings regarding the somatosensory ERP (SEP) obtained during sleep as follows: (1) latencies of SEPs become longer as sleep progresses from Stage 1 to 4; (2) the SEP during REM sleep is similar to that obtained during light sleep stages; (3) amplitude changes are not as consistent as those observed for latency, but early components are generally enlarged during slow-wave sleep; (4) the SEP gradually (perhaps as long as 30 minutes) returns to the presleep level after awakening.

Shagass and Trusty (1966) found a systematic relationship between visual ERP latencies and sleep stage, that is, progressive lengthening of latencies from Stage 1 to Stage 4. Weitzman and Kremen (1965) reported similar relationships between auditory ERP latencies and sleep stage.

Very early auditory ERPs, occurring between 1 and 10 msec

after stimulation, have been found by Jewett and Williston (1971) and related to activity evoked from brain stem auditory structures. Amadeo and Shagass (1973) experimented to determine whether these early ERPs would differ in awake and sleeping individuals. Their results showed little difference in amplitude and latency of these brain stem potentials either between waking and sleep or between sleep stages. They interpreted this finding as indicating that changes in later AEP components which occur during sleep are mediated by brain areas above the level of the brain stem, either at the thalamus or the cerebral cortex. Early components (latencies less than 40 msec) of the AEP were studied during REM and Stages 2, 3, and 4 sleep by Mendel and Kupperman (1974). These early components, obtained during REM sleep, had the same latency, amplitude and wave form as AEPs elicited during other sleep stages. Mendel et al. (1975) investigated the middle latency (8 to 50 msec) and late AEP components (50 to 400 msec) of adults in both sleeping and awake states. Sleep was induced by a drug (secobarbital) in 28 subjects. They found that in both the awake and sleeping states the middle latency AEP components were better measures of auditory thresholds than were late components. The authors suggest that the middle latency AEP components may be of use in measuring auditory functions in a clinical setting.

Buchsbaum et al. (1975) studied the effects of sleep stage and stimulus intensity on AEPs. Clicks ranging from 50 to 80 db were used as stimuli. They found that AEP amplitudes increased more with increasing stimulus intensity during Stages 2, 3, and 4 sleep than during REM sleep or when subjects were awake. More recently, Townsend et al. (1976) exposed 10 subjects to tone pulses 24 hours a day for 30 days. The intensity levels were at 80 and 90 db for 10 days each, in that order. The AEPs were examined in Stage 2 and REM sleep on every fifth night of the 30-day period. One finding was that the AEP in Stage 2 sleep was consistently larger than in REM sleep. The main finding was that during sleep there was little habituation of the AEP, even with long-term, daily exposure to the same stimulus. Thus, they concluded that the AEP during sleep is similar to the K-complex (see chapter 4) in terms of resistance to habituation. (It will be recalled that the K-complex is considered to be the sleeping

EEG correlate of the orienting response.) Thus the authors point out that during sleep the AEP behaves as though each succeeding stimulus is a "first" presentation.

In summary, the overall findings regarding ERPs during sleep indicate that they definitely occur and that the later components differ from waking ERPs in latency and amplitude. Sleep is an example, therefore, of a situation where a brain response occurs to a stimulus that is probably not consciously perceived.

Event-related brain potentials and various mental functions, including intelligence, meaning of stimuli, linguistic processing, learning, and hypnosis are covered in the next chapter. Sensory, attentional, and perceptual processes and their relations to ERPs are also presented in chapter 6.

Event-related Brain Potentials and Behavior: Mental Activities, and Sensory, Attentional, and Perceptual Functions

In this chapter we discuss some of the findings concerning the ERP and mental activities, including measures of intellectual functioning, meaning, linguistic processes, learning, and hypnotic suggestion. We also examine some ERP correlates of sensation, attention, and perception. The long-latency ERPs and steady potential shifts (e.g., CNV and P300) will be discussed in chapter 7 with regard to their observed relationships to higher cognitive processes such as attention, preparation for events, and information processing.

Event-related Potentials and Mental Activity

In this section we consider a number of human mental processes as they have been related to ERPs. Among these are intelligence, linguistic processes, learning, meaning, imagery, and ERPs produced during hypnotic suggestion.

ERPs and Intelligence

The approach in this area has been to attempt to relate some characteristic of ERPs (e.g., latency, amplitude, variability) to some measure of intellectual performance, most commonly, performance on an intelligence test. The original experiment was performed by Chalke and Ertl (1965), who postulated that latencies of ERP components may be an index of information-processing efficiency, that is, biologically efficient organisms process data more quickly than less efficient ones, and thus their ERP latencies should be shorter. In their study, Chalke and Ertl obtained ERPs to light flashes, using bipolar, F_4–P_4, electrodes. The measure of IQ was performance on a paper-and-pencil intelligence test developed by Otis (Higher Form A). The subjects were 33 graduate students with high Otis scores, 11 army cadets with average scores, and 4 mentally retarded individuals with very low scores. The results indicated that latencies of later ERP components (those occurring after 100 msec) were related to intelligence test scores (i.e., the higher the score the shorter the latency). This early study used a rather lopsided sample of subjects, since scores were clustered toward the high end. However, a much larger scale study by Ertl and Schafer (1969) based on a sample of 566 schoolchildren indicated significant correlations between test scores and ERP latencies.

Negative Findings

Several investigators have failed to confirm the relationship between ERP latencies and intelligence. Among them were Rhodes et al. (1969), who found that high intelligence scores were related to greater ERP amplitude but that performance was not related to latency. Davis (1971) reported no relation in a large-scale study in which visual ERP latencies were measured in more than 1,000 schoolchildren and compared to test scores and school performance.

In another study, the auditory ERP was measured using a bipolar placement with 84 persons in a first experiment and with 212 subjects in a second one (Rust, 1975). The measure of intelligence was the Mill Hill Vocabulary Scale in the first experiment and the Ravens Progressive Matrices in the second experiment. Neither study found a relation between intelligence and latency measures. Rust notes that more evidence has been produced for the visual ERP than the auditory in the intelligence context but saw no reason for a restriction of neural efficiency to any particular sensory modality, a comment similar to that made by Callaway (1975).

Positive Findings

Some additional investigators who have reported a relationship between the ERP and intelligence test scores are Osborne (1969), Galbraith et al. (1970), Shucard and Horn (1972), Gucker (1973), and Perry et al. (1976). Osborne (1969) found that test performance was negatively related to visual ERP latencies in a sample of 60 volunteer subjects. Galbraith et al. (1970) measured visual ERPs of retarded and normal young adults and found that long VEP latencies were related to low test scores. Shucard and Horn (1972) measured visual ERPs and intelligence scores of 108 persons under conditions of high, medium, and low arousal. They found the greatest degree of correspondence between fast latency and high scores under the low arousal condition. One suggested possibility was that brighter subjects were better able to maintain alertness in the boring low-arousal condition in which subjects merely watched light flashes. Shucard and Horn argued that arousal levels of subjects must be low in order to successfully use ERP latencies to predict intelligence. Gucker (1973) measured the VEPs of 17 children ranging in age from 8 to 13. Their WISC scores were correlated with measures of VEP latency and a high negative relationship was found, indicating that higher test scores were related to faster latencies.

A number of visual ERP and intelligence measures were studied by Perry et al. (1976). They administered a battery of abilities tests to 98 five-year-old children. Visual ERPs were recorded from left and right hemispheres (monopolar) and occipital midline (bipolar) under three stimulus conditions. The measures used were amplitude, latency, and complexity (number of peaks) of ERPs. They reported significant multiple correlations between these VEP measures and Wechsler Preschool and Primary Scale of Intelligence (WPPSI). An interesting aspect of this study is that the subjects were not selected on the basis of extreme IQ scores; in fact, the mean WPPSI IQ score was 119, with a range of from 94 to 141. Thus the relationships found between cortical functioning and intelligence seem to be encouraging, at least for the sample used. Perry and his colleagues intend to follow up this investigation with a series of studies on the same children.

Unlike investigations attempting to relate EEG to intelligence, the evidence appears to indicate some relation between the ERP and intelligence. Although Ertl and his colleagues deserve credit for stimulating research in this area, their neural efficiency hypothesis leaves much to be desired. As Callaway (1975) has argued, it is unlikely that a single neurophysiological factor, such as shorter ERP latencies, can be identified as the biological substrate of intelligence. In the meantime, investigations using multiple measures of the ERP and intelligence may prove to be more fruitful than more limited approaches. Hopefully, the experimental data derived from such approaches will enable the development of a satisfactory theoretical model to explain the relation between cortical function and intelligence.

ERPs and Stimulus Meaning

A number of studies have been conducted to determine whether significance or meaning of a stimulus, either natural or experimentally contrived, would affect the ERP. One early investigation in this area was that of Chapman and Bragdon (1964), who reported greater amplitude ERPs to relevant number stimuli as compared to irrelevant blank flashes. Begleiter et al. (1967) manipulated visual stimuli by giving them positive, negative, or neutral meaning through a conditioning procedure. Visual ERPs were recorded from over the right occipital hemispheres of 31 male college students. They found significantly lower ERP amplitudes to objects that had acquired negative and positive meanings, as compared to neutral stimuli. The authors suggested that the lower amplitudes for negative and positive stimuli, as compared to the neutral stimulus, indicate some sort of inhibitory brain activity for these affective stimuli.

However, Begleiter and Platz (1969a) used taboo words (e.g., fuck) and neutral words (e.g., tile), which were printed in capital letters and equal in area, to obtain visual ERPs. Blank flashes of light were also used. They reported that VEP components appearing shortly after 100 msec were larger in amplitude for taboo words than for neutral words or flashes. A later component was larger for both types of words than the blank flash. Thus, meaning seemed to alter the late VEP components but not in a manner consistent with the results of Begleiter et al. (1967).

Perhaps the taboo words produced more of a response in subjects than previously used stimuli because of the stronger inherent affective value of these stimuli as compared to those that attain such meaning through conditioning.

Sandler and Schwartz (1971) found that visual ERPs could be modified by content of a stimulus, independent of shape differences. For example, ERP amplitudes differed according to whether an ambiguous figure was seen as male or female (i.e., they were larger in amplitude for female perceptions). They concluded that change in stimulus content, or meaning, was more effective than structural change in producing ERP wave form variations.

An interesting demonstration of how internal factors such as expectancy might affect ERP amplitude was performed by Begleiter et al. (1973). In their experiment, moderate-intensity light flashes elicited either large or small amplitude ERPs, depending on whether a warning tone signaled that a bright or dim flash would follow. Thus the importance of subjective factors, independent of objective stimulus characteristics, in generating the ERP was again shown. Further, there have been reports of changes in the ERP which appeared at about the time when an expected, but absent, stimulus should have been presented. For example, Sutton et al. (1967) found that an ERP would occur in the absence of an expected click. Weinberg et al. (1970) referred to this as an *emitted* potential in contrast to potentials that are *evoked* by a specific stimulus. Ruchkin and Sutton (1973) reported the same result for visual stimuli, that is, a P300 response appeared with a peak latency of 400 msec at C_z and 480 msec at O_z, following the time of the missing flash. The lower amplitude and longer duration of the emitted P300 (compared to the evoked P300) was hypothesized to be due to the lack of a precisely timed external stimulus. In other words, the P300 associated with an expected, but missing, stimulus is an internally produced potential influenced by the variability inherent in subjective time estimates.

In summary, the studies reviewed in this section indicate that meaningfulness of stimuli appears to alter the ERP. Factors such as stimulus content, affective value, and expectancies exert an influence on the recorded brain response.

ERPs and Linguistic Processes

This section is primarily concerned with ERPs to language and nonlanguage stimuli. A number of investigators have reported differences in ERPs recorded over right and left hemispheres, depending upon whether stimuli were language related or not. For example, Wood et al. (1971) recorded ERPs during two auditory identification tasks: one task provided linguistic information and the other did not. Auditory ERPs from the left hemisphere differed for the two tasks but were identical over the right hemisphere. The authors concluded that different neural events occur in the left hemisphere during analysis of language versus nonlanguage stimuli. Morrell and Salamy (1971) reported that amplitude of auditory ERPs to natural speech stimuli were significantly larger in left hemispheric as compared to right hemispheric derivations.

Another approach was taken by Brown et al. (1973), who observed that wave forms of ERPs differed according to the meaning of a word. For example, ERPs to the word "fire" differed when it was presented in the phrase "sit by the fire," as compared to "ready, aim, fire." The wave form differences were significantly greater from over the left hemisphere than for right hemispheric locations (see Figure 6-1). In another part of this study, no hemispheric differences occurred when the meaning of the word "fire" was ambiguous. This was accomplished by using phrases such as "fire is hot" and "fire the gun."

To dispel possible criticisms that the words accompanying the critical stimuli were different and therefore could have produced the asymmetries found, Brown et al. (1976) conducted another experiment. They tested 15 young adults in a situation in which meaning was assigned immediately before the critical stimulus was delivered along with other words. That is, meaning was established for the ambiguous phrase "it was led" by telling subjects that the last word would be a noun, as in "the metal was lead," or a verb, as "the horse was led." The ERPs were recorded from two leads each over the left and right hemispheres. The leads were over F_7 (approximately Broca's area related to speech articulation); F_8, 3 cm from T_3 (Wernicke's area related to speech comprehension); and 3 cm from T_4. Again, as in the

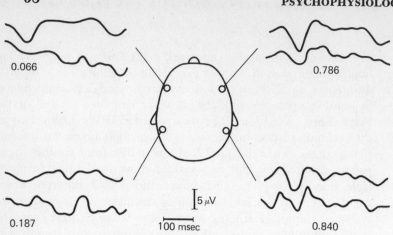

Figure 6-1. Averaged evoked potentials ($N = 100$) from one subject to the word "fire." For each pair of traces, the upper is the average response to the word "fire" presented in the phrase "sit by the fire." The lower is the response to "fire" in the phrase "ready, aim, fire." The coefficients of correlation below each pair are a measure of degree of similarity between the wave forms of the two traces. Upward deflections are positive with respect to the reference leads.

earlier study, Brown and associates reported that ERPs from over Broca's area were dissimilar for the two meanings, while they were similar at the other locations.

Friedman and colleagues (1975a) reported an experiment in which auditory ERPs were produced by real speech words and human sounds. An example of a real word was "kick" and a sound example was "pssst," uttered by the same person. The ERPs were measured under conditions in which the sounds and words were merely listened to and where one of them served as a signal for a finger movement. They found the P300 component amplitude to be largest to signal stimuli and smallest under passive listening. Sounds produced larger P300s than words at all electrode locations (left and right hemispheres, midline). The authors suggested that this might be due to the novelty of the sounds, since they occur less frequently in everyday speech.

Analyses of left-right hemispheric differences yielded only two greater left than right differences. The authors concluded that earlier studies reporting ERP correlates of differential hemispheric processing had design and statistical flaws and that reflection of hemispheric functioning by ERPs may not be as strong as indicated in the past.

Galambos et al. (1975) compared ERPs of subjects to speech sounds (pa or ba) and pure tones (250 to 600 Hz). They tested the hypothesis that the speech sounds would produce larger ERPs at the left hemisphere. They found the left and right hemisphere responses to speech or tones to be very similar and thus concluded, as did Friedman and co-workers, that the hemispheric differences to speech and nonspeech sounds are very small, at least under present recording conditions.

In still another experiment, Friedman et al. (1975b) recorded visual ERPs from over right and left hemispheres and vertex. The stimuli consisted of sequentially presented words that comprised a sentence. In one condition, an ingenious technique prevented the subject from knowing the meaning of the second word in the sequence until the last was shown.[1] In the other conditions, the meaning of the second word was known immediately. The latency of P300 to words that delivered information (last word or second word) was consistently longer than to other words in the sentence. No hemispheric differences were noted. The authors interpreted the finding that all words produced P300 components as indicating that the P300 system is engaged whenever task-related language stimuli are used.

In summary, it may be said that while early studies of hemispheric ERP differences to language and nonlanguage stimuli produced promising results, recent investigations, using stringent criteria for differences, have resulted in more conservative statements regarding ERP changes. However, studies that have related hemispheric differences to linguistic meaning have yielded more positive results.

[1] Subjects were told the form of the three sentences that were used throughout the experiment: The __eel is on the axle; The __eel is on the shoe; The __eel is on the orange. Thus, by omitting the wh, h, or p, the subject could not know the meaning of the second word until the last word in the sequence was presented.

Learning and ERPs

In relation to the number of ERP investigations in general, only a few have used the ERP in studies of human learning or conditioning. Begleiter and Platz (1969b) used a classical conditioning paradigm to study VEPs (occipital) to conditioned stimuli during acquisition, extinction, and reacquisition. The reinforcement consisted of a series of auditory clicks delivered over a loudspeaker. A positive conditioned stimulus (CS+) was reinforced on 50% of the trials, while a negative conditioned stimulus (CS−) was never reinforced. The CS+ consisted of an arrow (↑) pointing upward, while the CS− was a downward pointing arrow (↓). Prior to conditioning, VEP amplitude (negative peak at 155 to 160 msec) to CS+ and CS− did not differ. After conditioning, however, VEP amplitudes were significantly higher to CS+. During extinction (no reinforcement), amplitudes returned to preconditioning levels, while after acquisition, CS+ again resulted in higher VEP amplitudes than CS−. The authors hypothesized that their result was consistent with the notion of increased rate of neuronal firing to the CS+ after conditioning. In addition, stimulus generalization was shown, since when arrows were rotated 10 degrees from the original CS+ or CS− the same difference in VEP was found, that is, the "up" arrow at a 10-degree angle produced larger amplitude VEPs than the "down" arrow at a 10-degree angle from the original.

The auditory ERP was obtained from the vertex during a discrimination learning paradigm (Jenness, 1972). Auditory ERPs were closely related to improvement in discrimination performance. When identical stimuli served as feedback rather than as cues, the ERPs were of much greater magnitude.

Lelord et al. (1976) classically conditioned ERPs in children of three different intelligence levels. The three groups were (I) normal (nonretarded children), (II) mildly retarded (IQ between 50 and 60), and (III) severely retarded (IQ between 20 and 50). Sound was used as the conditioned stimulus (CS) and light as the unconditioned stimulus (UCS). After pairing of CS and UCS the Group I children showed increased amplitude of ERPs to the sound (CS), but the two retarded groups did not. That is, conditioning of ERPs occurred in normal children but not in retarded subjects.

The several studies reviewed here indicate that changes in ERPs occur under different learning paradigms. Namely, ERPs were larger in amplitude to a positively conditioned stimulus.

The ERP and Hypnosis (Suggestion)

Is there evidence that hypnotic or other forms of suggestion can influence the ERP? Some early evidence with patients undergoing brain surgery indicated that suggestion of higher or lower light intensities could influence visual ERPs in the expected direction (Hernandez-Peon & Donoso, 1959; Guerrero-Figueroa & Heath, 1964). Clynes et al. (1964) were able to alter visual ERPs of one person through hypnotic suggestion of selective blindness for peripheral aspects of her visual field, but they were unable to duplicate the effects with a second subject.

Studies conducted with larger numbers of subjects indicate that hypnotic suggestion does not alter ERPs to somatosensory stimuli even though subjects reported no perception of the stimulus under hypnotic anesthesia (Halliday & Mason, 1964; Shagass & Schwartz, 1964). Beck (1963) reported no enhancement of visual ERPs for 12 individuals under hypnotic suggestion of brightness, nor was there a decrease in ERP amplitude when dimness was suggested. Beck noted that the light appeared either brighter or dimmer to subjects, depending on the hypnotic suggestion, even though the light intensity remained the same throughout the experimental session. Beck et al. (1966) matched 10 hypnotically suggestible persons with 10 control subjects. While the controls showed increases and decreases in the VEP with intensity changes, the hypnotized subjects showed no changes with suggested brightness and dimness. The authors noted that the findings did not support the concept that hypnotic suggestion may selectively inhibit or enhance sensory transmission.

Galbraith et al. (1972) found that persons scoring high on a scale of hypnotic susceptibility had higher visual and auditory ERPs when instructed to selectively attend to these stimuli than did persons who had low susceptibility scores. No attempt was made to hypnotize any of the subjects. The authors suggested that hypnotically susceptible persons may be better able to comply with an externally imposed task, while unsusceptible persons appear to do just the opposite. That is, larger ERPs of unsusceptible subjects to irrelevant stimuli indicate that they pay attention to the distractors, not to the critical stimuli.

Andreassi et al. (1976a) measured VEPs of 12 subjects under hypnotic suggestions that equally intense light flashes were "very bright" or "very dim" and under no suggestion at all. No changes in VEP amplitudes or latencies were produced by the suggestions. In a second experiment, the VEPs of six subjects were obtained during hypnotic suggestion and no suggestion on two separate days. Again, no changes in the VEP were observed. Both experiments revealed remarkable stability of the VEP obtained during the hypnotic state.

Thus, while mental states have been demonstrated to affect ERPs in other situations, hypnotic suggestion does not appear to do so. The conclusion here is the same as that of Tecce (1970), who noted that the evidence for ERP changes with hypnosis or suggestion was largely negative whenever more than two subjects were studied. Experiments on the ERP correlates of hypnosis seem to emphasize the importance of attentional factors in this state and weaken the notion that hypnotic suggestion may selectively inhibit or enhance sensory transmission in the nervous system.

The lack of ERP change with hypnotic suggestion may be related to the fact that it is external to the person, that is, the suggestion comes from another individual. When stimulus characteristics are influenced by internal factors, the ERP may show appropriate changes. Some evidence for this stems from an experiment by Porjesz and Begleiter (1975) in which subjects set up their own internal expectancy by choosing to see a bright or dim flash. In that situation, the ERP amplitudes corresponded to the expectation, even though the stimuli were identical.

Sensation, Attention, Perception, and ERPs

As in chapter 4, the studies in this section are categorized according to whether the research is primarily concerned with stimulus variations, attentional aspects, or integrative perceptual functions.

Sensation and ERPs

Intensity of Stimulation

In general, more intense stimuli produce larger ERP amplitudes. For example, this has been found for visual stimuli by Vaughan and Hull (1965), for auditory tones by Bull and Lang (1972), and for somatosensory stimulation by Shagass and Schwartz (1963).

Vaughan et al. (1966) reported a decrease in visual ERP latencies with increases in light flash intensity. The latency of the somatosensory ERP depends on the part of the body stimulated (e.g., latency is about 10 msec longer with stimulation of the knee as compared to the wrist) (Shagass, 1972). The amplitude of the auditory ERP was found to increase in amplitude with increasing stimulus intensities (Picton et al., 1970). However, at intensities above 70 db, the relation was not as clear-cut. Bull and Lang (1972) varied the intensity of a 6-second, 700-Hz tone among five intensity levels while the ERP was measured from the vertex. The intensity levels were 50, 62.5, 75, 87.5, and 100 db. They reported that ERP amplitudes increased directly with increments in physical intensity. Schweitzer and Tepas (1974) used pure tone (1,000 Hz) at 10 intensities of stimulation and reported amplitude changes linearly related to intensity. Walsh and Tepas (1975) found that a temporary loss in hearing sensitivity after exposure to high-intensity sounds was reflected by decreased ERP amplitudes. These investigators measured ERPs to a 1,000-Hz tone at 80-db intensity level following 5 minutes of exposure to either a 720-Hz tone at either 45-db or 110-db intensity level. The ERPs immediately following the 110-db tone were smaller, thus correlating with temporary subjective loss of hearing sensitivity.

Frequency of Stimulation

The effects of stimulus repetition on ERPs have been studied by a number of investigators. For example, the rate of click presentation was varied between one per second and three per second while auditory ERP was measured by Fruhstorfer et al. (1970).

While continued stimulation at both rates produced some habituation, the higher presentation rate resulted in greater decreases in ERP amplitudes than the lower rate. Ritter et al.
(1968) noted a drop in amplitude of the positive ERP component occurring between 150 and 200 msec with a stimulus presentation rate of one per two seconds, but not with an interval
of 10 seconds. Butler (1973) reported interesting results which
indicated a decrease in ERP amplitudes with increased stimulation frequency up to 10 per second. Further increases in repetition rate reversed this trend. Thus, sounds presented at a rate
of 25 per second showed a revived N1–P2 amplitude as though
they were now perceived as a continuous 1-second duration
sound instead of a series of separate sounds.

Smell, Taste, Pain, and Acceleration

While the auditory, visual, and somatosensory systems have been
the most frequently investigated in ERP studies, it is possible to
study other forms of sensory stimulation, such as olfactory, gustatory, pain, and vestibular. For example, Smith et al. (1971)
studied smell-generated ERPs of three patients with surgically
produced smell deficits and three normal subjects. Streams of
compressed air containing odorous and nonodorous substances
were directed into the nostrils for 200 msec at 5-second intervals
to produce the ERP. The results indicated that the ERP (recorded from C_z) was elicited by stimulation of the nasal portion
of the trigeminal nerve and not by stimulation of olfactory receptors. No ERP was obtained when jets of air, passed over distilled water flasks, were directed into the nostrils. Substantial
ERPs, that is, components of 10 μV or more, could be obtained
by averaging 30 responses to the olfactory stimuli. The stimuli
used apparently stimulated both the olfactory and trigeminal
systems, a possibility that would pose problems for studying
responses of the olfactory system alone.[2]

The gustatory ERPs of humans were analyzed in detail by
Funakoshi and Kawamura (1971). Demineralized water, su-

[2] Another problem in work on smell, taste, and pain ERPs is that of synchronizing the stimulus presentations with the trigger pulse which initiates
the averaging computer.

crose, sodium chloride, tartaric acid, and quinine hydrochloride provided control, sweet, salty, sour, and bitter solutions, respectively. The ERPs were recorded from over the temporal cortex as 1 ml of each solution was poured over the tongue surface 40 times. The subjects rinsed their mouths between each application of a solution to the tongue. The researchers reported the onset of an "early" wave at 150 msec after the stimulus was applied (10 μV in amplitude) and a "late" wave at about 500 msec, which was approximately 20 μV in amplitude. The early wave occurred with all solutions and with tactile stimulation of the tongue. But the later wave only appeared with the salt and tartaric acid (sour) applications. Therefore, the early component was due to the mechanical stimulation of pouring the solution on the tongue surface, and the late wave was the taste ERP. The authors suggested that the lack of ERPs to sweet and bitter may be related to the relatively small tongue areas sensitive to sweet and bitter tastes. This, in turn, could result in smaller cortical responses to sweet and bitter, perhaps not visible within the limitations imposed by 40 samples.

Chatrian et al. (1975) produced a perception of pain in 17 persons by electrically stimulating the pulp of individual teeth. All subjects described the electrical stimulus to the tooth pulp as producing sharp pain of a very brief duration. The pain ERP was recorded from many scalp areas, including that over the postcentral cortex. The ERP was prominent over the somatosensory cortex, a finding that was interpreted as indicating the existence of a representation of tooth pulp sensation in the somatosensory area of the postcentral gyrus.

The vestibular sense provides information about body position. The receptors for linear and angular acceleration lie in the semicircular canals and utricles of the inner ear. The study of vestibular ERPs is more difficult than the study of visual or auditory ERPs, since it is difficult to produce a suitable means of stimulating the vestibular receptors. Salamy et al. (1975) studied ERPs to semicircular canal stimulation by using whole-body rotation (angular acceleration) as the stimulus. The ERP was summed for a 2-second period simultaneous with about 84 degrees of body rotation in a swing chair. The ERP was recorded from both hemispheres (central parietal, temporal, and frontal leads). The investigators obtained a consistent negative-positive ERP with peaks at about 193 and 345 msec, respectively. The negative peak seemed to be the most prominent feature related to angular acceleration. The negative-positive complex amplitude was greatest at the vertex (mean of 13.7 μV). This complex was not influenced by auditory and visual stimuli, since these were ruled out by experimental procedures. Salamy et al. also pointed out that somatosensory ERPs have negative-positive latencies peaking at about 135 and 220 msec, much earlier than ERPs obtained with acceleration, thus distinguishing somatosensory from vestibular components.

In general, greater intensity stimuli result in higher amplitude ERPs. Higher rates of stimulus presentation result in greater ERP amplitude decreases than do lower rates. This seems to follow up to a certain point, beyond which further rate increases may reverse the trend.

It is possible, though more difficult, to generate ERPs to smell, taste, pain, and body acceleration. One difficulty, for example, is that of synchronizing stimuli with the trigger pulse used to start computer sampling in obtaining ERPs. Another problem is that stimulation of the appropriate receptors is not as readily accomplished as with the visual and auditory systems.

Attention and Sensory ERPs

The definition of attention offered in chapter 4 will also be used here. Attempts to find neurophysiological bases of this complex mental phenomenon in humans have involved ERPs to a greater extent than the measurement of changes in ongoing EEG activity. It would appear that the demonstration of a physiological correlate of attention could be established if some change in ERPs occurred when subjects attended to a stimulus and if no alteration could be observed when they did not attend. In fact, there were a number of studies conducted during the 1960s which indicated that the amplitude of ERP components to attended stimuli was increased, while the ignored stimulus produced low-amplitude responses.

For example, Haider et al. (1964) measured visual ERPs to signal and nonsignal stimuli during a prolonged vigilance task.

They noted that lower amplitude ERPs were associated with lapses of attention, that is, failure to detect signals. Satterfield (1965) asked subjects to attend alternately to auditory clicks and electric shocks. The ERPs were greatly enhanced when subjects were attending to either the shock or click stimuli. A late positive peak (about 150 msec, recorded from C_z) was enhanced by the attended stimulus whether it was a shock or a click.

Groves and Eason (1969) provided evidence that ERP amplitude changed as a function of attention paid by subjects to the stimulus. They used four conditions in which VEP to light flashes were measured: (1) while passively watching a dim flash, (2) responding to each flash, (3) responding within a specified period to avoid a shock, and (4) reacting to each flash and receiving an occasional, unavoidable shock. Condition 3 resulted in enhanced ERP amplitude and significantly faster RTs. Groves and Eason concluded that the attentional aspect of avoiding a shock appeared to be an important factor in ERP enhancement.

While a number of other investigations produced similar positive results, Näätänen (1967) argued that the increased ERP amplitude did not reflect attention or cognitive activity per se, but rather that it was due to nonspecific arousal effects produced in response to expected, task-relevant, stimuli. That is, since stimuli were presented in a regular manner, subjects could anticipate, and be prepared for, the critical stimulus, and therefore, ERP amplitude increases could be due to increased cortical activation, not selective attention. In his own research, Näätänen (1967) randomly mixed relevant and irrelevant stimuli so that their occurrence could not be predicted. He found no ERP differences to relevant and irrelevant stimuli, suggesting that when differential preparation for these stimuli was precluded, ERP changes did not occur.

Karlin (1970) supported Näätänen's view regarding the importance of differential preparation in producing ERP changes in the attention experimental paradigm. Karlin (1970) and Näätänen (1967) pointed out possible uncontrolled variables in selective attention experiments, including stimulus intensity, duration, sensory modality stimulated, and peripheral orienting responses (e.g., pupil dilation and visual fixation).

However, a number of studies, which appear to avoid the

criticisms of Näätänen and Karlin, do indicate the role of selective attention in enhancing ERP amplitude. For example, Eason et al. (1969) presented unpredictable relevant stimuli to one visual field and irrelevant stimuli to the other field. The ERP component occurring between 120 and 220 msec increased in amplitude with presentations of relevant stimuli, presumably those to which subjects paid more attention. Harter and Salmon (1972) presented equal numbers of relevant and irrelevant stimuli in an unpredictable manner and found enhancement of an ERP negative component peaking between 220 and 250 msec and a positive component at 290 to 340 msec when the stimuli were attended to as compared to when they were not attended.

Thus, in general, it seems that event-related potentials are altered in the direction of greater response amplitude under conditions that require attention to stimuli. The finding of Harter and Salmon (1972) indicates the enhancement of long-latency components with attention. A discussion of attention as related to longer latency potentials is presented in the next chapter.

Perception and ERPs

In this section we examine the existing evidence to determine whether reliable relationships have been shown between the ERP and such perceptual activities as form and pattern perception, color perception, perceptual masking, and motion perception.

Shape, Pattern Size, Orientation and the ERP

Shape. The basic question here is whether stimulus shape and pattern will influence ERPs as well as perception. Spehlmann (1965) reported differences between VEPs produced by an unpatterned visual field versus a patterned one. A positive ERP component which peaked at 180 to 250 msec was much larger to patterned stimuli. John et al. (1967) found that different geometric shapes (e.g., square, diamond) produced different VEP wave forms. Little change in wave form of the VEP occurred with variation in the size of the figure (i.e., a small or large square evoked similar VEPs). They also reported that VEPs for a blank flash were different from those produced by geometric shapes.

Honda (1973) employed a pattern discrimination task that was designed to focus the subject's attention on either the size or shape of geometric figures (circles and squares). When subjects were required to make size discriminations and ignore form, the VEPs were affected by stimulus size. When shape discriminations were required, however, it was form and not size that resulted in VEP changes. These results were repeated by Honda (1974) with square and diamond stimuli. He concluded that the results showed the effects of selective attention on VEP wave forms and reflect electrical brain activities related to perceptual processing of patterns.

Pattern Size. White (1969), using four stimulus patterns: a checkerboard, a horizontal grating, a set of concentric circles, and a set of radial lines, found striking differences in VEP wave forms with the different stimulus patterns. He described an additional experiment in which VEPs were recorded to checkerboard patterns composed of different check sizes. It was observed that larger checks produced smaller amplitude VEPs (e.g., a check size that subtended 10 minutes of visual angle[3] produced a response approximately twice the amplitude of that produced by a check that was four times larger). Harter (1970) and Siegfried (1975) confirmed White's result with respect to the inverse relationship between VEP amplitude and check size. Harter (1970) also reported that this relationship depends on the portion of the retina stimulated. That is, when the foveal area (central 2 to 2.5 degrees of vision) was stimulated, relatively small checks (15 to 30 minutes of visual angle) evoked the greatest amplitude responses. However, when progressively more peripheral areas of the retina were stimulated (7.5 degrees out from the fovea), larger check sizes (up to 60 minutes of visual angle) produced the greatest amplitude ERPs.[4] Check size had little effect on VEP when the retina was stimulated 12.5 to 27.5 de-

---

[3] Visual angle depends on the size of an object and its distance from the eye. At a given distance, smaller size objects produce smaller visual angles at the eye. It is measured in seconds, minutes, and degrees.
[4] Sixty seconds of visual angle equal 1 minute, and 60 minutes of visual angle equal 1 degree.

grees from the fovea. Hypotheses regarding the factors that may be operating here include: (1) the greater number of edges separating light and dark areas, that is, patterns with many edges may produce larger responses, and (2) the angles, or total number of pattern elements, may affect VEP amplitude (Armington et al., 1971).

Harter and White (1968) noted that defocusing a checkerboard pattern resulted in lower amplitude VEPs. That is, with sharper checkerboard pattern images, the VEP was larger. This has led to suggestions by White (1969) that VEP amplitude differences may be used as a basis for testing vision, especially refractive errors in persons who cannot verbalize well enough for adequate testing by many of the currently used testing methods (e.g., retarded individuals or young children). This possible application is discussed further in chapter 13.

Eason et al. (1970) stimulated the upper and lower halves of the visual field and reported that VEP amplitude varied with visual field and check size. That is, checks subtending 10 minutes of angle produced larger VEPs in the upper field, while checks subtending 40 minutes of visual angle were optimal for lower field stimulation. The overall ERP amplitudes suggested to Eason and his colleagues that the cortical visual system is more responsive to patterned stimuli appearing in the lower visual field than in the upper. However, it also seemed that the system may be relatively more sensitive to smaller objects in the upper field. They speculated that the differential sensitivity of the upper and lower visual fields may have survival value for man as a ground-dwelling animal. That is, the upper field may be more attuned to "specks in the sky" which move rapidly and must be detected at a distance if the organism is to respond appropriately. However, ground objects that are close enough to pose a threat produce a larger visual angle. Thus the part of the visual system responding to them (lower field) may have greater sensitivity to objects subtending angles of 30 minutes or more.

Corners. Patterns that include corners have been found to produce larger amplitude visual ERPs than those containing stripes (MacKay, 1969; Rietveld et al., 1967). Moskowitz et al. (1974) measured ERPs to rounded and sharply cornered stimuli, which varied in angularity, in 45-degree steps, from 180 to 45 degrees. The visual ERP was greatest in amplitude for the 90-degree sharply-cornered pattern. This can be seen in Figure 6-2. Cornered and rounded corner patterns produced larger ERPs than straight lines (180 degrees). The peak latency of responses to cornered patterns was shorter than that of responses to rounded and straight patterns. Moskowitz et al. postulated a "center-surround receptive field" model of the visual cortex to explain the major portion of their findings. The argument presented was that interactions between excitatory and inhibitory areas of the visual cortex allowed maximal neuronal response to occur to the 90-degree cornered stimuli.

Orientation of Figures. Maffei and Campbell (1970) presented vertical, horizontal, and oblique sets of lines (moving gratings) to subjects while visual ERPs were measured. They found VEPs to vertical and horizontal arrays to be similar, but the amplitude in response to the oblique array was considerably smaller than to the others. The authors concluded that the resolving power of the visual system is greater in the vertical and horizontal orientation than in the oblique. Yoshida et al. (1975) postulated that human visual cortical cells may be more responsive to horizontally and vertically oriented stimuli because our visual world is oriented mostly in horizontal or vertical planes. Leaning towers, such as the one in Pisa, are relatively rare in our visual environment!

To summarize, we might conclude that perceptions of different forms, patterns, and orientations are paralleled by changes in visual ERPs. The various experiments with checkerboard patterns indicate that effects such as check size, sharpness of image, and location in the visual field can influence the ERP. That is, ERPs are larger with small check sizes, with sharp images, and with stimuli in the lower visual field. Patterns containing sharply angled corners appear to result in larger VEPs than those with corners that are rounded or not angled as sharply. It has been suggested that the greater responsivity of the visual cortical system to stimuli oriented vertically and horizontally may be due to experiential factors which determine sensitivity of visual cortical cells.

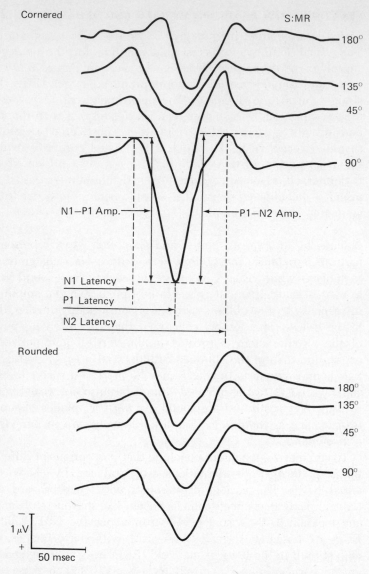

Figure 6-2. Typical summated wave forms for Subject M.F. for each of the eight experimental stimulus patterns. Positivity at the occipital electrode produced downward deflections in the recordings. Also shown is the method of amplitude and latency measurement.

112

Visual Masking and ERPs

There are instances in which stimuli may be presented to the visual system and yet not be perceived by the individual. For example, backward visual masking refers to a situation where presentation of a later stimulus (mask) interferes with the perception of an earlier presented stimulus (target). The question that concerns us here is the nature of the VEP to the stimulus that is not perceived.

Metacontrast, a type of backward visual masking, was studied in detail by Werner (1935), who showed that when two equally intense visual stimuli, having adjacent contours, were presented in rapid sequence, the first stimulus was not seen at all, and only the second was reported. For example, a filled-in square was presented for 20 msec and was followed 150 msec later by an outlined square, also presented for 20 msec. The interpretation of this was that the outlined square appropriated the contour of the solid square before it could establish itself in the visual system of the perceiver.

Schiller and Chorover (1966) investigated the question of whether or not the perceptual changes observed under metacontrast would be correlated with changes in the visual ERP. They reported no changes in the VEP with metacontrast and concluded that the VEP does not necessarily reflect changes in subjective perception. However, Vaughan and Silverstein (1968) reported attenuation of VEPs to foveal stimulation but not parafoveal during metacontrast suppression. They concluded that the failure of VEPs to reflect metacontrast suppression in the Schiller and Chorover study was because of the parafoveal conditions used.

Schiller (1969) has referred to metacontrast as visual masking involving contour interaction as distinguished from a situation where no contour interaction occurs, as when a large, intense patch of light follows a small relatively dim light flash. Studies of this latter type were carried out by Donchin et al. (1963), who measured the visual ERP under conditions in which a second (brighter) flash masked perception of the initial flash. At 20 msec ISI (intersignal interval), when visual masking occurred, the VEPs were similar to those elicited by the second flash presented alone, that is, the VEP to the first stimulus was completely suppressed. A similar result obtained by Donchin and Lindsley (1965) led them to conclude that the interference with the first flash by the second took place at or preceding the point at which VEPs were recorded (occipital cortex). They expressed the opinion that the same processes which are involved in perceptual suppression seem to be involved in the VEP change. It must be noted that in these two studies by Donchin and others, the second flash was many times more intense than the first one (from 100 to 10,000 times), and this is probably the reason why the VEP to the first stimulus was completely obliterated rather than merely attenuated as in the metacontrast study of Vaughan and Silverstein (1968).

Andreassi et al. (1971) studied the VEP under separate conditions designed to produce backward visual masking and no masking. Masking occurred when five equally intense Xs were displayed on a screen in an order that produced a disappearance of the first two in the sequence, namely, when presented in the˘ order 3, 1, 4, 2, 5, the Xs in locations 1 and 2 were not perceived by the subjects. The two masked Xs were the only ones spatially bounded by later appearing stimuli (e.g., 1 was bounded by 3 and 4). The main finding was that although the subjects did not perceive the first two Xs, they did produce a VEP in response to these stimuli that was similar to the VEP obtained under conditions in which no masking occurred, for example, presentation of Xs in the order: 1, 2, 3, 4, 5, resulting in the perception of all five Xs. Further experimentation (Andreassi et al., 1971) using the presentation order: 3, 1, 4, 2, 5, revealed that if the third, fourth, and fifth stimuli were three times more intense than the first two, then not only did perceptual suppression occur but there was also partial suppression of the VEP in the form of significant VEP latency delays in response to the perceptually masked Xs. The authors concluded that the excitation produced in the visual cortex by the early stimuli in the series was decreased in activity by the inhibitory activity of the later, more intense stimuli.

In another experiment, Andreassi et al. (1974) varied the intensity ratios of the masking (later) and masked (earlier) stimuli in a systematic manner while measuring VEPs. The intensity ratios used were 3 : 1, 5.8 : 1 and 10.8 : 1. It was found that the amount of delay in the occurrence of the VEP to the masked stimulus depended on the ratio of the intensity differences between the first two stimuli and the next three, that is, the greater the difference, the longer the delay in the appearance of the VEP to the first stimulus in the string. The results were the same from right and left occipital areas. Thus, it was concluded that as the ratio of the intensity difference between the earlier (masked) and later (masking) stimuli increased, the greater was the effect of cortical inhibitory fields upon excitatory receptive fields, and the greater was the VEP temporal displacement produced.

In backward masking, using single sequential stimuli, the earlier stimuli were never spatially bounded on more than one side, simultaneously, by later stimuli. To answer questions regarding changes in amount of contour interaction between sequential sets of multiple stimuli, Andreassi et al. (1976c) conducted three experiments. In the first, sequential sets of like stimuli (i.e., two grids, followed by three grids, followed by six grids) were presented, while VEPs were measured from O_z. The time between grid sets was 40 msec. The total light energy was equated for the three grid sets. The schematic of the spatial and temporal arrangement of stimuli as they appeared on a CRT screen in the first experiment is shown in Figure 6-3. In Condition A, all subjects reported two grids, in B they reported seeing only the second set of three grids, while in C they saw only the last set of six grids. The VEP component, which occurred at about 200 msec (P2), was significantly reduced in amplitude in Conditions B and C as compared to A. In Experiment 2, sets of the letter B were used to determine the reliability of the findings from Experiment 1 with a new stimulus configuration. The same results were obtained; that is, backward masking was accompanied by decreased P2 amplitudes. In Experiment 3, however, unlike sets of stimuli (two Bs, two Bs followed by three grids, and two Bs followed by three grids, followed by six grids) backward masking of the first set of two Bs did not occur, and neither did changes in VEP amplitude. Thus, when the amount of contour interaction between target and mask stimuli was increased to 50% (as compared to 25% in the single sequential blanking situation), VEP amplitudes decreased with backward masking.

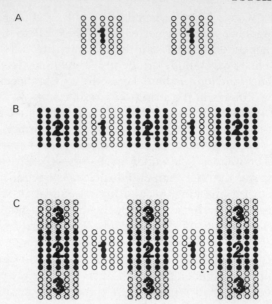

Figure 6-3. Schematic drawing of spatial and temporal arrangement of stimuli as they appeared in the Andreassi et al. (1976a) study. Numbers merely indicate order of presentation and were not part of the actual display.

When sets of unlike stimuli were used, the change in configuration reduced contour interaction between target and mask stimuli, thus preventing backward masking and the occurrence of VEP changes.

Andreassi et al. (1976b) investigated the effects of increasing amounts of target-mask contour interaction on perception of the target and the visual ERP. An experiment was designed in which a single grid stimulus (target) was followed by either one, two, three, or four grid stimuli. A final condition was the presentation of the target alone. In all instances the stimulus energy of target and mask was equated. Thus the amount of target-mask contour interaction was 0%, 25%, 50%, 75%, and 100%. Greater amounts of backward masking occurred with increases in contour interaction, and this was accompanied by increasing degrees of attenuation of the P2 component of the VEP. Samples of VEP recordings from one subject under the conditions of this experiment are presented in Figure 6-4.

In summary, a number of studies have indicated that backward visual masking was accompanied by changes in VEP amplitude or latency. The general explanatory mechanism may lie in the varying amounts of inhibitory-excitatory activity between groups of neurons at the level of the visual cortex. Thus, it is suggested that when a stimulus is presented to the visual system, it results in excitation being produced at a given location in the visual cortex. When similar stimuli follow the initial one closely in time and space, approximately adjacent areas of the visual cortex are stimulated, resulting in a reduction in response to the first stimulus. This inhibitory activity may not be sufficient to eliminate the VEP entirely, but it is enough to reduce it significantly, and the degree of VEP reduction may be related to the degree of spatial bounding of the first stimulus by later ones.

Color Perception and Visual ERPs

Pulses of electromagnetic energy (light) produce perceptions of color if they are within the visible spectrum for human subjects. The visible wavelength spectrum ranges from about 380 to 700 nm or billionths of a meter. The question that concerns us here is whether changes in wavelength (color) will be reflected in visual ERPs.

A number of investigators have reported that the wave form of the VEP was changed with different colors. For example, Clynes and Kohn (1967) indicated that VEPs to lines and dots were color-sensitive with respect to color of the surrounding field. Different VEP wave forms were obtained to stimulation with red, green, yellow, and orange stimuli. White and Eason (1966) also found that different components of the VEP varied as a function of stimulus color. Differences in VEP pattern were observed with stimulation by red, green, and blue and by the three colors simultaneously. Shipley et al. (1966) found that VEP wave form changed with wavelength over a range of 380 to 680 nm. For example, in the red range (640 and 680 nm) a larger positive component appeared at about 200 msec, while

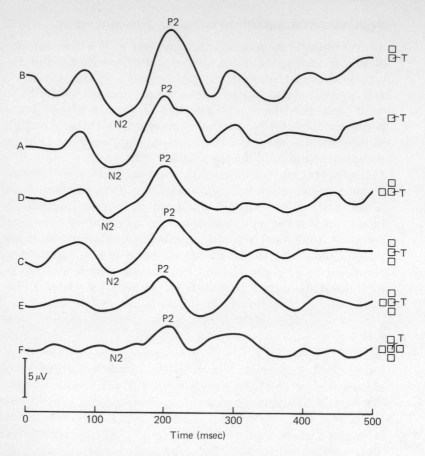

Figure 6-4. Visual ERPs obtained under the following amount of target-mask contour interaction: Condition B = 25%, A = 0%, D = 50%, C = 50%, E = 75%, and F = 100%. In the inset, the labeled squares (T) represent the earlier presented targets, while the unlabeled elements represent masking stimuli. The ERP traces show, in general, a decrease in N2-P2 amplitude with increased contour interaction. All subjects experienced apparent motion under Condition B in which the target appeared to jump upward to a new location. This could be the reason for a lack of amplitude difference between conditions B and A; i.e., contour interaction effects may be lost in apparent motion. Each trace is based on 100 responses to a target square (grid). Negativity is downward.

118

smaller, biphasic responses appeared with wavelengths in the violet range (380 and 20 nm). Regan (1972) criticized the use of large stimulus fields because they resulted in stimulation of both receptors in the fovea (cones) and receptors outside the fovea (rods and cones) which have different wavelength sensitivities. Another problem pointed out by Regan is that of equating the light intensity of different wavelengths, thus making it difficult to separate color and brightness effects.

Perry et al. (1972) used a technique that maintained intensity of red and green stimuli constant and their size small enough to be presented entirely within the fovea (i.e., they produced a size of .5 degrees of visual angle). Most estimates of foveal extent place it at 2 to 2.5 degrees of visual angle (e.g., see Ruch et al., 1965). The differences found in ERPs with red and green stimuli led Perry and associates to conclude that there appear to be fundamental differences in cortical processing of red and green.

Significantly different VEPs to patterned red, green, and blue stimuli in persons of normal color vision were reported by Kinney et al. (1972). Their results for one color-blind subject, who confused reds and greens but could distinguish them from blue (deuteranopia), showed VEPs that differed from normals. The VEPs for this deuteranope showed no differences in response to red and green but did show a different response to blue. Using six normal subjects and one deuteranope, Regan and Spekreijse (1974) compared their VEPs to two-colored visual patterns. They found that the appearance of a pattern of equal intensity red and green checks produced normal VEPs in persons with normal vision, but smaller VEPs in the color-blind individual. That is, when the brightness of the red and green checks were made equal, the amplitude of the color-blind subject's VEPs dropped sharply. Based on findings with subjects with normal color vision, these researchers concluded that the human visual system processes color information differently when the color is presented as patterned rather than as spatially-unpatterned stimulation.

The experiments of Kinney et al. (1972) and Regan and Spekreijse (1974) suggest possible methods for the objective detection of color blindness. This possibility was emphasized in a study by Kinney and McKay (1974) in which VEPs of persons with normal color vision and of others with different types of color defects were measured. The color defects were deuteranopia (red-green confusion), protanopia (insensitivity to deep red light), and tritanopia (red-blue-green confusion). Patterned stimuli varying in luminance (brightness) and color were used. The normals gave pattern responses (large positive wave at about 100 msec) for both color and luminance, while color defectives produced VEPs only to luminance and not to any of the colors to which they were insensitive.

Thus, it appears that studies which have used appropriate methodological controls result in findings indicating that different VEPs occur to stimuli varying in color. Some recent studies suggest the use of visual ERPs as objective indicators of color vision, which may be especially useful in cases where verbal responses are either not possible or purposely misleading.

Motion Perception and ERPs

Barlow (1964) found that sudden changes in the vertical position of a spot on an oscilloscope screen resulted in a definable visual ERP. Measurements of eye movements ruled out the contribution of this possible artifact in the production of the ERP. MacKay and Rietveld (1968) reported that a visual ERP occurred in response to movement of a single horizontal line, 7 cm in length. The line moved from rest at a velocity of 2 cm/sec. The presence of a reference line enhanced the VEP. Their finding may be related to the fact that perceived velocity of a moving figure is increased in the vicinity of a stationary reference point.

Andreassi et al. (1973) studied VEPs under two conditions of apparent motion and one condition that did not produce apparent movement. In all conditions, 20 Xs of identical stimulus energy and constant "on" and "off" times of 5 msec were presented sequentially on a CRT screen. Three different display orders resulted in three strongly different subjective perceptual experiences as follows: (1) an impression that "Xs converged toward the center from right and left," (2) "Xs diverged from the center with a small gap in the middle," and (3) the perception of "about 10 Xs with spaces in between." The VEPs, measured from O_1 and O_2, did not differ under the three conditions, indicating that the cortical mechanisms that produced the VEPs were similar even though the subject's perceptual experiences were very different.

Clarke (1974) produced VEPs through reversal in the horizontal motion of a visual noise pattern.[5] The velocity of motion was 10 degrees of visual angle per second, and motion reversal took 5 msec to occur. Clarke obtained suggestive evidence that motion-reversal VEPs were produced largely by direction-sensitive mechanisms within the human brain. He tentatively proposed that the mechanisms might be similar to the directionally sensitive neurons reported to exist in the visual cortex of the monkey.

In a recent study, Cooper et al. (1977) measured visual ERPs when stimuli such as cars, vans, and trucks moved at unpredictable and infrequent times in a televised landscape. Measurements were made from frontal, central, parietal, and occipital areas in nine subjects. They reported that the main cortical sign of detecting the moving target was the occurrence of a large (30 μV) positive potential at the vertex and parietal locations shortly after the eyes fixated in the area of the vehicle (300 msec). This response occurred when the subject saw the event he was told to detect. These investigators suggest that the potential they observed has origins in common with the P300, which has been reported to occur during discrimination and decision-making tasks.

In summary, investigations into the possible role of movement in producing an ERP have yielded positive results. Recent experiments have presented suggestive evidence for direction-sensitive mechanisms in the human brain and large amplitude responses accompanying the detection of a moving target.

In the next chapter, long-latency ERPs and steady potential shifts in recorded brain activity are discussed. These ERPs have been associated with the performance of various cognitive and information processing activities and have intriguing implications with respect to understanding brain-behavior relationships.

---

[5] Visual noise usually refers to a random dot pattern.

Event-related Slow Brain Potentials and Behavior

The brain potentials to be discussed in this chapter are "slow" in the sense that they take longer to develop than do the sensory evoked potentials and motor potentials discussed earlier. Two of these slow potentials are the contingent negative variation (CNV) and the readiness potential (RP), categorized by Vaughan (1969) as steady potential shifts. A third type of slow wave includes those positive or negative components of the ERP which occur at about 250 to 550 msec and are commonly referred to as "P300" responses.[1]

The Contingent Negative Variation

In the now classic paper by Walter et al. (1964), CNV was described as a steady, relatively long-lasting, negative shift in brain activity which developed between the time of a warning signal (S1) and a second stimulus (S2) which demanded a response. It was later found that CNV can occur without motor responses to S2. For example, Cohen and Walter (1966) obtained CNV in anticipation of pictorial stimuli that were used as S2. No motor response was made by the subjects. On the basis of this kind of result, Cohen and Walter suggested that the CNV reflects a state

---

[1] Some researchers prefer to call these long-latency components P3 without imposing a particular latency upon the responses. The terms P300 and P3 are synonymous. Sometimes P300 is used to indicate that, on the average, these late components occur at about 300 msec after the initiating stimulus.

of "expectancy" and have used the term "E wave" as a substitute for CNV. Other investigators proposed that CNV indicates an intention to act (Low et al., 1966), subject motivation (Irwin et al., 1966), or attention (McCallum, 1969; Tecce and Scheff, 1969). Whatever the terminology used, it is clear that CNV is related to psychological and performance factors, and some of these will be reviewed shortly.

The amplitude of CNV is about 20 μV, on the average, in young adults. It begins within 200 to 400 msec after S1 and reaches its peak within 400 to 900 msec if the S1–S2 interval is 1000 msec. The CNV amplitude drops abruptly with S2. The time needed to reach peak amplitude is related to CNV shape. Two basic shapes have been identified (see Figure 7-1) and are referred to as Type A (fast rise time) and Type B (slow rise time) by Tecce (1971). Type A CNVs have been found to occur when subjects were uncertain about when S2 would occur, and Type B occurred when they were more certain about its time of appearance (see Tecce, 1972). The magnitude of CNV appears related to stimulus intensity. When S2 intensity is very low (e.g., a barely audible tone) or very high (loud tone or intense elec-

Figure 7-1. Two types of CNV morphology based on fast (type A) and slow (type B) rise time to maximum voltage.

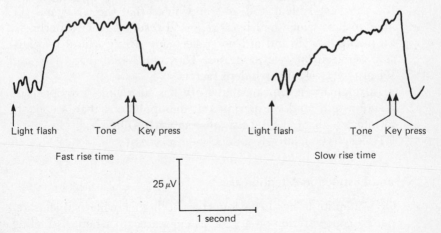

tric shock), CNV magnitude is increased, perhaps because of
enhanced attentiveness and alertness with regard to S2.

The CNV has been related to a number of performance parameters. We shall examine several of these here, including CNV
and speed of reaction, distraction-attention, effort, and stimulus
modality.

CNV and Reaction Time

There have been a number of reports in which an association
between CNV amplitude and RT was noted and several which
indicate no relation between CNV and speed of response. For
example, Cant and Bickford (1967) found that avoidable shock
increased CNV amplitude and quickened RT. Also, Tecce and
Scheff (1969) observed that distraction decreased CNV amplitude and slowed RT. They found, too, that reward increased
CNV and led to faster RTs. On the other hand, Naitoh et al.
(1971) reported that sleep loss produced decreased CNV amplitudes but did not affect RT. Further, Rebert (1972) observed
that feedback about speed of RT led to faster responses by subjects, but resulted in no CNV changes. Hillyard (1969) found
that larger amplitude CNVs were associated with faster RTs for
5 of 10 subjects tested, indicating that individual differences
may occur.

Rebert and Tecce (1973) performed a careful review of the
literature available at the time and noted that the CNV and RT
relationships which had been reported resulted from experimental manipulations and did not reflect any strong causal relationship between the two processes. They concluded that CNV and
RT are relatively independent factors.

In summary, it appears that CNV has been linked to speed of
reaction only under experimental manipulations that are likely
to affect both of them (e.g., distraction). Otherwise, CNV and
RT seem to be relatively independent processes.

CNV and Distraction-Attention

CNV amplitude has been found to be higher when subjects reported concentration on a task, as compared to when distracting

stimuli were introduced (McCallum & Walter, 1968; Tecce & Scheff, 1969). For example, Tecce and Scheff presented four letters or numbers during the S1–S2 interval and required subjects to recall them after their response to S2; this led to a reduction in CNV amplitude. This reduction was interpreted as being due to an interference with attention. Tecce and Hamilton (1973) introduced distraction into the S1–S2 interval by requiring that subjects do mental arithmetic (add 7's continuously). This resulted in reduced CNV amplitude and longer RTs to S2. The finding illustrates, incidentally, that longer RTs are not necessarily related to low-amplitude CNVs but rather to the experimental manipulation that affected both processes.

Tecce (1972) made two hypotheses: (1) that CNV amplitude is monotonically related to attention, that is, as attention increases, CNV increases; and (2) that the relationship between CNV amplitude and arousal[2] can be described by an inverted-U function, that is, at low and high levels of arousal, CNV magnitude is low, and at moderate arousal levels, CNV is at its highest amplitude. Tecce et al. (1976) found some evidence in support of these hypotheses. Subjects were required to respond to S2, after an S1–S2 interval in which letters were presented. In one condition, they were asked to recall the letters and in another, to ignore the letters. The letter recall task caused a lowered CNV amplitude, lengthened RT, and increased heart rate and eye blinking. The reduction of CNV and RT slowing was interpreted as a distraction effect. The increase of heart rate and eye blinking was interpreted in terms of increased arousal produced by distraction, an important factor in the disruption of CNV development. Thus, attention increases CNV amplitude, while distraction causes CNV attenuation.

CNV and Effort

The amplitude of CNV seems to increase when greater amounts of energy expenditure are anticipated to perform a task (Low & McSherry, 1968). These investigators found that the anticipation of greater energy expenditure was related to higher CNV

[2] Arousal is defined as a process that energizes behavior unselectively and affects only intensity of response (Tecce, 1972, p. 101).

amplitudes. That is, when greater amounts of force were required (and anticipated) to respond to S2, CNV increased in amplitude. Low et al. (1967) reported that CNV amplitude increased as S2 level decreased to a barely audible level. This was interpreted as indicating that greater attentiveness was required to detect the very low intensity imperative stimulus and that motivation has an effect. Briefly, then, CNV tends to be associated with degree of physical and psychological effort, and some investigators have related it to degree of motivation.

Stimulus Modality and the CNV

Although earlier studies indicated that modality of the stimulus did not appear to influence the CNV, there is some recent evidence that it may. Gaillard (1976) investigated the differential effects of auditory and visual warning signals on the CNV. Two S1–S2 intervals were used, 1 and 3 seconds. The CNV was composed of two waves: one following S1 at about 650 msec and a second which reached its peak at the end of the ISI. The first wave was called an orientation (O) wave and the second an expectancy (E) wave. A modality effect was shown, since the O wave was enhanced after an auditory S1, as compared to a visual S1. The finding that the CNV may not be a unitary potential had been previously reported in experiments by Borda (1970) based on his work with monkeys. Further, Loveless and Sanford (1974) and Weerts and Lang (1973) interpreted the O wave as a cortical component of the orienting response to S1, and the E wave as the traditional CNV. A brief discussion of the relationship between the CNV and P300 will be presented in a later section of this chapter.

Miscellaneous Processes and the CNV

In the course of development, a typical CNV may reach its peak amplitude at about 750 msec after presentation of the warning signal, with a 1.5-second ISI, continue at this level until a response is made (say for another 750 msec), and then return abruptly to baseline (prestimulus level). The question of the event associated with the return of CNV to baseline was investigated by Wilkinson and Spence (1973). They wanted to determine whether it was the movement in response to S2, the final decision made concerning the nature of the stimulus, or merely attention that was associated with the return to baseline. They set up an experimental situation to test this such that following a warning signal, the imperative stimulus either did or did not require an overt response and either did or did not give information that a third stimulus would be presented. They concluded that the return of CNV to baseline was due neither to the overt response made nor to the final decision but probably to a coarse identification of the stimulus as belonging to a relevant class of stimuli, for example, whether it was some type of tone or not. Further, they suggested that some P300 responses are related to the CNV, a point that will be taken up later.

The effects of stimulus uncertainty on the CNV, auditory ERP, and pupil diameter was studied by Friedman et al. (1973). The subject had to guess which of two auditory stimuli would be presented after a warning signal. The degree of certainty was manipulated by information about the second stimulus given prior to each trial. The CNV amplitude was higher in the uncertain as compared to the certain condition. In addition, P300 and pupillary diameter were also larger with uncertainty as compared to certainty. The results were interpreted as indicating a higher arousal level associated with greater task involvement on the part of subjects during the uncertain conditions.

The CNV was found useful as an indicator of sexual preference in groups of 12 male and 12 female college-age students (Costell et al., 1972). The subjects were shown paired visual exposures of male nudes, female nudes, and sexually neutral silhouettes. The first presentation, serving as S1, lasted 500 msec. The second presentation (S2) was the same slide and appeared after a delay of 1,500 msec and remained on for 2,000 msec. Both males and females responded with significantly higher CNV amplitudes to stimuli of the opposite sex than to either the same sex or neutral stimuli. Thus the interest value of, or attention to, nude persons of the opposite sex resulted in enhanced CNV amplitudes.

Weinberg et al. (1974) set up an experimental situation in which possible CNVs and ERPs would be produced to an expected, but absent, stimulus. Previous research had indicated that a brain potential could occur to an absent stimulus (Sutton et al., 1967; Weinberg et al., 1970). They also wanted to determine whether an emitted potential would be preceded by a CNV and whether the CNV would occur before and after feedback about correctness of the response. They found that emitted potentials occurred on occasions when the imperative stimulus was absent. A CNV was found to precede the emitted potential, which suggested that the expectancy of occurrence of a stimulus is important for the appearance of an emitted potential. This indicated that the CNV reflects the expectation to receive information.

The conclusion by Weinberg et al. (1974) that CNV represents expectation of information reception and not necessarily expectation to respond could also be used to interpret the results of Friedman et al. (1973), since more information was yielded by the uncertain as compared to the certain stimulus event, that is, subjects already knew what was coming in the certain situation. The suggested roles of the CNV in preliminary stimulus identification and as an indicator of sexual object preference present interesting possibilities for future research.

The CNV is a fascinating phenomenon, from both a psychological and a physiological point of view. As Tecce (1972) has pointed out, the main hypotheses regarding the psychological or performance correlates of the CNV have been expectancy, motivation, conation (intention to act), and attention. An arousal-distraction hypothesis of CNV production advanced by Tecce et al. (1976) is related to attention concepts. Demonstrations that distraction decreases CNV illustrates its relation to arousal and attentional mechanisms. This is also true for increased CNV amplitude with effort and sexual stimuli.

The Readiness Potential or Bereitschaftspotential

Readiness potential, or *Bereitschaftspotential,* was the term used by Kornhuber and Deecke (1965) to describe a slow-rising negative wave with amplitudes between 10 to 15 μV. It begins about 500 to 1,000 msec before a voluntary movement and peaks at the

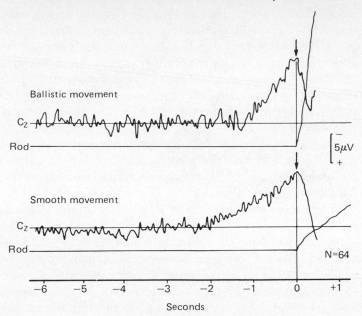

Figure 7-2. Brain potentials preceding rapid ballistic movements (upper plot) and slow smooth movements (lower plot) in the same subject. Upper trace of pair shows average potentials at the vertex ($TC = 5$ sec, 64 sweeps), lower shows rod positions. In both cases, there is a clear *Bereitschaftspotential*.

time of response (see Figure 7-2). It has been pointed out that this potential has a slow rise time and resembles a Type B CNV (see Tecce, 1972, and Figure 7-1). Tecce (1972) has observed that when a motor response (e.g., a key press) is required to S2 in a CNV paradigm, both CNV and RP occur, resulting in a hybrid wave or "CNV complex." However, when only attention to S2 is required, without an immediate motor response, only CNV occurs.

McCallum et al. (1976) recorded CNVs and RPs from areas of the human brain stem and midbrain. They reported that these slow potentials appeared to have similar, but not identical distributions throughout the brain stem. They caution that the results should be interpreted conservatively, since recording electrode placement was not confirmed. Deecke (1976) observed that CNV and RP have different scalp distributions. For example, CNV can be recorded from frontal areas, while RP cannot, and whereas RP is pronounced over parietal areas, CNV is minimal at that location. Thus, evidence derived from different experimental paradigms and as a result of recording over different brain areas indicates that the CNV and RP are separate phenomena.

McAdam and Seales (1969) reported that the amplitude of the RP was influenced by monetary reward. They recorded the RP under reward and no reward conditions and found that the amplitude of the RP could be approximately doubled in size with monetary reinforcement. Since CNV amplitude may also be influenced by subject motivational level, more research is required to determine the extent to which RP and CNV will vary together as a result of experimental manipulations.

Becker et al. (1976) measured RPs from 10 subjects who were instructed to vary the speed at which they pushed a 10-cm rod into a 10-cm tube. They were asked to produce fast movements as well as slow ones. The investigators reported that the RP started 800 msec prior to fast movements and 1300 msec before the slow, smooth movements. These results led them to conclude that it takes more time to prepare for voluntary, slow, smooth, movements than for quick movements. The latency results, plus the finding that the RP was greater in amplitude for smooth movements, also led them to suggest that different neural organization is involved in the production of quick movements versus slow, smooth ones.

In summary, the RP is a brain potential that precedes voluntary movements. Experimental evidence suggests that it is related to psychological and performance variables; that is, its amplitude is influenced by such factors as motivation level and speed of movement.

The P300 or P3 Potential

Sutton and colleagues (Sutton et al., 1965, 1967) discovered that a late-positive ERP occurred to task-relevant stimuli that delivered significant information. Since this component had a latency of about 300 msec after stimulus presentation, and it was positive going, it was referred to as P300. The P300 or P3 response has been associated with a variety of cognitive activities, including decision making, signal probability, attention, discrimination, uncertainty resolution, stimulus relevance, and information delivery. In fact, so many cognitive events have been related to P300 and other late waves that Beck (1975) has wryly commented, "One would not be greatly surprised to encounter a slow rising late wave of 'brotherly love'" (p. 243). The proliferation of terms is due, not to ambiguity of P300 as a physical occurrence, but to the variety of interpretations by different investigators who prefer to use their own labels to describe relationships found in a wide variety of experimental situations.

In this section we examine the association of P300 with decision making, stimulus probability, attention, signal detection, and discrimination. A final segment will briefly consider relations between P300 and the CNV.

Decision Making and P300

Some investigators have related P300 to decision making (e.g., Smith et al., 1970; Rohrbaugh et al., 1974). Rohrbaugh and associates devised an experimental situation in which only the second of two rapidly successive and relevant visual stimuli permitted subjects to make a decision. Analyses of the ERPs indicated that only this second stimulus produced a prominent and enhanced P300. Since P300 was not reliably enhanced in response to the first stimulus, the researchers concluded that neither relevance nor information delivery, per se, determines the amplitude of P300. Rohrbaugh et al. emphasized that the subject's activity as an *information processor* determined the amplitude of P300 and believe that the term "decision" is appropriate to describe its psychological correlate.

Hillyard et al. (1971) reported that confidence in a decision regarding detection was related to P3 amplitude; that is, higher amplitudes were associated with greater degrees of confidence. Squires et al. (1973) used a signal detection task in which subjects had to decide whether or not a very low level auditory signal was heard during a specified time interval. Based on their results, they made the suggestion that an early negative component of the ERP (N1, peaking between 140 and 190 msec) and P3 (354 and 450 msec) represented aspects of decision making. They also reported a relationship between P3 amplitude and decision confidence. In a later study, K. Squires et al. (1975) expanded this experimental design and were able to conclude that when the decision is difficult, P3 is mainly a function of decision confidence. When decision making is made easy, however, P3 varies with the probability of occurrence of a second stimulus, that is, higher amplitude P3 being associated with lower probability signals.

Begleiter and Porjesz (1975) compared ERPs generated by identical intensity flashes which were judged to be either "dim" or "bright" by subjects. Significant ERP amplitude differences to these identical "medium"-intensity stimuli were obtained, depending on the subject's decision about the physical properties of the stimulus; that is, those stimuli judged "bright" produced larger ERPs than those judged "dim." Two ERP components were enhanced: N1, which peaked between 100 to 140 msec and P2, which peaked between 140 and 200 msec.[3] The results were interpreted as demonstrating a relation between ERPs and a decision about the physical attributes of a stimulus. Further, they suggested that differential ERPs might reflect activation of memory traces about past experiences of "bright" and "dim." Donchin (1975) argued that the late ERP peaks shown in the Begleiter and Porjesz study could be categorized as P300 responses. Donchin cautioned that while P300 is associated with decision making, it tells little about the contents of the decision. Therefore, he concluded that ERPs cannot be regarded as carrying specific "memory traces" for past experiences such as stimulus brightness.

In summary, the general result is that P300 amplitude is enhanced when persons are required to make decisions about

---

[3] Donchin (1975) suggested that peaks labeled P2 by Begleiter and Porjesz in one of their figures actually had latencies ranging from 200 to 300 msec, i.e., within the latency range of P300.

stimuli. Furthermore, greater amplitude increases appear to be
related to increased confidence in the decision.

The P300 and Stimulus Probability

The studies to be reviewed in this section consider the relation
between P300 and relative certainty-uncertainty that a stimulus
will occur. Sutton et al. (1965) discovered that P300 was greater
in amplitude when subjects were uncertain about whether a
second stimulus would be a sound or a light. This pioneering
effort underscored the importance of a subjective reaction in the
production of late ERP components, as compared to stimulus
factors that influenced the earlier ERP components. Figure 7-3
shows auditory ERPs to certain and uncertain stimuli. Note the
large dips in the AEP at around 300 msec; this is the "P300."

Figure 7-3. Average wave forms for certain and uncertain ($P = .33$)
sounds for five subjects.

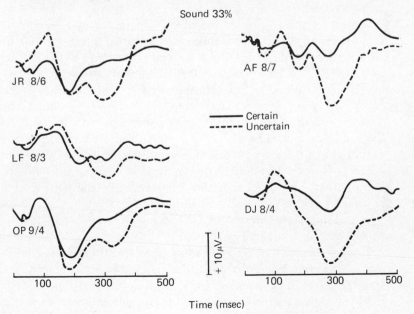

Teuting et al. (1970) found that P3 amplitude was high when the probability of a guessed outcome was low, and small when the probability of an event occurring was high. Thus, P3 was larger the more unexpected the outcome of the guess.

In an interesting experiment, Ruchkin et al. (1975) provided evidence that both evoked and emitted P300s were affected by stimulus probability. They devised a situation in which either the presence or absence of an auditory click provided information. The probability of stimulus presence or absence was varied between 25% and 75%. Both the emitted and evoked P300s were larger for the less frequent event and smaller for the event that had a higher probability of occurrence. The authors concluded, therefore, that evoked and emitted P300s are manifestations of the same brain processes.

Squires et al. (1977) conducted extensive computer analyses to measure ERP components that occurred in the time range of 150 to 600 msec after a stimulus. The subjects were presented with a series of tones. Any one tone was either loud or soft, and the probability of a given tone intensity was either high (.90) or low (.10). Subjects were told alternately to ignore or count tones, and measures were made from frontal, central, and parietal locations. Squires and colleagues reported three prominent ERP components: a large negative wave occurring at about 210 msec (N210), a large positive wave at about 350 msec (P350) and a slow wave (SW) which appeared over the last 200 msec of the 768-msec period. They noted that the P350 component was enhanced whenever the stimulus was rare and relevant to the subject's task. The same was true for the SW component, except that its scalp distribution was different from P350. The N210 component was most pronounced following rare stimuli. Hence, they concluded that the P350 and SW components are related to active processing of stimulus information (i.e., both stimulus probability and the tasks), while N210 reflects stimulus probability, independent of the task.

In summary, a number of studies have consistently associated P300 with stimulus probability; that is, higher P300 amplitudes were related to lower probabilities of stimulus occurrence. More detailed recent analyses reveal that there may be more than one component of the ERP, within the latency range of the classical

P300, related to stimulus probability and information processing (e.g., P3a and P3b of N. Squires et al., 1975, and P350 and SW of K. Squires et al., 1977).

Selective Attention, Orienting Responses, and P300

Hillyard et al. (1973) recorded auditory ERPs in persons who listened to a series of tones in one ear and ignored simultaneous tones in the other ear. The negative component (N1) of the ERP (peaking at 80 to 110 msec) was enlarged for the attended tones. A later, positive component, peaking at 250 to 400 msec (P3), also occurred to infrequent stimulus changes in the attended ear. These researchers interpreted the early ERP component as representing stimulus set and the later one as indicating response set in the selective attention situation. They proposed that stimulus set preferentially admits all sensory input to an attended channel, while response set facilitates recognition of these specific, task-related stimuli. They give an example of a cocktail party situation (with many competing auditory stimuli) in which there is a stimulus set for a particular speaker's voice and a response set to recognize the contents of his speech.

Picton and Hillyard (1974) measured auditory ERPs under a condition in which subjects had to detect and count occasional low-intensity signals and another condition in which the subject read a book and was instructed to ignore the ongoing auditory stimuli. Their recording system enabled the measurement of "early" (0 to 8 msec), "middle" (8 to 50 msec) and "late" (50 to 500 msec) ERP components. When attention was directed toward the auditory stimuli, a significant increase in two late waves was found. A component, labeled N1, occurred at approximately 83 msec, and P2 appeared at about 161 msec. In addition, a large positive wave which peaked at about 450 msec (P3) occurred in response to detected signals and to omitted stimuli in an otherwise continuous train. These researchers suggested that the N1–P2 complex represents activation of neurons involved in the analysis of auditory stimuli. They noted that P3 had been variously interpreted as representing resolution of uncertainty, an orienting response to an unexpected stimulus, a decision that an expected event has occurred, or a nonspecific change in arousal following such a decision. They favor the interpretation that P3 reflects a stimulus-independent perceptual decision process; that is, it indexes the decision that a certain signal has or has not occurred.

In a review of the literature concerning ERPs and selective attention, Musicant (1975) concluded that there is sufficient evidence to favor the hypothesis that selective attention has a direct effect on ERPs. He proposed that since P3 enhancement has been a more reliable finding than changes in earlier ERP components, there is less variability in ability of subjects to establish a response set as compared to a stimulus set.

A very detailed review of the selective attention-ERP literature was compiled by Näätänen (1975). In it he concluded that the ERP correlates of selective attention are by no means established. One basic criticism concerned the ability of subjects to predict the occurrence of relevant stimuli, at least to some extent. Another criticism was the lack of control over such factors as eye movements or pupil dilation, which could affect the ERP. Näätänen's criticisms seem to have had the effect of producing even more research to establish that reliable ERP changes do occur when persons attend to some stimuli and exclude others.

One reviewer who is more positive about the relationships demonstrated between ERPs and attentional mechanisms is Callaway (1975). He outlined some of the current notions in this area in the following statement: "The earlier AEP components (before 200 msec) seem to be affected by the simpler functions of attention (i.e., recognizing the stimuli as being in the relevant modality). Later components (200 to 400 msec) are most affected when more complex cognitive processes are involved. When very complex discriminations are called for there may be effects on very late (400 to 500 msec) components of the AEP" (p. 16). Some researchers disagree with the hypotheses regarding the late and early ERP components and their relation to attentional mechanisms. However, they are testable and suggest interesting research approaches.

Several recent investigations have helped to clarify some relations between attentional mechanisms and ERPs. For example, N. Squires et al. (1975) found evidence for two types of P3 waves. One of these they labeled P3a (latency about 240 msec), which was produced by unpredictable shifts in tone frequency and amplitude, regardless of whether instructions were to attend to or ignore the tones. The second, labeled P3b, with a latency of about 350 msec, occurred to tone changes only when subjects were actively attending to them. The P3a was distributed frontally-centrally, while P3b had a parietal-central distribution (see Figure 7-4). An experiment by Ford et al. (1976) supported the notion of more than one type of P3. They used a task designed to produce three levels of attention and found that P3 to the infrequent event became larger with increased attention. The P3 recorded from parietal leads was larger than the P3 from frontal areas during active attention. However, frontally recorded P3 was larger than parietal P3 during the ignore condition.

The effects of tone presentation rate on selective attention was examined by Schwent et al. (1976). The measures of attention were the auditory ERP and detection efficiency. The ISI's averaged 350 msec, 960 msec, and 1,920 msec in the fast, medium, and slow rate conditions. Interestingly, the early N1 component (latency 80 to 130 msec) was enhanced by attention only with the fast presentation rate, while P3 (300 to 450 msec) was enlarged to attended stimuli at all ISI's. Thus the enhancement of the early component was produced by imposing a high "information load" upon the subject. The authors commented that the fast stimulus presentation condition may have caused the subject to focus his attention more intensely, an observation supported by performance data, since signal detection was more efficient with the faster rates. The authors interpreted their results as further evidence that the N1 and P3 components reflect different selective attention processes.

Okita and Ohtani (1977) studied the effects of actively switching attention between the two ears on the AEP. They found that the AEPs were larger when subjects were required to switch attention to stimuli presented to one ear or the other in a random manner, as compared to presentations that allowed restriction of attention to only one ear.

In summary, attentional mechanisms have been found to produce changes in both early and late components of the ERP. Most of the studies conducted after 1970 have attempted to eliminate extraneous factors such as generalized arousal or prep-

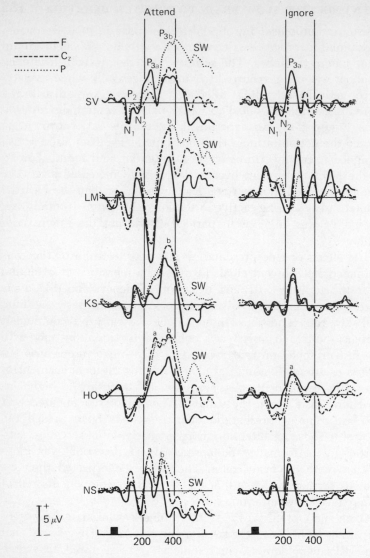

Figure 7-4. Evoked responses to infrequent stimuli ($P = .1$) at three electrode locations for five subjects in the attend (left) and ignore (right) conditions. The infrequent stimulus was soft for subjects SV, LM, KS and NS, and loud for HO. For each subject the wave forms from the three electrode sites, frontal (F), vertex (C_z) and parietal (P), are superimposed.

138

aration as the reason for ERP enhancement in selective attention. Some investigators have postulated that enhancement of
early ERP components with selective attention results from stimulus set, while a response set is responsible for enhancement of
later components. Recent studies reveal the complexity of the
situation, since ERP components may differ according to stimulus rate used, the brain area sampled, and the level of attention
required by the task.

The relationships that have been reported between the orienting response (OR) and P300 will be briefly reviewed here. The
suggestion that P300 accompanied the OR was first made by
Ritter and colleagues (Ritter et al., 1968; Ritter & Vaughan,
1969). Ritter et al. (1968) found that when the first of a series
of tones was presented unexpectedly it produced a P300 response. This also occurred when a change in pitch of the tone
was unexpectedly introduced. Predictable changes in pitch did
not produce a P300 response. They therefore concluded that the
P300 reflected a shift of attention associated with the OR. Ritter
and Vaughan (1969) reported P300 responses when signals
were detected but not with undetected signals or nonsignal
stimuli. They concluded that P300 could be associated with the
OR or stimulus discrimination and that it reflected brain processes concerned with the evaluation of stimulus significance.
Roth and Kopell (1973) expanded upon the work of Ritter and
colleagues by increasing the number of subjects and ERP
analyses. They obtained an ERP associated with infrequent, unpredictable stimuli, which had a positive component with a
latency of about 300 msec and interpreted this P300 as reflecting
the OR to unexpected stimuli.

The question of whether P300 is task-relevant or associated
with the OR to novel stimuli was investigated by Courchesne
et al. (1975). These investigators compared visual ERPs to rare,
task-relevant (counted) stimuli versus VEPs to rare, task-irrelevant stimuli, both types being presented randomly within a
sequence of other stimuli. The rare stimuli were of two types:
"simples," which were easily recognizable (e.g., geometric
forms) and "novels," which were not recognizable (e.g., complex, colorful patterns). The simple, task-relevant stimuli produced P3s (latency 380 to 430 msec) that were largest at Pz, but
the irrelevant novel stimuli evoked P3s (latency 360 to 380

msec) that were largest at C_z and F_z. The frontal P3s to novel stimuli were preceded by a large negative component (latency 240 to 300 msec). Thus, both types of unpredictable stimuli produced P300s, a finding consistent with previous ones. However, the stimulus novelty and task relevance resulted in P300s which differed in latency, depending on brain area sampled. Thus the authors concluded that the P300 is a complex brain response, made up of different components, related to different psychological processes. Similar conclusions had been reached by other investigators (e.g., N. Squires et al., 1975; Ford et al., 1976), who concluded that there is more than one type of P3 response.

P300 and the Detection and Discrimination of Stimuli

Stimulus Detection

Hillyard et al. (1971) used a signal detection procedure in which the subject's task was to decide on each trial whether or not an auditory signal (at threshold) had been added to continuous background noise. They found that P300 was several times larger when signals were detected than when they were not detected. It was concluded that P300 was enlarged only when stimulus information was being actively processed and that it was associated with the occurrence of a signal and its correct detection.

Sutton et al. (1967) and Ruchkin and Sutton (1973) found that a P300 appeared in the absence of a stimulus when the omitted signal was expected and provided information. For example, Sutton and associates asked subjects to guess, before each trial, whether the stimulus would consist of one or two clicks. The presence or absence of a second click told subjects whether their guess was correct or incorrect. A large P300 occurred at about the time of the second click, whether or not it had actually been presented. Sutton and colleagues interpreted the P300 as reflecting the delivery of information, or stimulus salience, to the subject. Ruchkin and Sutton (in press) have noted that the emitted P300 was of lower amplitude and broader duration than the evoked P300. They suggest that this may be due to the more imprecise internal timing that occurs when a subject is estimating the time of stimulus occurrence.

Variations in time estimation could lead to variations in the latencies of the emitted P300 components, thereby contributing to lower amplitudes and broader durations. Based on new experimental findings, Ruchkin and Sutton (in press) reported that emitted P300 latencies were longer and more variable than evoked P300 latencies. They suggest that longer latencies may be due to a longer time to decide that the second event is missing. They also postulated that the amplitude difference between evoked and emitted P300s is partly due to uncertainty and reduced information reception when a stimulus is omitted. Thus, it appears that the detection of the presence or the absence of some significant stimulus can produce an evoked *or* an emitted P300.

Discrimination of Stimuli

Hirsh (1971) compared ERPs when persons were merely required to count auditory stimuli and when they had to discriminate between the stimuli. A P300 (latency 300 to 375 msec) developed in 13 of 15 subjects during the discrimination, but not during counting trials. Ford et al. (1973) required their subjects to make discriminations between stimuli in the same sensory modality (e.g., flashes of lights) and between modalities (e.g., clicks and flashes). Stimuli were either made relevant or irrelevant through instructions. They found that the P300 was of high amplitude to relevant stimuli, medium sized if the stimulus was irrelevant but in the relevant modality, and nonexistent if in the irrelevant modality. The P300, therefore, seemed to reflect discriminations between and within modalities.

Poon et al. (1976) manipulated level of discrimination difficulty while measuring ERP and CNV to visual stimuli. One task involved simple RT, that is, subjects pressed a key as soon as they saw pairs of letters on a screen. In a more difficult discrimination, subjects pressed one key to indicate that two letters were both vowels or both consonants, and another key to indicate that the pair consisted of a vowel and a consonant. The mean RT was 221 msec for simple RT and 1,128 msec for the more difficult task. The CNV amplitude was smaller and P3 amplitude was enhanced under the more difficult discrimination task.

The general finding seems to be that tasks requiring discrimination of stimuli result in P300 responses, with larger responses being related to relevant stimuli and more difficult discriminations. This latter relationship is somewhat puzzling, since larger amplitude P300s have been found to accompany more confident, presumably less difficult decisions (e.g., Hillyard et al., 1971; Squires et al., 1973).

In summary, rather consistent relationships have been reported by various investigators regarding P300 and decision making and P300 and stimulus probability; that is, enhancement occurs with the decision process and with less probable stimuli. More recent studies of selective attention and the orienting response have indicated that the P300 is not a unitary process and may reflect variations in stimulus and response sets, in stimulus relevance, and in novelty of stimuli. Signal detection and discrimination processes have also been associated with P300.

Is there any common psychological process to which the P300 and its related components can be attached? A number of writers have suggested that P300 is related to active processing of stimulus information (Beck, 1975; Hillyard et al., 1971; Squires et al., 1975). A similar suggestion by Donchin et al. (1973) was that the amplitude of P300 is related to complexity of information processing required of a subject. Sutton's (1970) suggestion that salient stimuli enhance P300 is consistent with an active information processing interpretation, since, by salience, Sutton referred to information delivery and task relevance, which are aspects of information processing. In fact, all the processes reviewed in this section, including signal detection and discrimination, selective attention and the OR, stimulus probability and decision making, are aspects of active processing of stimuli. Hence, the brain function involved in the *active processing of information* may be a common denominator in the production of P300 responses.

The Relationship Between CNV and P300

Some investigators have suggested that P300 and CNV are related phenomena (Karlin, 1970; Näätänen, 1970), that is, that P300 is merely the return to baseline of the CNV. However, a number of studies have produced evidence that the two are separate phenomena. For example, Donald and Goff (1971) showed that P300 was enhanced by certain relevant stimuli but that enhancement was unrelated to CNV amplitude. Friedman et al. (1973) found that P300 changed systematically with changes in stimulus probability, but CNV did not. Donchin et al. (1975) reported that P300 amplitude was not affected by the presence or absence of a warning stimulus, whereas CNV was elicited only for warned trials. In addition, scalp distributions of CNV and P300 differed, indicating that they are generated by different neuronal populations in the brain. Poon et al. (1976) observed smaller CNV amplitudes and enhanced P300 with more difficult discriminations. Peters et al. (1977) measured CNV and P300 during verbal learning (paired-associates) and discrimination RT. They found that CNV amplitude showed an inverse relation to learning, while P300 increased with learning. Both wave forms were larger at central and parietal areas than at the frontal location during learning. During discrimination RT, however, the CNV was maximal at the frontal area and P300 was greatest at the parietal location. The CNV data were interpreted as reflecting early arousal and attentional processes, whereas P300 was related to the subject's decision about stimulus relevance. Peters and associates concluded that CNV and P300 could be regarded, on the basis of their data, as indices of learning activity taking place in the brain. The findings also indicated that they are separate processes.

The consensus at this writing seems to be that P300 and CNV are independent phenomena. No doubt their association with interesting psychological processes will lead to continued fruitful research on the nature of these slow potentials.

In the last few chapters we have seen how brain measures are correlated with different behaviors. In the next chapter we will examine how changes in muscle activity are related to various human activities. This is the first of the peripheral measures to be presented and it represents one of the consequences of processes that are initiated in the brain.

8

Muscle Activity and Behavior

In this chapter we briefly discuss the anatomy and physiology of muscle and the measurement of muscular activity in the form of the electromyogram (EMG). We then consider the relationship between the EMG and various activities, including motor performance, mental activity, and motivated performance.

Introduction

All of the outward behavior that we observe is the result of muscular activity. For example, an individual may have a notion to write a letter, but this is not possible without the fine motor coordination involved in moving a pen across a piece of paper to form the necessary words. The origin of the thoughts placed on the paper is in the brain of the person, and the initiation of these skilled movements is controlled by motor areas that also exist in the CNS. One of these motor systems is termed the pyramidal system, and its origins are primarily in the precentral gyrus of the cortex (motor cortex). It descends through various subcortical structures to the medulla, where an estimated 70% to 90% of the fibers originating in each hemisphere cross to the opposite side and descend within the spinal cord (Gardner, 1975). The area of the medulla at which the fibers cross over forms the shape of a pyramid, hence the term "pyramidal system." The pyramidal system is concerned with the initiation and control of fine muscle movements and is excitatory only; that is, it is involved only in the initiation of movements.

The extrapyramidal system, on the other hand, is a system that controls gross motor activities, such as those required to roll over in bed, and it has both excitatory and inhibitory components. This complex system has its primary origin in the prefrontal cortex, but it also has origins in the precentral, postcentral, and temporal cortex. It descends to the spinal cord in a very complicated manner, but it does not pass through the medullary pyramids, hence the name "extrapyramidal." The cerebellum is considered to be part of the extrapyramidal motor system and plays a role in the regulation and modification of motor activities, receiving input and having output to the rest of the brain and the spinal cord. This brief reminder of CNS mechanisms is presented here to emphasize the fact that muscles do not contract on their own.

Anatomy and Physiology of Muscles

There are three types of muscle tissue in the body: skeletal, smooth, and cardiac muscle. The skeletal muscles make up the voluntary motor system and are exemplified by such familiar structures as the biceps of the upper arm and the flexor digitorum of the forearm. Individual skeletal muscle fibers have striations and many nuclei, as shown in Figure 8-1. Smooth, or unstriated, muscles are considered to be part of the involuntary motor system, since we ordinarily do not exert control over

Figure 8-1. Types of muscle cells.

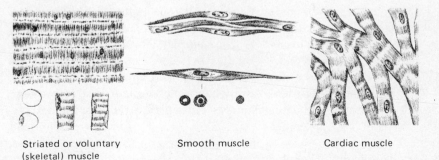

Striated or voluntary (skeletal) muscle   Smooth muscle   Cardiac muscle

them.[1] The smooth muscles of the blood vessels are good examples. These muscle fibers travel in a circular path and can change the diameter of the blood vessel by constriction or dilation. Individual smooth muscle fibers have a single nucleus and no striations. Cardiac muscle is also classified as involuntary muscle. It is striated, similar to skeletal muscle, but is considered to be a separate variety. Skeletal muscles make up approximately 40% of total body weight, while smooth and cardiac muscle account for another 5% to 10%. The primary focus of this chapter is on the activity of skeletal (voluntary) muscle.

Skeletal Muscle

Most voluntary muscles are attached to a bone through strong, nonelastic fibrous cords known as tendons. A muscle consists of groups of muscle fibers which form a primary bundle (fasciculus). A muscle is composed of a group of these fasciculi (see Figure 8-2). The fasciculus, in turn, contains many muscle fibers, and muscle fibers are composed of even smaller diameter myofibrils. Each muscle fiber contains several hundred to several thousand myofibrils. Each myofibril has about 1,500 myosin filaments and 3,000 actin filaments, which are protein molecules responsible for muscle contraction. Viewed under a microscope, the myosin filaments are thick and dark in appearance, while the actin filaments are thin and light colored. It is the myosin and actin filaments which cause the myofibrils to have alternate light and dark bands, imparting the striated appearance to skeletal muscle. The dark striations are also known as A-bands and the light ones as I-bands. Two other structures should be noted: the Z-band and the H-band (see Figure 8-3). The actin filaments are attached to the so-called Z-band or Z-membrane. The Z-band is located in the central region of the I-band. The portion of a myofibril that lies between two successive Z-membranes is called a sarcomere. The H-band appears as a light area in the center of the A-band when a muscle fiber is stretched and the ends of the actin filaments pull apart. Striated muscle fibers

---

[1] There is some evidence that control of smooth muscle may be learned when appropriate feedback is provided (see chapter 14).

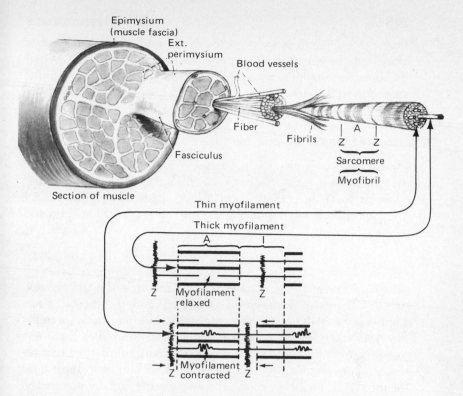

Figure 8-2. Detail of muscle showing structure and mechanics of muscular contraction.

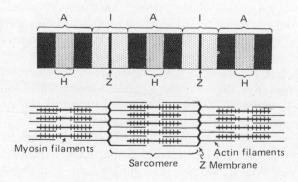

Figure 8-3. Arrangement of the myosin and actin filaments in the sarcomeres.

may vary in length from 1 to 40 mm (often extending the entire length of the muscle) and range in diameter between 10 and 80 μm. The sarcolemma is an electrically polarized membrane that surrounds each muscle cell. It is the cell membrane of the muscle fiber.

Mechanisms of Muscle Contraction

Action potentials in muscle fibers are responsible for the initiation of muscle contractions. We will briefly examine muscular contraction at the relatively gross level of the motor unit and at the molecular level, describing the interaction between actin and myosin filaments.

The Motor Unit

The basic mechanism of muscle contraction is the motor unit, which consists of a nerve cell, its axon, and the muscle fibers supplied by it. The motor neuron–muscle fiber link represents the last stage in the transmission of motor impulses from the cortex, down through the subcortical areas of the brain, over descending tracts of the spinal cord, and out over the motor neuron. The "final common pathway" was the name given by the noted neurophysiologist Sherrington to the motor pathway from the CNS to a muscle. The innervation ratio, or number of muscle fibers innervated by a single neuron, may range from 1 : 3 for those muscle fibers that control fine motor adjustments (e.g., the laryngeal muscles) to 1 : 1,000 for fibers involved in gross movements (e.g., gastrocnemius muscle of the upper leg).

Motor units obey the all-or-none principle discussed in chapter 2 in connection with neuronal action potentials. That is, the neurons and muscle fibers that comprise the motor unit either do not fire at all or fire with their full capacity. The information regarding action potentials in neurons applies to skeletal muscle fibers, except for some quantitative differences. For example, the resting potential is approximately −85 mV in skeletal muscle fibers, which is not too different from neurons. The duration of the muscle fiber action potential ranges from 1 to 5 msec, which is longer than that of the large myelinated neuron. The biggest difference is in the velocity of conduction along a muscle fiber;

that is, it is about 3 to 5 m/sec, or about 1/18th the velocity of conduction in large myelinated neurons. The skeletal muscles are normally innervated by large myelinated neurons at the neuromuscular junction (also known as the motor end plate). The neuromuscular junction is located near the middle of the muscle fiber. Thus the action potential spreads from the middle toward the ends, allowing all sarcomeres of the muscle to contract simultaneously. The strength of muscle contraction depends on the number of motor units contracting and the rate of contraction. The action potential of the fiber is brief, but the duration of muscle contraction may last up to 100 msec or more. Muscles are in a constant state of tonus to allow quick responses to external stimuli. The tonus is maintained by a steady flow of impulses from the spinal cord to each motor unit and varies with level of activity of the person and the nervous system. The loss of tonus may occur if the neuron supplying the muscle is damaged, thus preventing the constant flow of impulses. In the case of immobilized limbs, the flow of impulses is reduced, and some atrophy may occur.

Muscular Contraction at the Molecular Level

When a neuronal impulse reaches the neuromuscular junction, acetylcholine is released. The muscle fiber membrane thus becomes permeable to sodium ions and depolarization of the membrane occurs, resulting in the action potential. The presence of acetylcholinesterase at the neuromuscular junction causes the breakdown of acetylcholine, and the muscle fiber is ready to be stimulated again.

When an action potential travels down the muscle fiber, it causes the release of calcium ions into the sarcoplasm surrounding the myofibrils. This sets up attractive forces that cause the actin filaments to slide into spaces between the myosin fibrils. Thus the positive calcium ions produce an energy-releasing reaction which brings on the sliding of the myofibril filaments said to underly muscle contraction. It is believed that the energy for this contraction is derived from the enzyme adenosine triphosphate (ATP), which is broken down into adenosine diphosphate (ADP) when the motor neuron impulse reaches the muscle fiber. The ATP is broken down to form ADP, and the hypothesis is that large amounts of energy are thereby released. A relaxing factor has been discovered in muscle and has been postulated to react with the energizing substance of muscle to halt contraction until the next stimulus reaches the fiber (Jacob & Francone, 1970).

Muscle Fatigue

Prolonged and strong contraction of a muscle leads to muscle fatigue. This results from the inability of the muscle fibers to maintain work output because of ATP depletion. The nerves, as well as their action potentials, continue to function properly, but contractions become weaker and weaker with time (Guyton, 1977). Continuous muscle contraction contributes to interruption of the blood supply to muscle tissue and causes fatigue in about 1 minute because of nutrient loss.

Muscular Hypertrophy

Forceful exercise, in which muscles contract to at least 75% of their maximum tension, produces an increased number of myofibrils. Thus the diameters of the individual muscle fibers increase. In addition, the nutrients and metabolic substances, such as ATP and glycogen, are increased. Hypertrophy results from very forceful muscle activity, even though it might only occur for a few minutes each day.

The Measurement of Muscle Activity

Now that we have briefly reviewed the sources of electrical activity produced by muscles, methods for measuring this activity will be presented. We will then briefly review the literature to determine the kinds of changes in muscle activity that accompany the performance of various tasks.

Electromyography

Electromyography is the technique for measuring and recording electrical potentials which are associated with contractions of muscle fibers. Thus the measurement of muscle activity results in a record called the electromyogram (EMG). The EMG is often used in the clinic to study muscular disorders. Very thin needle electrodes can be inserted into muscle tissue, and recordings can be made from limited muscle regions or even from single motor units. The EMG can also be recorded from the skin surface, since some portion of the action potentials produced in muscle fibers is transmitted to the skin. The closer the muscle tissue is to the skin surface, and the stronger the contractions, the greater will be the amount of electrical activity recorded at the surface. Most studies relating EMG to human performance deal with the activity occurring in large muscle groups. Therefore, the information in this chapter is derived mainly from surface EMG recordings.

General Properties of the EMG

The surface EMG records the electrical activity of motor units, which occurs prior to contraction of a muscle (Thompson et al., 1966). Electrodes placed on the skin over an active muscle record the algebraic sum of a large number of depolarizations which occur when a group of motor units are activated (Lippold, 1967).

Muscular Effort and the EMG

Studies that have examined the relation between EMG level and degree of muscle tension indicate that the EMG is a fairly good indicator of tension in skeletal muscles. For example, in a study by Malmo (cited by J. F. Davis, 1959), EMG was recorded from the flexor muscles of the forearm while subjects varied the amount of squeeze on a hand dynamometer.[2] The recordings showed regular increases in EMG amplitude (in microvolts) as grip strength increased. The data for the 9 families and 11 males indicated that, on the average, a higher EMG level was produced by females than males to maintain a given grip level. Essentially similar results were obtained by Wilcott and Beenken

[2] A hand dynamometer is a device to produce and measure variations in hand grip strength.

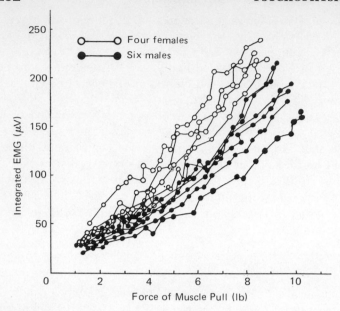

Figure 8-4. The relation between the force of muscle pull in pounds and integrated EMG in microvolts for the bicep muscle.

(1957) for their four female and six male subjects. Their results are shown in Figure 8-4. The male-female differences indicate that females must bring more motor units into action to accomplish the same amount of work.

The EMG Wave Form

The surface EMG that accompanies muscle contraction consists of a series of spiked discharges from motor units underlying the electrode. The frequency of the components may range from 20 to 1,000 Hz, with an amplitude of about 100 to 1,000 μV, depending upon the mass of muscle tissue beneath the recording electrodes and the degree to which they are contracting. However, amplitudes as low as 2 to 3 μV may be recorded when a muscle is in a relatively relaxed state. The recorded EMG wave form is not as regular as some of the other physiological meas-

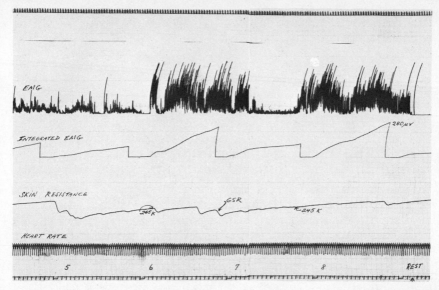

Figure 8-5. Right forearm EMG measured during trial 5-8 in a verbal learning situation. The totally integrated record shows that EMG over a 30-second trial (trial 8) was 280 μV. Note the sharp cessation of EMG activity at the end of trial 8 (rest). The very top line is a time marker (one sec), and the bottom line indicates the serial presentation of items to be learned. Also shown are the records of skin resistance (245 kΩ) and heart rate. (From author's unpublished data.)

ures, e.g., the alpha wave of the EEG. This is why, in studies that attempt to quantify EMG and relate it to behavior, the integrated surface EMG is often derived. This is accomplished by feeding the EMG into an integrator circuit which will show the total amount of activity over a certain period of time (e.g., 10 seconds). An example of an integrated EMG record is presented in Figure 8-5. The EMG is shown in two stages in Figure 8-5: (1) a first level of integration produces the EMG (first line) with no activity shown below baseline; and (2) a second line shows the summed EMG and its calibration in microvolts and provides a measure of total muscle activity in a given time period. The investigator in this experiment was studying the amount of forearm EMG produced during a 30-second verbal learning trial. The other measures depicted are skin resistance and heart rate.

Electrode Placement for EMG Recording

The general principles for electrode application are the same as for other physiological measures. That is, the skin must be cleansed with either alcohol, acetone, or some abrasive material to remove dead skin or oils. Then, after electrode paste is rubbed into the area and the excess removed, the recording electrode containing a new supply of paste is placed into the desired position. The EMG is best recorded with a bipolar electrode arrangement, with both electrodes located over the muscle of interest. The resistance between the electrodes should not exceed 10,000 Ω and should be lower if possible (e.g., 5,000 Ω). Too low a resistance, say less than 1,000 Ω, should be regarded with suspicion, since it could mean that there is a conducting bridge of paste between the electrodes or that they are too close. This situation could result in a short-circuiting of the EMG potentials. The subject, the EMG recorder, and the electrical equipment close to it should all be grounded to protect the subject and to prevent 60-cycle interference in the recording. Once exposed to electrode paste or jelly, the electrodes will start to deteriorate. They must be scrubbed in hot water and soap after each use and then rinsed thoroughly in clear water to remove all traces of electrolyte.

Specific Electrode Placements

In order to place electrodes over the muscle of interest, some standardization is necessary. The exact specifications for placement of electrodes over 11 different muscle areas have been outlined by J. F. Davis (1959). Examples of two common placements are given in Figure 8-6, adapted from J. F. Davis (1959).[3] The examples are for the frontalis muscle of the forehead and

[3] Specifications for other placements in the original J. F. Davis publication are contained in a chapter by Lippold (1967).

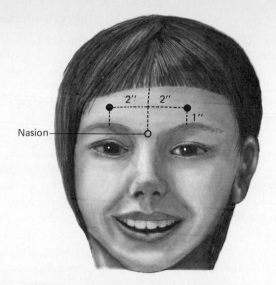

Standard Forehead Lead (frontalis muscle)

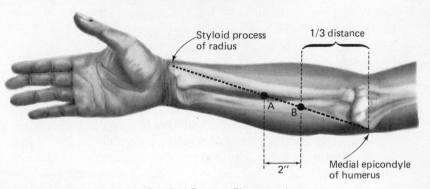

Standard Forearm Flexor Lead

Figure 8-6. Standard forehead and forearm leads for measurement of EMG.

the flexor muscles of the forearm. The placements for the frontalis muscle are obtained by measuring 2 in. to the left and right of midline (nasion as the midline reference point) and placing each electrode 1 in. above the eyebrow. One must be careful to watch for eye-blink and EEG artifact with this placement.

The forearm flexor (flexor carpi radialis and flexor digitorum sublimis) leads involve measuring the distance from the medial epicondyle of the humerus to the styloid process of the radius, while the subject has his forearm on a table with his palm up. Next, a point that is one-third of the distance from epicondyle to styloid is taken. The center of Electrode A is placed over this point. Electrode B is placed 2 in. distally from the center of A. This placement should show visible movement with flexor movement of the middle finger of this hand. The ground may be placed at the elbow or wrist of the same arm to reduce ECG artifact. Since the EMG is susceptible to movement artifact, it is best to use relatively small electrode surfaces and an attachment that is flexible as opposed to rigid. Placement over a pulsating artery should be avoided.

Recording the EMG

Since the EMG is a relatively small signal, a similar level of amplification as that required in the recording of EEG is required. Although the EMG produces a wide range of frequencies, some experts agree that the maximal activity occurs at the lower end of the spectrum (Goldstein, 1972). The frequencies of interest range from approximately 20 to 400 Hz. This means that the filtering system must allow at least this frequency range of EMG to be recorded. Since ink-writer pen systems cannot follow the signal very well after 150 Hz, one approach has been to record the EMG on magnetic tape for later playback into a computer or to record at a slowed rate which the ink-writer can follow. Still another method utilizes a cathode-ray oscilloscope to display the EMG recording during experimental trials, since it has no difficulty in following and displaying even very high frequencies. As mentioned previously, the technique of integration helps considerably in the analysis of EMG activity. Essentially, the integrator provides a measure of total EMG output over a given period of time. Or, alternately, it may be designed to automatically reset when a certain level of activity has occurred, for example, reset occurs after every 300 μV of accumulated EMG activity. The total integrated activity is proportional to both the positive and negative components of the EMG wave form. Goldstein (1972) points out a possible problem inherent in the use of integrators. That is, since they do not discriminate between artifacts and real muscle action potentials (MAPs), the artifacts may be integrated along with MAPs. An encouraging note concerns the reliability or consistency of the EMG measures in the same individual, performing some standard task, over a period of time. Goldstein (1972) cites several studies which indicate that the EMG yields good test-retest reliability, suggesting that it is a consistent measure.

The EMG and Behavior

Many studies relating EMG to various kinds of human behavior and performance have been reviewed by Duffy (1962, 1972) and by Goldstein (1972). An examination of the EMG literature for the period from 1970 on indicates that relative to other physiological measures, investigations using the EMG have been few in number. The reason for this relative decrease in EMG research is not known. During this same time period, however, there were quite a few studies of EMG in a biofeedback context. Several EMG biofeedback studies that relate to basic learning processes will be presented in this chapter, while representative EMG studies aimed at using biofeedback to treat some specific disorder will be examined in chapter 14.

Motor Performance and the EMG

The EMG has been recorded by investigators during the performance of various kinds of motor activities, including time to react, tracking, speech production, and fatigue-producing muscular activities. Some of these studies are briefly reviewed in this section.

EMG and Reaction Time

The electromyogram was recorded from the forearm extensor muscles while a subject waited to obtain a signal for his response (R. C. Davis, 1940). Muscle tension began about 200 to 400 msec after the ready signal and increased up to the moment of reaction. Two other findings were of interest: (1) the higher the muscle tension at the end of the foreperiod, the faster the RT; and (2) muscle tension was higher and RT was quicker at the end of regular foreperiods as compared to irregular ones. The finding that RT is faster with regular foreperiods is not surprising, since other investigators before and since have obtained this result. It is interesting, however, that muscle tension should be higher with regular foreperiods. Davis attributed this to a form of set or an increased readiness to respond.

It is also of interest to relate these findings to those of other studies using different physiological measures. For example, the alpha-blocking response begins about 300 msec after the stimulus (Lansing et al., 1959) or at a similar interval for the start of muscle tension buildup. Also, skin conductance has been found to be higher and RT faster during experimental conditions under which there were regular intervals between stimuli as compared to irregular intervals (Andreassi et al., 1969).

Kennedy and Travis (1948) investigated the relationship between EMG, RT, and level of performance in a continuous (2-hour) tracking task. Thirty-two subjects performed a pursuit tracking task while EMG was recorded from the frontalis muscle. A warning light was placed 24 degrees peripherally from the main task and flashed on when muscle tension fell below predetermined levels. The subject was required to lift his foot from a pedal when the light flashed, and this RT was measured. Thus, RT and tracking performance were measured at various tension levels. Kennedy and Travis reported that RTs became progressively slower with low levels of tension and faster when tension level was high. The number of failures to respond greatly increased at the low tension levels, indicating that the subjects were probably drowsy at those times. On the basis of this and other studies (Kennedy & Travis, 1947; Travis & Kennedy, 1948; Travis & Kennedy, 1949), they proposed that frontalis muscle tension might serve as an indicator of alertness in situations where persons were involved in monotonous tasks over prolonged periods of time.

In the Davis (1940) study the muscle group actually involved in the response showed an increase in tension during the foreperiod while in the Kennedy and Travis investigation, the frontalis muscle was not involved in the response, but the task was a visuomotor one in which subjects had to follow changes in a visual display by making hand and arm movements. Goldstein (1972) noted that with increased practice, activity in muscles not involved in the reaction tends to decrease. For example, Obrist et al. (1969) reported decreased activity in chin and neck muscles just before and during the time that subjects depressed a telegraph key with their hand. This was correlated with decreased heart rate. They interpreted this to indicate a decrease in irrelevant muscular activity that might otherwise interfere with the task the subject was to perform. Further study led them to suggest that EMG measured from chin muscles may be a good index of irrelevant motor activity. Obrist et al. (1970) obtained additional evidence that the decreased chin EMG was related to cardiac deceleration. Again they found inhibition of task-irrelevant somatic activities during the foreperiod, just as the response was made, in a simple RT task.

EMG has been measured from the masseter muscles (jaw) while 19 subjects performed in an RT experiment (Holloway & Parsons, 1972). The warning signal (chime) preceded the execution stimulus (buzzer) by a variable interval (8 to 17 seconds), and subjects were instructed to terminate the buzzer as quickly as possible by pressing a foot switch. Their results were similar to those of Obrist and associates in that fast RTs were associated with less EMG activity during the preparatory foreperiod of the task. Notice that in this experiment, as with previous ones showing decreased EMG in the period just preceding the response, the muscle tension was measured from muscles other than those involved in the task and the response. It would have been informative if these investigators had also provided information on EMGs from responding muscle groups to enable some statement regarding the relative activity of task-involved and noninvolved muscle groups. The implication is that only activity in muscles not concerned with task execution would be reduced during the time just before and during the response.

To briefly summarize, it appears that when a muscle group is involved in the execution of a RT task, progressively increasing activity during the foreperiod is related to faster responses. However, noninvolved muscles show a decrease in activity, presumably lessening the possibility of interference with the relevant motor response.

EMG and Tracking

Tracking involves the movement of some control (wheel or stick) to keep an indicator on a moving target. Continuous motor adjustments must be made to perform the task correctly. A pilot maintaining a correct altitude and heading and a driver keeping a car in her own lane are performing tracking tasks.

Kennedy and Travis (1948) obtained results which indicated that low frontalis EMG was related to poor tracking performance. A number of tracking studies have indicated a relation between subjective effort and EMG. For example, experiments by Eason and his colleagues have shown, in general, that conditions which required increased effort led to increased EMG levels and improved performance (Eason, 1963; Eason & White, 1960, 1961). Eason and White (1960) observed that EMG level increased and tracking performance improved as a function of practice trials, up to a certain point. After this point, performance dropped even though EMG increased, suggesting that fatigue was occurring. When subjects were given either 0, 10, 20, or 40 seconds between trials, performance improved with intertrial interval, but the EMG level was lower. This inverse relationship between EMG and performance was interpreted as evidence that muscular fatigue is partly responsible for the commonly observed superiority of distributed over massed practice in pursuit rotor tracking and other perceptual-motor tasks. Eason and White advanced a two-factor hypothesis of muscular tension. They proposed that muscular tension is positively related to both motivation and fatigue. Since motivation facilitates performance and fatigue hinders it, the tension level at any given time is a summation of the motivation and fatigue components.

Eason (1963) recorded EMG from forearm, biceps, trapezius (neck), and splenius (neck) muscles, while subjects performed pursuit tracking tasks over a number of days. He found that EMG level stayed constant over days even though performance improved, indicating increased tracking efficiency. Neck muscle tension alone was found to reflect changes in effort as well as the activity level of all four muscles. Eason and Branks (1963) found increases in EMG as subjects exerted greater degrees of concentration in a pursuit rotor task. Irrelevant stimulation in the form of a lifted weight increased EMG level and enhanced performance. However, when the irrelevant stimulation was intense, performance decreased despite an increase in EMG. This last study suggested that there was an optimal EMG level in the accomplishment of the task. Below and above this obtained EMG level, performance was not as efficient.

To briefly summarize, it seems that efficient tracking performance is related to some moderate to high EMG level. Very low muscular tension (possibly indicative of drowsiness) and very high tension (perhaps associated with overexertion or fatigue) seem to be associated with less efficient performance.

EMG and Speech Activity

Behaviorists have long maintained that thinking is nothing more than subvocal speech. This peripheral theory of thinking emphasizes that mental phenomena are related to skeletal muscle activity. Goldstein (1972) reviewed a number of studies which indicated that EMGs occurred during thinking, but they were not confined to the vocal mechanism (laryngeal muscle activity), since EMG changes were observed in many different muscle groups. Recent studies have examined subvocal speech as it occurs during reading in some individuals. Such occurrences limit the rate of reading for these persons to about 150 words per minute, or approximately the maximum attainable while reading aloud. In one study, Hardyck et al. (1966) recorded EMG activity from the surface of the throat, over the laryngeal muscle, of 50 subjects. The presence of subvocalization was determined by noting EMG changes that occurred when the subjects were asked to read silently and then to stop reading. The presence of

EMG activity during reading indicated subvocalization. Out of the 50 subjects tested, 17 were found to be subvocalizers. These 17 persons were tested further in the following manner: first, they were allowed to hear their own amplified EMG activity over headphones, then they were shown how it could be controlled, and finally they began to read under instructions to keep the EMG level at a minimum, that is, to maintain silence in the headphones. Most of the subjects showed a reduction in speech muscle EMG level within 5 minutes. After 30 minutes, all 17 subjects were able to read at an EMG level that was comparable to their resting level. Follow-up tests after 1 and 3 months revealed no subvocalization during reading, using the EMG as the criterion. The authors attributed this rapid, and apparently long-term, disappearance of subvocalization to the ability of subjects to make fine motor adjustments of the speech musculature on the basis of auditory cues. This is in contrast to the situation in which attempts to reduce the speech muscle activity by instructions alone were not successful. The authors cited the work of Basmajian (1963), who reported that subjects can learn to control the contractions of single motor units, with auditory and visual cues, within 15 to 30 minutes.

In a later study, Hardyck and Petrinovich (1969) identified 50 college and 13 high school students who were habitual subvocalizers during silent reading. Forty-eight of the college students learned to eliminate the subvocal activity within 1 hour. The 13 high school students required from one to three sessions to eliminate the subvocal speech. The researchers noted that speed of eliminating the subvocal pattern was quicker for those persons who scored higher on intelligence tests. The immediate effect of eliminating subvocalization was that subjects reported a reduction of fatigue previously associated with reading for periods of 1 to 3 hours. Hardyck and Petrinovich suggested that both elimination of subvocal speech and reading improvement instruction should enable a high speed of reading, with good comprehension, for students with sufficient ability to benefit from the techniques.

McGuigan and his associates have found increases in chin, lip, and tongue EMGs during silent reading as compared to resting levels (McGuigan et al., 1964; McGuigan & Bailey, 1969; Mc-

Guigan & Rodier, 1968). In addition, McGuigan and Rodier (1968) observed increased amplitude of chin and tongue EMG for college students during the memorization of prose materials. They also found that EMG levels were higher during silent reading when they presented auditory "noise" in the form of prose different from that being read. They interpreted this latter finding as indicating that subjects changed the amplitude of their covert oral behavior to facilitate the reading process. McGuigan (1973) suggests that the higher level of oral EMG activity during silent reading in children and less proficient adults indicates that these individuals exaggerate their covert oral behavior to bring their comprehension up to a proper level. Likewise, under demanding conditions (e.g., noisy environment) the average individual enhances reading proficiency by exaggerating the amplitude of covert oral activity, sometimes reading aloud to do this, perhaps to overcome a distracting conversation in the vicinity. Contrary to the view of others who would eliminate subvocal activity related to silent reading, McGuigan believes that the covert oral response is beneficial to this and other types of linguistic tasks.

In summary, EMG studies have reliably detected subvocal speech during silent reading. Feedback of EMG may have practical applications in terms of eliminating this habit in adults if they are hindered by it. However, children appear to subvocalize naturally while reading silently, and perhaps teachers should not try to eliminate this activity if it helps in comprehending the material at an early learning stage.

EMG and Muscular Fatigue

Investigations have indicated that persons can maintain maximum muscular effort (i.e., 100%) for less than 1 minute (McCormick, 1976). However, a level of about 25% of their own maximum can be maintained for 10 minutes or more. The implications of these findings are that muscular efficiency decreases when a high level of exertion is required over a continuous period and that this is due to muscle fatigue. With respect to performance in tracking, Eason and White (1960) have argued that muscular fatigue is partly responsible for the superiority of distributed practice over massed practice. They also suggest that a fatigued subject would have to increase muscular tension in order to continue making rotary pursuit movements. Thus, additional motor units would be recruited to compensate for the reduced activity of fatigued units.

Some support for this notion is derived from a study by Wilkinson (1962), although a completely different type of task was used. Twelve persons were required to perform a 20-minute pencil-and-paper addition test under the following conditions: (1) after a normal night of sleep, and (2) after 32 to 56 hours of sleep deprivation. The EMG recorded from the inactive forearm indicated that subjects who maintained performance best after deprivation had the greatest increases in EMG over normal levels. Thus the maintenance of performance level under somewhat stressful conditions seems to be at the cost of extra energy expenditure.

Örtengren et al. (1975) conducted studies of localized muscle fatigue in both laboratory and factory assembly-line conditions. Two assembly-line stations, considered to be heavy work, were examined, and results were found to be comparable for both the laboratory simulation and the actual assembly line. At one station the muscles were under heavy static load for periods of 60 seconds at a time. The other station required that individuals perform much of their work above their shoulders. The EMGs were recorded from biceps, triceps (upper arm), forearm, deltoid, and trapezius muscles of five experienced male workers. Subjective incidents of localized fatigue corresponded highly with increased EMG level of various muscles. The technique enabled comparison of muscle strain for different work tasks and may be used to provide information about how work situations can be changed to make tasks less strenuous.

The effect of desk slant on EMG and fatigue ratings was tested by Eastman and Kamon (1976). They photographed back posture and recorded EMG from deltoid, trapezius, and spinae erector (lower back) muscles while six subjects performed reading and writing tasks at either a flat desk, a 12-degree tilt desk, or a 24-degree tilt desk. The subjects participated in 2½ hour sessions on each of 3 days. The major finding was that EMG activity from the lower back muscles was significantly lessened with the 24-degree desk slant. Fatigue ratings were also least for the desk slanted at 24 degrees of angle.

The several studies reviewed in this section indicate that feelings of localized fatigue are associated with increased local EMG activity. Studies of EMG activity may be useful in reducing fatigue produced by different types of work tasks and work places.

EMG and Mental Activity

In this section we briefly consider studies of EMG in conditioning, cognitive activities, and sleep.

Conditioning of the EMG

The control of single motor units through conditioning procedures is well established, and much of the relevant work has recently been summarized by Basmajian (1977). The emphasis in this section is on EMG changes during conditioning as revealed by surface recordings.

Operant conditioning of the EMG was demonstrated by Cohen (1973). Two groups of subjects were reinforced for producing either 40 to 60 μV of activity or 90 to 110 μV of chin EMG, for a minimum duration of .5 second. Both experimental groups learned to emit the correct EMG level to obtain reinforcement. Basmajian and Newton (1974) recorded EMG from the upper and lower buccinator (cheek) muscles of nine clarinet players during musical exercises. When visual EMG feedback was provided via an oscilloscope, the musicians rapidly learned to suppress or activate specific parts of these muscles (in less than 10 minutes). The investigators concluded that subjects can rapidly learn to control the contraction patterns in different parts of the same small muscle, and electronic feedback may offer a method to teach alterations in muscle responses while performing on musical instruments.

A comparison of EMG biofeedback with more commonly used verbal relaxation instructions in reducing frontalis muscle tension was made by Haynes et al. (1975). During EMG feedback conditions, 22 subjects heard a tone that decreased in pitch as they became more relaxed and increased in pitch as muscular tension increased. Four other subjects received verbal instructions to relax according to either the techniques of Wolpe (passive relaxation) or Jacobson (active relaxation). A control group of 17 subjects were told to become as relaxed as possible but received no other assistance. A final group received noncontingent feedback in the form of a tone that was presented at random intervals and was not related to low or high EMG levels. The EMG biofeedback group achieved greater degrees of muscle relaxation than either of the other two relaxation groups and much greater than that achieved by persons in the two control conditions.

In another study of frontalis muscle relaxation training Kinsman et al. (1975) compared continuous EMG biofeedback with verbal feedback in reducing EMG level. The verbal feedback was based on changes in EMG level, e.g., if electrical activity lessened the subject was so informed. The training of the 64 male subjects (aged 18 to 31) consisted of three consecutive daily sessions. The researchers found that while verbal feedback facilitated muscle relaxation the direct EMG feedback was superior. Subjects who received no feedback were unable to reduce muscle tension over the course of the training sessions.

Alexander (1975) questioned two basic assumptions implicit in the use of EMG feedback to achieve lowered muscular tension. These were (1) that tension reduction in one muscle (e.g., the frontalis) is generalized to other skeletal muscles, and (2) that the subjective feeling of being relaxed is related to EMG reduction. Alexander's experimental group achieved significant decreases in frontalis EMG feedback, but this lowering of tension did not spread to two other skeletal muscles (forearm and leg). In addition, a comparison of the ratings of relaxation made by experimental and control groups (no feedback) indicated that "mild" relaxation was achieved by both groups over the 5-day period of the experiment. Thus, Alexander proposed that his data do not support a claim that frontalis EMG reduction is either related to or produces general feelings of relaxation. However, this study was preliminary in nature, and further studies using other muscle groups and additional ways to measure feelings of relaxation must be conducted before it can be definitely concluded that EMG reduction is not related to subjective feelings of relaxation. In this context it is interesting to note that Eason and White (1961) found neck EMG to be the best single indicator of effort in a tracking task and the best representative of tension level in the group of muscles they examined (i.e., neck, trapezius, deltoid and biceps). This kind of result suggests that some muscle groups may be superior to others in terms of indicating general tension level of different bodily muscles.

To summarize, it is clear that operant conditioning of the surface EMG, using appropriate feedback, has been obtained by a number of researchers. It seems that by providing accurate information about internal processes, EMG feedback can lead to instrumental control of muscle tension level. The studies mentioned here are general in nature, since they deal primarily with the learned control of EMG. Investigations that have studied EMG biofeedback in the context of treating certain disorders, such as tension headache, will be discussed in chapter 14.

The classical conditioning of EMG has been demonstrated in several studies. For example, Van Liere (1953) measured EMG from the masseter and forearm muscles in an experimental group, in which the CS (tone) was followed by the UCS (another tone), and in a control group, which received the CS only. As conditioning progressed the experimental group showed a larger EMG increase to the CS than the control group, indicating conditioning of these muscles. Obrist (1968) also showed EMG activity of neck, chin, and forearm muscles during classical conditioning. In another study (Obrist, 1969), using a blue light as the CS and an electric shock as the UCS, it was found that chin EMG activity decreased in anticipation of the aversive UCS. The drop in EMG activity reflected a decrease in discrete movements, not in tension level.

EMG and Cognitive Activities

Included in this section are a number of studies that have related EMG to cognitive activities, including problem solving, verbal learning, and concept identification. Clites (1936) measured the forearm EMGs of subjects solving a verbal problem. He found that EMGs were greater when subjects were successful in problem solving than when they were unsuccessful. Perhaps success led to more interest and involvement in the task and was reflected in the higher EMG levels.

The question of probability of success and its effect on muscular effort expended in a task was investigated by Diggory et al. (1964). These experimenters measured EMG from the forearms of three groups of subjects: (1) those who were led to believe that they had a high probability of success (Ps) in a task, (2) subjects who believed that Ps was very low, and (3) those who believed that Ps was 50-50. The investigators manipulated Ps by showing the subjects predetermined graphs of past performance and extrapolations to future performance after each trial. The results supported the conclusion that persons who expected to succeed exerted more effort, as measured by EMG level, than those who expected to fail. Thus, there would seem to be some support for the idea that the experience of success influences EMG in an upward direction.

The picture is slightly complicated, however, when one considers results of studies which have varied difficulty without considering success or failure. For example, R. C. Davis (1938) measured forearm and neck EMGs while subjects solved number problems that became progressively more difficult. He reported that with increased task difficulty, EMGs at both locations increased correspondingly. The difficulty of a problem was judged by the proportion of subjects who failed it. Pishkin and Shurley (1968) measured frontalis EMGs of psychiatric patients during a concept identification task. The EMG was higher with unsolvable than with solvable problems. The investigators concluded that the EMGs represented tension associated with difficulty in processing complex information. In a later study, Pishkin (1973) reported that schizophrenics produced higher EMGs than normals as complexity of problems to be solved increased. Both groups, however, showed higher EMG activity with increased complexity.

Hence, some of the obtained results indicate heightened EMG activity when subjects were "successful" in their tasks. However, other findings show increased EMG with increased task difficulty. In the latter instances, the increased EMG was related to less successful performance. The reason for this discrepancy is not clear. Perhaps some complex interaction exists between level of task difficulty and degree of involvement of the subjects tested in the various studies. It could also be related to extent of subjectively experienced success or failure. An examination of motivation (involvement) effects will be reviewed shortly.

EMG During Sleep

The question of EMG activity during sleep and dreaming was reviewed by Goldstein (1972). The consensus of several studies that she examined was that the onset of dreaming was marked by a reduction in neck and head EMG activity. This general conclusion was supported in an investigation conducted by Bliwise et al. (1974). These researchers measured chin and lip EMGs during sleep on three consecutive nights. They found that EMGs decreased toward their lowest levels starting 5 minutes before the onset of REM sleep. The lowest EMG levels of the night occurred throughout REM sleep. A sample of EEG, eye movements, and integrated EMG obtained by Bliwise and colleagues is presented in Figure 8-7. The chin EMG was superior to lip recordings in identifying REM sleep. However, the authors caution that the elaborate instrumentation required to obtain adequate EMG data may not be worth the effort when routine identification of sleep stages is the main objective.

EMG and Motivated Performance

Several studies have shown that EMG increased progressively from the beginning to the end of a task (e.g., Bartoshuk, 1955; Surwillo, 1956). These increases have been termed EMG gradients. There is evidence suggesting that the slope of these gradients is related to level of motivation. Bartoshuk (1955) reported that EMG gradients were related to quality of performance in mirror tracing. With subjects equated for practice, the gradient slope (especially for right forearm EMGs) was found to be directly related to speed and accuracy of performance. Surwillo (1956) tested the hypothesis that the slope of the EMG gradient could be increased by raising the level of incentives in a tracking task. In his first experiment, two incentive levels were produced. The higher incentive task resulted in steeper

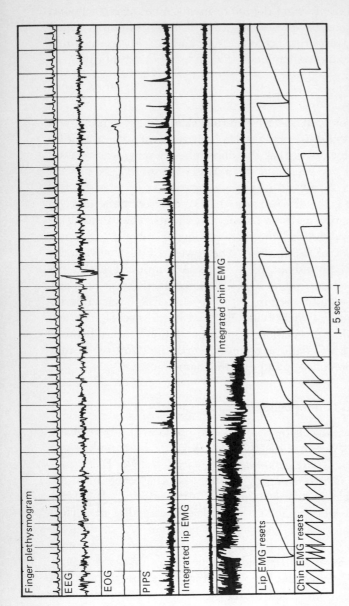

Figure 8-7. Polygraph tracing. This example shows a marked decline in integrated chin EMG 10 seconds prior to the transition to REM sleep (which starts at the end of the K-complex in the middle of the EEG tracing). The decline is paralleled by a slowing of chin EMG reset rate. Integrated lip EMG and reset rate are already low pre-REM and do not decline further during REM sleep. Four single phasic spikes can be seen in the integrated chin EMG and one in the integrated lip EMG during REM sleep. Such spikes may appear simultaneously with or independently of spikes from the periorbital electrodes (PIPs). Note the simultaneous appearance of PIPs and phasic inhibition in the integrated chin EMG about 7 seconds prior to the chin EMG drop.

EMG gradients as measured from the biceps, wrist, and frontalis muscles. In a second experiment, a new group of subjects was tested at three incentive levels. Again, incentive level was found to be a factor in raising the EMG gradient.

Bartoshuk (1956) reported a positive relation between frontalis EMG gradient slope and motivation to listen to a story. The EMG gradients of listeners who rated the stories high in interest value were steeper than those who gave the story low ratings. Pishkin and Wolfgang (1964) also found evidence that EMG gradients were related to motivated performance in a study in which monetary rewards were manipulated during a concept identification task. In a more recent investigation, Zucchi and Galeazzi (1971) found evidence for EMG gradients in a group of 26 children ranging in age from 7 to 14 years. The task used was a variation of mirror tracing.

The effects of an experimenter's presence on EMG gradients were tested by Chapman (1974). Three groups of subjects listened to a recorded story under three conditions: (1) unobserved, (2) experimenter present in the same room, and (3) experimenter in an adjoining room. The story was Maugham's, "The Dream," which took 11 minutes 15 seconds to present. Frontalis EMG showed a regular gradient from the beginning of the story to the end. The gradients were significantly higher under both conditions in which the experimenter was present, as compared to the completely unobserved condition. Chapman concluded that the mere presence of the experimenter was a source of arousal. The rise in frontalis gradient while listening was also found in the original study by Wallerstein (1954) and the follow-up by Bartoshuk (1956).

Malmo (1975), in his book *On Emotions, Needs, and Our Archaic Brain,* discusses EMG gradients and their significance at some length. He hypothesizes that the appearance of an EMG gradient indicates the occurrence of an organized behavior sequence. Further, the steepness of the gradient reflects degree of subjective involvement in the task.

To summarize briefly, it has been shown that EMG may vary with motivational level. EMG gradients have been reported for both mental (e.g., listening to a story) and physical activities (e.g., tracking). Thus, it would appear that level of involvement in a task can affect EMG activity and could be a confounding element in studies that do not take this factor into account.

In the next chapter, we discuss electrodermal activity (EDA) and behavior. This measure, like the EMG, is another peripheral physiological response that is sensitive to changes in behavioral states.

Electrodermal Activity and Behavior

It has been known for some time that changes in electrical activity of the skin can be produced by various physical and psychological stimuli. Changes in electrodermal activity (EDA) were first reported in 1888 by Féré, who passed a small current between two electrodes on the skin surface and observed changes in skin conductance when a subject was presented with a variety of physical stimuli (Woodworth & Schlosberg, 1954; Venables & Martin, 1967). A galvanometer was used to measure increases in skin conductance that occurred when visual, auditory, or olfactory stimuli were introduced. This phenomenon was soon labeled the psychogalvanic reflex (PGR) or the galvanic skin response (GSR) by early investigators.

In 1890, another researcher, Tarchanoff, found that he could obtain similar galvanometer deflections without the use of externally applied current; that is, there were natural differences in electrical potential between two skin areas, and this potential changed when the subject was stimulated. Féré and Tarchanoff contributed what were to become two basic methods for the measurement of EDA: the recording of skin conductance (SC) and skin potential (SP). Figure 9-1 shows a typical change in SC and SP levels with stimulation.[1] The physiological bases for these responses are still not fully understood, but changes in sweat gland activity have been strongly implicated in a variety of research studies (Edelberg, 1972). Since sweat glands are lo-

[1] The skin potential response is shown in millivolts (mV), while skin resistance is measured in kilohms (kΩ) or thousands of ohms.

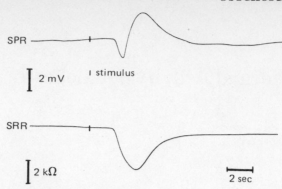

Figure 9-1. Characteristic skin resistance and skin potential responses.

cated in the skin, we will now briefly consider the anatomy and physiology of the skin in order to more fully understand the nature of the phenomena being examined in this chapter.

Anatomy and Physiology of the Skin

The skin consists of two layers: an epidermis, or outer layer, which is about 1 mm or less in thickness, and a dermis, or inner layer, which ranges from about 0.5 mm over the eyelids to 6 mm over the upper back, palms of the hands, and soles of the feet. The epidermis consists of five separate cellular layers: stratum corneum (outermost layer, also known as the keratinous or "horny" layer), stratum lucidum, stratum granulosum, stratum spinosum, and stratum germinativum (see Fig. 9-2). The dermis contains blood vessels, nerves, lymph vessels, hair follicles, smooth muscle, sweat glands, and sebaceous glands. Just below the dermis is the hypodermis (subcutaneous connective tissue), which contains blood and lymph vessels, the roots of hair follicles, sensory nerves, and the secretory portions of the sweat glands (Woodburne, 1973).

The eccrine sweat glands are the ones with which we are most concerned. They have a wide distribution over the body surface and are found everywhere in the skin except at the margins of the lips, the concha (outer ear), the glans penis, the prepuce,

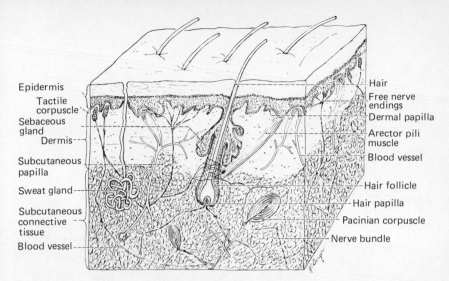

Figure 9-2. The structure of the skin.

and the clitoris. They are most numerous in the palms of the hands and the soles of the feet. One estimate is that a square inch on the palm contains 3000 sweat glands (Jacob & Francone, 1970). The eccrine glands are simple, tubular structures with a rounded secretory portion and a duct that leads to the surface of the skin. The secretory portion is formed by several unequal coils rolled into a ball of about 0.3 to 0.4 mm in diameter. The secretory duct from the eccrine gland opens as a small pore at the surface of the epidermis. An example of surface epidermal sweat pores is shown in Figure 9-3. This is a photograph of a fingertip, which was prepared in order to count the number of active sweat glands present, as indicated by chemical reactions at the pores.

The secretory portion of the eccrine sweat gland has a profuse nerve supply via cholinergic fibers of the SNS. That is, although innervated by SNS fibers, the transmitting agent is acetylcholine, a chemical usually associated with PNS functions. Discussions by Edelberg (1972) and Venables and Christie (1973) indicate that EDA is a complex reaction with a number of con-

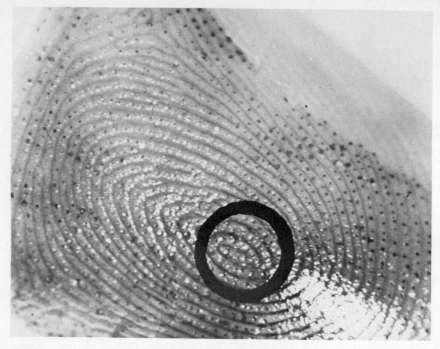

Figure 9-3. A photograph of a fingertip prepared for a sweat gland count. The circle indicates the usual area of the ridge pattern used for counting. Active sweat glands produce black dots because of the starch-iodine reaction at the tips of the ducts.

trol centers in the CNS. The EDA does, however, strongly reflect SNS activity, and behavioral researchers often interpret EDA as indicative of arousal level or emotional reactivity of an organism.

While an important function of the skin is to protect the organism it covers, for example, by keeping bacteria, parasites, and noxious chemicals out and keeping vital fluids in, it also has a role in thermoregulatory activities. The thermoregulatory contribution is produced by dilation of blood vessels in the skin and increased sweating, both of which result in decreased skin and body temperature. Conversely, constriction of blood vessels in the skin (which reduces blood flow to the surface) and pilo-erection ("goose bumps") help to maintain body heat. Piloerection produces its effect by increasing the area of the insulating air that surrounds the skin, thus preserving heat.

An interesting aspect of sweating is that it is not only thermo-regulatory. This fact forms the basis for the behavioral studies in this chapter. Sweating, or sweat gland activity, is reflected as changes in skin potential (SP) and skin conductance (SC) in a variety of situations, including ones that are emotionally arousing. For example, eccrine glands of the palms and fingers of the hand respond weakly at certain levels of heat and strongly to psychological and sensory stimuli. You may have noticed wet or "clammy" palms in situations that were fear- or anxiety-provoking but that were otherwise not very warm. The sweating to psychological stimuli has sometimes been termed "arousal" sweating, and some workers believe it has adaptive value (Darrow, 1933; Wilcott, 1967). Wilcott (1967) has suggested that arousal sweating in any part of the body may toughen the skin and protect it from mechanical injury. He notes an observation by Edelberg and Wright (1962), who found that palmar skin was difficult to cut during profuse sweating. When sweating is blocked the skin is more susceptible to mechanical injury (Wilcott, 1967). Thus, this interpretation of arousal sweating suggests that it has survival value for the organism, as do other SNS responses in emergency situations. In contrast to eccrine glands of the fingers and palms, those on the forehead, neck, back of the hands, and other areas respond quickly and strongly to thermal stimuli but weakly to psychological or sensory stimuli.

Types of Electrodermal Activity

As already noted, changes in EDA will occur with a wide variety of sensory and psychological stimuli. The momentary fluctuations of EDA that occur with stimulation have been termed phasic responses, while the relatively stable EDA is referred to as the tonic level. A classificatory scheme for the various terms relating to EDA was suggested by Venables and Martin (1967). They proposed the following designations and abbreviations:

SRR = skin resistance response
SRL = skin resistance level
SCR = skin conductance response
SCL = skin conductance level
SPR = skin potential response
SPL = skin potential level

The first four of these are related to the Féré effect, since they rely on an external source of current for their observation (exosomatic), while the last two (Tarchanoff effect) do not require the application of current and may be thought of as endosomatic. Skin conductance and skin potential will be considered separately, since, despite their apparent common origin, they are different phenomena.

Skin Conductance

The term *skin resistance response* (SRR) refers to momentary fluctuations in SR as did the older GSR terminology. *Skin resistance level* (SRL) indicates the baseline SR at any given time. *Skin conductance response* (SCR) and *skin conductance level* (SCL) are conductance unit measures of SRR and SRL, respectively. Units of conductance are preferred by many investigators instead of resistance values. One reason for this is that conductance values are more suitable for averaging and other statistical manipulations; that is, since conductance is the reciprocal of resistance, it is more likely to conform to the normal distribution of measures required for many statistical analyses. Another reason is that conductance increases with higher levels of arousal or activity of the organism and decreases at low levels, a relationship that is more logical for most persons.

The unit of conductance is the mho (ohm spelled backward) to distinguish it from the ohm, which is the unit of resistance. To give an example of a reciprocal transformation, a micromho (μmho) of conductance is equal to 1,000,000 Ω of resistance, and 10 μmhos equals 100,000 Ω. Log conductance measures go one step further and take the log of micromho values. The log conductance measures also conform to assumptions required for parametric statistical analyses of SC measures, such as analysis of variance or t tests. Venables and Christie (1973) have recently proposed, since the case for the use of conductance units is strong, that the terms SCR and SCL be used to refer to exosomatic measures of EDA, and this will be the usage in the remainder of the present chapter.

The amplitude of the SCR will depend on electrode size and might vary from .01 μmho to 5 μmho. Latencies of the SCR vary from 1.3 to 2.5 seconds after stimulus presentation.

Skin Potential

The *skin potential response* (SPR) refers to changes in SP, while *skin potential level* (SPL) is the level of SP at any point in time. The recordings depicted in Figure 9-1 show the SPR to be a biphasic (negative then positive) response measured in millivolts. However, SPR can also have a uniphasic negative wave or a uniphasic positive wave. The amplitude of the negative wave of the SPR may typically be about 2 mV, and the positive portion about 4 mV. Measures of SPR amplitudes may be difficult, since SPL is not always easy to establish. The latency of the negative SPR component is similar to that of the SCR (Venables & Christie, 1973).

Origin of EDA

In research relating performance and psychological factors to EDA, measures of SC or SP can be interpreted as mainly reflecting changes in sweating activity. For a subject during a single recording period, the amplitude of palmar SCRs and SPRs and the amplitude of sweating responses are usually found to be highly correlated (Wilcott, 1967).

The Measurement of Electrodermal Activity (EDA)

Skin Conductance Level (SCL)

Fortunately, there are good commercial instruments available today that contain the appropriate amplification, filtering, and ink-writing characteristics to enable the recording of SCL. This includes the availability of appropriate input couplers which convert activity recorded at the skin surface into conductance units (μmhos). The circuits used to measure SCL are of two basic types: those that employ a constant voltage and those using a constant current.[2] The constant-voltage system holds the voltage across the electrodes constant, and the current through the skin varies with conductance changes; this is what is measured on the ink writer. If, however, the current through the skin is held constant, then the voltage, or potential difference between the two electrodes placed on the skin surface, varies with resistance. This latter system is the constant-current technique. Edelberg (1972) recommends a current density of 8 μA/cm^2 (measured at either site) with the constant-current method. For the constant-voltage technique, he suggests a source of 0.75 to 1.0 V across the sites. Lykken and Venables (1971) recommend the use of a constant-voltage circuit limited to 0.50 V.

Skin Potential

While the bipolar placement of electrodes is preferred for SCL measures, a unipolar arrangement is essential to record SPL. The active electrode may be placed on the palm of the hand and referred to a relatively inactive site on the forearm. Edelberg (1972) mentions the inner portion of the earlobe as an inactive area. Alternatively, an experimenter may produce an inactive area by using a dental burr to remove a portion of the epidermis or by pricking the skin under the electrode with a needle (e.g., Shackel, 1959; Wilcott, 1959). Stimulation in the form of mental multiplication or having the individual participate in making word associations, will produce changes in SP. The SP may be measured with a sensitive dc amplifier.

A diagram illustrating the placement of electrodes to measure both SP and SC is presented in Figure 9-4. The figure shows a bipolar placement on the medial phalanges of two fingers for

[2] Most commercially available instruments for the measurement of SC use the constant current technique, and it has proven satisfactory for many researchers. For the student or researcher interested in more detail regarding the electronic circuitry involved in SC measurements, there are several excellent sources (see, e.g., Edelberg, 1967, 1972; Venables & Christie, 1973; Venables & Martin, 1967).

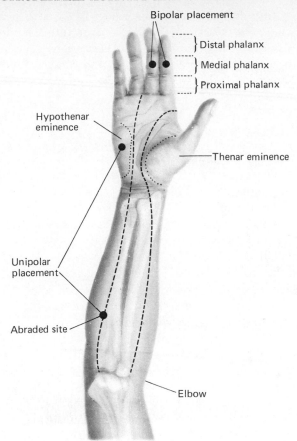

Figure 9-4. Recommended placements of electrodes for measuring SC and SP.

the SCL recording. Venables and Christie (1973) recommend that the electrodes be placed on two adjacent fingers: either the second and third, or the fourth and fifth fingers. For the SPL measure, the active electrode is placed on the palm of the hand, while the reference electrode is located on the forearm. The inactive electrode should be placed on an abraded site (accomplished by skin pricking, rubbing with sandpaper, or skin drilling). The fingers or soles of the feet may also be used as the site of the active electrode in SP recording. The researcher must be careful to avoid skin areas that have cuts or other kinds of blemishes, since this may interfere with the response obtained. Difficulty in preparing the reference site and the possibility of skin injury are factors that should be considered in the use of SP measures.

Electrodes for Recording EDA

Nonpolarizing electrodes should be used for both SC and SP measurements, and these are commercially available. An appropriate technique is to use a metal coated with the salt of that metal. For example, Ag/AgCl (silver/silver chloride) or Zn/ZnSO$_4$ (zinc/zinc sulphate) electrodes. Venables and Martin (1967) recommend the use of Ag/AgCl electrodes with solutions of either KCl or NaCl as the electrolyte. Wilcott[3] recommends the use of zinc electrodes, since they are easier to use than silver and are entirely adequate if kept clean and polished.

Electrode size is significant in the recording of SCL, since resistance of the electrodes varies inversely with area. Therefore, the larger the area, the smaller the resistance. This fact argues for the use of as large an electrode as possible. The electrolyte used should not be allowed to spread beyond the electrode site, since it increases the effective area of the electrode. Edelberg (1972) recommends the following electrolyte paste: 6 g of corn starch mixed into 100 ml of .05M NaCl and brought to a boil while stirring; after boiling for 30 seconds, the mixture is ready for use.

A typical electrode for use in palmar or plantar (sole of foot) placements may be 1.5 to 2.0 cm in diameter, while those used on the fingers may be 1.0 cm or less in diameter. Electrodes may be held in place by strips of surgical tape, plastic adhesive, or elastic bands.

Ground Electrodes

A ground lead may not be necessary in SC or SP measurement if there is no interference present, for example, 60 Hz from room

[3] Personal communication, R. C. Wilcott, September 1, 1977.

outlets. If artifact does occur, a ground electrode should be placed on an inactive site, on the same side of the body as active electrodes.

Analysis of EDA Data

If one records directly in conductance units, three kinds of measures are possible: (1) the level of conductance (SCL) during a given period of time, (2) the number of conductance changes (SCR) during the same period, and (3) the magnitude of the SCR. The first and third measures will be micromhos, while the second will be based on the number of times a change of a given magnitude takes place. For example, if SCL is at 10 μmhos, a response may be defined as any change of 1.0 μmho or greater that occurs within a specified time, say, 1.5 to 2.5 seconds. The magnitude of the SCR can be treated as a percentage of SCL and thus be related to prestimulus baseline level.

When baseline changes occur, the pen may have to be reset by hand and the new SCL level recorded. If many SCRs occur, this constant resetting could be cumbersome. One way to solve this problem is to use automatic resetting or, alternatively, to feed the EDA data into two channels of the polygraph: one channel for baseline SCL and another for SCR. With this latter procedure, the gain for SCL is adjusted so that it is relatively insensitive to small changes, while the SCR gain is set to make it sensitive to the SCRs regarded as significantly large. Some commercial devices provide automatic recentering when SCRs occur or when SCL extends beyond certain predetermined ranges.

In the treatment of SP data, counts of the number of SPRs occurring in a given time period may be made. In addition, level of SP (mV) can be recorded directly on the ink-writer paper. The SPR measure is complicated by the fact that it has negative and positive components. Investigators commonly measure the degree of negativity and positivity of the waves (in mV) and the latencies of their occurrence. Edelberg (1972) suggests that the magnitude of the positive response should be measured from the peak of the negative component to the peak of the positive wave (in mV) without regard to whether the baseline is crossed or not. Paper speeds of 15 mm/sec are suitable for observing baseline changes in SCL or SPL and the more rapid SCRs and SPRs.

Electrodermal Phenomena and Behavior

This section briefly reviews a number of areas in which EDA has been related to behavior and performance. Investigations in this area may be categorized in the following manner: motor performance, mental activity, positive and negative affect (emotional responses), motivation, signal detection, the orienting reaction, and conditioning of EDA. It will become obvious to the reader that SC is used much more frequently than SP by investigators seeking to relate EDA to behavior. Basically, this is probably because SC is easier to measure and offers fewer problems of interpretation than SP.

Electrodermal Activity and Motor Performance

Freeman and Simpson (1938) found that when subjects exerted pressure against spring scales with their feet, SCL increased. The degree of SCL increase was proportional to amount of pressure exerted. Pugh et al. (1966) suspected that this finding, as well as others like it, may have been due to effects of preparatory set rather than muscular effort per se. In addition, the effects of tactual stimulation had not been separated from effort. Pugh et al. found that a signal preparing subjects to lift different weights resulted in larger SCRs than the lift itself. Also, SCRs varied according to the mass of the object placed in the hand prior to lifting when no muscular effort was involved. Thus, Pugh and colleagues concluded that SCRs were not due to muscular effort per se but resulted from the preparation to work and amount of tactile stimulation.

Reaction Time

One of the early studies of the relation between SCL and speed of reaction was conducted by Freeman (1940). He studied the RT of a single subject under various states of alertness, with the subject's condition ranging from half asleep to extremely tense. The results of 100 experimental sessions were recorded over a number of days, and Freeman found an inverted-U-shaped relation between SCL and RT, in which RTs were slower at high and low SCL levels and fastest at moderate levels. Schlosberg (1954) reported that Freeman's results had been duplicated with another subject, but a later study, using a greater number of subjects (Schlosberg & Kling, 1959) failed to replicate these findings. In a study by Andreassi (1966b), SCL was measured continuously as 16 persons reacted to a fixed number of "random" signals occurring over a 40-minute experimental period. Andreassi found evidence for the conclusion that at the highest SCL, RT is significantly faster than at moderate or low SCLs. Decreases in SCL over the course of the experimental session correlated significantly with a slowing of RT. The plotted results did not approach an inverted-U function, and it was suggested that this may have been due to a limited range of arousal in a situation where level of activity was not purposely manipulated.

Surwillo and Quilter (1965) measured RTs and SPRs of 132 healthy males, aged 22 to 85 years, in an hour-long vigilance situation. The subjects were required to monitor the movements of a clock pointer and to press a key as quickly as possible when it traveled through twice the usual distance. The median number of SPRs that occurred in the 18-second period before critical signals was calculated, and subjects were divided into two groups, those above and those below the median. Those above the median in SPR production were termed "labiles" (mean of 2.27 SPRs), and those below were called "stabiles" (mean of .73 SPRs) in accordance with the terminology of Lacey and Lacey (1958). The RT for "labiles" (488 msec) was significantly faster than that of "stabiles" (540 msec). This confirmed a hypothesis of Lacey and Lacey (1958), who proposed that autonomic labiles (those with a large number of spontaneous autonomic responses) would have faster RTs than stabiles.

Andreassi et al. (1969) measured SCL and SCR while subjects detected critical signals which occurred at either fixed or variable intervals. Individuals were required to make responses, which required some effort, in order to have the opportunity to detect the signals. The results showed that SCL and SCRs were significantly higher when signals came at fixed intervals (30 seconds) than when they were variable (between 11 and 66 seconds). Further, reaction times were significantly faster with regularly appearing signals. Andreassi and colleagues suggested that the term "improved expectancies" seemed to describe the superior RT performance with regular signal patterning. The elevated EDA observed with fixed intervals was attributed to an increased readiness to respond when subjects could anticipate the occurrence of a signal.

Cowles (1973) found that faster RTs were related to higher SCL. Another measure used was the latency of the SCR. Cowles found that longer SCR latencies were associated with poorer performance in the simple RT task used. He suggested that SCR latency, as well as SCL, may be a measure of long-term or tonic arousal level. This would be in contrast to the number and magnitude of SCRs, which are considered to be measures of short-term or phasic arousal. Baugher (1975) measured the number of spontaneous SCRs that occurred during a 40-minute vigilance task. The 36 male subjects were divided into low-arousal and high-arousal groups on the basis of the SCL value at the time of occurrence. The RTs to critical signals were found to be significantly faster for the high-arousal as compared to the low-arousal group. The author concluded that the direct relationship between SCRs and RT was expected (i.e., instead of an inverted-U function) because of the limited range of arousal conditions used. This was similar to the conclusion reached by Andreassi (1966b).

To summarize, it seems that faster RTs are associated with higher SCL. In addition, the number of spontaneous SPRs and SCRs is also related to speed of reaction, that is, a greater number of these responses being associated with faster RTs. Whether there is an inverted-U-shaped relation between SCL and RT performance has not been established. Perhaps the subject's level of arousal (as indicated by EDA) must be actively manipulated by the experimenter to show this relationship.

Mental Activity and Electrodermal Phenomena

Changes in electrodermal responses have been observed to occur while persons were involved in a variety of mental activities, including adding numbers, learning, and producing word associations. This section examines electrodermal activity during verbal learning, conditions of positive and negative affect (feeling), motivation, and relaxation.

Verbal Learning and EDA

Brown (1937) found that words which were learned faster were accompanied by larger magnitude SCRs than those not learned as quickly. Berry (1962) measured SCL during the learning of paired-associates and when subjects were asked to recall the learned materials. He found that moderate SCL in the first minute of the learning session was related to better recall. In addition, moderate SCL in the first minute of the recall period was also associated with best performance. He suggests that these data support an inverted-U function relating arousal and performance. Andreassi (1966a) required Navy enlisted men to learn three lists of nonsense syllables, on three successive days while SCL and heart rate were recorded. The lists had 100%, 53%, and 0% association values, corresponding to easy, moderately difficult, and difficult learning materials, respectively. He found that SCL and HR were significantly higher during the learning of the easy list as compared to the other two. The findings were interpreted in terms of greater subject involvement in the learning task when their performance was more successful. This conclusion was given some support from the performance of the only subject whose physiological responses did not vary with list difficulty. This subject did not show differential performance with any of the lists, that is, responses were uniformly poor, and he was the only subject to fall asleep during some of the 2-minute rest periods between lists!

Lists of eight high-arousal words (e.g., vomit) and eight low-arousal words (e.g., swim) were presented to 40 male and 40 female students (Maltzman et al., 1966). They were asked to listen to these words while EDA was recorded. They were told that the physiological correlates of relaxation were being measured. The investigators reported that the high-arousal words produced significantly larger SCRs than the low-arousal words. Further, retention tests administered after all the items had been presented revealed that the subjects could remember more of the high-arousal than low-arousal words. Maltzman and his associates hypothesized that the SCRs were evidence that orienting responses (OR) occurred and that the OR facilitated the reception of words and their retention.

Andreassi and Whalen (1967) measured SCL, SCRs, and heart rate (HR) during verbal learning. In a first experiment, after lists of materials were learned to perfection, the same material was presented for 20 overlearning trials. The `overlearning phase was accompanied by significant decreases in all of the physiological measures. However, when a new list was presented subsequent to overlearning, there were increases in SCL, SCRs, and HR. In a second experiment the initial learning phase was followed by two overlearning sessions with the same list. This time all three measures showed progressive decreases during the first and then the second overlearning phase. The results indicated that new learning, perhaps because of the novelty of the situation and the materials to be learned, produced the highest levels of physiological activity. Overlearning, because of stimulus and situational habituation, led to significant decreases in activity.

To briefly summarize, studies of EDA and verbal learning indicate that more successful learning, in general, tends to be associated with greater amounts of activity. The higher levels of EDA may be associated with increased levels of alertness when subjects are involved in the acquisition of novel stimulus materials. Electrodermal activity has been identified as an important component of the orienting response to novel stimuli, an area that will be covered later in this chapter.

Positive and Negative Affect and EDA

Affect refers to subjective feelings roughly related to like or dislike of objects, people or events, that is, feelings that produce an emotional reaction. Music is one example, and the effects of three types of music on the SCR and HR of 18 college students were investigated by Zimny and Weidenfeller (1963). The three musical pieces had been previously judged to be exciting, neutral, and calming by 59 other students. Selected 6-minute portions of Dvorak's *New World Symphony*, Chopin's *Les Sylphides*, and Bach's *Air for the G String* were judged as exciting, neutral, and calming, respectively. Significant SCRs occurred in response to the exciting music but not to the calming or the neutral pieces. No HR changes were observed as a function of music played. The authors interpreted the SCR results as indicating that different kinds of music produce differential EDA and that this reflects emotional responsivity.

The interpretation that a subject is encouraged to use with respect to observed violence appeared to influence SCRs in a study by Geen and Rakosky (1973). The subjects were 55 male undergraduates whose SCRs were measured while they viewed a prize fight sequence from the film *Champion*. The showing of the film was preceded by narratives that described events leading to the 6-minute fight scene. The narratives depicted the sequence as either aggression, vengeance, or fictional vengeance. In the introductory remarks relating to fictional vengeance, subjects were reminded that the fight was not real and that the injuries were only makeup. The greatest number of SCRs were observed following the aggression narratives, while significantly fewer SCRs occurred after the remarks emphasizing the fictional (make-believe) aspects of the fight scene. The interpretations offered by Geen and Rakosky suggest that by emphasizing the fictional aspect of the fight scene, the subjects were able to dissociate the observed violence from their own lives.

A sample of 22 female and 3 male college students rated the five most upsetting words in the following categories: sex, bathroom, social and political issues, diseases and violence (Manning & Melchiori, 1974). These investigators then measured the SCRs of a different sample, consisting of 27 females and 3 males, to these upsetting words. In addition, responses to 25 matched neutral words were obtained. Significantly larger SCRs were evoked in response to upsetting words as compared to neutral words. Within the five categories, larger SCRs occurred to the sex and bathroom items as compared to the other three categories.

The effects of erotic and neutral stimuli upon SCR, HR, and subjective ratings of 52 females were studied by Hamrick (1974). The erotic stimuli (slides of nude males) resulted in significant increases in SCR and decreases in HR. The changes in SCR and HR to the nude males were accompanied by subjective ratings that indicated sexual arousal and positive affective reactions. The decreased HR is consistent with the work of Lacey et al. (1963) in which HR deceleration was found to accompany situations in which subjects paid attention to perceptual materials.

Lanzetta et al. (1976) tested Charles Darwin's assertion that freely expressing an emotion will intensify the emotional experience, while suppressing it will lead to a reduction of experienced intensity. In a series of experiments, subjects were asked to either conceal or exaggerate facial expressions associated with the anticipated reception of electric shocks. It was found that suppression of expressive responses led to smaller SCRs and lower pain ratings than when exaggeration of the emotional response was required. They interpreted these results as supporting hypotheses regarding the role of nonverbal displays of emotion in regulating the emotional experience itself, as well as serving a social-communicative function. Darwin's hypothesis was also supported, suggesting that a "cool" response to an emotional situation could aid in preventing reactions from spiraling out of control.

In summary, it appears that EDA can serve as a rough index of affective value of stimuli for a subject. This would seem to be true both for nonverbal stimuli (music, film sequence) and for emotionally tinged words and opinions. The recent findings of Lanzetta et al. (1976) may have important implications for the study and control of various types of emotional behavior and should be pursued further.

Motivation and EDA

A new measure of SCL, called electrodermal recovery rate was introduced by Edelberg (1970). It is used with exosomatic measures of EDA and is based on the time it takes for SCL to return to a level midway between the peak of the response and its initial level. Edelberg (1970, 1972b) has related this recovery rate, also called recovery half-time, to the degree to which a subject is goal-oriented. That is, the half-time recovery is faster under conditions of goal-oriented activity than under other conditions of arousal. For example, recovery times are faster when a subject is involved in a mirror-tracing task as compared to resting with eyes open. Edelberg (1972b) concluded that the measure is stable over time and that it is related to relative quality of performance of an individual. He also suggests that slow recovery in aversive conditions may indicate a defensive reaction. Waid (1974) obtained results that supported those of Edelberg in that electrodermal recovery rate was faster during goal-oriented activity than during less directed behavior. The finding that recovery rate was slower during a timed arithmetic task, as compared to a verbal RT task was interpreted as being similar to previous findings in which recovery time was slower when electric shock was threatened. Waid altered the original Edelberg procedure somewhat by requiring that the response recover 33% instead of 50%. This change increased the number of measurable responses. These studies of electrodermal recovery rate and goal orientation provide another way of analyzing EDA and correlating it with performance, as well as providing information about EDA correlates of motivation. The finding that this measure of EDA is related to degree of task involvement corresponds to earlier findings of Andreassi (1966a) who suggested a similar relationship for SCL and performance.

Signal Detection and EDA

In a previous section, we discussed EDA associated with RT to detected signals. In this section, we examine some studies that have related EDA to efficiency or accuracy of signal detection in vigilance-type situations. Ross et al. (1959) investigated SCL and its relation to signal detection over a 2-hour period. They found, for nine subjects, that higher SCL was associated with better vigilance performance. In the Surwillo and Quilter (1965) study previously mentioned, the number of SPRs that occurred within the 18-second period before the critical signal was significantly greater for detected signals than for missed signals. Various measures were studied (i.e., SCL, HR, and neck EMG) during a vigilance task that required subjects to attend to a flashing light and to report when it stayed on longer than usual

(Eason et al., 1965). The most consistent finding was that during the course of a vigil, performance and SCL decreased significantly. Eason and colleagues interpreted the decreased SCL as representing a drop in SNS activity, which in turn was due to the drowsiness producing effects of the experimental situation.

Krupski et al. (1971) measured SCL while 31 persons performed a vigilance task. The investigators were interested in the number of commission errors, that is, responding in the absence of a signal, and its relation to EDA. They found that subjects who had large-amplitude SCRs when they detected a signal made fewer commission errors than those who had small detection-related SCRs. The larger SCRs were interpreted in terms of greater attention level, which resulted in superior vigilance performance. In addition, subjects who had large orienting responses (defined as the SCR amplitude to the first signal) also made fewer commission errors, a finding that would support the conclusion regarding attention level and vigilance performance.

The results of studies briefly reviewed in this segment indicate that higher levels of skin conductance and greater numbers of SPRs are associated with superior signal detection. Krupski et al. (1971) interpreted this type of finding in terms of higher levels of attention (reflected in EDA) which led to more efficient detection.

The Orienting Response and EDA

In his book *Attention, Arousal and the Orientation Reaction,* Lynn (1966) details a variety of physiological changes that occur when an organism is presented with a novel stimulus. Among these are pupil dilation, increased EMG activity, increased frequency and lower amplitude EEG, increase in amplitude and decrease in frequency of respiration, a slowing of heart rate, and changes in EDA. Berlyne (1960) categorized characteristics of stimuli that have the potential to elicit the OR as follows: novelty, intensity, color, meaning, surprise, complexity and incongruity, and conflict. Many recent studies have investigated EDA correlates of the OR. Only a few of these will be presented here to give an idea of the type of research being done and some representative findings.

Bernstein (1969) habituated subjects to a given stimulus intensity and found that the OR (indicated by SCR frequency) was greater when the stimulus was changed to a greater intensity than when the change involved lowering the intensity. He concluded that the direction of stimulus change was an important variable in eliciting the OR, that is, after the original OR had been habituated. Bernstein hypothesized that increased stimulus intensity might signify "something approaching the organism" (p. 128) and that this could lead to a more intense OR. This hypothesis was tested by Bernstein et al. (1971), who measured SCRs in a situation where patterned stimuli were stationary or appeared to move either toward or away from the individuals tested. Frequency and amplitude of SCRs were greater under the apparent motion than with the stationary perceptual condition. Further, the physiological changes were more prolonged when objects appeared to approach the subjects than when they appeared to recede. These results indicated to the authors that the onset of movement in the visual field is associated with a momentary increase in perceptual receptivity. In addition, stimuli that move toward the person are more significant than those that move away, as indicated by the respective ORs.

The hypothesis that an OR to stimulus change can attenuate a subsequent OR to a second stimulus change was examined by Maltzman et al. (1971). This hypothesis was confirmed with a group of 96 subjects who experienced the two stimulus changes at 5-, 10-, or 30-second intervals. In addition, Maltzman and colleagues noted that the magnitude of the SCR was greater when the stimulus change was an increase in illumination as opposed to a decrease, a similar finding to that of Bernstein (1968). Yaremko et al. (1970) examined the OR (magnitude of SCR) as a function of degree of deviation from an expected stimulus. The numbers 10 through 19 were presented serially to subjects. On the next trial (when 20 should have been presented) the numbers 31, 21, 19, or 9 were delivered. Thus the critical number was either 1 or 11 places out of sequence in either the positive or negative direction. The SCR magnitude was related to degree of discrepancy between the expected and the observed number, that is, the 11-unit discrepancies produced larger SCRs than the smaller ones, regardless of direction. The results were interpreted as supporting Sokolov's (1963) hypothesis that OR magnitude depends on the amount of stimulus change.

The effects of repeatedly imagining a stimulus, upon habituation of the OR was studied by Yaremko et al. (1972). Subjects who imagined hearing a tone showed greater habituation of the SCR component of the OR to a 500-Hz tone when compared to subjects who imagined seeing a light or those in a control group. The habituation rate did not differ from that of subjects who had previously received 10 trials with a 500-Hz tone. It was suggested that the imagery process aided in the formation of a "neuronal model" (Sokolov, 1963[4]) and facilitated habituation. Namely, the repeated imagery of a tone primed the formation of a neuronal model of the stimulus, and the partially formed model functioned to inhibit responding to the actual tones. Yaremko and Butler (1975) found that imaginary electric shocks prior to receiving actual shocks attenuated SCR to later-presented real shocks.

Siddle and Heron (1976) used SCR magnitude, HR, and finger pulse volume (FPV) to test OR to a change in tonal frequency. Following habituation to a 1000-Hz tone at 70 db intensity, new tones of either 670 Hz or 380 Hz (both 70 db) were presented to subjects. Significant changes in all measures occurred to changes in auditory stimulus frequency. The results were contrary to O'Gorman's (1973) contention that the OR is only sensitive to changes in stimulus intensity or modality. In addition, SCR magnitude was significantly larger to the greater degree of stimulus change (i.e., with 380 Hz as compared to 670 Hz). The HR and FPV measures did not vary as a function of degree of difference between training (habituated) and test (new) stimuli. Thus, EDA was the most sensitive OR component to a change in tonal frequency.

In a recent study, Waters et al. (1977) tested the hypothesis that selective attention consists of at least two processes: (1) responsivity of phasic and tonic ORs to relevant stimuli, and (2)

[4] Briefly, Sokolov's concept assumes that incoming stimuli are compared with representations of past stimuli which reside in the cortex of the brain. If a stimulus is novel, i.e., if it does not match any of the existing "neuronal models," an orienting response occurs. If the incoming stimulus is familiar, it matches a model in the cortex, and the orienting reaction does not occur.

habituation of these same ORs to irrelevant stimuli. Tonic OR would be reflected by elevated SCL, for example, and phasic OR, by magnitude of SCR. The experimenters devised an attention-demanding task and made provisions for the introduction of distracting stimuli that would disrupt task performance. Some subjects, however, had exposure to the distracting stimuli prior to the demanding task. The prior exposure continued until the phasic OR to the distracting stimuli was habituated. Two other groups of subjects either had no prior exposure to any stimulus or were exposed to a completely different stimulus (500-Hz tone). A final group received both types of preexposure but no distraction during problem solution. In the experimental task, subjects were required to solve mathematical problems from memory. The problems were presented by a male voice, and irrelevant stimuli were presented by a female voice. Those subjects who received prior exposure performed better and produced significantly fewer SCRs than subjects in the other two groups. The authors concluded that their hypotheses were confirmed. That is, prior exposure to distractors enhanced problem solution by permitting learned inhibition of phasic ORs to those stimuli and thus eliminated their competition with task-relevant stimuli.

In summary, EDA seems to have provided a useful physiological indicator in experimentation on the nature of the OR. Frequency and amplitude of SCRs are affected by changes in stimulus direction. Magnitude of conceptual deviation and imagery have been related to magnitude of SCRs and tendency of the OR to habituate, respectively. The EDA measure of OR also indicates that it can vary with changes in stimulus quality as well as intensity. Finally, the EDA measure of OR may be useful in studying aspects of selective attention.

Conditioning and Electrodermal Activity

In the well-known Pavlovian classical conditioning paradigm, a conditioned stimulus (CS) for example, a bell, eventually leads to a conditioned response (CR), for example, salivation, after it has been paired with an unconditioned stimulus (UCS), such as food, a sufficient number of times. The classical conditioning of EDA and of other autonomic responses (e.g., HR) has been an extensively studied phenomenon with both animal and human subjects. Edelberg (1972a) points out that because of the well-defined nature of SCRs and SPRs, they serve well as the CR, since it is often possible to distinguish them from the orienting response to the CS. A wide variety of unconditioned stimuli have been used in the classical conditioning of EDA in humans. Some examples are white noise, electric shock, a puff of air, and sexually arousing stimuli (Prokasy & Kumpfer, 1973). A good UCS must produce effective ANS activation, and it should habituate slowly.

In the instrumental conditioning paradigm, the subject must emit some kind of response to obtain a reinforcement. The response is not defined for the subject, and in the case of EDA the required response might be an increase in the rate of SCRs. At one time, it was believed that ANS responses could not be instrumentally conditioned. However, there is now considerable evidence that some degree of instrumental conditioning can be demonstrated with EDA (Kimmel, 1973). Some reinforcers that have been used in the instrumental conditioning of EDA include pleasant odors, lights presented to subjects in a dark room, lights or sounds that indicated monetary rewards, pictures of nude women presented to male subjects, and cool air for persons in a hot and humid chamber (Kimmel & Gurucharri, 1975).

Classical Conditioning of EDA

A discussion of a variety of independent variables that have been manipulated in studies of electrodermal conditioning has been presented by Prokasy and Kumpfer (1973). Some of these variables include the effects of interstimulus interval upon the magnitude of the conditioned EDA, percentage of reinforced trials, and the modality of the CS (e.g., light or sound). Successful EDA conditioning has been observed to occur in a variety of experimental conditions. Complex variables in the classical conditioning situation were examined in a review by Grings and Dawson (1973). These included the effects of instructional variables, for example, regarding the CS-UCS relation, and individual differences, for example, the effects of age, sex and intelligence, on the classical conditioning of EDA. Since the classical conditioning of EDA has been presented in detail elsewhere (Prokasy & Kumpfer, 1973; Grings & Dawson, 1973), a sample of only one recent experiment will be presented here.

Prokasy et al. (1975) tested the hypothesis derived from Pavlov's (1927) work that if a CS is greater than or equal to the intensity of a UCS, then conditioning to that CS should not occur. The amplitude and probability of SCRs were used as the criteria of conditioning. The results indicated that conditioning was obtained even when the CS was greater in intensity than the UCS, thus refuting Pavlov's proposition. No difference in the amount of conditioning was associated with either CS or UCS intensity.

Instrumental Conditioning of EDA

Much of the experimental work on the instrumental conditioning of EDA has been reviewed by Kimmel (1973). Basically, the review indicates that EDA, for example, the frequency or magnitude of SCRs, will be increased or decreased when the delivery of some reinforcement is contingent upon this response. The reinforcement may involve either the presentation of some pleasant stimulus (e.g., monetary reward) or the avoidance of some unpleasant stimulus (e.g., electric shock). The review by Kimmel will serve the student who desires more detail about this topic.

A recent study that explored the instrumental conditioning of EDA was done by Kimmel and Gurucharri (1975). Two groups of 20 subjects each were placed in a hot (115°F), humid (100% humidity) chamber while SCRs were measured. The first group of 20 experimental subjects received cool air whenever a SCR was emitted. As the experimental session progressed, the number of SCRs increased, indicating that the cool air was an effective reinforcer for producing the SCR. Twenty control subjects who were individually matched with each experimental subject on the basis of preexperimental level of spontaneously produced SCRs were then tested under the same conditions. Each control subject then received cool air at the same time, based on the record of when his matched experimental subject received the

SCR contingent reinforcement. Thus, both groups received the same number of cool air presentations, but the control group's rewards were not contingent on producing a SCR. Nevertheless, the control group showed an increase in unelicited SCRs, although not at the same accelerating rate as the experimental subjects. Detailed examination of the SCR records of the controls indicated that they coincidentally received cool air with 38% of their SCRs, and this accounted for their increased rate of SCR production. The researchers further noted that the SCR responses of the experimental subjects resembled results from traditional instrumental conditioning studies more closely than any previously conducted SCR investigation.

In summary, the classical conditioning of EDA has been achieved under a variety of experimental conditions. Similarly, there is recent evidence that instrumental conditioning of EDA is possible with a variety of reinforcers. However, the effects of subjective thoughts, or cognitive mediation, have not been clearly delineated in instrumental EDA conditioning paradigms. Some investigators (e.g., Shean, 1970; Stern, 1970; Stern & Kaplan, 1967) suggest that cognitive mediation plays a role in EDA conditioning. For example, a subject might find that a certain type of thought (e.g., a favorite activity) is related to receiving cool air, whereas, in actuality, it was the SCR produced by the arousing thought that resulted in delivery of the reinforcement. Therefore, it may be that the number of SCR-producing thoughts are increased rather than a subject's ability to influence sweat gland activity. This possibility must be investigated.

The next chapter considers two different peripheral responses, both involving the eyes. The student may be surprised to learn that a wide variety of behavioral states and activities have been associated with changes in pupil diameter and eye movements.

Pupillary Response, Eye Movements, and Behavior

This chapter considers two kinds of responses involving the eye and how these relate to human activities. Pupillography refers to the measurement of variations in the diameter of the pupillary aperture of the eye under various conditions. Electrooculography (EOG) is concerned with measuring changes in electrical potential that occur when the eyes move. A discussion of the pupillary response and its relation to behavior will be presented first, followed by a presentation of eye movements and their relation to psychological activities.

Anatomy and Physiology of the Pupillary Response

The pupil is the opening at the center of the iris of the eye through which light passes. A major function of the iris is to increase pupillary diameter in dim light and to decrease it in bright light. This adjusts the amount of light allowed to enter the eye according to the environment of an individual. The pupil of the human eye can constrict to 1.5 mm in diameter and dilate to about 8-9 mm or more in diameter and can react to stimuli in .2 seconds (Guyton, 1977; Lowenstein & Loewenfeld, 1962). The constriction and dilation of the pupillary aperture is produced mainly through control of the ANS exerted upon the muscles of the iris. More specifically, neurons of the PNS innervate circular fibers of the iris, causing pupillary constriction, while excitation by SNS fibers causes the radial fibers of

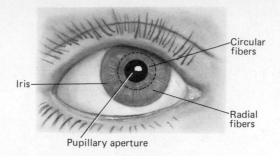

Figure 10-1. Diagram of the eye. The diameter of the pupillary apperture is the measure used in pupillography. Pupillary constriction occurs with contraction of circular fibers, while dilation results from contraction of radial fibers.

the iris to produce dilation of the pupil. Both the circular and radial fibers are smooth muscle (see Fig. 10-1). The circular muscle fibers are also termed the sphincter pupillae, and the radial fibers are the dilator pupillae.

The ANS is intimately involved in emotional behavior. A strong emotional stimulus (e.g., an unexpected pistol firing) will cause the pupil to dilate. Thus, a dilated pupil will appear as part of a fear reaction, with a response occurring in as little as .2 second and peaking in .5 to 1.0 second. The dilation will persist even though a bright light is presented to the eye, indicating that the emotional response can override the pupillary constriction response to intense light stimuli. Animal studies have shown that pupillary dilation occurs with stimulation of the hypothalamus, thalamus, and reticular formation. These are brain areas that have been implicated in emotional behavior and behavioral arousal.

The Measurement of Pupillary Size

Although many observations about changes in pupil size under different emotional or performance conditions have been reported over the years, it is only within the last 20 years that the development of practical and reliable instrumentation has enabled the precise measurement of pupillary aperture under different experimental conditions and psychological states. One problem in the measurement of pupil size is the constant fluctuation in pupil diameter that occurs during waking hours. These spontaneous changes occur simultaneously in the two eyes and are about 1 mm in amplitude. They are thought to be under control of brain centers that continuously regulate pupil size according to intensity of light stimulation. Measurements obtained under normal lighting conditions must take these fluctuations into account.

Early devices in the measurement of pupil size included the use of infrared photography, which made it possible to get pictures of pupil diameter in dim light. Photoelectric methods, which measured reflected light from the iris, were also used. Both were cumbersome and not too accurate. Hakerem (1967) considered the best available device at that time to be the "Lowenstein pupillograph," which used an infrared scanning of the iris to determine the amount of reflected light. This device can measure the diameters of both pupils and provide information about the rate of change in pupil size. Hess (1972) described his own device in some detail along with procedures for its use. Essentially, his device consists of a movie camera, a projector (movie or slide), a screen, and reflecting mirrors. The use of infrared film enables recordings of pupil diameter regardless of the subject's eye color. For any given visual stimulus the averaged pupil diameter for 20 individual frames is used as the measure of pupil size for that stimulus. Hess emphasizes the importance of holding constant the factors of stimulus brightness and brightness contrast. Brightness contrast refers to the relative brightness of a stimulus and its background.

A recently developed and widely used pupil-measuring technique is the Whittaker Corporation TV Pupillometer. This electronic device uses a closed-circuit TV system to observe the eye and a signal processor to measure and display pupil diameter. A low-intensity infrared light source illuminates the eye, and a low light level silicon matrix tube camera is used to record pupil size. Pupil diameter is presented as either a direct numerical readout or appears on a chart recorder showing continuous changes in size. The system also has automatic circuitry to maintain proper measurement over a wide range of recording conditions. Pupil diameter may be measured over a 0- to 10-mm range, with provisions for expanding subintervals of this range.

Fatigue and Pupil Size

Lowenstein and Loewenfeld (1964) have noted that pupil diameter is maximal in a well-rested individual, decreases with fatigue, and reaches a minimal diameter just before sleep. Kahneman and Peavler (1969) observed a continuous decrease in pupil size between the beginning and end of an experimental session. Hess (1972) cautions experimenters to avoid presentation of an excessive number of stimuli in studies of pupil size, since fatigue causes the pupil to decrease in diameter.

Geacintov and Peavler (1974) measured pupil sizes of 11 telephone operators to determine whether pupil constriction would reflect fatigue in a work environment. Each subject was measured before and after a full day's work of providing directory assistance with either the usual telephone book or an automated microfilm reader. The average pupil size for all subjects at the beginning of the day was 4.6 mm at the book position and 4.5 mm at the microfilm location. Pupil diameter decreased on the average, between morning and evening measures. However, the data analyses indicated that a significant decrease (.43 mm) occurred only for the microfilm condition. Thus, a size difference between prework and postwork measurements was found with the microfilm reader but not with the book. Subjects reported more fatigue symptoms, such as backaches, headaches, and eyestrain when using the microfilm device than when they used the telephone book. However, performance was superior with the microfilm reader because of the greater access speed of this automated device.

A recent article by Tryon (1975) lists a number of factors that may have an effect on pupil size. Some of these variables which are not otherwise mentioned in this chapter are listed in Table 10-1.

Table 10-1   Factors That May Influence Changes in Pupil Size

Factor	Effect on Pupil Size
Darkness reflex	Momentary dilation due to interruption of a constant adapting light
Consensual reflex	Stimulation of one eye affects both eyes equally
Near reflex	Constriction due to decreasing the point of focus, i.e., the pupil constricts with convergence of the eyes on a near object
Lid-closure reflex	Momentary contraction followed by redilation
Psychosensory reflex	Restoration of diminished reflexes due to external stimulation
Age	Decreased diameter and increased variability with age
Habituation	Pupil diameter decreases, speed of contraction increases, and magnitude of reflex decreases with continued stimulus presentations
Binocular summation	Constriction greater when both eyes are stimulated simultaneously

Source: Adapted from W. W. Tryon, Pupillometry: A survey of sources of variation. *Psychophysiology*, 1975, *12*, 90-93.

Pupillography and Behavior

This section considers pupil size as it has been related to various kinds of mental activity, attitudes and affective states, information processing, and perception. Comprehensive reviews of this area have been presented by Hess (1972) and by Goldwater (1972).

Pupil Size and Mental Activity

Hess and Polt (1964) measured pupil size before and during mental multiplication. Comparisons showed that pupil size was greater in diameter just before the answer was given as compared to measurements made just before the question was asked. The increases ranged from 4% to 30% in diameter from prequestion to preanswer period. Pupil size decreased after the answer was given. In another experiment (Polt, 1970), the threat of a mild electric shock for incorrect answers resulted in greater amounts of effort to solve problems, and this, in turn, produced greater pupil dilation.

Pupil size was observed as subjects listened to strings of three to seven digits presented at a rate of one per second (Kahneman and Beatty, 1966). After a 2-second pause, each string was repeated by subjects at the same rate. The researchers found progressive pupillary dilation with the presentation of each digit, with maximum dilation being reached after all digits were presented. Then, as each digit was repeated, pupillary constriction occurred and reached its baseline when the last digit was reported. Also, the amount of pupil dilation at the pause was a function of the number of items in the string, that is, it was greatest with seven digts (4.1 mm) and least with three digits (3.6 mm). These researchers suggested that pupillary dilation varied directly with momentary cognitive load. In another study, Beatty and Kahneman (1966) found similar pupillary size variations when digits were retrieved from long-term memory, for example, with a familiar telephone number. Subjects were required to recall a telephone number when presented with a one-word cue such as "home" or "office" and to present the digits at a 1-second rate. The magnitude of pupil dilation was larger with these familiar digits as compared to a string of seven unfamiliar digits presented for recall. As before, pupil diameter decreased with each digit reported, returning to baseline as the last digit was given.

Pupillary dilation has been related to the difficulty encountered by subjects in a pitch discrimination task (Kahneman & Beatty, 1967). When the difficulty in distinguishing between two tones became greater, subjects showed increased dilation. Paivio and Simpson (1966) studied pupil size when individuals were asked to generate images to abstract and concrete words. They found that imagery increased pupil dilation, with greater amounts occurring to abstract words as compared to concrete words. Furthermore, time to reach maximum dilation was greater with abstract words, perhaps because it was more difficult to generate images to abstract terms. Simpson and Hale (1969) found greater pupil dilation in subjects who were required to decide in which direction a lever was to be moved than with yoked controls who were told how to move the lever. Paivio (1973) suggested that the cognitive activity involved in making a decision regarding the occurrence of an image is responsible for pupillary dilation. That is, the overt decision increases arousal level and pupillary dilation.

Kahneman and Peavler (1969) measured pupil diameter during a verbal learning task. The learning trials were presented under conditions of either high incentive (5 cent reward for each item learned) or low incentive (1 cent reward). The high-incentive items were more efficiently learned than the low-incentive ones (55% vs. 18%), and they produced larger pupillary dilations (4.04 mm vs. 3.97 mm). Colman and Paivio (1970) measured pupillary activity during a paired-associates learning task. The abstractness of the words were varied, and subjects learned the pairs under standard conditions or using imagery as a mediator. Pupillary dilation was greater under the standard, more difficult learning condition. The results also showed larger pupil size with the abstract word pairs that were more difficult to learn.

In summary, the studies reviewed in this section indicate that pupil dilation occurs during mental activity. Increased pupillary dilation has been observed with greater effort and task demands. Further, pupil size appears to vary with momentary processing load imposed by the task. Imagery can produce pupillary response, and there is suggestive evidence that images which are harder to generate result in greater magnitudes of dilation. Pupil size has also been found to increase under conditions of greater incentive and more difficult verbal learning.

Positive and Negative Affect, Attitudes, and Pupil Size

Positive Affect

One of the most intriguing results of the original Hess and Polt study (1960) was that pupil size appeared to be related to affect or "feeling tone" generated by various stimuli for different individuals. For example, Hess and Polt reported that when viewing pictures of a male nude and of a baby, female subjects gave larger pupil dilation responses than did male subjects. On the other hand, male subjects reacted with larger pupillary dilation to a female nude. Hess et al. (1965) found that homosexual males had greater pupil dilations to photographs of male nudes as compared to female nudes, while the results for heterosexual males showed the opposite pupillary response. In addition, Hess (1965) presented pictures of food to some subjects before lunch and to others after they had eaten. The pupil responses of persons tested before lunch ("food-deprived") showed significant increases to food pictures as compared to the nondeprived subjects. Hess has interpreted the results of studies such as these just mentioned in terms of "interest" or "motivation" of the subject with respect to the stimuli presented. Others have also found pupillary diameter to be related to affect. For example, Simms (1967) reported greater pupil response to photographs of the opposite sex, especially when the photographs were retouched to produce enlarged pupils. The implication of this finding is that pupil dilation in others may be subtly perceived as signifying interest on the part of that other person. Bernick et al. (1971) measured pupil size of male subjects while they viewed an erotic "stag movie," a suspense movie (mystery), and an erotic homosexual movie. The degree of reported penile erection corresponded closely to increases in pupil diameter.

Negative Affect

Hess (1972) has noted in various studies that certain types of negative stimuli may produce a constriction in pupil size, for example, pictures of crippled children. However, if the negative picture has "shock content" (e.g., a picture of a mutilated person), dilation may occur initially, followed by constriction after repeated presentations. Thus the emotional reaction produces a SNS response (pupil dilation), and after it wears off, the constriction occurs and reflects aversion or "perceptual avoidance." Hess contended that ". . . there is a continuum of pupil responses to stimuli, ranging from extreme dilation for interesting or pleasing stimuli to extreme constriction for material that is unpleasant or distasteful to the viewer" (1972, p. 511). Other investigators have challenged this claim of bidirectionality of the pupil response. For example, Loewenfeld (1966) reviewed effects of various sensory and psychological stimuli and concluded that none, except increased light intensities, caused pupillary constriction. Woodmansee (1967) reported an opposite response, that is, pupillary dilation in 13 of 14 female college students who viewed a picture of a murder scene. Peavler and McLaughlin (1967) did not find constriction to negative word stimuli. Libby et al. (1973) reported that unpleasant visual stimuli produced greater dilation than pleasant stimuli. Several of their 34 subjects, however, did show consistent pupillary constriction to a few stimuli. Janisse (1974) found a positive relationship between pupil size and affect intensity but no evidence of constriction to negative stimuli. In general, the results of other investigators cast doubt on Hess' hypothesis regarding pupillary constriction to unpleasant stimuli.

In summary, there appears to be substantial research support for the claim that pupillary diameter increases with stimuli that produce positive affect. Pupillary constriction with negative stimuli is still controversial and may be a response limited to a few individuals and a small range of stimulus conditions.

Attitudes

It has been suggested that pupil size might be a more valid index of attitude toward persons or things than more traditional methods, for example, interviews or questionnaires (Hess, 1972). One example is a study of Barlow (1969), who showed slides of three political leaders (Lyndon Johnson, George Wallace, and Martin Luther King) and one unknown person to subjects classified as "liberal" or "conservative." The liberals showed pupillary dilation to Johnson and King and constrictions to Wallace. The conservatives showed an opposite response pattern. The question of attitude and pupil size requires a great deal of additional work.

Information Processing and Pupil Size

A number of studies by Kahneman and his associates have indicated that progressive pupil dilation occurred when lists of materials were presented for processing (e.g., Kahneman & Beatty, 1966; Kahneman & Wright, 1971). In addition, Kahneman and Wright (1971) have suggested that increased mental effort results in greater pupil dilation. They showed that pupillary response was greater when subjects were required to recall an entire series of items than when they recalled only part of the information. In addition, Wright and Kahneman (1971) observed that pupillary diameter was increased during listening when persons were asked to repeat sentences as compared to when they had to answer questions about the information contained in the sentences.

Pupillary dilation did not occur during reading or listening to passages that varied in difficulty (Carver, 1971). He suggested that pupil size cannot be used as an objective indicator of whether or not the subject is processing information. However, Stanners et al. (1972) observed that systematic increases in pupil size occurred as information was presented via a tape recorder. Further, there was suggestive evidence that more complex sentences produced larger pupillary responses. In another experiment, Stanners and Headley (1972) reported that pupil diameter showed greater increases if subjects were asked to recall information from memory as compared to a requirement to recognize items presented, that is, a mean difference of about .2 mm. They suggested that this could reflect different processing in recall and recognition or more intense rehearsal produced by the requirement to recall information.

Poock (1973) found that pupil diameter was related to information-processing speed. He first determined maximum processing capacity (100%) by having subjects press buttons corresponding to displayed numerals as fast as possible. Then subjects alternately processed numerals at 50%, 75%, 100%, and 125% of maximum capacity. Significant increases in pupil diameter over baseline levels (viewing a blank slide) were found when subjects were required to process information at 75% and 100% of capacity. However, when the requirement was raised to 125% of capacity, pupillary constriction occurred.

Peavler (1974) measured pupil sizes of 14 female college students while they processed digit strings of various lengths (5, 9, and 13 digits). There was a trend toward increased pupil size with each successive digit in the five- and nine-digit conditions. However, the 13-digit condition revealed that dilation leveled off immediately after presentation of the 10th digit. This suggested to Peavler that information-processing effort was momentarily suspended at this point. This point of no further dilation corresponded to the short-term memory capacity of the subjects, which was approximately nine digits in this experiment. Average pupillary diameter increased from about 5.0 mm with the first digit to 5.6 mm with the ninth.

The studies reviewed in this section seem to indicate that pupillary diameter changes occur during information processing and that the change is related to degree of mental effort required. The increases in pupillary dilation observed with heavy information-processing loads may be related to elevated CNS activity under higher load conditions.

Perceptual Processes and Pupil Size

Hakerem and Sutton (1966) measured pupillary response to threshold (barely perceptible) visual stimuli. No pupillary dilation occurred to stimuli that were not detected or when the subject was not asked to detect the weak light flashes. However, when subjects were required to detect whether a flash was present or absent, and they correctly discriminated a flash, pupillary dilation occurred. Beatty (1975) found similar results when subjects were required to detect a weak tone that was present during one-half of the experimental trials. Pupil dilation occurred only when a presented signal was detected by the subjects. Beatty concluded that the pupillary dilations reflected changes in nervous system activation which accompanied perceptual processing.

Libby et al. (1973) presented 30 pictures to 34 male subjects while measures of pupil diameter and heart rate were obtained. The main finding was that an interesting stimulus evoked a physiological response characterized by pupil dilation and a decrease in heart rate.

Three groups of 11 subjects each (introverts, ambiverts, and extroverts, so classified by the Eysenck Personality Inventory) were presented with affective and taboo words while pupillary response was measured (Stelmack & Mandelzys, 1975). They were also presented with matched neutral words. There were 12 affective words (e.g., vomit), 12 taboo words (e.g., whore), and 24 neutral words (e.g., field). The introverts had the largest average pupil size under all conditions. This result supported Eysenck's hypothesis that introverts have generally higher levels of physiological arousal.

In summary, results indicate that pupillary dilation can index the perception of very weak sensory stimuli. One recent finding implies that degree of pupillary change may be related to personality; that is, introverts show a high degree of response.

The modern era of pupillography was ushered in by the provocative work of Hess and his associates. It continues as a very interesting research area that has implications for the study of various forms of human behavior. In addition, studies of pupillary responses have been conducted in advertising research (see, e.g., Krugman, 1964; Bortel, 1968; Hess, 1975). Those students who wish more detailed information on the general topic of pupillography and performance are referred to reviews by Hess (1972) and Goldwater (1972) and the books of Janisse (1974) and Hess (1975).

Eye Movements

The Control of Eye Movements

Eye movements are controlled by cerebral systems in conjunction with cranial nerves and sets of eye muscles attached to the outside of the eyeball. The cerebral areas involved in eye fixations are the occipital and frontal cortices. Innervation of the eye muscles is by the third (oculomotor), fourth (trochlear), and sixth (abducens) cranial nerves. They influence movements of three separate pairs of eye muscles: the superior and inferior rectus, the lateral and medial rectus, and the superior and inferior obliques (see Fig. 10-2). The superior and inferior recti contract to move the eyes up or down. The lateral and medial recti allow movements from side to side, and the obliques control rotation of the eyeballs. The three sets of muscles are reciprocally innervated to allow one pair to relax while another pair contracts.

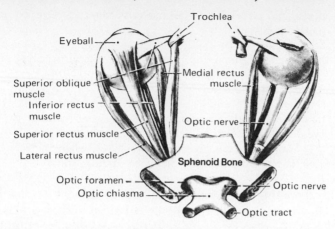

Figure 10-2.   Extrinsic muscles of the eye. (Inferior oblique muscle not shown.)

The purpose of eye movements is to direct images of objects so they stimulate the foveal region of the eye, that is, the area of best acuity.

Fixation movements of the eye are controlled by two different neural mechanisms (Guyton, 1977). Voluntary fixations, or the selective convergence of the eyes on some object of choice, are controlled by a small area in the premotor cortex of the frontal lobes. The maintenance of involuntary fixation is controlled by areas in the occipital cortex. Shackel (1967) identified three common types of eye movements:

1.   *Saccadic*—This refers to movements of the eyes from one fixation point to the next. A fixation pause lasts for about ¼ to 1 second, and the saccade (movement) lasts for approximately 1/50th to 1/10th of a second, depending on how long it takes to make the next fixation. Saccadic movements occur so quickly that they only occupy 10% of the total time spent in eye movements, while fixation accounts for 90% of the time (Guyton, 1977). (Perception generally takes place only during fixations.)

2a. *Smooth Pursuit*—This is the eye movement that occurs when a moving object is fixated and followed by the eyes. The rate of movement can closely approximate that of the object, up to 60°

per second and beyond. (In this case, perception can occur while the eye is in motion.)

2b. *Smooth Compensatory*—This is a movement to correct for body or head tilt to maintain an upright view of the visual field. (It is an "automatic" or reflex activity.)

3. *Nystagmoid*—These are oscillations of the eyes often consisting of slow horizontal sweeps and quick returns to the original eye position. There are three causes of nystagmoid movements: (a) where eye defects or the visual field prevent adequate fixation; (b) when the vestibular system is impaired; or (c) when there is impairment of visual or vestibular pathways in the CNS.[1]

To these three basic varieties of eye movement we should add the rapid eye movements (REM) of sleep and eye blinks. The REMs of sleep occur sporadically, are variable in amplitude, and last from a few minutes to a half hour or more. Blinking of the eye lids lasts about .2 to .4 second and, on the average, occur at 2- to 10-second intervals, with wide individual variability.

Recording Eye Movements

Three of the basic methods commonly used to measure eye movements were described by Shackel (1967). These are the contact-lens method, the corneal reflection method, and a technique termed electrooculography (EOG). The EOG will be briefly outlined here. The basis for the EOG is the steady (approximately 1 mV) potential that exists between the cornea and retina of the eye. The cornea is electrically positive, while the back of the eye at the retina is negative. When the eyes are fixed straight ahead, recording electrodes detect a steady baseline potential. When eye movements occur, the potential across the electrodes changes and a corresponding deflection is produced in the pen of a recorder. Electrode pairs placed horizontally on the skin surface, at the corners of the eyes, detect horizontal

---

[1] It should be noted that small spontaneous saccadic drifts, and other movements, occur in the normal eye at rest. When these small movements are effectively eliminated, e.g., by stabilizing an image on a certain portion of the retina through optical techniques, a fixated image gradually fades and disappears.

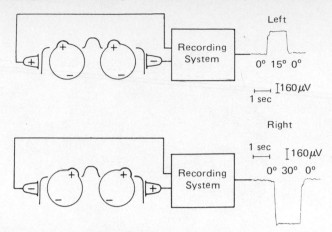

Figure 10-3. Basis of electrooculography. The eyeball is like a minute battery. As it rotates, the poles of the "battery" come nearer to the respective electrodes on the adjacent skin. The change in direct potential, and thus the angle of rotation, can be recorded.

movements. Electrodes placed above and below the eyes detect vertical movements. What is really being detected is a change in dc potential that is produced when the eyes move (see Fig. 10-3). The pen deflection in the ink-writing system will be either positive or negative, depending on the polarity of the connections, and the amplitude of the deflection is linearly related to the extent of movement, up to about 30° from center. Horizontal movements may be recorded by measuring across one eye or across both eyes with electrodes placed near the external canthus (outside) of each eye (see Fig. 10-4). For monocular recording, one electrode must be at the side of the nose near the internal canthus with the other at the external canthus. The EOG recorded from one eye is considered to reflect the position of the other eye unless stated differently. The binocular measure provides more reliable results (Shackel, 1967). For precise recordings, the electrodes must be placed adjacent to the horizontal plane passing through the cornea of the eye. Researchers commonly use a binocular placement for horizontal eye movement and monocular for vertical movements.

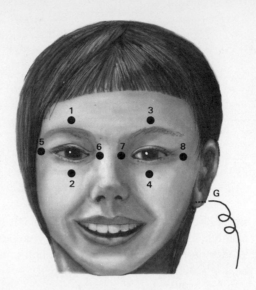

Figure 10-4. Placement of electrodes for eye movement recordings. Electrodes 1 and 2, 3 and 4 are for vertical movement recordings. Electrodes 5 and 6, 7 and 8 are for horizontal recordings (monocular). The most common horizontal placements are 5 and 8 (binocular). Vertical recordings are usually monocular. G, ground electrode at mastoid area, behind ear.

Problems in EOG Recording

Shackel (1967) describes three problems in the recording of EOG: (1) the small magnitude of the EOG signal, (2) the existence of skin potentials in the same frequency band as EOG signals, and (3) slow drift, often caused by unclean electrodes and poor contact. The first of these problems can be overcome through the use of a suitable, sensitive recorder. Most physiological recording devices are satisfactory, provided they have the appropriate couplers for dc recordings. The skin potential response can be minimized by careful preparation (e.g., removing the outer layer of skin) or by using aluminum salts to inhibit sweat gland activity. Another possible problem, that of slow drift, may be minimized by following the preparation routine outlined below (see Shackel, 1967, pp. 318-320).

Preparation of Electrodes and Subject

The electrodes used for EOG measurement are similar to the small disc or cup electrodes used in EEG recordings. They may be made of either silver or stainless steel. The electrodes should be nonpolarizing, small, and light enough to enable attachment with surgical tape or an adhesive collar. The dc drift caused by electrode polarization can be recognized as a steady deflection of the recording pen in one direction. Electrodes should be kept in an airtight container, washed in distilled water, and then placed in a saline solution with the leads shorted together before use. Paste is then applied to the electrodes before they are placed on the skin. After proper preparation, skin resistance between the electrodes should be less than 2000 Ω. The subject's head must be held in one constant position with regard to the center of the visual field. Some researchers employ a chin rest to accomplish this, while others make an impression of the subject's teeth in dental plastic and have the subject position his mouth on this "bite board" before each trial. While the head is fixed in place, the system is calibrated directly in degrees of eye movement by having the subject fixate a series of points at known angles of eye rotation. The gain may be adjusted so that one division on the recording paper equals 1° or 2° of eye movement (Shackel, 1967). Typical recordings of saccadic and pursuit movements are depicted in Figure 10-5.

The records shown in Figure 10-5 are monocular for the vertical movements and binocular for the horizontal ones. The careful recording of EOG can result in a great deal of stability and repeatability of the results over a period of time (Shackel & Davis, 1960).

Eye Movements and Behavior

There has been a fair amount of research relating eye movements and behavior over the past several years. In the next few sections, we will discuss the measurement of eye movements during mental activities, visual search, and perception.

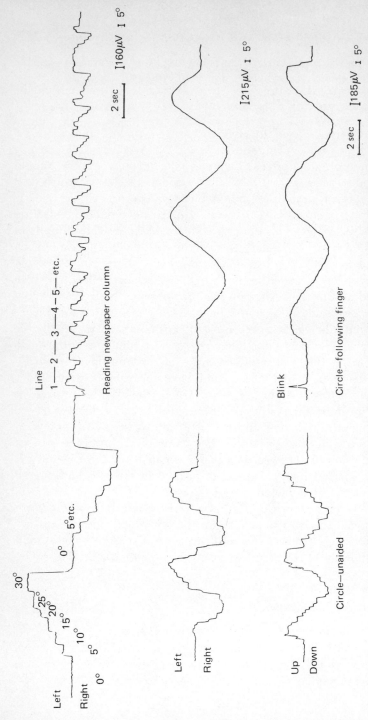

Figure 10-5. Typical recordings of saccadic and pursuit movements. The subject fixates a series of points at 5° intervals, reads a newspaper column, tries to scan smoothly round a circle by himself, and follows a fingertip drawn round the circle. Note also the typical wave form of a blink, on the vertical record only, with sharp rise and fall and short duration.

Mental Activity and Eye Movements

The primary function of eye movements is to allow the eyes to alter their position and focus upon objects of interest. Saccadic movements bring objects into foveal vision through quick adjustments, while pursuit motions adjust eye movements to moving objects. However, eye movements have also been related to mental activities such as learning and problem solving.

Eye Movements and Learning

A series of experiments by McCormack and colleagues have used eye movements in conjunction with paired-associate learning to support a two-stage conceptualization of verbal learning. It is hypothesized that subjects consolidate responses during an initial or "response-learning" phase and then connect responses to stimuli in a second or "hook-up" stage. They have found, for example, that efficient performers spend more time fixating on the stimulus word from the outset in a learning task as compared to inefficient learners of paired-associates (Haltrecht & McCormack, 1966). (In paired-associates learning, a set of stimulus words must elicit a specific set of response words for successful completion.) In another experiment, it was found that fixation of response words decreased as learning progressed, while time spent viewing the stimulus words increased (McCormack et al., 1967a). Furthermore, viewing time of response and stimulus words diverged more quickly when subjects learned an easy list (high response similarity) than when they performed with a difficult list (low response similarity) (McCormack et al., 1967b). Thus, there is evidence here consistent with the notion that eye movement pattern varies with stage of learning, and it may differ for slow and fast learners.

Eye Movements, Problem Solving and Cognitive Mode

Nakano (1971) measured the eye movements of undergraduate subjects when they were presented with two horizontal arrays of pictures. The pictorial stimuli were presented under three conditions: (1) when no problem solving was required, (2) when the pictures were used in the solution of a problem, and (3) after problem solving. The average number of eye fixations was greatest under the problem solving condition and lowest after problem solving.

An interesting observation by Teitlebaum (1954) concerned the movement of a person's eyes either to the left or right when reflecting on a question asked by another. This observation was investigated in more detail by Day (1964), who confirmed that the eyes move leftward or rightward in a consistent manner after persons had been asked a question requiring some thought. The individual is usually unaware of the lateral movement, which can easily be observed by another person sitting opposite to the subject. It has been hypothesized that those persons who move their eyes rightward are left hemisphere dominant, while those who move their eyes to the left are presumed to be right hemisphere dominant (Bakan, 1969).

Some evidence to support this proposal was obtained by Kinsbourne (1972), who found that right-handed subjects had a tendency to move their eyes to the right for verbal problems and either up or to the left for spatial problems. Hence, the eyes moved in a direction opposite to the hemisphere involved in the solution of the problem. However, Kinsbourne did not find these differences for numerical problems. He also reported that in left-handed subjects the direction of movement did not correspond to problem type. This may be related to the fact that about 60% of left-handers are left hemisphere dominant in language functions, while 40% are right hemisphere dominant. Kocel et al. (1972) observed that verbal and arithmetic questions elicited more rightward movements of the eyes than did spatial and musical questions. This result was interpreted as further support for the hypothesis that direction of lateral eye movement indicates activation of the contralateral hemisphere of the brain.

Gur (1975) tested 32 right-handed male students on spatial and verbal problems when sitting behind the subjects and when facing them. The filmed eye movements showed that they moved leftward with spatial problems and rightward for verbal problems when the experimenter sat behind the subjects. This finding corroborated previous ones. However, when the experimenter faced the subjects the eyes moved predominantly in one direction, either left or right, regardless of problem type. Thus the influence of problem type appears to be maximized when the experimenter's presence is minimized. Gur et al. (1975) reported that the eye movements of 17 left-handed subjects were haphazard even when the experimenter sat behind them and, therefore, were uncorrelated with problem type. This result supports the view that right-handers show a higher degree of hemispheric lateralization for various functions than do left-handed persons.

In summary, recent studies of eye movements during problem solving suggest that lateralization of brain function may be reflected by the direction of this movement. The eyes move rightward for verbal analytic problems and leftward for spatial problems, suggesting activation of the contralateral hemisphere, a finding that has been demonstrated in EEG studies of cognitive function. A greater degree of lateralization for right-handers is also indicated by the experimental results.

Eye Movements and Reading

The study of eye movements during reading has been an area of basic laboratory research since the early 1900s (Woodworth, 1938; Woodworth & Schlosberg, 1954). Comparisons of eye movement patterns of slow and fast readers have been conducted in applied contexts to determine whether this information could be used in the development of remedial reading programs. A study by Buswell (1922), cited by Woodworth and Schlosberg (1954), examined the eye movement reading patterns of students at 13 levels from first grade to college. The results indicated the following regarding the development of reading skills: (1) there was a steady decrease in number of eye fixations per line of reading material with higher grade levels (18.6 in first grade and 5.9 in college); (2) the fixations became shorter in duration (660 msec in first grade and 252 msec at college level); and (3) the number of regressive movements decreased from an average of 5.1 per line for first graders to .5 for college students. Regressive movement refers to returning the eyes to earlier portions of the material being read. Studies of slow and fast readers at the same grade level indicated that more efficient readers made fewer and shorter duration eye fixations and did not regress to early material as did inefficient readers.

The study of eye movements and reading continued through the 1930s and 1940s (see a review by Tinker, 1946), but not much has been done in this area since then. An early position which held that vision did not occur during eye movements was supported in a study by Uttal and Smith (1968). They found that blurring of alphabetic characters occurred during quick voluntary saccadic movements. A review of research on reading, including some of the early eye movement studies, was recently written by Venezky (1977).

Eye Movements in Visual Search

Visual search refers to examining the visual field to locate a desired object, for example, searching for a familiar face in a crowd of people. Ford et al. (1959) studied eye movements during free search for targets in a circular field subtending 30° of visual angle. By "free search" the authors meant the kind of visual task involved in monitoring an empty visual field in which objects could appear at any time and at any location as, for example, in the case of an airplane pilot watching the sky for significant objects. The researchers found that in free search subjects averaged three eye fixations per second. The mean duration was found to be 280 msec for each fixation, while the average eye sweep covered 8.60° of visual angle. The eye fixations were not distributed evenly over the search area, and the investigators suggested that patterns of eye movement would be influenced by extent and shape of the field searched and the time available for search. Their last suggestion was confirmed in a study by White and Ford (1960), who investigated eye movements during radar search and found eye patterns to be very different from the "free search" situation. The presence of the rotating scan-line[2] on the radar set resulted in much more predictable, circular, search patterns. The mean fixation time was 370 msec (vs. 280 msec in free search), and the authors suggested that this was due to the greater restraints on eye movements produced in the more restricted radar task; that is, more fixations were made in free search. The greatest number of fixations occurred at about 4° to 7° from the center of the circular radar display.

[2] The scan-line represents the radar antenna sweeping the sky for targets.

Mackworth et al. (1964) studied eye movements during a vigilance task. The detection task involved noticing a .5 second pause in a revolving dial pointer. Under the four experimental conditions, subjects monitored either one or two dials, with frequent or infrequent signals. They found that (1) detection probability for two dials was one-half that for one dial, and (2) in the one dial condition, every missed signal was fixated without being detected. This latter point is noteworthy, since it indicates that fixation of a signal or target does not necessarily mean that it will be detected or recognized as such by the visual system. Mackworth has referred to this phenomenon as "looking without seeing."

Based on studies of eye movements, Gould (1969) concluded that the location of eye fixations on a display depends on four general factors: (1) the search task itself, (2) prior information about the target, (3) the purpose (as contained in instructions) of the subject, and (4) previous experience. For example, Gould and Schaffer (1965) found that subjects practiced in tachistoscopic perception required fewer fixations to find targets than those without this experience. These investigators recorded eye movements while subjects scanned patterns to compare the sum of three digits in each of four peripheral cells with that of three digits in a central (target) cell. Both larger target sums and greater target-nontarget similarity caused longer fixations.

Gould and Peeples (1970) recorded eye movements during a search task in which subjects had to determine how many of eight comparison patterns matched a standard pattern. One finding was that standard patterns were fixated longer than target patterns even though they were identical. In addition, target patterns were fixated longer than nontarget patterns, suggesting that with unlike patterns, fixation stopped as soon as a difference was noted, while identical patterns led to fixation that ended only when all identical elements had been verified.

Volkmann and Volkmann (1971) studied saccadic eye movements in a search task by varying the position of a target stimulus (triangle) among 13 locations along a horizontal line. The target position was randomly varied, while the other 12 positions were occupied by circles. Target stimuli located near the center of the array were detected faster than those on either end. The mean number of fixations paralleled search latency; that is, the number of fixations was smallest near the center and increased with distance from the middle area. Coren and Hoenig (1972a) found that the presence of irrelevant (nontarget) stimuli can influence the extent of saccadic movements made to detect a target. Target stimuli (red asterisks) appeared in a location 10° left of right of center immediately after disappearance of a central fixation point. The target was accompanied by zero, one, two, or three nontarget stimuli (black asterisks) spaced at 1° intervals, either between target and fixation point (inside) or beyond the target (outside). The saccades extended to an average 10.75° with extraneous stimuli outside the target and 9.01° when nontarget stimuli were horizontally located inside the target. The authors concluded that saccadic movements are influenced by the locus of nontarget stimuli in the general surrounding portions of the visual field such that the fovea is moved close to the geometric center of those stimuli.

Williams (1967) studied eye fixations upon stimuli coded in different ways. He found that color, shape, and size of objects on a display influenced eye fixations. For example, color resulted in a greater number of fixations, while size and shape did not have much of an effect. In another study, Williams (1973) reported the greatest number of eye fixations with orange colored targets. The least fixated were green targets.

The effects of different methods of coding a target on search time and number of eye fixations were studied by Luria and Strauss (1975). They reported that color coding alone led to the fewest number of eye fixations and shortest search time. A combination of color and shape coding was second best, while shape alone was next best. The intermediate performance with the color-shape code may indicate that the subjects used color primarily and were slightly distracted by shape. The least efficient detection, in terms of the number of eye fixations required, was for the uncoded targets.

In summary, studies of eye movements during visual search have produced some basic information about the number and duration of eye fixations in the first stages of visual information processing. Mackworth's data indicated that fixation of a target may not be sufficient for detection. The mean number of fixations tends to parallel detection time, and the presence of irrelevant (nontarget) stimuli influences the extent of saccadic sweeps made to detect targets. Irrelevant stimuli also result in longer eye fixations during visual search. Color coding of targets seems to improve search time.

Eye Movements and Perception

The measurement of eye movements has been utilized by several investigators interested in the problems of pattern recognition and discrimination. In a study by Gould and Schaffer (1967), subjects were alternately instructed to find patterns that either matched or did not match a standard pattern. Eye movement recordings indicated that subjects spent more time fixating patterns that exactly matched a memorized standard than on those which differed, suggesting that detailed comparisons of features were being made.

Noton and Stark (1971a,b) analyzed eye movements of subjects while they viewed different patterns in a "learning" phase and during a "recognition phase." In the first or learning phase, they merely viewed five different patterns for 20 seconds each. In a second or recognition phase, these five patterns were again viewed, along with five new ones. Analyses of eye movements indicated that subjects followed similar paths for a given pattern, and the sequence of movements was usually the same in the recognition phase as it was in the learning phase. This led Noton and Stark to suggest that memory for features of a picture is established sequentially by the memory of eye movements required to look from one feature to the next. The characteristic pattern of eye movements for a given subject viewing a given stimulus has been termed a "scan path" by Noton and Stark. Gould and Peeples (1970) also reported consistent scan paths for their subjects. However, Luria and Strauss (1975) did not find consistent scanning strategies among their subjects. This led the latter investigators to suggest that the use of a characteristic scanning technique may depend on the type of search task.

What have eye movement studies revealed about how people look at pictures? A study by Mackworth and Morandi (1967) indicated that portions of a picture that were rated as highly informative by one group of people were fixated more frequently by another group of individuals who examined the pictures while their eye movements were measured. Yarbus (1967) found different patterns of eye movements while subjects viewed the same painting of a family scene under a variety of instructions. For example, when asked to estimate the wealth of the family, fixations centered on furniture and on clothing worn by women. When asked to estimate the ages of persons in the picture, eye fixations on faces became the most numerous. Thus, it seems that the information one wishes to derive from a visual scene will determine the pattern of eye movements used in examining the picture. Loftus (1972) found that durations of eye fixations did not affect recall of a picture but that the number of fixations made during a fixed period of viewing did affect later recognition. That is, the greater the number, the more likely was the person to recognize the picture at another time.

Antes (1974) had 20 subjects rate the informativeness of various regions in 10 pictures. Another 20 subjects viewed each of the pictures for 20 seconds while their eye movements were measured. The findings corroborated those of Mackworth and Morandi in that informative regions of pictures were fixated immediately. However, Antes also found that while initial fixations were on informative areas, the less informative detail received a greater proportion of the fixations later in the viewing sequence. Data from this and previous experiments also suggest that observers use information from peripheral vision to fixate immediately on informative areas. Gould (1974) points out that people tend to fixate on contours more frequently than on other areas of a picture. This is because contours carry critical information as to the shape, and therefore the identification of objects in the picture.

To briefly summarize this section, it seems that significant portions of visual stimuli attract eye fixations. Characteristic scan paths appear to exist, but their role in pattern recognition has not been determined. In looking at pictures, people tend to fixate those areas that contain the most information, especially in the early stages of viewing. The purpose of a viewer will also determine how he or she looks at a picture. A higher number of fixations during a viewing period seems related to superior recall of that picture.

Eye Movements and Illusions

In recent years, a good deal of attention has been given to the study of eye movements while persons experience various kinds of visual illusions. The familiar Muller-Lyer figure is one example. It will be recalled that the line with an attached arrow head pointed inward looks shorter than an identical line with the arrow head directed outward. It has been found that with prolonged inspection, the magnitude of the illusion decreases, although it does not disappear completely. One explanation for this concerns feedback provided by erroneous eye movements regarding the nature of the distortion. If eye movements are restricted to one portion of the figure, less information will be fed back, and the illusion will persist to its full extent. An experiment that supports this eye movement hypothesis was conducted by Festinger et al. (1968). They found that the Muller-Lyer illusion

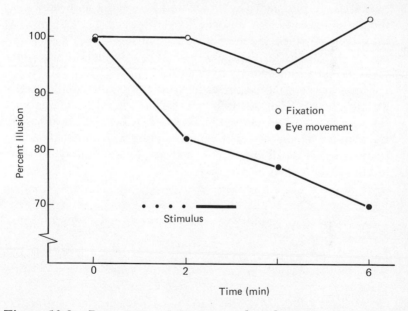

Figure 10-6. Percentage of illusion is plotted against inspection time in minutes. The inset shows the Oppel-Kundt stimulus configuration used in the experiment.

became less powerful when eye movements were made over the entire figure than when only one part of the figure was fixated. A similar result was found for the Oppel-Kundt figure, which also produces illusory differences in length of line (Coren & Hoenig, 1972b). In the Oppel-Kundt illusion, a divided horizontal space (e.g., five equally spaced dots) is seen as having greater linear extent than a solid horizontal line of identical length (see inset of Fig. 10-6). Two groups of 15 subjects each observed this illusion. One group made saccadic eye movements over the entire length of the illusion, while the other group fixated on the junction between the divided and undivided space. The illusion decreased over time for the eye movement group but not for the fixation group (see Fig. 10-6).

Eye movements were recorded while subjects experienced a "rebound illusion" (Mack et al., 1973). The rebound illusion occurs when the eyes pursue a luminous object in the dark. When the object comes to an abrupt stop, it appears to rebound sharply backward. Experiments by Mack and colleagues indicated that the illusion is caused by an overshoot of the target by the eye, at the point at which the target stops. Thus, it appears that eye movement studies may provide valuable information regarding the bases for various kinds of visual illusion.

The next two chapters cover measures of cardiovascular activity and their relation to behavior. A representative summary of the voluminous research on the associations between heart activity and psychological functioning is presented in Chapter 11, while discussions of blood pressure and blood volume are the topics of Chapter 12.

Heart Activity and Behavior

Changes in heart activity that occur in fear-provoking situations undoubtedly were noticed by men living thousands of years ago. The association of the heartbeat with love also reflects the common association of this organ with emotional reactions. Today we use scientific methods to study changes in heart activity not only during obviously emotional situations but also in the performance of more subtle tasks such as signal detection and problem solving. In this chapter, the changes in heart activity that occur during the performance of various tasks will be considered. More specifically, we will examine the effects of the following factors upon heart activity: motor performance, mental tasks, perceptual and emotional situations, and conditioning. The section on conditioning will briefly consider investigations of classical and instrumental conditioning of heart activity. But, first, we briefly review the anatomy and physiology of the heart and how its activity is measured.

Anatomy and Physiology of the Heart

The heart is a muscular, four-chambered organ whose main function is to supply blood, which contains nutriments and oxygen necessary for the functioning of body cells, to the tissues of the body. The heart is about the size of a man's fist. It weighs approximately 300 g in the male and 250 g in the female. The four chambers are the right and left atria (on top) and the right and left ventricles (on the bottom). Figure 11-1 is a cutaway drawing that shows the various heart chambers. The atria are receiving chambers for blood that has been returned to the heart by the veins. The ventricles pump blood via arteries to the lungs and the rest of the body.

Heart Structures Involved in Blood Circulation

The right atrium receives blood from all body tissues except the lungs. The veins that bring blood to the right atrium are (1) the superior vena cava (blood from the upper body), (2) the inferior vena cava (blood from the lower body), and (3) the coronary sinus (blood from the heart itself). The blood flows from the right atrium to the right ventricle and from there to the lungs (via the pulmonary artery). In the lungs, carbon dioxide is removed from the blood and oxygen is added. The oxygenated blood is then returned to the left atrium by four pulmonary veins. From there it goes to the left ventricle, which then pumps the oxygenated blood through the aorta to the rest of the body.

Control of the Heartbeat (Cardiac Cycle)

The heartbeat, which we can hear from a stethoscope and record with the electrocardiograph, represents the contracting that the heart does to pump blood to other body areas. The human heart normally contracts at a rate of about 72 beats per minute (bpm) at rest. The control of this beating is by mechanisms both internal and external to the heart.

Internal Cardiac Control

The internal mechanism of the heartbeat consists of a system of specialized fibers including: (1) the sinoatrial (S-A) node, (2) the atrioventricular (A-V) node, (3) the A-V bundle, and (4) the left and right bundles of conducting fibers (Guyton, 1977). The S-A node is located in the right atrium, and its regular electrical discharge produces the normal rhythmic contraction of the entire heart. The S-A node is also known as the pacemaker, with a rate of 120 bpm at normal body temperature. However, the

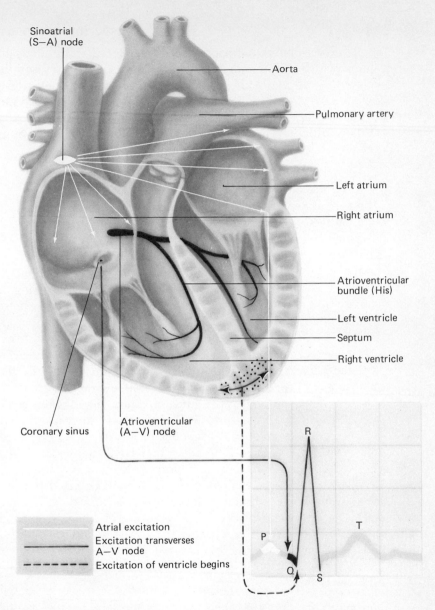

Figure 11-1. Conducting system of the heart showing source of electrical impulses produced on electrocardiogram.

vagus nerve inhibits the pacemaker and holds the rate down to approximately 70–80 bpm. The impulse for contraction is slightly delayed at the A-V node before passing into the ventricles. The A-V bundle then conducts the impulse into the ventricles, and Purkinje fibers conduct the impulse for contraction to all parts of the ventricles. The contraction phase of the heart is known as systole, while the relaxation phase is termed diastole.

External Cardiac Control

The normal regular rate of contraction may also be influenced by external factors, that is, by nerves from the ANS and CNS. The PNS influences the S-A and A-V nodes via the vagus nerve. Its influence results in a slowing of the heartbeat. This influence is produced by the release of the neurotransmitter acetylcholine at the vagus nerve endings, which, in turn, results in the slowing of activity at the S-A node and a slowing of the cardiac impulse passing into the ventricles (Guyton, 1977). The SNS has the opposite effect; that is, it produces an increase in heart rate. It exerts this effect through the release of norepinephrine at the sympathetic nerve endings. This results in (1) an increase in the rate of S-A node discharge, (2) increased excitability of heart tissue, and (3) an increase in force of contraction of both atrial and ventricular musculature. The SNS acts to increase cardiac output in certain emotional situations or at extreme levels of exercise. However, it should be noted that HR increases are often due to decreased vagus nerve inhibition (PNS).

At one time it was thought that the medulla exerted the primary control over certain reflex actions concerned with influencing heart rate. However, it is now known that other CNS structures, including the hypothalamus, cerebellum, and amygdala, also contribute to these reflexes.

Carotid Sinus Reflex

Baroreceptors (pressure sensitive) are present in the carotid sinus, located in the neck at about the level of the chin. The carotid sinus is supplied by fibers from the glossopharyngeal (IXth) cranial nerve. When pressure on the walls of the carotid sinus is low, because of decreased blood pressure, this information is transmitted to a cardiac acceleration center in the medulla. At this point, sympathetic fibers are brought into action to increase heart rate and, in addition, to bring the pressure of the carotid sinus up to an acceptable level. The basic function of the baroreceptors is to ensure an adequate blood supply to the brain. Thus, we see the operation of a feedback mechanism which maintains heart rate and blood pressure within certain limits. The reader interested in more detail on this topic may want to consult a review of central mechanisms in the control of heart rate by Cohen and Macdonald (1974). There are other internal and external factors that can influence heart rate, including the metabolism of the heart itself, chemical factors, and hormonal influences.

Measurement of Heart Activity

A portion of the electrical impulse that passes through the heart during contraction spreads to the surface of the body. If electrodes are placed on the skin, the electrical potentials generated by the heart can be recorded. When these potentials are amplified and recorded on an ink writer, the resulting measurement is called the electrocardiogram (ECG). The normal ECG is composed of characteristic deflections referred to as P, Q, R, S, and T waves. These wave components of the ECG are depicted in Figure 11-2. The relatively small P wave is produced by electrical currents generated just before contraction of the atria. The QRS complex is caused by currents generated in the ventricles during depolarization just prior to ventricular contraction. Note that the R wave is the most prominent component of the QRS component. The T wave is caused by repolarization of the ventricles. Atrial repolarization does not result in a separate ECG wave because it is masked by the more pronounced ventricular related changes. The depolarization and repolarization that occurs in cardiac muscle fibers is similar in principle to the depolarization and repolarization which occurs in neurons. That is, depolarization occurs as the ionic activity inside of the fiber becomes positive with respect to the outside, and repolarization is a return to internal negativity and external positivity.

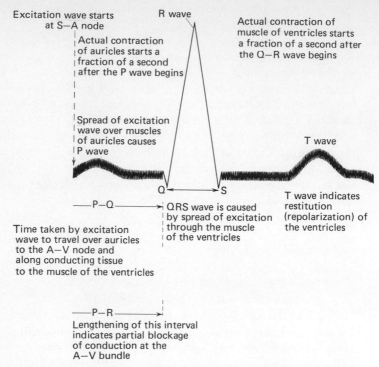

Figure 11-2. Electrocardiogram.

Wave Component Durations

The time between the start of the P wave and the beginning of
the QRS complex (or P-Q interval) is about 160 msec (Guyton,
1977). The Q-T interval, or the time from the beginning of the
Q wave to the end of the T wave, is about 300 msec. Since the
cardiac cycle lasts about 830 msec (based on a rate of 72 bpm),
there are approximately 370 msec between the end of the T
wave and the beginning of the next atrial contraction. The heart
actually spends less time contracting than relaxing; for example,
with a cycle of 800 msec, it is in ventricular systole for 300 msec
and in diastole for 500 msec.

Limb Leads for Recording the ECG

There are several standard limb leads for ECG recording. They are as follows:

Lead I—Electrodes are attached just above the wrists on the insides of the right and left arms. The polarity is selected so that when the left arm lead is positive, with respect to the right, there is an upward deflection of the P and R segments of the ECG.

Lead II—Electrodes are attached above the right wrist and above the left ankle. The polarity is chosen such that there is an upward deflection of the P and R waves of the ECG when the ankle lead is positive relative to the arm placement.

Lead III—Electrodes are attached above the left wrist and above the left ankle. Again, the polarity is selected so that there is an upward deflection of the P and R waves when the ankle placement is positive relative to the arm lead. Normal ECG records obtained through the use of these three lead placements are shown in Figure 11-3.

The leads described above are adequate in situations where subjects are lying down or sitting or standing in one place. However, for active subjects, sternal or axillary leads are preferred. Sternal leads are placed over bone (sternum) and are therefore relatively immune to movement artifacts (see Fig. 11-4). The placement of chest leads illustrated in Figure 11-4 shows the upper electrode placed on the manubrium of the sternum and the lower lead on the xiphoid process of the sternum. An upward deflection of the ECG is obtained when the upper electrode is positive relative to the lower one. The axillary (underarm) leads are also depicted in Figure 11-4 and show placements at the level of the heart. They are moderately free from movement artifacts, but since they are over muscle tissue, arm movements may produce EMG artifacts.

Amplitude and Recording Characteristics of the ECG

In the normal ECG, lead II produces an R wave that ranges in amplitude up to about 2 mV (Brener, 1967). This 2-mV peak is

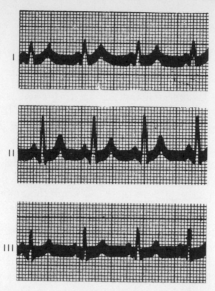

Figure 11-3. Normal electrocardiograms recorded from three standard electrocardiographic leads.

much larger than that encountered in either EEG or EMG recordings. The 2-mV peak amplitude must be amplified by a factor of about 2500 to bring it to a usable level. The procedure in clinical work is to use a gain setting that will allow a vertical deflection of 1 cm equal to 1 mV. A slightly higher gain would be used by researchers in psychophysiology. Paper speeds of 25 mm/sec enable good resolution of the various components of the ECG and are necessary when investigators want information on interbeat intervals. When information on rate only is desired, speeds of 5 or 10 mm/sec are adequate.

Measures in Research

In studies of human performance, heart rate or heart period (HP) are commonly used as measures of heart activity. The HR is based on the number of beats per unit of time, for example, in beats per minute. It is based on the occurrence of the most

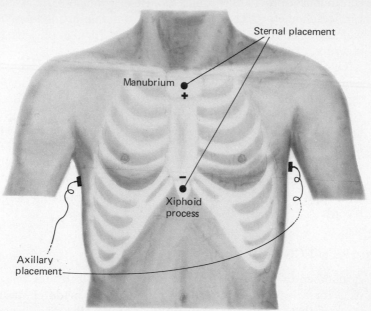

Figure 11-4. Placement of electrodes at manubrium and xiphoid process of sternum enables recording of ECG with active subjects. The axillary placements are not as free from EMG artifact as are the sternal leads.

prominent component of the ECG, that is, the R wave. Thus, continuous recordings of HR may be taken and then beats per minute may be computed. Alternatively, 10 or 20 seconds of the activity in a given minute may be sampled and taken as the HR for that period. The HR may also be continuously monitored by electronic counters which can automatically print out the rate for given time periods.

The HP measures the time between one R wave and another. This time is usually in milliseconds or seconds and may be automatically measured by an event per unit time (EPUT) meter (Brown, 1972). This device is commercially available and can be connected to a printer to obtain a numeric readout of each heart period. Information regarding interbeat variability can be continuously provided through the use of commercially available cardiotachometers. These devices are available as modular units which can be plugged in for use with a particular physiological recorder.

The ECG may be recorded on any physiological recorder which provides a pen deflection of 1–15 mm for each millivolt of signal and can process frequencies from 0.1 to 125 Hz (Brown, 1972). The ECG is not difficult to obtain, since it is a relatively large signal and does not require as much amplification as some other measures (e.g., EMG). With lower degrees of amplification, you are less likely to pick up unwanted electrical activity. However, as with other physiological measures, the proper use and application of electrodes is critical in obtaining a good record.

Electrodes in ECG Recordings

A number of good commercially available electrodes may be used for research purposes. Electrodes can be made of stainless steel or silver. They are usually in the shape of flat discs, or cups, measuring from ½ in. to 2 in. across. They may be held in place by adjustable rubber straps, suction cups, surgical tape, or adhesive plastic strips. Some excellent electrodes have been developed in connection with the space program and are especially suited for long-term recordings, that is, 24 hours or more. One example is a silver disc embedded in a rubber suction cup with a center-mounted sponge that contains the electrolyte.

Electrodes should be applied to hairless sites, if possible. The area of application may be briskly rubbed with a gauze pad until the skin is slightly pink. Then electrode jelly is rubbed in and the excess wiped off. Electrolyte jelly or paste is applied to the electrode before it is attached to the recording site. Electrodes should not be so tightly attached that they cause discomfort or muscle tremor. The latter can cause artifacts in the record. On the other hand, they must be prevented from moving, since this will also result in distorted recordings. As mentioned previously, the sternal lead is preferred for the moving subject. It also has the advantage of producing a large R wave. Leads II and III also produce large R waves. The large R wave is important in terms of ease of analyzing the data and providing a suitable signal for triggering automatic counters. Brown (1972) recommends that the amplified R wave be used to activate a Schmitt trigger, a device that will enable signals to reach counters or cardiotachometers in a reliable manner.

For a freely ranging subject, telemetry or portable recorders may be used. Telemetry is far more comfortable for the subject. The subject wears electrodes and a small FM or AM transmitter (as light as 18 g), capable of sending heart signals to a recorder at another location, where the information may be recorded on FM tape. Miniature portable recorders enable ECGs to be obtained from subjects or patients as they go about their daily activities (e.g., see Gunn et al., 1972). Electrodes attached to the sternum and rib cage are fed into a small recorder which amplifies the signal and records it on a tape. Such recording units weigh about 3 to 4 lb and are attached around the patient's or subject's waist with a belt. Usually, the recordings are made for a 24-hour period. The large mass of data obtained are amenable to analysis by modern computer techniques in a matter of minutes.

Heart Activity and Behavior

In recent years, the number of studies concerned with heart activity and human behavior appears to have increased considerably. The studies described in the remainder of this chapter are, by necessity, only representative of the large volume of research conducted over the last several years. We will consider relationships between heart activity and the following: motor performance, cognition, attention, perception, motivation, emotional reactions, and conditioning.

Motor Performance and Heart Activity

It is well known that vigorous muscular activity produces a requirement for increased blood supply and that heart activity speeds up under these conditions. Hence, under continued strenuous motor performance, higher HR would be expected. However, there are some tasks, for example, simple RT, that require only periodic and brief movements, involving muscles to a minimal degree. In this section we will examine two categories of motor activities: (1) the type associated with quick unstrenuous reactions, and (2) those in which continuous, complex, or strenuous motor performance is required.

Reaction Time

An interesting body of literature has grown concerning the relationship between cardiac activity and RT. A number of investigators have found that HR decreases during the fixed foreperiod of simple RT experiments (e.g., Lacey, 1967; Obrist, et al., 1969; Webb & Obrist, 1970). There have been suggestions that greater magnitudes of HR slowing are related to faster RTs. However, this contention is still controversial, and more recent work has resulted in fascinating findings regarding changes in the heartbeat that depend on the time of event occurrence within the cardiac cycle.

Although HR deceleration has sometimes been associated with faster RTs in situations where foreperiods are used, this does not appear to hold when the HR is controlled by external factors or when no warning signal is used. For example, Nowlin et al. (1970) manipulated the HR of 14 cardiac patients (with pacemakers) and found no relation between RT and different rates of cardiac pacing. The authors proposed that a sudden change in HR did not influence RT performance. Heart rate varied from a low of 45 bpm to a high of 115 bpm. Thus, when HR changes were externally controlled the relationship between deceleration and RT was not obtained. In another study, Surwillo (1971) measured HR and RTs of 100 healthy males in three experimental sessions. Stimuli occurred at random (no warning or foreperiod), and RTs were collected in three experimental sessions as HR varied spontaneously. Cardiac deceleration to stimuli was not observed under these conditions. Although HR varied naturally over a range of 30 bpm, there was no evidence of a relationship between RT and HR. Thus, these two last studies indicate that HR slowing and RT were unrelated when an external cardiac pacemaker was used and when stimuli were presented without regular foreperiods.

Botwinick and Thompson (1971) measured RTs at different phases of the cardiac cycle of 13 elderly males. Stimuli were programmed to occur at the R wave, or at .2, .4, or .6 second after the R wave. The preparatory interval was kept constant among these four conditions of stimulation. The RT did not vary with the phase of the cardiac cycle of these 13 subjects or in another group of 31 younger male subjects.

Obrist et al. (1973) studied the relationship between RT, HR, and measures of task-irrelevant somatic activity (eye movements and blinks, chin EMG, general bodily activity, and respiration). The subjects were four groups of children (4-, 5-, 8-, and 10-year-olds) and an adult reference group. The purpose was to study the cardiac-somatic hypothesis that HR and ongoing somatic activities vary in a similar direction. The investigators expected that the younger children would show more somatic activity because of inability to inhibit restlessness. They reported that for all groups a decrease in HR and a drop in task-irrelevant somatic activities were coincident with making the relevant responses. However, they failed to find a lawful developmental trend (i.e., changes with age) of incremental HR deceleration, although RT was faster in older children. Klorman (1975) measured HR and RT in groups of preadolescent (10 years of age), adolescent (14 years), and young adult (19 years) males. The task was simple RT with a relatively long (5 second) foreperiod. His HR findings agreed with those of Obrist et al. (1973), since there were no systematic age differences in cardiac deceleration even though older subjects had quicker RTs.

Lacey and Lacey (1977) used a fixed-foreperiod RT paradigm and measured heart period (R–R interval) as a function of time at which an imperative stimulus was presented in the cardiac cycle. They found that magnitude of HR deceleration during the preparatory interval depended on where in the cardiac cycle the imperative (response) signal was presented. If it occurred early in the cardiac cycle, deceleration was much greater than if the imperative signal came late in the cycle. The finding that HR deceleration was differentially affected during a single cardiac cycle indicates a greater sensitivity of the HR response than had previously been suspected. Lacey and Lacey attributed the speed of this deceleration to control exerted by the vagus nerve upon HR.

Phasic cardiac responses of eight subjects were studied during choice RT (Jennings and Wood, 1977). The cardiac cycle time was varied by presenting stimuli at either the R wave or 350 msec later. An interesting finding was that when responses occurred early in the cycle, anticipatory deceleration ended and shifted to acceleration within the same heartbeat. However, if responses occurred later than 300 msec after the R wave, the shift from slowing to speeding was delayed until the next heartbeat. To explain this, Jennings and Wood hypothesized that the vagal inhibitory activity responsible for slowing of HR ends when a task is completed, and therefore, the shift to speeding depends on the time course of vagal inhibition. The RT data showed that magnitudes of both HR deceleration and accelerative recovery were larger for faster responses. However, speed of RT was not related to time of stimulation in the cardiac cycle. The authors note that while this finding is not definitive, since only two points in the cycle were studied, it is consistent with previous reports of negligible or unreliable effects of cardiac time on RT.

In summary, it is well established that HR deceleration occurs during the fixed foreperiod of a RT task. The relationship between magnitude of HR slowing and speed of RT is still a point of controversy. It seems clear that when an RT task is performed under conditions in which HR is externally manipulated, or without fixed foreperiods or warning signals, there is no HR decrease associated with the period just prior to the response or during the response itself. The general findings suggest that unmanipulated cardiac deceleration represents a preparation to respond when an individual expects a significant stimulus. Developmental changes in HR deceleration have not been found, although RT is faster in adolescents and young adults than in children. Recent findings indicate that magnitude of HR deceleration during the preparatory interval of an RT task depended on time of event occurrence within the cardiac cycle. In addition, it has been found that when RT responses occurred early enough in a cardiac cycle, deceleration terminated and shifted to acceleration within the same heartbeat.

Complex Motor Performance and Heart Activity

Ohkubo and Hamley (1972) obtained measures of HR during a 5-day period while individuals learned to drive a car. The subjects were 12 young males who were instructed in driving along an isolated course five times during each day of training. As proficiency increased, a marked decrease was observed in HR during both rest and driving periods.

The effects of simulated sonic booms on tracking performance and HR were studied by Thackray et al. (1972). The subjects were exposed to four unexpected simulated sonic booms (indoors) over a 30-minute period. Tracking performance improved after boom stimulation, and HR showed a sustained deceleration. The authors proposed that the simulated booms produced an alerting reaction and that the reduced HR reflected a state of heightened attention.

Laurell and Lisper (1976) measured HR and RT of young women in three experimental conditions: (1) driving a car on a closed 5-km track, (2) being driven as a passenger on the same track, and (3) sitting in a stationary car. Each condition lasted approximately 2 hours. While RT did not differentiate between the three conditions, there was a progressive slowing in RT as a function of time in the testing session. The slowing of RT was interpreted as resulting from drowsiness produced by monotony. The HR was generally higher in the driving and passenger conditions than in the stationary condition.

Heart Activity and Mental Performance

In this section, we consider heart activity and mental performance in situations where the task or task situation was not intended to be stressful or provoke an emotional reaction. The latter type of relationship will be examined in a subsequent section. This section focuses on the relationship between cardiac activity and verbal learning, problem solving, and cognitive activity (thoughts and imagery).

Verbal Learning

In one study of verbal learning, Andreassi (1966) investigated the relationship between HR, SCL, SCRs, and difficulty of materials to be learned. (The SCL and SCR findings were discussed in Chapter 9.) The mean HR was significantly higher when the subjects learned the easiest list than when they performed with lists of moderate or high difficulty. Thus, superior performance was related to elevated HR. The results suggested that during superior performance the individuals became more involved in the learning task, and this effect was reflected in the increased HR. A similar finding was reported by Malmo (1965), who found that HR was consistently higher during tracking trials where performance was better as compared to the poor performance trials.

Andreassi and Whalen (1967) reported that the HR of 15 college students was elevated during learning to criterion than it was during resting. When the same list was presented for 20 additional trials after original learning, HR showed a significant decrease. Finally, the requirement to learn a new list of materials produced a significant increase in HR. In a second experiment, these researchers asked 16 new subjects to learn a list of verbal materials to a criterion of perfect recitation. After this, the list was practiced for two sets of trials. The original learning was associated with an average increase in HR of from 79 to 87 bpm. The mean HR decreased to 83 bpm in the first overlearning session and to 81 bpm in the final set of 20 list repetitions. The decreased HR was interpreted in terms of an habituation of physiological responsivity when the individuals were no longer required to assimilate novel materials.

To briefly summarize, elevated HR occurs during the acquisition phase of verbal learning, especially if performance is successful. Continued repetition of familiar materials will produce a decrease in HR.

Problem Solving

Lacey has presented a theoretical framework that relates HR to a subject's interaction with his or her environment (e.g., Lacey et al., 1963; Lacey, 1967). According to this theoretical orientation, decreased HR during performance of a task is associated with increased sensitivity to stimulation and occurs when a situation requires mental intake of environmental stimuli. This theory further states that increased HR accompanies stimulus rejection or mental elaboration, as during the solution of a problem. Steele and Lewis (1968) found support for the second of these hypotheses. They measured HR of subjects in four age groups while the individuals solved problems involving mental arithmetic. The age groups were 6 to 8 years, 9 to 11, 12 to 15, and 16 to 27. They found an immediate acceleration in HR with each problem, which lasted for three cardiac cycles and then fell below resting levels. This was true for subjects in all age groups. The degree of cardiac acceleration did not vary as a function of age. Thus the results support the hypothesis that cardiac acceleration accompanies the mental elaboration involved in problem solving.

Goldstein et al. (1975) monitored HR and SCL continuously while 20 male undergraduates solved either seven riddles (humorous) or seven problems. One theory of humor (cognitive) suggests that humor is basically a problem-solving process, involving both a perception of and a resolution of certain features of the humor stimulus. Riddles were chosen for comparison with problems because they resemble them structurally; that is, they have a similar question (Q) and answer (A) format. The researchers tested the hypothesis that physiological arousal would occur during the Q portion of the riddle or problem and drop to the prestimulus level shortly after the punch line or answer is provided. The riddles were unsolvable because the subjects never heard them before, and the problems were also insoluble since the 3 seconds between Q and A was not sufficient time to allow solutions. A sample riddle used was: Q: "How can you tell an honest politician?" A: "When he's bought, he stays bought." A sample problem was: Q: "What is the least common multiple of 3, 8, 9 and 12?" A: "72." The results showed that cardiac activity did not differentiate between riddles and problems. Heart rate increased once a riddle or a problem was presented, and decelerated when the solution was given. However, for SCL there was a significant reduction for riddles from Q and A but not for problems. Thus, while heart rate did not differentiate between riddles and problems, SCL did. The SCL results led Goldstein et al. to doubt the underlying similarity of the riddle and problem-solving situations.

Imagery and Meditation

The question here concerns the effects of thoughts and images upon heart activity. Although common experience might tell us that thinking about certain activities can produce a physiological response, the verification of this intuitive notion is not simple. Suppose an experimenter asks a subject to imagine being fearful while HR is being measured? If a change is observed, the problem then arises concerning whether the physiological response results from the instruction to "image" or the imagery itself. Although there has not been much research in this area, the findings that have been obtained are suggestive. For example, Schwartz (1971) developed a procedure to obtain cardiac responses to specific internal (thought) stimuli in the absence of external stimuli. Upon the presentation of a tone, subjects were asked to think of a number sequence. The number sequence was followed by thoughts of letters (e.g., A, B, etc.) or of emotional words (e.g., rape, death). The subjects were asked to experience any thoughts that accompanied these letters or words. The results were that the 10 subjects (5 males, 5 females) had significantly higher HRs when thinking about emotional words than when thinking about letters. The data clearly indicated that different thought sequences can produce different cardiac responses.

A number of physiological responses were recorded while 36 subjects practiced transcendental meditation or TM, according to the method of the Marharishi Mahesh Yogi (Wallace & Benson, 1972). During meditation, HR slowed, SCL decreased, and EEG alpha activity increased, among other changes, and the subjects were described as being in a wakeful but very relaxed state. In fact, the investigators observed that the physiological changes during TM, a relatively easily learned technique, were very similar to those noted to occur in highly trained experts in yoga and in Zen monks, who have had 15 to 20 years of experience in meditation. These results led the authors to suggest that the possibilities for clinical application of this relaxing technique should be investigated.

Klinger et al. (1973) studied HR and other physiological variables while subjects engaged in a variety of tasks, including ones calling for imagining and concentration. In the imagery condition, subjects were asked to imagine a person they liked in eight separate 30-second trials. In the concentration condition, subjects were required to do moderately difficult mental tasks, for example, forming as many words as possible from the word "demonstrate." The authors found that the imagery task resulted in relatively low HR, while the task requiring concentration produced high HR. The results could be interpreted in support of Lacey et al.'s (1963) hypotheses that HR is low during perceptual activity and higher during cognitive activity.

In summary, the studies reviewed indicate that HR can be influenced by images and thoughts. There is much need for further work in this area to indicate the cardiac effects of various qualities and intensities of mental experience.

Heart Activity and Perception

This section examines cardiac correlates of perceptual thresholds and stimulus significance.

Perceptual Thresholds

Edwards and Alsip (1969) measured auditory thresholds under conditions designed to test Lacey et al.'s (1963) suggestion that lowered HR could lead to greater sensory sensitivity. Twenty-five tones (near threshold levels) were presented during high HR and 25 during periods of low HR. They found no difference in the number of correct detections under high and low HR. Saxon and Dahle (1971) measured auditory thresholds during periods of induced low and high HRs. The subjects exercised for 2.5 minutes and auditory thresholds were measured after 3 to 4 minutes of rest. These thresholds were compared with those obtained at resting HR levels. There was a mean increase of 18 bpm after exercise compared to the resting level. Detection thresholds were lower, that is, sensitivity was greater, at resting levels than after higher HR was induced. The researchers noted that in the Edwards and Alsip study the difference between low and high HR was only 13.8 bpm, perhaps accounting for the lack of a HR-threshold relationship observed. Saxon and Dahle interpreted their results in support of the Lacey et al. formulation.

Elliott and Graf (1972) tested the hypothesis that subjects would be most sensitive to visual stimuli during the P wave, and least during the QRS complex, of the cardiac cycle. They presented 25 subjects with 96 stimuli at four phases of the cardiac cycle: P, QRS, T, and T–P. No detection differences were found at any of these four phases. Velden and Juris (1975) also failed to find variations in perceptual performance with phases of the cardiac cycle. Their subjects were required to detect a 1000-Hz tone from a white noise background while heart activity was measured.

Although a relationship between sensory sensitivity and cardiac cycle has not been established, Schell and Catania (1975) have presented some evidence that a general cardiac deceleration is related to increased sensory acuity. Their 24 subjects were tested under conditions in which a warning signal preceded the threshold stimulus by a time sufficient to allow a cardiac response. Greater HR deceleration occurred when the threshold visual stimulus was detected than when it was not. The authors concluded that degree of sensitivity to the environment may be predicted by observing cardiac activity. Carriero and Fite (1977) also found superior perceptual performance related to cardiac deceleration. In their experiment, 10 subjects judged the relative positions of a black bar which was projected on a screen. They found that accurate judgments were accompanied by greater cardiac deceleration to stimulus onset than were inaccurate judgments. However, they noted that this relationship existed only during the first half of the experiment.

In summary, the suggested relationship between perceptual sensitivity and phase of the cardiac cycle does not seem to have been confirmed by research findings. However, there is some evidence that cardiac deceleration, in general, may be related to superior perceptual performance. These results are similar to those reported for RT and cardiac activity.

Stimulus Significance

The effects of a 1000-Hz tone (about 70 db) upon HR were studied by Keefe and Johnson (1970). They report a complex

HR response that consisted of an initial small deceleration followed by a more marked acceleration and then by another deceleration. A similar finding for a 1000-Hz tone (85 db) was reported by Graham and Slaby (1973), that is, a triphasic HR response of deceleration-acceleration-deceleration. However, for broad-band white noise (50–10,000 Hz at 85 db), a diphasic cardiac response was obtained, that is, acceleration followed by deceleration (see Fig. 11-5). The differential effects of these two types of auditory stimulation should be taken into account in studies of cardiac response to auditory stimulation.

Hatton et al. (1970) found that if sound intensity is high enough, rapid rise time produces HR acceleration which occurs within the first second of stimulus onset. However, if rise time is

Figure 11-5. HR change from prestimulus averaged over 10 presentations of 5-second, 85-db white noise of 1000-Hz tone ($N = 12$).

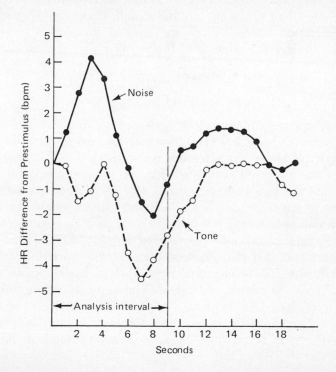

gradual, acceleration begins only after a 1- or 2-second delay, even with high intensities.

The heart responses of 38 female students to a high-speed dental drill were measured by Gang and Teft (1975). Sixteen of the persons tested were dental hygiene students, and 22 were liberal arts and science majors. The sound level of the dental drill ranged from 90 to 95 db. Cardiac accelerations were obtained to the sound of the dental drill, but they were most pronounced in those subjects who had unpleasant experiences in the dental office as a patient and who were not familiar with the high-speed drill. Those who had pleasant experiences in the dental office and were familiar with the drill had the smallest amount of HR acceleration. The authors concluded that the subjects were responding not only to the intensity of the stimulus but also to its meaning.

In summary, sound stimuli will result in HR changes. The responses to pure tones versus white noise appear to differ. The response to a meaningful stimulus (dental drill) tended to be greater than to nonmeaningful stimuli. However, the results are difficult to evaluate, since the level of stimulation (90–95 db) was greater than that used in the other two studies mentioned here.

Heart Activity, Attention, and the Orienting Response

Graham and Clifton (1966) reviewed the hypotheses of Sokolov (1963) and the Laceys (Lacey et al., 1963) regarding heart activity during the orienting response (OR). They noted that Sokolov proposed cardiac acceleration as the OR to novel stimuli, while the Laceys hypothesized HR deceleration as facilitating the reception of stimuli. Graham and Clifton reviewed a number of studies in which HR changes took place in response to weak and moderate stimuli and showed habituation over trials. They concluded that the OR was accompanied by HR deceleration and that HR acceleration most likely represented a "defense reaction" to stimuli of "prepain" intensity. Germana and Klein (1968) tested the hypothesis that the HR component of the OR is deceleration. They used three levels of auditory tone stimuli: 50 db, 70 db, and 90 db. If the Graham and Clifton hypothesis held true, then the OR to the 50-db tone would be deceleration, while the 70- and 90-db tones would produce a diphasic response, that is, acceleration-deceleration. Instead, acceleration-deceleration-acceleration was obtained for all stimulus levels. Thus, they concluded that the OR to a new stimulus appears to be an increase in HR.

Pursuing this question further, Raskin et al. (1969) found that an 80-db stimulus resulted in a brief HR deceleration, while one of 120 db produced HR acceleration (see Fig. 11-6). Thirty males received 30 presentations of .5 second white noise at each level of stimulation. The brief HR deceleration to the 80-db stimulus was interpreted as representing the OR, while it was concluded that the acceleration to the 120-db stimulus reflected a defensive reaction (DR). These results supported the Graham-Clifton formulation of the OR and DR. It should be noted that the 120-db noise was of far greater intensity than that used by Germana and Klein in their experiment. Also note that the HR

Figure 11-6. Beat-by-beat changes in mean PA, BC, and HR from prestimulus beat 3 produced by 30 presentations of the two stimulus intensities.

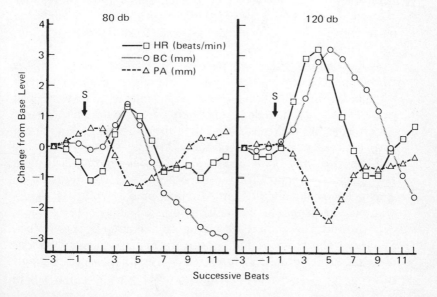

analysis in Figure 11-6 is based on beat-by-beat changes. The abbreviations PA and BC in Figure 11-6 stand for forehead-skin pulse amplitude and forehead-skin blood content, respectively.

Hare (1972) used slides of homicide victims to study HR response to unpleasant stimulation. Forty-nine college students participated in this experiment in which a beat-by-beat analysis of HR was performed. Hare reports three different groups of responders based on the HR data. One group of 9 subjects showed acceleration, 12 gave marked deceleration, while the remaining 28 persons produced moderate deceleration. The results support the contention that the OR consists of HR deceleration and that the DR consists of HR acceleration. However, the generalizability of the finding is somewhat limited as a result of the individual differences found. The result regarding individual differences was followed up by Hare (1973). In this study, he recorded HR of 10 females who feared spiders and compared them to 10 others who did not fear spiders. The 20 subjects viewed six spider slides and 24 slides of neutral objects, for example, landscapes. It was predicted that those persons who feared spiders would show a DR in the form of accelerated HR. The prediction was confirmed, since Hare reported that subjects with spider fears showed HR acceleration and those without showed deceleration, especially when they found the slides to be interesting. The two groups showed no differences with respect to the neutral slides.

Similar findings were reported by Hare and Blevings (1975), who found HR acceleration to slides depicting spiders with fearful subjects but HR deceleration with nonfearful persons. The results were also like those obtained by Klorman et al. (1975, 1976). Thus, it would seem that the type and intensity of stimuli used and the possible role of individual differences should be considered in studies of the OR and DR. There appears to be a fair amount of support for the hypotheses that HR deceleration is associated with the OR and stimulus intake, while HR acceleration accompanies the DR and stimulus rejection.

In a study of subjects listening to continuous verbal text, Spence et al. (1972) found a decrease in HR when individuals directed their attention to external stimuli. The 40 subjects listened to a taped psychoanalytic interview while HR was measured. Cardiac deceleration was associated with the main theme of the therapeutic interview, that is, references to termination of the patient's treatment. Although this experiment did not investigate the OR in terms of a reaction to a discrete stimulus, the general result is congruent with the notion that attention to external stimuli results in cardiac deceleration.

Heart Rate and Emotional Responses

Emotion, as considered here, will include HR changes that have been recorded in situations of stress, fear, and motivation.

Stress

Many studies have used electric shock as a stressful stimulus and have investigated cardiac activity in response to the shock itself or in anticipation of the shock. Elliott (1974) reviewed several studies that showed a decrease in HR just prior to the shock. However, he points out that this change was a phasic one; that is, it occurred in the few seconds before the stressful stimulus. Elliott observed that when one looks at the longer term (tonic) effects, say, over a period of minutes, HR increases occur under threat of an electric shock. An example of a short-term (phasic) decrease in HR is a result obtained by Obrist et al. (1969) in which deceleration took place in anticipation of a "very painful" electric shock. On the other hand, tonic acceleration was reported by Deane (1969), who told subjects that they would receive a shock at a specific point in a sequence of numbers. Interestingly, Deane's subjects showed increased HR at the beginning of the number series and a decrease just before and during the expected time of the shock.

Bankart and Elliott (1974) found that a large HR increase (about 20 bpm) occurs in a situation where a subject is waiting for the first shock to occur. This "first trial" effect habituates rapidly over subsequent trials. Elliott (1975) measured HR and eye blinks of 32 subjects who expected shocks at different probability levels. There was a 30-second countdown period in which the experimenter counted from 10 to 0. The shock probability varied among 0%, 50%, and 100%. Anticipation of a shock resulted in significantly higher HR than when no shock was expected. The cardiac response did not show evidence of habituation under the 50% and 100% probabilities, and there was no difference in HR under these two conditions. The "first trial" effect was again reported.

The effects of a real-life stress upon HR of 12-year-old females was studied by Shapiro (1975). An interesting aspect of Shapiro's experiment is that he compared the responses of 17 girls raised in a kibbutz with those of 19 other Israeli girls raised in an urban environment. The measures were taken as the girls received immunization injections. In addition to HR, three behavioral measures were taken: (1) a self-rating about fear of needles, (2) a self-rating regarding expected intensity of pain, and (3) ratings of reactions by a nurse in the injection area. The measures of HR were taken one day before the injection, at the time of the injection, and one week after. The lower HR for the kibbutz girls (mean of 72 bpm) as compared to the urban girls (79 bpm) corresponded with their behavioral measures, indicating a more relaxed attitude to needle penetration. Shapiro postulates that educational policies in the kibbutz, which emphasize the helpfulness of medical personnel, may have been responsible for the physiological and behavioral differences observed.

Another technique that has been used to produce stress involved the introduction of a demanding task for subjects to perform. Frankenhaeuser and Johansson (1976) had subjects perform three tasks of varying difficulty while they measured HR and epinephrine excretion. They found, as have previous investigators, that performance did not deteriorate much when the task became more demanding. However, physiological arousal did increase as a function of task difficulty; that is, both HR and epinephrine excretion increased. In addition, subjective ratings of distress increased with demanding tasks. The authors interpreted the results as showing the high physiological cost of adapting to stressful situations. In other words, our performance may not drop under stressful conditions, but we pay for this with increased bodily energy expenditure.

In summary, both phasic decreases and tonic increases in HR have been obtained in studies where the anticipation of an electric shock is a prominent component. These results are not contradictory but merely indicate momentary HR decreases just prior to the occurrence of the shock and a generally elevated HR over the extended course of an experimental session. Investigations into the effects of shock probability on cardiac response merely seem to indicate a relation between no shock (low HR) and shock (higher HR), rather than a systematic function dependent on probability levels. The experiment by Shapiro regarding a real-life stressful situation, and its differential effects on two social groups, is provocative and, hopefully, this type of research will be repeated in a variety of situations. Other real-life stress situations have revealed higher HR in naval pilots during takeoff and landing on aircraft carriers than during bombing runs (Roman et al., 1967), and elevated HR in physicians during stressful periods of daily life (Ira et al., 1963).

Emotional Reactions

This section briefly considers several studies that deal with various emotional reactions to stimulus situations. These emotional reactions are, in reality, defined by the experimental situation and may roughly be classified as fear, frustration, anger, and excitement. There is little doubt that HR will rise under the threat of shock or in an anger-producing situation (Elliott, 1974). Other studies of fear and frustration also indicate HR increases related to these feeling states. One of the difficult questions over the years, however, has been whether HR level will enable one to differentiate between emotional reactions, for example, fear and anger. In a classic experiment by Ax (1953), pulse rate and blood pressure showed greater increases in fear than in anger, among other differences. However, although this result suggested different patterns of physiological response in fear and anger, Elliott (1974) believes that the finding may be related to whether the subjects were more inclined to action by a fear of electrocution than they were by anger toward an insult. Elliott is of the opinion that the accumulated research has not shown HR to be useful in differentiating emotional states.

The effects of frustration on cardiac response were studied by Rule and Hewitt (1971). Subjects were asked to learn lists of verbal materials. During the learning sessions verbal reinforcement was provided by a peer. Three groups of 30 subjects each received either an easy list with neutral comments from their peers, a difficult list with neutral comments, or a difficult list with derogatory comments. This last condition was considered to be "highly thwarting" in that it involved both frustration and insult. The other two conditions were considered as being low or moderate in amount of "thwarting" and thus merely frustrating. The persons subjected to both frustration and insult did not differ in cardiac rate during the learning period, but when made aware of an opportunity to administer electric shock to their peers, in a role reversal, this "high-thwarted" group displayed elevated HR compared to the low and moderate groups. Thus the insulted subjects did not show HR increases over the other groups until given the opportunity to retaliate against their tormentors.

Klorman and his colleagues have conducted a series of studies in which HR measures were taken while subjects viewed fearful or neutral stimuli. In one study, Klorman (1974) identified 45 females who had a high fear of snakes. Measures of cardiac activity were obtained as they watched films of seascapes or snakes. The main finding was that the cardiac response habituated with repeated presentation of the feared stimuli. Habituation was reduced when high fear stimuli were introduced earlier. A second study by Klorman et al. (1975) categorized 32 female subjects as either high or low in fear of mutilation. The subjects viewed neutral (photographic poses), mutilation (burn and accident victims), and incongruous slides (e.g., a bald man with lemons attached to his ears) as HR was measured. The fearful subjects showed increased HR to mutilation slides, while the low-fear persons showed cardiac deceleration. Both groups responded to incongruous stimuli with HR deceleration. These results were interpreted as indicating defensive reactions in fearful individuals and orienting responses in the low-fear subjects.

The authors see these results as extending Hare's (1973) results with spider-fearful persons to those with a fear of mutilation. Similar results were obtained by Klorman et al. (1976), when mutilation slides produced cardiac acceleration in 13 fearful persons and lowered HR in 13 low-fear subjects. Neutral (standard photographs) and incongruous (e.g., a young woman with shaving cream on her face and an electric razor in her hand) resulted in HR decreases in additional samples of 13 high- and low-fear persons. The results support Hare's (1972) conclusion that individual differences in reaction to a supposed "fear" stimulus will determine whether HR acceleration or deceleration will occur.

In summary, there is suggestive evidence in the literature that frustration plus insult will lead to an increase in HR when the victim has a chance to retaliate. A series of investigations of reactions to "fearful" stimuli support the notion that HR will accelerate in persons who actually fear the stimulus and will decelerate in those who do not fear the "unpleasant" stimulus but instead find it morbidly interesting.

Motivation

Elliott (1974), on the basis of his own prior research, concluded that the effects of increasing the amount of an incentive (e.g., money) usually produced an increase in tonic HR during the performance of the relevant task (e.g., Elliott, 1969; Elliott et al., 1970). Evans (1971) reported that rivalry (a desire to win) caused significant increases in tonic HR, that is, HR measured over at least a 1-minute period. He interpreted this increase as indicating the incentive nature of competition. In a follow-up study, Evans (1972) measured HR of 64 men and 64 women while they participated in placing objects of different sizes and shapes into a form board. Half of the males and half of the females completed the task under competitive and noncompetitive conditions. The introduction of competition resulted in an average increase in HR of 10 bpm, regardless of resting HR level. Evans interpreted this result as supporting Elliott's work, indicating that incentive increases are accompanied by elevations in tonic HR.

Evans (1974) further pursued the question of competition effects on HR. He told 16 persons that their performance would be compared with other persons and gave another 16 subjects neutral instructions. Mean HR was recorded while the 32 subjects performed a series of four different forms of a digit-symbol substitution task. The mean HR associated with completion of the fourth form (trial) was used as the basal rate. Then subjects in the "social comparison" group were told that their performance on the next digit-symbol form would be compared with 25 other students who had the same amount of practice. Subjects in the control group were merely told that they would perform another digit-symbol task. The social comparison group showed a significant increase from 95 bpm on the fourth (basal) trial to 107 bpm during the critical trial. The control group showed an increase from 92 to 93 bpm. In addition, performance of the social comparison group improved significantly more than performance of the control subjects.

To summarize, it appears that increased incentive level can produce an elevation in cardiac rate. In addition, the introduction of competition may be inferred to have incentive or motivational effects, since it results in tonic HR acceleration. However, the possible roles of fear of failure or apprehension about comparisons, or individual reactions to rivalry, have not been delineated in HR studies that have used competition as an independent variable.

Conditioning of Heart Activity

A brief discussion of classical and operant conditioning procedures was presented in Chapter 9. In this section, we will consider some studies concerned with classical and instrumental conditioning of cardiac activity.

Classical Conditioning

It has long been known that ANS responses can be modified by classical conditioning. For example, Kimble (1961) mentions changes in GSR and respiration which were produced by the CS in various experiments, in addition to the well-known (e.g., Pavlov's dog) salivary response. Heart rate has also been classically conditioned, that is, a CS formerly paired with a pleasant (food) or unpleasant (electric shock) stimulus can produce a change in HR. For example, Notterman et al. (1952) measured HR in a classical conditioning situation and reported cardiac deceleration just before the onset of the UCS (shock). Obrist et al. (1969) also observed a conditioned HR deceleration that took place in the CS (light)-UCS (shock) interval. Although these studies indicate conditioned deceleration of HR, Van Egeren et al. (1972) obtained results that revealed individual HR differences in an aversive classical conditioning experiment. These investigators used two experimental paradigms in studying the cardiac responses of two groups of subjects during classical conditioning. The HR changes indicated three kinds of response during the CS–UCS interval: initial acceleration followed by deceleration, deceleration only, and initial deceleration followed by acceleration. The findings illustrate the importance of considering individual differences in experiments dealing with the conditioning of heart activity. Recall also that a previously mentioned study by Hare and Blevings (1975) showed HR acceleration in high-fear subjects prior to the UCS (spider slides).

The possible effects of respiration on concurrent HR changes during conditioning were examined by Headrick and Graham (1969). Three groups of 20 persons each were given conditioning trials as follows: respiration controlled at normal rates, controlled at fast rates, or uncontrolled. Significant HR responding occurred in all three groups during the CS (tone) UCS (electric shock) interval. There were three components to the HR response: deceleration immediately after the CS, followed by a brief acceleration, and a large deceleration just prior to the UCS. Thus, this study seems to rule out respiration effects in classical conditioning of HR. Obrist (1976) has offered explanations of anticipatory HR deceleration during the CS–UCS interval in terms of both behavioral and biological strategies. The behavioral approach explains the phenomenon as a function of stimulus parameters, for example, the effects of UCS intensity. The biological strategy explains the HR changes in terms of physiological interactions. For example, Obrist's data have indicated that HR deceleration is due to a momentary increase in vagal (parasympathetic) excitation which overrides sympathetic acceleratory effects.

Furedy and Poulos (1976) explored the possible use of body tilt as a UCS in conditioning a decrease of HR. In a first experiment, they established that tilting the body from a head-up

to a head-down position produced a mean cardiac deceleration
to less than 60 bpm by the ninth second after UCS onset. (The
duration of the tilt was 9 seconds, and 32 separate tilts were performed.) In a second experiment, Furedy and Poulos demonstrated that classical conditioning of HR deceleration could be
accomplished by using a tone as the CS and body tilt as the
UCS. This time 32 tilts were each performed .5 second after a
1.7 second duration tone. However, the 12 subjects produced a
mean conditioned deceleration of only 4 bpm. This was a small
conditioned response relative to the large unconditioned response of over 30 bpm in the first experiment. An encouraging
aspect of this study is that the classically conditioned cardiac
deceleration was obtained with a stimulus other than the often
used electric shock.

In summary, the classical conditioning of HR has been reported in a number of experiments. The most common UCS has
been electric shock, which has usually produced cardiac deceleration. The role of individual differences may explain variations
in cardiac patterning sometimes observed in the CS–UCS interval. The possible influence of respiratory variations on HR
changes seems to have been ruled out. Recent data have implicated vagal (parasympathetic) excitation in producing HR deceleration in the CS–UCS interval.

Instrumental Conditioning

The term "instrumental conditioning" is used here to refer to
changes in physiological activity that occur as a result of reinforcement. For example, an individual is provided with a continuous display of his heart activity and is reinforced when HR
rises above a certain level. The rise in HR is thus instrumental
in obtaining the reinforcement. The reinforcement may be the
achievement of a desirable event (e.g., monetary reward) or
the avoidance of something unpleasant (e.g., an electric shock).
The terms "instrumental" and "operant" conditioning will be
used interchangeably, although some workers in the field (e.g.,
Kimmel, 1973) prefer to use the word "operant" to refer to
unique instrumental conditioning procedures in which responses
are "emitted" independently of identifiable external stimuli. It

will be recalled that in the classical conditioning situation the reinforcement (UCS) is presented whether or not the subject makes a particular response.

For quite some time (from the late 1930s to the early 1960s), most investigators agreed that the modification of ANS responses by instrumental conditioning was not possible but that these same visceral responses were amenable to classical conditioning. Kimble (1961) reflected the thought of the time when he stated that "autonomic responses apparently cannot be instrumentally conditioned at all" (p. 108). However, some research findings have accumulated since then indicating that subjects may possibly learn to modify their HR and other autonomic responses in an instrumental conditioning paradigm. An important aspect is the provision of feedback, or knowledge of results, to the individual so that he or she knows that the desired response is being achieved (e.g., see Bergman & Johnson, 1972). Early demonstrations of instrumental conditioning of HR were provided by Shearn (1962) and Hnatiow and Lang (1965). Shearn (1962) used a conditioning paradigm in which HR increases postponed the delivery of an electric shock. The experimental subjects produced more HR accelerations over the five sessions as compared to control subjects. Shearn reported changes in respiration which, he suggested, could have mediated the HR change. However, after being alerted to this possible contaminating effect of respiration, experimenters have either monitored or controlled breathing in studies conducted since then. Hnatiow and Lang (1965) reported the successful stabilization of HR when subjects were instructed to keep their heart rates as steady as possible and were provided with a visual display of HR. Control subjects, who were provided with false feedback did not show a reduction in HR variability. Lang (1974) pointed out that the magnitude of HR control achieved in various studies has been modest, especially HR deceleration, and he attributes this partially to the difficulties in providing all the environmental controls necessary to perform instrumental conditioning studies with humans (e.g., subject isolation, powerful reinforcers). He also suggested that HR control is a type of skill learning, and some individuals are better at it than others.

The importance of individual differences in learning control of HR was underscored by McCanne and Sandman (1976) in an extensive review of operant HR conditioning. They suggested that individual differences in physiological responding occur during instrumental HR conditioning and that a study of these differences might help to understand how voluntary control is achieved over HR. They had earlier ruled out changes in respiration, muscle activity, and cardiac-somatic interaction (with the CNS as the control mechanism) as possible bases for operant control over HR. However, this is controversial, since critics have emphasized the difficulty of demonstrating HR changes without concurrent somatic changes, for example, respiration (Blanchard & Young, 1973; Katkin & Murray, 1968). Thus the student should be cautioned that this area is controversial and also rather unsettled in terms of comprehending the underlying mechanisms which allow instrumental control of HR. Examples of recent investigations into the possible instrumental control of HR, utilizing persons with normal cardiovascular function, will now be presented.

Wells (1973) provided 9 subjects with 13 sessions of learning to increase or decrease their HR. The subjects were also instructed in keeping respiratory rate at a steady level. Feedback of HR was provided by means of a meter in all but three sessions. The subjects spent one portion of each session in attempting to increase HR and another segment in decreasing it. The decrease-increase segments were counter-balanced. The subjects, who were selected on the basis of being highly motivated to do the task, were very successful at increasing HR. Six subjects produced HR increases ranging from 17 to 35 bpm. However, HR decrease was not as successful, with very small changes being observed. The greatest mean HR decrease for any person was 3 bpm.

The effects of varying incentive (monetary) on the voluntary control of HR speeding and slowing were investigated by Lang and Twentyman (1976). Fifty subjects received four HR control sessions over a 3- to 4-week period. The results showed that subjects can alter HR directionally and that performance was improved with monetary incentives. Frequent reinforcement, additional incentives and practice with feedback produced optimal HR change performance. The researchers postulate that the findings support an interpretation of HR feedback training as being similar to the learning of a psychomotor skill. This implication is stronger for HR speeding than for HR slowing, since only incentive altered slowing, while speeding was also influenced by other factors manipulated. Recently, Lang (1977) discussed the difficulty of demonstrating HR slowing, the small size of the effect, and its possible dependence on respiratory changes.

In summary, research on the instrumental conditioning of HR indicates that cardiac activity may be brought under some degree of voluntary control. It appears that increases are more easily attained than decreases. The exact mechanisms underlying this voluntary control are not known. Researchers have variously suggested that the HR changes are mediated by respiratory factors, by muscle activity, and by factors similar to those that influence the learning of a motor skill (e.g., practice with feedback, motivation, and frequent reinforcement). This area is controversial. However, the possibility of voluntary control over HR has important clinical implications, regardless of the source of this control. Clinical applications of biofeedback will be discussed in Chapter 14.

Research on the relationship between cardiac activity and behavior continues to occupy the time of many researchers. Many empirical findings and some interesting concepts have stemmed from these studies, for example, those of the Laceys and Obrist and colleagues, which will be discussed more fully in Chapter 15. Chapter 12 discusses two physiological measures, blood pressure and blood volume, and their relation to behavior.

Blood Pressure, Blood Volume, and Behavior

This chapter examines two physiological measures, blood pressure and blood volume. Blood pressure (BP) indicates the amount of force exerted by the blood on a blood vessel. Blood volume (BV) refers to the amount of blood present in a certain portion of body tissue. The blood pressure and blood volume responses, and their relation to behavior, will be presented after a brief discussion of the anatomy and physiology of these measures.

Anatomy and Physiology of the Blood Vessels

Blood vessels may be divided into several categories on the basis of their size, function, and microscopic characteristics. These categories include the large elastic arteries, medium-sized muscular arteries, small arteries (arterioles), capillaries, and veins (Jacob & Francone, 1970). The blood vessels are composed of three layers: an inner tunica intima, a middle tunica media, and an outer tunica adventitia. Table 12-1 outlines the structures of these various kinds of blood vessels. Figure 12-1 illustrates the structural layers of arteries and veins.

Basically, the arteries are tubes with thick walls, branching out from the aorta to carry blood to all parts of the body. Arteries are made up of smooth muscle fibers and elastic membrane tissue. This gives them an elastic property, enabling them to stretch when pressure is applied and then readily return to

Table 12-1 Structure of Blood Vessels

Vessel	Outer Layer: Tunica Adventitia	Middle Layer: Tunica Media	Inner Layer: Tunica Intima
Large arteries (elastic)	Thick layer, consisting of connective tissue	Layer consists largely of elastic fibers with some muscle	Thin endothelial cells resting on connective tissue
Muscular arteries (medium)	Thick layer, consisting of connective tissue	Fewer elastic fibers, more smooth muscle	Thin endothelial cells resting on connective tissue
Small arteries (arterioles)	Thin	Consists of muscular tissue	Layer composed almost entirely of endothelium
Capillaries	Absent	Absent	Endothelial layer, one cell thick
Veins	Thin layer	Thinner, little muscle or elastic tissue	Endothelial lining with scant connective tissue

Source: Taken from S. W. Jacob and C. A. Francone, *Structure and function in man* (2nd ed.). Philadelphia: W. B. Saunders, 1970.

normal when pressure is relaxed. The arterioles are the smallest arteries in the body. They enable blood to enter capillary beds (Guyton, 1977). The capillaries are tiny vessels, one cell layer thick (about 10 μ), which allow the actual exchange of carbon dioxide and oxygen in the lungs and of nutrients and wastes in body tissues. The blood leaves the capillary beds by small venules, which form into small veins and eventually into larger veins, which carry blood back to the heart. Veins are not as muscular as arteries and have valves that prevent the backflow of blood.

Innervation of Blood Vessels

All the blood vessels of the body, except the capillaries, are innervated by nerve fibers from the SNS alone (Guyton, 1977).

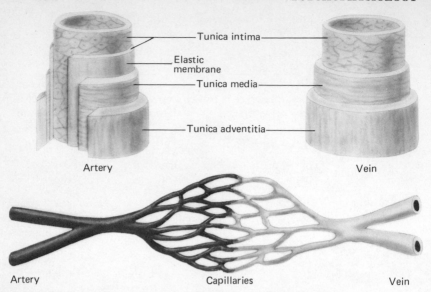

Figure 12-1. Component parts of arteries and veins.

The SNS produces varying degrees of constriction of the blood vessels. This is controlled via the vasomotor center, which is located in the reticular substance of the brain (lower pons and upper medulla). The hypothalamus of the brain can exert powerful inhibitory or excitatory effects on the vasomotor center. Cortical effects have not been as well defined.

The vasomotor center maintains what is called sympathetic vasoconstrictor tone, which is essential in keeping arterial blood pressure at an appropriate functioning level. Normal sympathetic tone keeps almost all the blood vessels of the body constricted to about half of maximum diameter. With increased SNS activity vessels can be further constricted. On the other hand, by inhibiting the normal tone, blood vessels can be dilated. Thus, normal sympathetic tone allows both vasoconstriction and vasodilation of blood vessels. The PNS exerts no direct influence over the peripheral blood vessels (Gardner, 1975). The sympathetic vasoconstrictor substance is norepinpephrine, which acts upon the smooth muscle tissue of blood vessels.

Regulation of Blood Pressure

Jacob and Francone (1970) list five factors that function to maintain arterial blood pressure:

1. *Cardiac factor*—This refers to the volume of blood expelled each time the left ventricle contracts.
2. *Peripheral resistance*—This is produced primarily by the arterioles, which vary their diameter over a wide range.
3. *Blood volume*—Blood volume refers here to the relatively constant volume of blood cells and plasma within the whole circulatory system. If blood volume is low, then blood pressure is reduced.
4. *Viscosity*—Increased viscosity of blood causes a greater resistance to flow and, therefore, a higher arterial pressure. If blood hematocrit[1] increases, so does the friction between successive layers of blood, and viscosity increases drastically. The hematocrit value of a normal man is about 42, while that of a normal woman is about 38 (Guyton, 1977).
5. *Elasticity of arterial walls*—When elasticity of the larger arteries decreases, systolic pressure rises. Systolic blood pressure refers to the pressure exerted on arterial walls during ventricular systole (contraction), while diastolic pressure is related to ventricular diastole.

Stretch receptors (baroreceptors) in the carotid sinuses and in the aorta transmit signals to the vasomotor system of the brain stem according to arterial pressure. The baroreceptors are not stimulated by pressures between 0 and 60 mm Hg, but above this level they progressively increase their firing rate until a maximum is reached at about 180 mm Hg. (Guyton, 1977). If blood pressure becomes elevated, reflex signals from the vasomotor center slow the heart and dilate the blood vessels. Thus, stimulation of baroreceptors by pressure in the arteries reflexly causes arterial pressure to decrease, while low pressure produces the opposite effect, that is, pressure is reflexly caused to rise back toward normal. While the baroreceptor reflex is important in regulating moment-to-moment changes in arterial pressure, it is

---

[1] Blood is composed of cells and plasma. The hematocrit refers to the percentage of blood that is composed of cells. Thus, if a person has a hematocrit reading of 42, it means that 42% of the blood volume is cells and 58% is plasma.

unimportant in the long-term control of blood pressure since the baroreceptors adapt in 1 or 2 days to a given pressure level.

Blood pressure varies within the cardiac cycle, for example, it rises sharply with ventricular systole. Blood pressure level also changes from beat to beat, posing difficulties in measurement (e.g., see Tursky et al., 1972).

Regulation of Blood Volume

The normal adult has a blood volume of approximately 5000 ml (5 liters). This figure varies with such factors as age, sex, build, race, environment, and disease (Grollman, 1964). In this chapter, we are interested in examining changes in blood volume that occur in the performance of various mental and physical tasks. That is, shifts in the blood volume of various body parts that occur in different kinds of activities. These shifts in blood volume are dependent upon the arterial blood flow into an area and the venous outflow from an area. Therefore, those factors mentioned earlier with respect to vasoconstriction or vasodilation of blood vessels (e.g., SNS activity, baroreceptor reflex) are also of importance in regulating blood volume. There is also a reflex for the control of blood volume (Guyton, 1977). For example, if blood volume of the body increases, stretch receptors in the atria and large veins transmit signals to the vasomotor center. Reflex signals involving both the vasomotor center and the hypothalamus then cause the kidneys to increase their fluid output, thus reducing total body fluid and blood volume.

Measurement of Blood Pressure

The methods we will describe for the measurement of blood pressure are known as indirect techniques. The true measurement of blood pressure can only be achieved by penetrating an artery to insert a sensing device. This direct measurement technique is not indicated in the laboratory with human subjects because of possible medical complications and the need for sterile conditions.

The most familiar blood pressure measuring technique involves the use of a sphygmomanometer (from the Greek word *sphygmos*, meaning "pulse"). The method involves the use of a pressure cuff, a rubber bulb, a mercury manometer, and a stethoscope. The pressure cuff is wrapped around the upper arm and inflated to a level well above the expected systolic pressure (say, 200 mm Hg). The stethoscope, which has been placed on the brachial artery, picks up no sound at this level, since the artery has been collapsed by the cuff pressure. The cuff pressure is then gradually reduced, until sounds are heard. The sounds are produced by small amounts of blood passing through the cuff and are called Korotkoff sounds, after the man who first used this method. The pressure on the manometer is noted when the first sound is heard. This is taken as the systolic pressure and, for a normal adult, ranges between 95 and 140 mm Hg, with 120 mm Hg being average (Cromwell et al., 1976). The pressure in the cuff is then reduced further, until the sounds are no longer heard. When the sounds disappear, the manometer is again noted and taken as diastolic pressure. Normal diastolic pressure ranges between 60 and 90 mm Hg for the adult. This technique is termed the auscultatory method of obtaining blood pressure and is adequate for the physician who is mainly concerned that his patients fall within a normal range for their age. However, for psychophysiological research, it is necessary to have automated, accurate techniques that enable continuous measurements of blood pressure.

Tursky (1974) has pointed out that the auscultatory method leads to an underestimate of systolic blood pressure. This is because the pressure in the cuff must be lower than that in the artery in order for the Korotkoff sound to be heard. A problem also exists in measuring diastolic pressure by this means, because it also depends on changes in sound. Tursky et al. (1972) developed an automated constant-cuff pressure system to overcome this error of measurement. This technique determines the relationship between a fixed-cuff pressure and arterial pressure at each heartbeat. The presence and absence of the Korotkoff sound is then used to establish a median (average) pressure. The system was tested on a patient who had arterial pressure recorded directly from the brachial artery of the left arm while median systolic pressures were obtained from the right arm with the constant-cuff procedure. Measures on five sets of 32 beats showed a close correspondence in systolic pressure obtained with each method (all comparisons were less than 2 mm Hg apart). Steptoe et al. (1976) described an adaptation of a technique for measuring pulse wave velocity (PWV) in which the interval between the R wave of the ECG and radial pulse pressure is obtained. The resulting transit time is used as an indirect measure of blood pressure change. Test trials indicated a high relation between transit time (PWV) and mean blood pressure measured directly from an artery.

Another automated device, which uses ultrasound to measure movements of the brachial artery, has been described by Cromwell et al. (1976). The principle used is similar to sonar in that high-frequency sound is directed at the artery and reflected. Changes in the sound produced as the artery expands and contracts are detected (Doppler shift)[2] and translated into blood pressure. That is, the Doppler signals clearly identify the opening (diastole) and closing (systole) of the artery as the cuff pressure decreases. These sounds are analogous to the Korotkoff sounds and allow continuous measures of systolic and diastolic pressures.

Gunn et al. (1972) briefly describe a portable device for the automatic measurement of blood pressure. A cuff is inflated on a programmed schedule and records systolic and diastolic pressure on a miniature tape recorder. The instrument can be worn by a freely moving person and enables the continuous recording of blood pressure (up to 10 hours) as he goes about his daily activities.

Measurement of Blood Volume

Brown (1967) points out that plethysmography is a term used to describe various techniques of measuring blood volume changes in a limb or segment of tissue. The term is derived from the Greek *plethysmos,* which means "an enlargement." Three basic types of devices for recording blood volume changes are described by Brown (1967):

[2] The Doppler shift refers to changes in pitch as an object moves toward or away from a listener.

1. *Hydraulic or pneumatic systems,* in which fluids or air detect a volume change in an observed part and transmit this to a recording device.
2. *Electrical impedance,* which reflects changes in impedance by tissue to the passage of high-frequency alternating current, as a function of volume change.
3. *Photoelectric transducers,* which measure changes in the intensity of a light passed through a tissue segment, for example, a fingertip or an earlobe. The intensity varies as a function of the amount of blood in the tissue from moment to moment. It should be noted that photoelectric techniques do not reflect absolute blood volume but only changes within a given person. Comparisons across subjects cannot be made.

Photoelectric devices to measure blood volume changes have been described by Tursky and Greenblatt (1967) and Lee et al. (1975). The device described by Tursky and Greenblatt involves the use of a pair of fiberoptic light guides. One guide is connected to a regulated light source which transmits light to the skin, and a second, attached to a photocell, records changes in reflected light corresponding to volume changes. Lee et al. (1975) use a reflective transducer which combines an infrared light-emitting diode (LED) and a silicon phototransistor. This device can be applied to almost any area of the body to measure changes in vascular activity (see also Tahmoush et al., 1976).

Cook (1974) points out that there are two elements of plethysmographic change that can be measured. These are the relatively slow engorgement of an area, just described as blood volume, and a rapid component referred to as pulse volume or pulse amplitude. Pulse volume represents the pumping action of the heart as represented in local blood vessels. Blood volume and pulse volume can be measured with the same photoplethysmographic device, using different coupling and gain settings, on separate channels of a recorder. Blood volume measurements obtained with a photoplethysmograph require dc coupling and low gain, while pulse amplitude requires ac coupling at high gain.

Figure 12-2 shows sample traces of blood volume, pulse amplitude, and blood flow. The tracings show that all the meas-

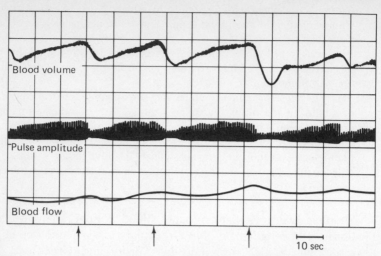

Figure 12-2. Blood volume, pulse amplitude, and blood flow responses from the finger to a 95-db, 1000-Hz tone. Arrows mark the onset of stimulus presentation.

ures are sensitive to an environmental stimulus; in this case a 95-db tone presented binaurally.

A vaginal photoplethysmograph has been developed (see Geer et al., 1974; Sintchak & Geer, 1975) for measuring changes in vaginal blood volume. This device, in addition to a penile strain gauge, was used by Heiman (1977) in a study on sexual arousal patterns in males and females. Briefly, the vaginal device is a hollow cylinder, 1¾ in. long and ½ in. in diameter, and houses a small lamp and a photocell. It is inserted into the vagina, and the indirect light reflected back to the photocell from the vaginal wall is measured. The amount of reflected light varies with changes in vaginal vasoconstriction.

The penile strain gauge fits around the shaft of the penis, near the coronal ridge, and measures changes that occur with erection or return to normal size. Laws and Bow (1976) describe a penile strain gauge of this type in detail. Figure 12-3 illustrates some data obtained by Laws and Bow from a single subject during the viewing of a 3-minute segment of pornographic film. De-

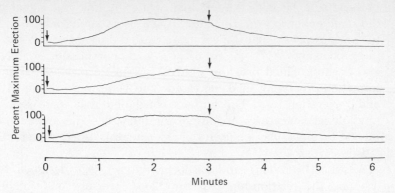

Figure 12-3. Sample polygraph tracings showing measurement characteristics of penile transducer. Arrows indicate onset and offset of 3-minute film segments.

picted are the course of penile erection from zero to maximum and the return to baseline.

Blood Pressure and Behavior

In this segment, we examine a number of studies that have employed blood pressure as one of the physiological variables in studies relating to human behavior. The studies to be briefly reviewed fall into the following categories: mental activity and blood pressure, blood pressure and emotional behavior, and conditioning of blood pressure.

Mental Activity and Blood Pressure

The relationship between a number of physiological variables and "mental load" was investigated by Ettema and Zielhuis (1971). The physiological measures included blood pressure, HR, and respiration rate. The researchers manipulated mental load by varying the amount of information processed by subjects in a given period of time. High and low tones were presented over earphones in a random sequence. The high tone required pressing a pedal with the left foot, while the low tone signaled the same action by the right foot. Each of 24 young adults had the various physiological measures recorded during rest and during processing of 20, 30, 40, or 50 signals per minute. Systolic and diastolic blood pressure showed systematic increases as information-processing load increased. The same was true for HR and respiration rate. The authors concluded that increases in physiological measures are useful for indicating the amount of mental load and may be useful in assessing this aspect of various jobs in industry.

A study by Wilkie and Eisdorfer (1971) was designed to examine the relationship between blood pressure and intelligence test scores (WAIS) of elderly persons. They hypothesized that intellectual decline over time would be related to elevated blood pressure. The subject sample included 207 persons, initially aged 60 to 79 (mean of 69), 87 of whom completed the follow-up study 10 years later. Diastolic blood pressure was used as the measure. Elevated diastolic pressure was found to be related to significant intellectual loss among individuals initially examined in their sixties. Their age peers, with normal or mild elevations of blood pressure, showed no loss. None of the hypertensive persons initially examined at 70 to 79 years of age completed the follow-up, while those with normal and mildly elevated blood pressure showed some intellectual decline over the 10-year period. The authors suggest that intellectual decline associated with aging might be related to some disorder, such as elevated blood pressure, and is not merely a part of the "normal" aging process.

Emotional Reactions and Blood Pressure

It has been reported that both frustration and attack produced an increased level of diastolic and systolic blood pressure (Gentry, 1970). In that study, 30 males and 30 females were subjected to frustration (interrupted and not allowed to complete an intelligence test) attack (personal insults by an experimenter), or control conditions. A sex difference was found in that males generally had greater increases in systolic pressure than did females, with no differences noted for diastolic changes. Sex differences in response to 1 minute of painful electric shock were found by Liberson and Liberson (1975). Eighteen male and 18 female subjects (ranging in age from 23 to 55) had blood pressure, respiration, and HR measured just prior to, and immediately after, the painful stimulus. The males responded to the shock with a significant increase in systolic blood pressure, while females had significant increases in respiration rate. The authors postulate that if stress affects the cardiovascular system to a greater degree in men than in women, this could be a contributing factor to a higher rate of heart disease in men.

Doob and Kirshenbaum (1973) measured blood pressure and digit-symbol performance in four groups of 10 persons each, after they were subjected to various combinations of frustration and aggression. The blood pressure and digit-symbol performance were recorded both before and after the following conditions: (1) not frustrated, viewed neutral film; (2) not frustrated, viewed aggressive film; (3) frustrated, viewed neutral film; (4) frustrated, viewed aggressive film. Persons in Group 4 showed the greatest increase in systolic blood pressure from the first to second reading; those in Groups 2 and 3 showed a small increase; and individuals in Group 1 had slight decreases. The authors interpret the results as contrary to the idea that movies depicting aggression are tension-reducing for either frustrated or nonfrustrated persons; rather, the effects of frustration and aggression seem to be additive in terms of arousal level.

Along similar lines, Geen and Stonner (1974) found that subjects who were given electric shocks, and who then viewed an aggressive film about revenge, showed higher BP levels at the conclusion of the film than did persons who were not shocked and who were told that the theme of the identical film was either altruism or professionalism. Geen and Stonner suggest that the meaning attached to observed violence affects aggression by lowering inhibitions against aggressiveness and by raising arousal levels. Geen (1975) followed this study with another in which the effects of being shocked and viewing "real" violence were compared with neutral treatment and observing a film of "fictional" violence. The combination of prior shock (attack) and observation of real violence produced the highest levels of BP. This and the prior study indicated to Geen that the observation of violence facilitated the expression of aggression by raising the viewer's level of emotional arousal.

To summarize, it would appear that changes in blood pressure occur in laboratory situations where subjects are frustrated or threatened with electric shock. The combination of being attacked or frustrated and viewing an aggressive film seems to result in reliable increases in BP. The idea that the observation of violence facilitates aggressive activity by raising level of physiological arousal is an interesting one that should be explored further.

Conditioning of Blood Pressure

Much of the basic research on changing BP levels through instrumental conditioning has been motivated by the possible development of a technique for the treatment of patients who suffer from essential hypertension. This disorder is one of elevated blood pressure without a demonstrable cause and is implicated in heart disease and strokes. In this segment, we will consider attempts to instrumentally condition blood pressure level in normal subjects, while in the chapter on biofeedback the use of this technique with hypertensive patients will be considered.

The pioneering work of DiCara and Miller (1968), in which instrumental conditioning of blood pressure of rats was attempted, has prompted other researchers to try a similar approach with humans. For example, Shapiro et al. (1969) provided 20 normal male subjects with information (feedback) about their systolic pressure and reinforced half of them for decreasing it and the other half for increasing it. They developed an application of the auscultatory technique to provide automatic feedback of systolic pressure at each successive heartbeat, that is, feedback regarding upward or downward changes in pressure was given with each beat. Short duration lights and tones signaled blood pressure which was in the right direction. After every 20 signals of this type, the subjects received a reinforcement. The reinforcer was a nude centerfold from the pages of *Playboy* magazine, projected on a screen for 5 seconds. The results indicated that systolic blood pressure can be modified by external feedback and operant reinforcement. This occurred in a single session consisting of 25 trials.

In a follow-up study, Shapiro et al. (1970) found that the changes in blood pressure levels were independent of HR. Shapiro et al. (1972) extended their findings to diastolic pressure in another study of instrumental conditioning in 20 normal males. This time the reinforcers consisted of slides of landscapes, slides of nude women, and money. Measures of HR and respiration were also obtained. The group reinforced for pressure increases had a mean diastolic pressure difference of 7.0 mm Hg (10% of baseline level) as compared to the decrease group (up increased 4 mm Hg, down decreased 3 mm Hg). Respiration patterns were similar in the two groups, ruling out breathing rate as a possible influence. However, HR was slightly influenced when diastolic blood pressure was reinforced. Further analysis showed that this was due to coincidental reinforcement of HR, since HR effects did not persist on trials without feedback and reward. The authors expressed encouragement about the possible application of this technique to hypertensive patients, especially in view of the relatively brief (25 or 35 minutes) training periods used in the studies.

The work of Shapiro and colleagues has been criticized by Blanchard and Young (1973) for using different feedback modes (visual and auditory) and reinforcers (slides and monetary rewards). They also criticize the lack of a no-feedback control group. These criticisms were addressed in a study by Fey and Lindholm (1975), in which two groups of normal subjects received feedback contingent on either increases or decreases in systolic pressure, and two other groups received either noncontingent feedback or no feedback at all. The subjects all participated in three 1-hour experimental sessions over a 3-day period. Progressive, and significant declines in systolic pressure were obtained by the decrease group over the 3-day period. No systematic changes were observed in the other three groups. The authors pointed out that visual feedback alone seemed to be as effective as the feedback-reinforcer combination previously used in the instrumental conditioning of blood pressure. They concluded that contingent feedback is effective in lowering blood pressure and that ability to do this is improved with practice over a few days.

To summarize this section we might conclude that modest, but consistent, decreases in blood pressure have been instrumentally conditioned in a number of studies. These results were achieved with normal persons. The possible extension of this type of conditioning to individuals suffering from essential hypertension could have important implications for the treatment of this disorder.

Blood Volume and Behavior

The studies in this section fall into three main categories. These are (1) blood volume and sexual response; (2) orienting responses and blood volume; and (3) conditioning of blood volume responses.

Blood Volume and Sexual Response

The measurement of genital blood volume has become an increasingly important method of studying sexual behavior and preferences over the past several years. As Geer (1975) has observed, nongenital measures have not proven as useful in sex research as have genital ones. Zuckerman (1972) examined the use of various physiological measures in studying human sexual response and noted that EDA, HR, respiration, and pupillary diameter did not appear to be sensitive to arousal produced by sexual stimuli or to accurately reflect sexual preferences. Blood pressure, however, did show a graded response to erotic stimuli. Zuckerman concluded that penile erection measures have proven to be the most sensitive indexes of sexual arousal in the male and have differentiated between preferred and nonpreferred sexual objects.

In recent years, the work of researchers such as Geer and his associates has resulted in the development of more satisfactory devices for the measurement of genital blood volume in the female (Geer, et al., 1974; Sintchak & Geer, 1975). Geer and his colleagues have also been responsible for much of the contemporary research that has used genital measures, in both males and females, to study sexual responsivity (e.g., Geer & Quartararo, 1976; Heiman, 1977). Let us now review some of the more recent studies in this field.

McConaghy (1974) measured changes in penile blood volume of 12 medical students as they viewed moving and still pictures of female and male nudes. The penile volume increases to moving pictures of nude women were greater than those to still pictures. The penile volume tended to decrease to moving and still pictures of nude males.

Geer and his coauthors (1974) describe the use of a vaginal blood measurement device, which could be inserted by subjects in privacy. They used this device to measure vaginal blood volume and pulse volume during the presentation of erotic and nonerotic films to 20 female college students. Two female experimenters described the research to subjects in detail during the first session. In the second session, the subjects inserted the vaginal probe and after a 3-minute rest period viewed the two films. The erotic film was 8 minutes in duration and showed a young man and woman engaged in foreplay, oral-genital sex, and intercourse. The 8-minute nonerotic film depicted scenes of battles and court life during the time of the Crusades. Both blood volume and pulse volume were significantly higher during viewing of the erotic film than during the nonerotic film. This led the authors to conclude that they had developed an instrument which could detect sexual arousal in women.

Geer (1974) described a procedure used in his laboratory in which young men and women were asked to imagine an arousing sexual scene while they were alone in a private, comfortable room. Measures of penile volume and vaginal pulse volume were made in the room without observers and with no erotic stimuli present. After 2 to 3 minutes, increases in the size of the penis and elevated vaginal pulse volume were observed. A postrecording questionnaire indicated that the subjects were sexually aroused by their fantasies. Thus, Geer concluded, it is apparent that cognitive factors influence sexual arousal.

In another study, Geer and Quartararo (1976) measured vaginal blood volume and pulse volume as seven adult women (aged 19 to 35) masturbated to orgasm. Pulse volume increased greatly during masturbation and postorgasm periods over baseline levels. However, while blood volume increased during masturbation and postorgasm, it decreased dramatically at the onset and during orgasm. The researchers postulated that the drop in blood

volume during orgasm reflects SNS activity. This is consistent
with the model of sexual activity which proposes that sexual
arousal is controlled by the PNS, while orgasm is under SNS
influence.

Heiman (1977) compared the sexual arousal of males and females, using a combination of genital and subjective measures.
In Heiman's study, 59 female and 39 male undergraduates completed three sessions during which genital blood volume and
pulse volume were measured. The subjects listened to various
kinds of tapes which were: erotic, erotic-romantic, romantic, or
control (contained neither erotic nor romantic materials). A
2-minute subject-generated fantasy preceded and followed each
tape. The main findings were that (1) erotic and erotic-romantic
contents resulted in similar increases in genital pulse amplitude
and blood volume in both sexes, (2) there was high agreement
between subjective ratings of sexual arousal and the genital
measures, and (3) individuals became aroused during sexual
fantasy.

In summary, a number of recent studies that have used measures of genital blood volume or pulse volume indicate genital responses to sexual stimuli, sexual activity, subjective sexual
arousal, and sexual fantasy. The genital response is apparently
more sensitive to sexual arousal than other physiological measures because it is directly involved in the various sexual behaviors.

Blood Volume and the Orienting Reflex

Changes in blood volume form an important part of the orienting
response as described by Sokolov (1963). Sokolov reported increases in forehead blood volume with novel or unexpected stimuli and decreases when stimuli were painful or threatening. According to Sokolov, increases in cephalic blood volume reflect
the orienting response (OR), and the OR leads to improved
perceptual ability. Conversely, decreases in blood volume reflect
a defensive response (DR) which protects the organism by making it less sensitive to threatening or painful stimuli. The OR is
said to habituate with continued stimulus presentation, and the
DR is said to be immune to this effect. While Sokolov's theory

still remains to be established, it has been found that blood volume changes occur in various parts of the body as a result of unexpected or novel stimuli.

The orienting response and its speed of habituation were investigated by Levander et al. (1974). Nineteen young male subjects were presented with a series of 100-db tones (1-second duration) at intervals varying between 35 and 60 seconds. Decreases in finger blood volume and pulse volume were used as the physiological measures of the OR. Both responses were relatively large with the presentation of the first tone, and both habituated (i.e., decreased in response amplitude) as a function of additional tone presentations. The researchers noted that the pulse volume responses habituated faster than the blood volume responses, suggesting a degree of independence between these measures.

The effects of stimulus repetition on habituation of the OR was also studied by Ginsberg and Furedy (1974). They measured finger blood volume and pulse volume of 20 subjects who listened to a series of 80-db tones. They found that pulse volume responses habituated to the repetitive stimulation, but blood volume did not.

The effects of stimulus intensity and rise time on the OR were tested by Oster et al. (1975). They used tones of 70 and 90 db, with fast (10 μsec) and slow (100 msec) rise times. Sixty subjects had blood volume responses recorded from the head (temporal artery) and finger. As Sokolov predicted, head (cephalic) blood volume shifted from dilation to constriction with increased sound intensity. However, the constriction response habituated, thus not meeting one of Sokolov's criteria for a DR. Completely different types of stimuli and procedures were used by Hare (1973) in assessing blood volume as an indicator of the orienting and defensive responses. The subjects were 20 young females, 10 of whom feared spiders and 10 who did not. The fearful group responded with decreased forehead blood volume to pictures of spiders, while the nonfearful group had the opposite response. The vasoconstriction would indicate the DR, while the vasodilation would suggest the OR, thus providing results in line with Sokolov's theory.

In summary, blood volume and pulse volume appear to change

with the introduction of new or unexpected stimuli. With regard to blood volume responses, some of the research findings partially support Sokolov's theory regarding the relation between cephalic vasoconstriction and vasodilation and the DR and OR, respectively. Differences between habituation rate of the blood volume and pulse volume responses may indicate a partial physiological independence of these two measures.

Conditioning of Blood Volume

Conditioning of the vasomotor response has been reported with both classical and instrumental approaches. For example, Shean (1968) produced a classically conditioned finger blood volume decrease in a situation where the CS was the word "boat" and the UCS was an electric shock. Acquisition and extinction of the vasoconstriction response was observed in all the subjects who later indicated they were aware of the relationship between the CS and UCS.

Blood volume changes have also been instrumentally conditioned. For example, Christie and Kotses (1973) found that cephalic (head) blood volume could be brought under stimulus control in eight subjects who participated in six separate sessions. A photoplethysmographic device was positioned over the temporal artery of the head to detect blood volume changes. Four of the subjects received feedback and reinforcement for vasodilation, while the other four were conditioned to produce vasoconstriction. The four persons reinforced for vasodilation showed this response in the period during which the reinforcement was available, while the other four reliably produced vasoconstriction. The authors suggested the further investigation of this technique for possible use in the treatment of migraine headache, since this disorder has been linked to vasodilation of cephalic arteries.

The next two chapters consider practical applications of physiological measures. Chapter 13 is concerned with a number of diverse applications ranging from lie detection to attempts at better understanding of behavior disorders. Chapter 14 presents applications of biofeedback in various clinical situations.

Applications of Physiological Measures to Practical Problems

The basic question addressed in this chapter is: "How can the measurement of physiological responses help in the solution of practical problems?" In order to answer this question, we will examine a number of research studies in a variety of areas. The main difference between the studies to be described in this chapter and those in earlier ones is that applied research is generally performed in order to provide a solution to an immediate problem. This is not to say that basic research, that is, research accomplished with no particular application in mind, is not of practical value. It is often the case that basic research leads to applications of techniques and information which are very useful, and many times basic and applied studies support and complement one another.

The applications that we will consider are concerned with lie detection, sensory system testing, mental retardation, nervous system disorders, behavior disorders, and vigilance.

Detection of Deception

The use of physiological measures to determine when an individual is lying has a long history. Woodworth and Schlosberg (1954) observed that the principle of SNS discharge (arousal) and its effects on salivary secretion[1] was supposedly used by primitive people in lie detection. The unfortunate suspect was given dry

[1] SNS effects include a reduction and thickening of saliva flow.

rice to eat and the fear involved in lying presumably interfered with salivation. Obviously, a guilty person would not be able to swallow the rice!

About 70 years ago, Munsterberg (1908), in his book *On the Witness Stand,* suggested that measures of emotional reactions such as respiration, heart rate, blood volume, and changes in skin conductance should be investigated as possible aids in distinguishing between the innocent and the guilty suspect. He recommended caution in the use of this approach, since "the innocent man, especially the nervous man, may grow as much excited on the witness stand as the criminal when the victim and the means of the crime are mentioned; his fear that he may be condemned unjustly may influence his muscles, glands and blood vessels as strongly as if he were guilty" (1908, p. 132). Munsterberg suggested instead that the measures be used in situations where a certain item of information could only be known to a witness of the crime.

The approach suggested many years ago by Munsterberg has more recently been described by Lykken (1974) as the guilty knowledge test (GKT). Lykken distinguishes the GKT from the lie detection (LD) approach, since in LD the interrogator asks direct relevant questions such as, "Did you rob the bank?" mixed with irrelevant ones such as, "Are you sitting down?" In contrast, the GKT involves the preparation of questions so that a multiple-response situation is created. Thus, for example, in a situation where a robber pretended that he wanted to take out a loan for paying doctor bills, before showing his gun, the interrogator would tell the suspect that the guilty person will know the supposed purpose of the loan. Then the interrogator lists five possibilities (e.g., car, vacation, gift, doctor bills, new appliance) and the suspect repeats each of them while the various physiological measures (e.g., SCR, respiration, blood pressure) are recorded. Lykken found only one field-study of the LD technique which he thought adequate in terms of the criteria against which LD validity could be measured. This real-life study by Bersh (1969) unfortunately did little to establish the validity of the physiological response portions of the test. Lykken believes that the GKT, in association with physiological measures, has potential for improving the efficiency of police work. However, he deplores the increasing use of the LD test in industry and suggests that it is worthless in both screening employees and in detecting thieves. He estimates that there are 3000 persons giving over several million polygraph[2] tests in industry each year.

Woodworth and Schlosberg (1954) describe a laboratory demonstration of a lie detection technique, one that is sometimes referred to as the card test. A member of the class picks a card from a stack of 10 cards, remembers it, and returns it to the pack. Then, as skin conductance is measured, the subject responds "no" to each card as it is shown to him by an experimenter. There will be a SCR to each card, but the largest response will usually be to the card that was picked. The GKT and card test are both classified as information tests by Podlesny and Raskin (1977), since their use presumes that a person's critical information can produce differential physiological responses to various items. Information tests are distinguished from deception tests which are based on the assumption that differential physiological response occurs to certain questions when the person is deceptive. Such differential responding may be due to arousal, emotion, or attention, and underlies the "control question" and "relevant-irrelevant question" tests (Podlesny and Raskin, 1977).

Two recent extensive reviews of lie detection have appeared as chapters in books (Barland & Raskin, 1973; Orne et al., 1972). In addition to the criminal investigation and industrial applications of LD, Orne et al. (1972) point out that it is commonly used for screening individuals for security purposes in certain government agencies. Orne and his colleagues detail the procedures followed by interrogators in real-life situations. Apparently, professional polygraphers rarely vary their techniques in a systematic way, a practice that makes it difficult to establish the validity of the various aspects of the procedure. For example, Orne et al. ask whether the polygrapher makes his decision of "guilty" or "innocent" on the basis of a pretest interview, the person's dossier, the physiological responses, a posttest interroga-

[2] The polygraph merely refers to a recorder that measures more than one physiological response at a time. The lay public has come to associate the word "polygraph" with lie detection. Many law enforcement agencies use the Keeler polygraph, which measures respiration, skin resistance, and cardiovascular activity (relative blood pressure).

tion, or some other subtle behaviors that an experienced criminal investigator might notice. Orne et al. (1972) conclude, as did Woodworth and Schlosberg (1954), that LD in a real-life situation is an art rather than a science. Scientific evaluation of the contribution of physiological responses to the LD situation is, therefore, very difficult, since it is only one part of the total procedure. A potentially serious contamination of the whole procedure, mentioned by Orne and associates, is the interrogator's possible bias regarding the suspect's guilt and the effect this may have on the LD procedure.

Barland and Raskin (1973) discuss interrogation techniques used in LD. The questioning techniques advocated by recognized polygraph schools utilize a variety of procedures including peak-of-tension tests, relevant-irrelevant questions, control questions, and guilt complex questions. The peak-of-tension test assumes that the subject will show increasing autonomic response as the critical item in a list, usually the middle one, is approached. A list of about seven questions is shown to the subject before actual testing. The person is required to answer "no" to each. Autonomic responding will be assumed to peak near the point of lying and then decrease as the person relaxes afterward. The relevant-irrelevant test may involve the asking of several relevant questions in each series. Irrelevant questions are sandwiched in between, and physiological responses to the two types of questions are compared. Control questions are formulated during a pretest interview and represent areas about which the individual may be very concerned, for example, "Can you remember stealing anything before you were 18 years old?" (Barland & Raskin, 1973). The purpose of the so-called guilt complex question is to determine whether a person responds emotionally to any question that is accusatory in nature. For example, a question which implies that the subject committed a fictitious crime might be, "Did you steal that gold coin collection?" (Barland & Raskin, 1973). Thus the questioning procedures in LD can have subtle nuances and may involve comparisons of more than responses to only relevant and irrelevant questions.

The validity and reliability of polygraph techniques in the detection of deception were recently assessed by Raskin et al. (1977). They evaluated the results of eight experiments which included field studies of criminal suspects and laboratory "mock crime" experiments. They also evaluated the belief that psychopathic criminals can "beat the polygraph." The main conclusions were that polygraph examinations using control questions or GKTs were approximately 90% accurate when properly conducted and evaluated. They also found that deception in diagnosed psychopaths was as easy to detect as in nonpsychopaths. Polygraph examiners were encouraged to use measures of finger blood volume and finger pulse amplitude in addition to the commonly used respiration, SCR, and relative blood pressure.

In another study of LD in psychopaths and nonpsychopaths, Raskin and Hare (1978) obtained additional results to dispel the notion that psychopaths can defeat the polygraph test. They used a sample of 48 prisoners, half of whom were diagnosed psychopaths. Half of each group were "guilty" of taking $20 in a mock crime and the other half were "innocent." A polygraph examination was conducted after a field-type interview. The measures were respiration, electrodermal activity, and cardiovascular response. The test results yielded 88% correct decisions, 4% wrong, and 8% inconclusive. Again, the psychopaths were as easily detected as nonpsychopaths. In addition, psychopaths showed evidence of stronger electrodermal responses and HR decelerations in the control question test used.

Lieblich et al. (1976) used a GKT and measures of SCRs to detect information held by a sample of 30 inmates of a maximum security prison. The questions were based on 20 items of personal information obtained before the testing began. The items included the inmate's name, his father's name, place of birth, and so on. The subjects listened quietly while SCL was monitored, and the experimenter asked 20 questions followed by five alternate responses, one of which included the correct personal item. On the basis of the SCRs, a significant proportion of subjects were matched with their questionnaire responses. The matching, however, was not as close as had been obtained in a previous study with a sample of college students. Although the situation used was not a real-life one, that is, the individuals were not being interrogated about a crime, the use of a criminal population was similar to one that might be encountered in an actual field detection situation.

Laboratory Studies in the Detection of Deception

In their recent review, Podlesny and Raskin (1977) point out that the main advantage of laboratory studies is that the truthfulness of the response can be controlled and compared with the physiological response given. This is in contrast to real-life situations in which the decision about truthfulness or deception may never be verified in some cases. On the other hand, the laboratory subject may not be highly motivated to evade detection and may not be representative of a typical population of criminal suspects.

In an early laboratory study (Thackray & Orne, 1968), 30 subjects were told that they would be interrogated as though they were suspected of being espionage agents. They were given a set of code words and were questioned by an experimenter who did not know the words but who had a list of questions that related to these words. The physiological measures obtained during interrogation were respiration amplitude, changes in skin conductance, skin potential, systolic blood pressure, and finger blood volume. They found that SCRs, SPRs, and finger blood volume were effective in discriminating deception in this situation. They observed that several previous studies had indicated SCR as the best single index of deception. Systolic blood pressure and respiration amplitude gave inconsistent results. Orne et al. (1972) noted that most laboratory studies agree that SCR is superior to other physiological variables in the detection of deception. Similarly, Barland and Raskin (1973) concluded that the physiological response which has shown the greatest success in discriminating between truthfulness and deception in the laboratory has been electrodermal activity. The usefulness of SCR in field situations, however, has been a subject of controversy. Most field examiners claim that blood pressure and respiration are more useful in detecting deception than EDA measures. In their opinion, the SCR is too sensitive to be useful in differentiating between relevant and irrelevant questions in a highly emotional criminal interrogation (e.g., Arthur, 1971). The issue is still not resolved.

Cutrow et al. (1972) evaluated nine physiological measures

in the detection of deception: breathing amplitude and rate, eye blink rate and latency, finger pulse volume, HR, palmar GSR, forearm GSR, and voice latency (time it took subject to answer each question). All measures were found to be indicators of deception. A combined index of six measures (breathing amplitude, rate, eye blink rate, finger pulse volume, palmar GSR, and voice latency) were found to be more effective than any single index in detecting deception.

Barland and Raskin (1975) employed a mock crime situation in which the physiological variables included measures of cardiovascular activity (relative blood pressure, pulse amplitude), skin conductance responses, and respiration cycle time. Thirty-six subjects were "guilty" of taking $10 and 36 were "innocent." A pretest interview was conducted during which control questions were formulated. One purpose of their experiment was to evaluate, in the laboratory, techniques commonly used in the field. They found that deceptive subjects showed larger increases in cardiodiastolic level in response to relevant questions, while truthful persons had larger responses to control items. The SCR measure successfully distinguished between truth and deception, and longer respiratory cycles were found during lying. Pulse amplitude did not differentiate between lying and telling the truth. The authors concluded that the effectiveness of field techniques and equipment was demonstrated in their laboratory experiment.

Measures of EDA, respiration, blood pressure, pulse amplitude and volume, and heart rate have been commonly used in studies of deception. Podlesny and Raskin (1977) suggest that several other measures may have potential value as correlates of deception and should be further investigated. These include muscle activity, ocular activity (including eye blinks and eye movements), pupillary diameter, EEG, micromomentary expressions, and voice analyses. Micromomentary expression refers to analyses of filmed sequences of facial changes in a deception situation. Voice analyses include the study of frequency and amplitude changes in the vocal pattern during deception. Kubis (1973) evaluated two voice analysis techniques in LD and compared the results with those yielded by a polygraph test in a mock crime situation. Accuracy obtained with both voice analysis techniques gave results that were no different from chance, while the traditional polygraph test produced significant numbers of correct detections.

In summary, a recent increase in the number of well-designed studies, and the results obtained, seem to support the use of physiological measures in the detection of deception. Although polygraph techniques have yet to reach the status of a science, there are some promising developments in this approach:

1. Psychophysiologists are becoming more aware of the practical and theoretical implications of the lie detection paradigm in studying the effects of cognitive, attentional and motivational factors upon physiological responses to verbal stimuli (Barland & Raskin, 1973; Orne et al., 1972).
2. The use of multiple physiological measures in laboratory studies have indicated the value of this approach (e.g., Raskin et al., 1977).
3. Investigators are attempting to create some realistic lie detection situations in the laboratory (e.g., Barland & Raskin, 1975).
4. Improved experimental designs and statistical analyses in lie detection studies are being encouraged (Podlesny & Raskin, 1977).
5. The use of more realistic subject populations (e.g., prison inmates) has yielded promising results (Lieblich et al., 1976).

If the encouraging trends continue and, perhaps, new measurements and techniques are developed, we may someday witness a science of lie detection based on physiological measurements.

Clinical Applications of Physiological Measures

The utilization of physiological measures has been applied in a variety of clinical situations in the past few years. Some of the applications have included testing of vision, hearing (audiometry), brain responses in retarded individuals, and brain activity in neurological and behavioral disorders. Examples of how physiological responses have been used in these various clinical situations will be briefly described in the sections that follow.

Auditory System Tests

The use of auditory evoked potentials (AEPs) to assess hearing deficits in retarded children, infants, and children with multiple handicaps (e.g., those with cerebral palsy) has been increasing in recent years. Since traditional auditory testing requires that the subject indicate verbally or by gesture that he has heard a sound, a technique which can evaluate the integrity of the auditory system without requiring such a response would be of value for testing certain individuals. Rapin (1974) has observed that the AEP is a powerful physiologic test of hearing because it indicates that stimulation by sound has caused a response to occur in the auditory system and the brain. She has found that early diagnosis of hearing deficit with AEPs can allow early remediation, for example, several infants were fitted with hearing aids before they were 6 months of age because AEPs showed their hearing to be impaired. Rapin is of the opinion that evoked potential audiometry is too demanding a technique for routine use with cooperative patients but is justified for use with selected cases, similar to those mentioned above.

Rapin et al. (1969) studied behavioral responses to sound and the AEPs of 51 children whose mothers had German measles during the first 3 months of pregnancy. Only 13 of the children were classified as normal in response to sound (i.e., they had some minimal vocabulary, were responsive to vocal sounds, and localized sounds accurately). Twelve of these 13 had normal AEPs. Of the remaining 38, judged to be hearing impaired through behavioral responses, 27 had AEPs that indicated moderate or severe hearing deficits. The other 11 manifested brain damage that may have obscured behavioral responses to sound even though hearing was normal as judged by AEP records.

Shimizu (1968) studied the AEP to determine whether it could be used to diagnose damage to the auditory nerve. The subjects were four patients known to have auditory nerve pathology in one ear. The AEPs from the damaged ear were longer in latency and lower in amplitude than those recorded from the normal ear. Rose et al. (1972) determined auditory thresholds by evoked response audiometry (ERA) and by routine clinical audiometry. The patients were 50 adults who were tested by five audiologists. The investigators found that the greater the hearing loss, the better the agreement between the two tests. They caution, however, that the differences between ERA results and routine audiometry indicate that caution should be taken in the use of ERA in routine clinical situations, thus agreeing with the opinion of Rapin (1974).

In summary, the brief review presented here indicates that AEPs can be especially useful in detecting auditory system deficit in cases where other testing is not feasible, for example, with infants or certain retarded individuals. On the other hand, its use as a routine technique in the clinic is not currently recommended because it is more demanding and less accurate with cooperative patients than are traditional tests.

Visual System Tests

A number of studies have indicated that visual evoked potentials could be used to detect the presence of lesions at various levels of the visual system (Regan, 1972). In an early study, Vaughan et al. (1963) found that patients suffering from hemianopia produced VEPs which were 50% greater in amplitude from over the unaffected hemisphere. Hemianopia refers to defective vision in which there is blindness in half of the visual field. The patients studied by Vaughan et al. had homonymous hemianopia which affected either the right or left halves of the visual fields of both eyes; thus damage involved either the right or left occipital areas. The hemianopic patients could be differentiated from both normal and from brain-damaged persons who did not have visual defects, with VEP measurements. The most striking difference was the depressed amplitude of an early positive wave peaking between 50 and 60 msec. A follow-up study by Vaughan and Katzman (1964) confirmed the usefulness of positive (latency 50–60 msec) components of the VEP in identifying patients with hemianopic defects involving the central 10° of the visual field, that is, a 50% depression on the affected side. In addition, they reported that visual disorders could be localized by recording both VEPs and electroretinogram (ERG). For example, retinal disease was found to be associated with changes in both VEP and ERG (electrical activity of the retina) with stimulation of the involved eye. Optic nerve disease was indicated by loss or suppression of the VEP with stimulation of the involved eye, accompanied by a normal ERG. Damage of areas before the optic chiasm (optic nerve) were associated with loss of the VEP. Damage in areas between the lateral geniculate bodies and visual cortex were associated with loss of the early VEP components and preservation of the late ones.

The results of a number of studies suggest that the VEP may be used as a test of visual acuity. For example, Harter and White (1968) found that when a checkerboard stimulus pattern was in sharp focus, there was a large negative VEP component at 100 msec and a positive wave at 180 msec. As the image was defocused (contours of the checkerboard pattern were degraded), there was a progressive decrease in amplitude of these two components. White and Bonelli (1970) found that VEP amplitude with binocular stimulation was greater with focused images than defocused ones. Further, the degree of binocular summation shown by the VEPs was also related to quality of the image, since summation was maximal with sharply focused patterns. In another study, White and Hansen (1975) tested the effects of presenting images, which differed in focus, to the two eyes. This technique produces image relationships which are similar to clinical cases of amblyopia in which the image seen by one eye is extremely dim or defocused. In some cases, it was observed that one eye gave a stronger contour response than the other. The studies by White and his colleagues suggest very strongly that the VEP can be used to test visual acuity and may prove useful in the prescription of corrective lenses to a population that is difficult to test, for example, the very young or the retarded.

Lombroso et al. (1969) measured the VEPs of 22 children suffering from amblyopia and compared their responses to unpatterned (light) and patterned (checkerboard) stimulation. Each eye was stimulated individually with both plain and patterned light. The VEP to patterned light was abnormally depressed when derived from the amblyopic eye. The unpatterned light showed no VEP differences for amblyopic and normal eyes. The researchers concluded that the cortex is the major site of defect in this condition since it is here that cells responding to pattern or shape are found.

An interesting possible application of the VEP technique has been described by Kinney and McKay (1974), who have used it to distinguish between individuals with differing types of defects in color perception. They tested 16 normals, 8 deuteranopes (red-green confusion), 8 protanopes (insensitivity to deep red), and 1 tritanope (red-blue-green confusion). The persons with normal color vision produced VEPs to patterns formed by color differences, while the color defective individuals produced no VEPs to targets formed of colors they could not discriminate. Again, this type of approach could possibly be used in testing color vision of persons incapable of giving accurate verbal responses.

Evaluation of Mental Retardation

The approach here has been to compare various aspects of the ERP produced by retardates and normals. For example, Rhodes et al. (1969) compared the VEP of 20 bright and 20 dull children. The bright children had an average full-scale WISC score of 130, while the dull group averaged 79. Only children who had no record of brain damage or emotional disturbance were tested. The subjects were 10 or 11 years old, and each group was composed of 10 boys and 10 girls. The VEP components (latencies between 100–250 msec) recorded from occipital and central areas were larger for the bright children. These same VEP components were consistently larger over the right hemisphere (C_4) than the left (C_3). This central hemispheric amplitude asymmetry was not observed for the dull group. No latency differences were noted between the two groups.

Bigum et al. (1970) measured visual ERPs and somatosensory ERPs from normal children and a sample suffering from Down's syndrome (mongolism). Down's syndrome is characterized by consistent physical features (e.g., protruding tongue, flat nose), and mental retardation. The subjects were 24 retarded children ranging in age from 6 to 16 years, who were matched in age with 24 normal children. They found hemispheric VEP, amplitude asymmetries for the normals but not the Down's syndrome subjects, a result similar to that of Rhodes et al. (1969). The SEP for Down's syndrome children was also different, that is, components beyond 150 msec were greater in amplitude than those of normals. Amplitude asymmetries in the VEP were also found in normal children, but not in retardates, by Richlin et al. (1971). Again, the amplitudes were higher from right hemisphere derivations. Richlin et al. did not find auditory ERP differences (amplitude or latency) between their normal and retarded subjects.

The habituation of the auditory ERP to clicks in normal and Down's syndrome infants was studied by Barnet et al. (1971). They found that normal infants, aged between 5 and 13 months, showed progressive amplitude decreases in the AEP with repetitive stimulation. However, Down's syndrome infants of similar age did not show such habituation. The researchers suggest that habituation may reflect development of normal sensory capacities, since normal newborns also did not show it. In another study the AEPs of young adults with Down's syndrome were compared with those of normal young adults (Straumanis et al., 1973). The AEPs were larger in amplitude for the retardates than for the controls. These investigators propose that the increased amplitude AEP reflects a defect in brain inhibitory mechanisms. The finding of larger AEPs for Down's syndrome adults may be related to a slow habituation similar to that reported for Down's syndrome infants by Barnet et al. (1971).

One finding that seems to be consistent in the studies reviewed here is the amplitude asymmetries found in the VEPs of normal children but not in retarded subjects. Dustman and Beck (1976) observe that this lack of asymmetry in VEPs has been found in Down's syndrome, in dull children and following the ingestion of alcohol. They speculate that the reticular formation produces differential activation in the hemispheres of normal persons and that in the less efficient brain this hemispheric differentiation is less developed, reduced, or completely missing.

It is apparent that additional research is needed before the mechanisms underlying ERP differences in normals and retardates are elucidated. However, the findings to date may be useful. For example, John et al. (1977) used sophisticated computer analyses of ERP data in attempts to classify learning disabilities, mental retardation, and a variety of other disorders. The approach used by John and his colleagues is termed "neurometrics" and employs ERP and EEG analyses of responses to a variety of visual, auditory and somatosensory stimuli.

ERPs in the Evaluation of Nervous System Disorders

Beck et al. (1975) compared the VEPs of 27 epileptics of a particular type (centrencephalic) with those of 27 normal subjects. The epileptics had significantly larger parietal VEPs than did the normals. The most prominent differences were in a negative wave at about 100 msec and a positive one around 250 msec. These investigators have found ERPs to be more useful in the determination of "brain death" than the EEG. They cite a case of a 41-year-old woman in a coma who produced a flat (isoelectric) EEG. However, stimulation with flashes of light resulted in a VEP indicating that her brain, although severely damaged, was still alive.

The finding by Jewett et al. (1970) that responses from the subcortical brain stem of humans could be elicited by auditory stimuli and recorded at the vertex on the scalp has led to the use of this technique in evaluating subcortical function. Since the cells generating the activity are a considerable distance from the recording electrodes these brain stem potentials have also been referred to as "far-field potentials" (Jewett & Williston, 1971). Starr and Achor (1975) report that they have found auditory brain stem potentials to be useful in evaluating the mechanisms of coma and in localizing midbrain and brain stem tumors. They point out that the brain stem potential is independent of attention level, latencies and components vary systematically, and they are abolished by damage to the auditory system. The response consists of a series of seven components (labeled I through VII) which occur during the first 10 msec after stimulation and are of very low amplitude (less than a microvolt). Responses to binaural stimulation can be measured by placing an active electrode at C_z and the reference electrode on the right earlobe. Stimulation may be provided by auditory clicks at a rate of 10 per second. Figure 13-1 shows an auditory brain stem potential.

Starr and Achor (1975) compared the brain stem responses of six normal subjects with a variety of patients whose potentials were measured at bedside. They concluded that the finding of normal brain stem potentials in a comatose patient suggests that the coma is due to metabolic (e.g., uremia) or toxic (e.g., drug

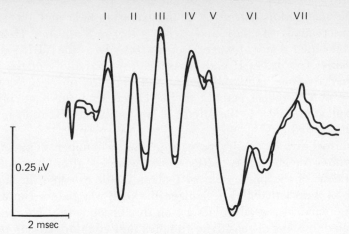

Figure 13-1. Auditory brain stem responses from normal subject in response to monaural click signals, 65 db SL, presented at 10 per second. Clicks were presented to right ear and recordings derived from vertex and right earlobe electrodes (C_z-A_2). Total of 2048 click trials were used to form each of two averages presented. Roman numerals I through VII designate sequence of upward peaks comprising response. Note that amplitude calibration is in submicrovolt range and sweep duration is 10 msec. In this figure, positivity at vertex (C_z) electrode is in upward direction.

overdose) causes and that the brain stem has been spared. The absence of all components after wave III was associated with a tumor which damaged the midbrain. The absence of all waves after I was correlated in another case with damage to the cochlear nucleus (in the medulla). Wave I was related to activity of the auditory portion of the VIIIth cranial nerve.

In another set of clinical observations, Starr and Hamilton (1976) correlated abnormalities of the auditory brain stem potential with confirmed (at operation or autopsy) locations of brain damage. They reported that the midbrain must be intact for waves IV through VII to occur. Widespread brain stem lesions were correlated with the absence of all components after wave I. Extensive brain stem lesions followed anoxia in three patients who showed a wave I that was normal in amplitude

but delayed in latency. On the basis of these and the earlier
observations of Starr and Achor (1975), Starr and Hamilton
concluded that (1) wave I reflects activity in the VIIIth cranial
nerve; (2) waves II and III coincide with activity of the cochlear nucleus, trapezoid body, and superior olive; (3) waves
IV and V reflect activity of the lateral lemniscus and inferior
colliculus; and (4) the origins of waves VI and VII remain to be
discovered.

Noel and Desmedt (1975) described a number of patients in
whom somatosensory ERPs were measured after they suffered
lesions of the brain stem or thalamus. For example, in one patient with left thalamic damage the SEP was reduced in amplitude and increased in latency on the affected side. This was related to a loss of sensitivity to touch and vibratory stimuli on the
right side of the patient's body.

Thus, there are a number of recent findings which indicate
that ERPs and brain stem potentials are useful in the diagnosis
of some neurological disorders. Although only a few representative studies have been presented here, there are many investigations in progress at various hospitals and laboratories, indicating
that the ERP may become an important diagnostic tool for the
neurologist.

Physiological Responses and Behavioral Disorders

Brain ERPs and Psychiatric Diagnosis

Regan (1972) expresses the belief that the application of ERPs
to the study of behavior disorders is a difficult task, both scien-
tifically and conceptually. However, several investigators have
developed approaches that result in differential results with psychiatric patients and normal subjects. For example, Callaway
et al. (1965) recorded auditory ERPs to 1000-Hz and 600-Hz
tones from schizophrenic patients and normal control subjects.
The tones were presented randomly and were equated for loudness at about 65 db. In normal subjects the two tones produced
very similar ERPs, while in schizophrenics the ERPs were different. A later study by Callaway et al. (1970) indicated that
this difference between the ERPs of normals and schizophrenics

to the two tones was due to a greater variability in the responses of schizophrenics, that is, the ERPs of the patients were not as consistent as those of the normals. Callaway (1975) suggested that the high degree of ERP variability in schizophrenics is partly related to the unstable and variable thought processes of these patients. However, he believes that ERP variability is of limited value in studying schizophrenia, since, among other reasons, patients differing in diagnostic category (e.g., depression) also produce highly variable ERPs.

Another approach has been that of Shagass and associates, who used the somatosensory ERP to study "recovery functions" in psychiatric and nonpsychiatric patients (see Shagass, 1972). The technique involved the presentation of two electric shock stimuli, in close succession (intervals between stimuli may vary from 20 to 200 msec), and measuring the amplitude of the second ERP relative to the first. The amplitude ratio of the second ERP to the first is the measure of recovery of cortical excitability after stimulation. The higher the ratio, the greater the recovery. Figure 13-2, from Shagass and Schwartz (1964), shows that somatosensory ERP recovery ratios during the first 20 msec were greater in nonpatients than in patients. That is, this initial phase of recovery was delayed or reduced in the patients with behavior disorders. The amount of recovery in the visual ERP was also found to be reduced in psychiatric patients in a number of studies cited by Shagass (1972). A modified somatosensory ERP recovery function has been used by Shagass and colleagues in more recent years (Shagass, 1977). The procedure involves the use of a constant interval between the two stimuli (10 msec), varying the intensity of the first stimulus, using trains of stimuli, and using a second stimulus of constant intensity. Although the modified procedure was developed in an attempt to enable differential diagnoses of psychiatric patients, it has not yet proven to be any more successful than the original procedure (Shagass, 1977).

The ERP approach of Callaway in the studying of psychiatric disorders tended to emphasize changes in the response which took place 100 msec or more after the stimulus, and that of Shagass focused on components that occurred within 100 msec after stimulus presentation, especially the first 20 msec. Another approach is to examine the relationship between psychiatric disor-

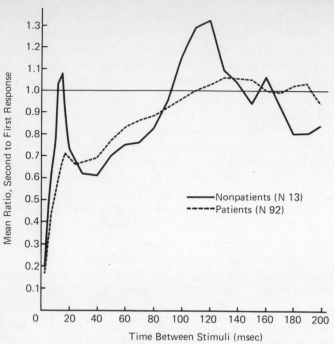

Figure 13-2. Mean somatosensory (primary component) recovery curves for 13 nonpatients and a heterogeneous sample of 92 psychiatric patients. Note biphasic pattern of curve in nonpatients and greater recovery of 20 msec. than by patients.

ders and the CNV. For example, McCallum and Walter (1968) reported that persons suffering from severe anxiety neurosis had contingent negative variation (CNV) waves that were much lower in amplitude than those of normal controls, especially when a distracting stimulus was introduced. Other patient groups that have reportedly evidenced reduced CNVs, when compared to nonpatients, were schizophrenics (McCallum & Abraham, 1973) and psychopaths (McCallum, 1973). Although the CNV distinguished between patients and nonpatients, there seems to be little or no differentiation among patient categories.

Another ERP that has been studied in relation to behavior disorder is the P300. For example, Roth and Cannon (1972) compared this late positive wave in 21 schizophrenics and a group of controls matched for age and race. The late waves of the schizophrenics were significantly lower in amplitude than for the nonpatients. When studies of the relationship between ERPs and behavior disorders were first begun in the early 1960s, researchers had high hopes for the use of the technique both for differential diagnosis and as a possible aid to understanding the neurophysiological bases of these disorders. These early goals have not yet been realized, but work continues in this important area.

EEG and Schizophrenia

In a recent review, Itil (1977) concluded that the most important finding in EEG research relating to schizophrenia is that patients have less well-organized alpha activity and more low voltage fast activity (beta) than normals. He postulates that available data support the position that desynchronized high-frequency beta activity may be the physiological correlate of a genetic predisposition to schizophrenia. In a representative study, Itil et al. (1972) found that a sample of 100 schizophrenics had significantly higher voltage beta activity (ranging from 24 to 33 Hz) than a sample of 100 normal subjects. In addition, the schizophrenics had alpha waves that were lower in amplitude and frequency than those of control subjects. Itil (1977) suggests that further work is needed to correlate quantitative EEG findings with possible biochemical factors in schizophrenia. Hare (1975) reviewed a number of EEG studies and concluded that somewhere between 30% and 60% of diagnosed psychopaths show some EEG abnormality. This is usually in the form of widespread slow-wave activity.

Electrodermal Activity and Behavioral Disorders

Lader and Noble (1975) noted that patients categorized as anxiety neurotics show elevated levels of skin conductance (SCL) and greater numbers of spontaneous fluctuations (SCRs) than do normal controls. Venables (1975) reviewed a number of studies which investigated the relationship between EDA and schizophrenia. The trend of results seem to indicate that (1) higher than normal levels of skin conductance occur in some schizophrenics; (2) chronic schizophrenics appear to show a faster recovery to baseline SCL than normals; (3) chronic schizophrenics show higher levels of spontaneous SCRs than normals; and (4) schizophrenics who give orienting responses do not habituate to the stimulus as quickly as normals. The general trend for EDA seems to support the contention of some investigators that chronic schizophrenics are overaroused, since high levels of EDA indicate elevated SNS activity.

Schalling et al. (1973) measured SCRs and finger pulse volume of criminal subjects who scored either high or low on a scale of psychopathy. They found that the group scoring high in psychopathy had fewer spontaneous SCRs during a tone stimulation period and a poststimulation rest period than the other group. The investigators suggested that the lower degree of responsivity to stimuli in the more psychopathic subjects might be related to the hypothesis that states of low cortical arousal are a main correlate of psychopathy (see Hare, 1975). No differences in finger pulse volume were found.

Skin conductance responses, penile volume, and ratings of slides depicting sexual scenes were measured by Kercher and Walker (1973) in a group of 28 convicted rapists and 28 inmates convicted of crimes unrelated to sex. No significant differences were found between the groups on the penile volume measures. However, the rapists produced larger SCRs to the erotic material and gave more negative ratings to the sexual themes than the control inmates. These findings were interpreted as suggesting that the erotic stimuli were unpleasant for the rapists.

Cardiovascular Activity and Behavioral Disorders

Venables (1975) indicates that there has been little research attempting to relate heart activity to schizophrenia. A sample study is that of Spohn et al. (1971) who reported HR deceleration to slides in both normal and schizophrenic subjects. These results would be in line with those mentioned earlier which indicated HR deceleration to be related to attention to external stimuli by normal subjects. Obviously, much remains to be done in this area.

Pulse rate and forearm blood flow were measured in 31 cases of psychotic depression, before and after a series of electroshock treatments (Noble & Lader, 1971). Clinical improvement subsequent to shock treatments was accompanied by increased forearm blood flow. Pulse rate did not change. These investigators suggested that depressive illness is related to decreased blood flow which may involve a disturbance of hypothalamic control.

In a review of physiological measures that have been studied in relation to psychopathy, Hare (1975) indicates that most of the cardiovascular research in this area is conceptually based on the orienting response and on the Laceys' (1967) hypothesis that sensory intake is associated with HR deceleration and sensory rejection with HR acceleration. In a representative study, Hare (1968) found that the cardiovascular components of the OR (i.e., HR deceleration and finger vasoconstriction) were relatively slow to habituate in psychopaths. The slow rate of habituation was regarded by Hare as consistent with the position that cortical mechanisms of arousal are at a low level for psychopaths.

In summary, the work briefly reviewed here only scratches the surface with respect to the number of studies that have attempted to relate behavior disorders to physiological measures. However, it is hoped that a feeling for the type of work in the area has been conveyed. Much more remains to be done and established in this potentially fruitful area.

Physiological Correlates of Vigilance Performance

The problem of vigilance decrement, enunciated so well by Mackworth (1950), is still with us. There has been increasing attention in recent years to the physiological changes that occur during the course of a vigil. A book on vigilance edited by Mackie (1977) reveals a variety of performance situations and measures that are currently being used. For example, prolonged night automobile driving and physiological changes were studied by O'Hanlon and Kelley (1977). In three separate experiments the performance of 41 young males was monitored while measures of EEG and HR were taken. The main performance indicator was the frequency of drifting out of lane, that is, the number of times the white line or road shoulder were touched during the drive. All driving was done on actual roads in California. The time of driving ranged from 109 to 315 minutes and averaged 200 minutes. Each driver used the same vehicle and started the run at 10:00 P.M. An observer was present in the vehicle with the driver at all times. The subjects were divided into groups of 21 "better" and 20 "poorer" performers on the basis of the lane drifting measure. The better drivers tended to have higher rates of heart activity and lower amounts of heart rate variability than the poorer drivers. The HR of both groups decreased progressively over the course of the drive. In three cases the experimenter took control of the vehicle when the subject's performance became very erratic and they appeared more asleep than awake. The EEG records of these three subjects confirmed this, revealing bursts of delta or theta activity. The drivers were unaware that the experimenter took control, suggesting that persons who are at a dangerously low level of arousal while driving may not realize it. More studies of this type are needed, especially when the tremendous losses in traffic accidents and other kinds of accidents are considered. One might possibly visualize night drivers, or radar operators, or pilots of the future wearing physiological monitors that sound an alerting bell or buzzer when the recorded activity signals a potentially dangerous low level of activity.

This chapter has indicated the diversity in potential applications of physiological measures. A relatively new area of application is that of biofeedback. A virtual avalanche of published reports has appeared on this topic over the past decade. As a result, the next chapter is devoted solely to a consideration of those biofeedback applications whose expressed purpose has been to treat various ailments, ranging from tension headache to high blood pressure.

Biofeedback Applications to Clinical Problems

Biofeedback represents an area on which much research interest is currently focused. The voluminous research conducted on biofeedback training (BFT) over the past several years has necessitated a separate chapter to provide a representative summary of the work performed.

Biofeedback means providing a person with immediate and continuous information regarding certain physiological processes about which the individual would normally be unaware. Thus, a person might be provided with information regarding muscle potentials in his left forearm, his level of blood pressure, his heart rate, or perhaps the type of brain wave being produced at the moment. The basic premise in BFT is that if an individual is given information about his biological processes and changes in their level, he can learn to regulate this activity. Therefore, with appropriate conditioning and training techniques the individual can presumably learn to control body processes which were long considered to be automatic and not subject to voluntary control. The basic premise regarding learned control over physiological responses has theoretical and practical implications. On the theoretical side, it means that certain physiological processes that are under the control of the autonomic nervous system (e.g., blood pressure, heart rate) must be reexamined to determine the extent to which they are subject to voluntary regulation. On the practical side, it implies that symptoms of certain physical maladies such as hypertension (high blood pressure) or cardiac arrhythmias (irregular heartbeats) may be alleviated by self-regulation.

The literature review of this chapter represents only a small portion of the large volume of clinically oriented biofeedback research that has been generated in the past few years. The attempt has been to describe what researchers have been doing and concluding about their applications of biofeedback to specific human disorders. The potential benefits of this research are great. However, overenthusiastic or premature claims about therapeutic effectiveness could harm the field by reducing its credibility. In general, biofeedback researchers would do well to heed the advice of Neil Miller, who said, "This is a new area in which investigators should be bold in what they try but cautious in what they claim" (1974, p. xviii).

There are a number of questions regarding BFT which require answers. For example, (1) What is actually learned as a consequence of BFT? Is it an awareness of some internal response, or is it an awareness of associations between stimuli and responses? (2) What are the variables that influence learning, and how do they exert their effect? For example, what are the effects of the quality and quantity of reinforcements used to promote learning? (3) Which physiological responses are best to modify with respect to a specific disorder? (4) To what extent does transfer of training take place from the laboratory situation to real life? (5) How are the factors of motivation and expectancies to be handled in BFT? (6) To what degree does the BFT situation operate as a placebo effect? (7) How does BFT compare with other possible approaches to altering physiological response, such as relaxation, meditation, or hypnosis? At the conclusion of this chapter the reader should have some preliminary notions about the extent to which these questions have been answered by the representative summary of BFT research presented. Problems of a theoretical and empirical nature which confront biofeedback researchers are discussed in a thoughtful paper by Black and Cott (1977). Prior to examining some BFT literature a typical biofeedback situation, aimed at training a person to increase production of alpha wave activity, will be described.

An Example of a BFT Situation

The production of alpha waves[1] may be achieved by almost any person who relaxes with his eyes closed in a quiet room. We will define alpha activity here as a regular EEG signal, occurring between 8 and 13 cycles per second, at an amplitude of approximately 20 to 60 μV. It is more difficult to produce alpha activity with the eyes opened (e.g., see Brown, 1974). Let us suppose that our objective is to attempt to train increases in the production of alpha activity under eyes-opened conditions and compare this with alpha training under an eyes-closed condition.

The EEG may be recorded by some standard bipolar or monopolar electrode placement from over the occipital or parietal areas. Some commercially available equipment only permits the use of the bipolar technique. In this case an O_2–P_2, or an O_1–P_1 derivation may be used. The EEG activity is filtered and amplified by equipment[2] which is set to produce a signal whenever the activity meets the criteria set up for alpha; in this instance, waves that occur at a frequency of 8 to 13 Hz and at an amplitude between 20 and 60 μV (see Fig. 14-1). Assume that the equipment provides the subject with a tone over headphones every time activity in the alpha range is detected. This tone is the feedback which tells the person that he is achieving the desired response. The output of our alpha detecting equipment will also go to another device which records the amount of alpha activity produced during a given time period, for example, during a 1-minute or a 10-minute interval. Hence, a tone is produced when a person is producing alpha waves and no tone when he is not. The subject might be simply asked to keep the tone on as long as possible. At the end of each 1-minute trial the person might be informed about the actual amount of alpha produced, or he might simply be told, "Very good, keep up the

---

[1] There is no scientific evidence that the production of alpha waves in a normal person enables him to have any special mental powers or benefits. In addition, Johnson (1977) questions whether the learned control of brain wave activity has ever been adequately demonstrated.

[2] An evaluation of various commercially available alpha feedback devices was compiled by Schwitzgebel and Rugh (1975).

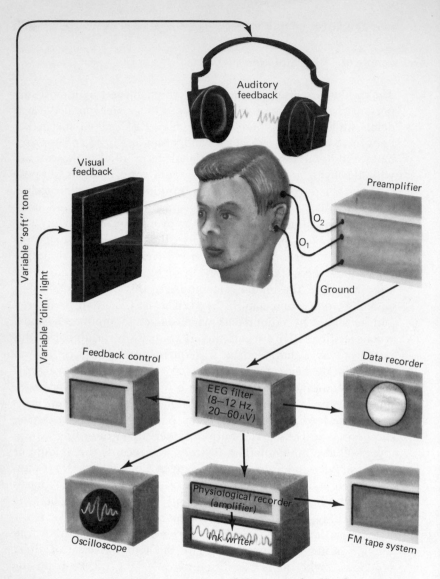

Figure 14-1. Schematic drawing of alpha wave feedback instrumentation similar to that which might be used in a research setting. The physiological recorder and oscilloscope enable monitoring of the accuracy of EEG biofeedback. The amount of alpha activity is accum-

306

good work," and to try to keep the tone on for a longer period of time during the next training interval. Monetary rewards or other incentives can also be provided for good performance. The experimenter keeps a record of the amount of alpha activity produced over a number of training trials.

The BFT may continue for a number of days or weeks, and a record of performance plotted as a "learning curve" over the period of the experiment can be kept. The procedure should include the alternation of "alpha on" trials with "no alpha" trials. In the latter case the person is asked to keep the tone from sounding. The object of this procedure is to allow the subject to clearly differentiate between the alpha and nonalpha situation, and it also ensures that increased alpha production is not merely due to unlearned baseline changes.

An eventual goal of BFT is to have the person produce the desired physiological response without the benefit of the electronic equipment providing the feedback. One possible way to achieve this might be to have the person practice the production of alpha between training sessions at home and after training has been completed. Certain trials during the training sessions can be conducted without providing feedback. Performance with and without feedback can be determined, that is, in terms of the percentage of alpha activity, under the two conditions. Alternatively, the feedback signal can be gradually removed so that it is less and less frequently presented over sessions, until it is completely absent. During the gradual removal of the feedback signal the subject is informed about his level of alpha production after each trial. Subjects may return several months after the completion of training to test their retention of alpha producing skills and for possible retraining sessions. This same basic procedure can be used in attempts to train regulation of blood pressure, heart rate, EMG, or some other physiological activity. A simple equipment configuration for providing EMG feedback

---

ulated on the data recorder, which can provide numerical readout or printout. Information about amount of alpha production is fed back to the subject via headphones (tone), visual display (light), or both.

is shown in Figure 14-2. Many persons practicing BFT use this simpler form of instrumentation.

In the next section, we consider physiological measures that have been used in a BFT context in attempts to alleviate specific disorders.

The Electromyogram (EMG) in Biofeedback Applications

The EMG has been used extensively in biofeedback applications ranging from the treatment of tension headache to attempts at the alleviation of stuttering.

EMG and Tension Headache

Tension headache results from the sustained contraction of skeletal muscles of the forehead, scalp, and neck (Friedman & Merritt, 1959). Budzynski et al. (1970) have reported alleviation of tension headache by having patients reduce EMG levels in frontalis (forehead) and splenius (neck) muscles through BFT. In another report, Budzynski et al. (1973) demonstrated that a combined program of frontalis EMG feedback and relaxation practiced at the patient's home was effective in treating tension headaches.

The effectiveness of frontalis EMG biofeedback and passive relaxation instructions in treating tension headache was studied by Haynes et al. (1975). The 21 college student subjects were assigned to either a BFT group, a relaxation group, or a control group (no treatment). Both of the treatment procedures were more effective than no treatment in reducing the frequency of headaches. Essentially the same results were obtained by Cox et al. (1975), who compared the efficacy of frontalis EMG/BFT, relaxation instructions, and a medication placebo on the frequency, duration, and intensity of tension headaches. The 27 subjects, who were equally divided among the three conditions, ranged in age from 16 to 64 years and had a history of chronic headache ranging from 1 to 39 years. The EMG feedback and relaxation instructions were found to be equally superior treatments to the glucose placebo in reducing headache activity and

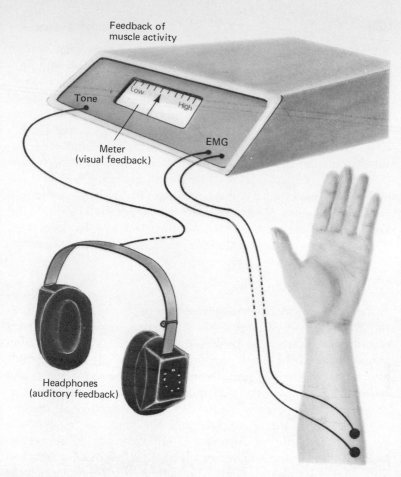

Figure 14-2. A much simpler biofeedback system than that depicted in Figure 14-1 would be used in most clinical applications. The EMG system shown above illustrates the provision of a subject with information regarding changes in forearm EMG level. Decreases or increases may be reflected by changes in tonal frequency or deflections of a dial pointer to the left or right.

frontalis EMG. The feedback and relaxation effects were similar.

Stoyva (1977) reviewed a number of studies which indicated an alleviation of tension headache through the use of feedback-assisted muscle relaxation. Budzynski (1977) notes that although EMG feedback in a clinic setting can be successful with chronic tension headache, the addition of home practice helps. He believes that the motivation for home practice is enhanced by cassette tapes that teach relaxation skills that can then be refined by EMG/BFT. Thus, it would appear that reduction of head and neck muscle tension levels through BFT helps to alleviate tension headaches. More information is needed about the duration of the beneficial effects and the relative effectiveness of other muscle relaxation techniques in treating tension headache.

EMG Feedback and Stuttering

It has been estimated that between 40 to 50 million children in the Western world stutter badly (Coleman, 1976). This speech disorder is characterized by blocking of speech or the repetition of initial sounds of words, especially in a socially stressful situation. Legewie et al. (1975) recorded EMG of facial and throat muscles in two patients, one mild case (25 years of age) and one severe case (a 24-year-old who had stuttered since the age of 4). EMG recordings of face and neck muscles revealed increased activity during stuttering in both patients. Subsequently, training to relax the muscles involved in speech was undertaken with the 24-year-old-patient. The patient learned to anticipate the occurrence of excessive EMG during speech blocks and was eventually able to converse with several people in the laboratory without stuttering. However, the patient was not able to do this outside of the laboratory. Legewie and his associates suggested that progressive fading out of feedback and the use of other therapeutic measures simultaneously might help in the transfer of the newly learned behavior to situations outside the laboratory.

In another application of EMG feedback to stuttering, Guitar (1975) trained three adult male stutterers to reduce facial and neck EMG prior to speaking selected sentences. Decreases in stuttering were associated with decreased lip EMG in one patient, lower EMG at a laryngeal site in another, and a combination of lip and laryngeal EMG decreases in the third. A systematic program was then instituted with a 32-year-old male stutterer in which feedback training to reduce EMG during speech resulted in the elimination of stuttering during both face to face conversations and telephone calls. A follow-up showed that stuttering was still substantially improved 9 months after laboratory training ended.

Lanyon et al. (1976) found that feedback regarding EMG in the masseter (jaw) muscle led to a reduction of muscle tension. The reduction in tension was associated with a major reduction in stuttering in the six persons studied. In a follow-up investigation, Lanyon (1977) taught 19 stutterers to relax their masseter muscles under conditions of EMG feedback. In a series of three experiments it was found that reduced muscle tension was followed by reduced stuttering. Lanyon also reported that relaxation was generalized to periods of no EMG feedback after explicit instructions and constant reminders to do so were given.

The use of EMG biofeedback may offer a viable way of treating the common speech disorder known as stuttering. As with any new application, further clinical trials and experimental investigations are required to confirm the degree of usefulness and delineate limitations of the approach.

EMG Feedback in Neuromuscular Disorder

The amplification and feedback of EMG signals has been found to be helpful in neuromuscular reeducation. Basmajian and associates (1975) have used EMG feedback to assist patients in improving the strength and voluntary control of muscles that are weak, unreliable, and poorly controlled as a result of a stroke. One condition that may occur after a stroke is "foot drop." Paralytic foot drop is characterized by an inability to contract the muscles that bend the ankle to raise the foot. The patient often wears a brace to assist in walking. Basmajian and colleagues divided 20 patients with foot drop into two therapeutic groups: (1) 40 minutes of exercise, three times a week for 5 weeks, and (2) 20 minutes of exercise and 20 minutes of EMG/BFT over the same period. The tibialis anterior muscle (lower leg) was selected for training, since it is the main muscle involved in lifting the ankle. The group receiving BFT showed an improvement in both strength of flexion and range of movement which was approximately twice as great as the other group. In addition, three patients in the BFT group were able to discard their braces. In another clinical study, Takebe and Basmajian (1976) found that patients treated with a peroneal nerve (leg) stimulator for 5 weeks and those treated with BFT for 5 weeks showed and maintained improvement of their walking pattern as compared to patients who received physical therapy only. These investigators believe that instant BFT can play an important role in muscular reeducation in stroke patients. They call for additional research to study effects of parameters such as patient age and duration of illness.

Middaugh (1977) reported on the use of EMG/BFT with 12 patients suffering from neuromuscular dysfunction because of nervous system damage. The subjects were asked to produce 30-second contractions in a muscle that was below functional strength. The EMG feedback, in each of two sessions, was a continuous tone that varied in pitch proportional to the amount of activity. A comparison of results for feedback versus no feedback trials revealed that EMG activity was an average of 16% higher on feedback trials (a significant difference). Time since injury was not a factor, and all patients showed a positive effect. Thus, Middaugh concluded that EMG feedback had a substantial effect on motor unit recruitment which was independent of locus of nervous system damage or time since occurrence of the injury.

Engel-Sittenfeld (1977) discusses a number of clinical studies in which EMG feedback was used in attempts to treat the muscular symptoms of a wide variety of disorders including cerebral palsy, poliomyelitis, hemiplegia, torticollis and rectosphincter incontinence. Fairly successful results were achieved with torticollis and rectosphincter responses. Torticollis is a painful disorder in which spasms in the neck muscles cause the head to be twisted back in a painful position. Alleviation of torticollis through the reduction of muscle tension via EMG feedback has been reported by several investigators (e.g., Cleeland, 1973). Control of the rectal sphincter muscle was achieved by six incontinent patients, aged 6 to 54, with BFT (Engel et al., 1974). Follow-ups at periods ranging from 6 months to 5 years found four patients completely continent and the other two improved.

The promising results obtained thus far seem to argue for the further clinical evaluation of BFT in treating neuromuscular disorders.

EMG Feedback and Anxiety

It is estimated that 5% of persons in the United States suffer from chronic anxiety: "a persistent or recurrent state of dread or apprehension accompanied by signs of physiological arousal" (M. Raskin, et al., 1973, p. 263). The effects of deep muscle relaxation, achieved through frontalis muscle BFT,[3] on 10 chronically anxious patients was investigated by M. Raskin et al., (1973). The patients had not been helped by psychotherapy or medication for the 2-year period before this study was undertaken. All 10 patients reached the criterion of 2.5 $\mu V/min$ of EMG activity or less, averaged over a 25-minute period. The training time of the daily sessions varied from 2 to 12 weeks. Four of the 10 persons improved in self-ratings of anxiety level. The relaxation training had impressive effects on the insomnia of five of the six patients with sleep disturbances. In addition, the four patients with headaches experienced a reduction in the frequency and intensity of their headaches.

Reeves and Mealiea (1975) report the successful use of EMG/ BFT in three adult males with an extreme fear of flying. The procedure involved training the individuals in muscle relaxation using frontalis EMG biofeedback. A self-generated cue word, "relax," was paired with low levels of frontalis EMG. Training continued over 12 one-half hour sessions. All three subjects were able to travel by air on several occasions subsequent to treatment and experienced only slight discomfort.

Budzynski (1977) suggests that EMG feedback is useful for

---

[3] Middaugh has pointed out (personal communication, December 22, 1977) that frontalis feedback primarily involves facial muscles and simultaneous relaxation of muscles throughout the body does not necessarily occur. The term "deep muscle relaxation" implies generalized effects that are not yet established.

treating anxiety when (1) there is a muscle tension component to the anxiety pattern; (2) the person cannot learn to relax with nonmachine relaxation procedures; (3) the individual is not aware of his or her muscle tension level; (4) the person believes that BFT will help in learning to relax. The results of the few studies which exist suggest that EMG/BFT may be useful with certain types of anxiety.

Frontalis EMG relaxation has been used in a BFT situation with asthmatic patients (Fried, 1974). Asthma is characterized by episodes of bronchospasm during which the person has great difficulty in breathing. The episode or bronchospasm may be initiated by allergens in the environment, by emotional reactions, or both (Bates et al., 1971). In Fried's study, the feedback of auditory clicks provided information about rising EMG in the forehead muscles. The patients were trained to keep the EMG at a low level during the presentation of slides depicting flowers, trees, dust, or whatever was usually effective in the induction of an asthmatic attack. This procedure seemed to reduce the number and severity of attacks and enabled the person to feel that he had more control over the situation.

In another study of this type, Kotses et al. (1976) investigated the effects of operantly produced frontalis muscle relaxation on peak expiratory flow rates (PEFR) scores in asthmatic children. The PEFR is a measure of efficiency in expelling air from the lungs. The subjects were 36 asthmatic summer campers ranging in age from 8 to 16 years. They were divided into a contingent feedback group, a noncontingent feedback group, and a no treatment group. The contingent feedback group received a tone for changes in EMG, while the noncontingent received tones that were not related to EMG in any systematic fashion. These two groups participated in nine sessions spread over 3 weeks. PEFR was obtained daily from all 36 subjects by persons who were unaware that it would be used in a study. The EMG training group showed an increase in PEFR over the pretraining level, while the noncontingent and no treatment groups did not evidence a change. The researchers concluded that the reduction of frontalis EMG through BFT was associated with the alleviation of some symptoms of bronchial asthma. Kotses et al. indicate that the underlying mechanisms for this improvement are unknown at this time.

EMG Feedback and Hyperactivity

The term "hyperactivity" is used to describe a group of symptoms that include overactivity, short attention span, impulsivity, and in some cases, aggressive behavior. Hyperactivity is often associated with learning disability. Frontalis EMG was recorded and fed back to a hyperactive 6-year-old boy during 11 sessions over an 8-week period (Braud et al., 1975). The boy was asked to turn off a tone that signaled the presence of muscular tension. EMG level decreased within and across training sessions. Improvement was observed in school and at home as long as the boy continued to practice and use the techniques of relaxation learned in the laboratory. This study is suggestive and encouraging. However, it is based on only one subject, and obviously replication is needed with larger groups of hyperactive individuals.

It had been noted in chapter 8 that the number of general EMG studies had apparently declined over recent years. However, EMG is obviously being widely used in BFT applications.

The EEG in Biofeedback Applications

EEG Biofeedback and Epilepsy

Three delineated forms of epilepsy—grand mal, petit mal, and psychomotor—produce seizures or attacks that are accompanied by disturbances in the EEG pattern. Attempts to treat epilepsy have focused on influencing the EEG pattern through BFT. For example, Sterman and Friar (1972) reported the suppression of seizures in an epileptic patient who had been conditioned to produce 11 to 14 Hz EEG through BFT. This 11 to 14 Hz EEG activity is recorded from over the central or sensorimotor cortex and is referred to as the sensory motor rhythm (SMR). Sterman (1973) has suggested that the SMR may be an EEG phenomenon related to brain mechanisms that mediate motor suppression.

The reduction of seizures in severe epileptics using SMR training has been reported subsequently by Sterman et al. (1974), Seifert and Lubar (1975), Lubar and Bahler (1976), Finley (1976), and Finley (in press).

Sterman et al. (1974) reported that four epileptics had a reduction in seizure frequency when biofeedback was used to train the production of 12 to 14 Hz EEG from over the Rolandic (central) cortex. Seifert and Lubar (1975) worked with three male and three female adolescent epileptics whose seizures were not well controlled by drugs. The patients were provided with feedback whenever they produced ½ second of 12 to 14 Hz activity of a specified magnitude. They observed a significant reduction in the number of seizures during the first 3 to 4 months of treatment in five of the six epileptics. The BFT sessions were 40 minutes long and scheduled three times a week.

Sensory motor rhythm training was used with eight epileptics whose seizures were frequent, severe, and not controlled by anticonvulsant drugs (Lubar and Bahler, 1976). Six of the eight patients were studied in an extension of SMR training initiated by Seifert and Lubar (1975). In addition to 12 to 14 Hz activity patients were provided feedback of 4 to 7 Hz activity which indicated epileptiform spike activity. They were to suppress their epileptiform activity. The patients continued to show improvement in the form of decreased seizure frequency. The addition of feedback regarding epileptiform activity enabled some patients to develop the ability to block many of their seizures. The more successful patients demonstrated an increase in the amount and amplitude of SMR during the training period.

Finley (1976) reported on 1 year of SMR training with a young male patient. The frequency of seizures decreased from an average of eight an hour to one every 3 hours over the training period. In addition, the amount of SMR activity (11 to 13 Hz) increased from 10% of the EEG activity to 70%, and epileptiform discharges decreased from 45% to 15%. Finley (in press) reported on an adult male psychomotor epileptic who showed benefit from SMR training. Finley points out that as a result of the long-term and intensive nature of the feedback procedure, only about 30 epileptic patients have received SMR training in the United States, and thus the efficacy of the procedure has not been established. In fact, several investigators using SMR training with epileptics have not observed beneficial effects with the procedure. One of these was Kaplan (1975), who reported that biofeedback training of 12 to 14 Hz Rolandic activity had no effect on clinical EEG or seizure incidence in two epileptics. She then attempted to train three other epileptics to produce 6 to 12

Hz Rolandic activity. Two of them experienced reductions in seizure frequency, but this was not attributed to EEG training, since no learning of 6 to 12 Hz activity was achieved. Kaplan suggested that the BFT procedure provided the patients with new techniques of relaxation and that specific EEG changes associated with seizure reduction had not yet been reliably demonstrated. Gaustaut (1975) believes that claims regarding the beneficial effects of "alpha states" and the conclusions about the relation between SMR training and seizure reduction are premature. He supports Kaplan's position that a cause-effect relationship between EEG feedback and epilepsy has not been established.

A lack of relation between the SMR and seizure reduction was reported by Kuhlman and Allison (in press). These investigators used both contingent and noncontingent feedback to train 9 to 14 Rolandic EEG activity. Although seizure reduction occurred in three of the five patients, it was associated with increases in the amount and frequency of alpha and not with enhancement of the SMR. Johnson and Meyer (1974) used a sequence of relaxation training, EMG feedback, and feedback of alpha and theta EEG frequencies with an 18-year-old epileptic who had suffered severe grand mal seizures since the age of 8. After the relaxation and EMG feedback phases, EEG training was administered in 36 sessions over a 1-year period. Seizure frequency dropped by 46% during the 12-month period. A 3-month follow-up subsequent to the end of training indicated that seizure rate remained at the lower level.

In summary, it would appear that some suggestive findings indicate a relation between SMR training and seizure reduction in epilepsy. However, the limited number of cases studied and some negative findings (e.g., Kaplan, 1975) indicate the need for further study. Positive findings with other EEG frequencies (e.g., Johnson & Meyer) indicate that the possible benefits of training with other waves (e.g., alpha, theta, or beta) should be investigated.

EEG/BFT: Drug Use and Chronic Pain

The effects of EEG alpha and EMG feedback on anxiety, marijuana use, and sleep were studied by Lamontagne et al. (1975).

Three groups of eight persons each were assigned to either EEG, EMG, or control conditions and did not know which treatment they were receiving. Training was limited to 40-minute sessions on four consecutive days. The EMG group maintained an improved level of muscular relaxation during training, while the EEG group failed to retain gains in alpha from one session to the next. A slight reduction in drug use was observed during training and at follow-up periods of 3 and 6 months. Improvements in duration and quality of sleep were made in all groups (including control subjects), suggesting a possible placebo effect associated with participating in the study.

Melzack and Perry (1975) worked with 24 patients suffering from chronic pain of pathological origin, including cancer. A combination of alpha feedback training, hypnotic training, and placebo effects reduced pain in a significant number of patients. Although the majority of patients learned to increase alpha activity during training sessions the investigators concluded that pain relief results, not from the increase in this EEG activity, but from suggestion, relaxation, and the feeling of being able to control pain that resulted from participation in the study.

The studies briefly reviewed here suggest some possible important applications for EEG biofeedback training. There is a need for a cautious attitude with regard to claims of beneficial effects stemming from EEG biofeedback training. This is because the exact nature of the BFT contribution is obscure with regard to the beneficial effects observed. We return to the questions: What is being learned, and are we observing placebo effects?

Biofeedback of Heart Activity

Weiss and Engel (1971) used operant conditioning of HR with eight patients who suffered from premature ventricular contractions (PVCs). The PVC is a dangerous irregularity in the heartbeat. The training included approximately 30 sessions, 10 of which involved learning to increase the HR, 10 in which HR decrease was taught, and 10 in which HR decrease and increase were alternated throughout the session. Decreases in the number of PVCs were associated with the slowing of HR. Five of the eight patients were able to control their PVCs in the laboratory and to transfer the learned effect outside the laboratory. Training with the other three patients was not successful. In two of these cases the hearts may have been too diseased to beat regularly for prolonged periods of time.

A 29-year-old woman with sinus tachycardia (periodic occurrence of occasional very fast HR, in this case from 200 to 240 bpm) was taught to regulate her HR with BFT (Bleecker & Engel, 1973). The patient was alternately trained to increase and decrease her HR. The presence of a green light indicated that HR was to be quickened, while a red light meant that she was to slow her HR. A yellow light indicated the desired state. The patient was ultimately able to control her HR away from the laboratory without feedback.

However, Weiss and Engel (1975) were unable to consistently increase ventricular heart rate (VHR) in three patients with complete heart block. The three patients suffered from a condition in which the atria and ventricles beat with independent rhythms. The atrial rhythm was normal, but the ventricular rhythm was abnormally slow (e.g., 30 to 45 bpm). The inability to alter VHR with BFT was attributed to the interruption of impulse conduction between the atria and ventricles of the heart in these patients.

Patients with ischemic[4] heart disease were not as capable as an age-matched sample of healthy males or a group of college students in learning to modify their HR via BFT (Lang et al., 1975). The college students had the best performance in terms of ability to learn to increase and decrease HR. The authors interpreted the results as supporting the hypothesis that age and disease interfere with ability to profit from feedback training in the control of HR.

This brief presentation suggests that heartbeat irregularities may be amenable to biofeedback training. As Engel (1977) has indicated, there is insufficient data to allow a definitive evaluation of BFT as a primary therapy or as an adjunct therapy in

---

[4] Inadequate blood supply to the heart muscle usually caused by coronary artery disease.

these cardiac disorders. However, sufficient evidence exists to encourage the clinical testing of BFT alone and in conjunction with other therapy in the treatment of various heart irregularities.

Blood Pressure and BFT Applications

The cardiovascular abnormality known as high blood pressure, or hypertension, is estimated to occur in 5% to 10% of the general population in the United States (Shapiro et al., 1977). One of the first studies to use BFT in an attempt to regulate hypertension via BFT was that of Benson et al. (1971). They used BFT with seven patients suffering from high blood pressure. Decreases in systolic blood pressure, ranging from 16 to 34 mm Hg, were obtained in five of the individuals. The effectiveness of the training in terms of transfer outside of the laboratory situation is not known because no follow-up data were obtained.

Schwartz and Shapiro (1973) discussed general procedures, findings, and theoretical issues in the biofeedback training of blood pressure regulation. They noted that a common training procedure is to provide "binary" feedback, that is, the subject knows with each heartbeat whether blood pressure has gone up or down. In the binary feedback-reward situation the subject is provided with information regarding momentary fluctuations in blood pressure, and a reward is presented for a sustained (tonic) change in some direction (e.g., when systolic pressure has decreased by at least 5 mm Hg). They also point out that "baseline" blood pressure values may change either up or down over a session, independent of learning. For example, increases may occur if the stimuli used for feedback or reward are arousing, and decreases will be observed as subjects adapt to the experimental situation. Thus, researchers must be careful to control for these in order not to misinterpret changes from baseline as indicating a therapeutic effect. Schwartz and Shapiro mention that the novelty of the experimental situation plus expectancy may operate as a placebo effect, thus making it difficult to assess the effects of BFT alone. However, the placebo effect should not be regarded in a negative light. Stroebel and Glueck (1973) point out that the novelty of a BFT situation with its equipment, feedback displays, and the possibility for self-regulation of certain processes may produce a placebo effect that has good results, especially, for example, if it can produce a reduction in the blood pressure of hypertensives. There are difficulties associated with depending on placebo effects since not enough is known about the conditions and types of persons in which they are operative. Hence, the utility of a placebo as a method of treatment is limited, since these unknowns make the control of this effect very difficult.

Motivation looms as an important factor in any learning situation and is crucial in BFT. The problem of motivating hypertensive patients is discussed by Schwartz and Shapiro (1973), who note that, unlike the tension headache patient, individuals with high blood pressure typically have little or no discomfort from this condition. The rewarding effects of blood pressure reduction, therefore, are not readily recognized by the patient, and it is important to ensure that these patients are properly motivated in the BFT situation.

Yoga exercises for complete mental and physical relaxation, combined with BFT of skin conductance level, led to improved blood pressure levels in 16 of 20 hypertensive patients (Patel, 1973). Patel used SCL instead of continuous blood pressure feedback, since he wanted to avoid entering an artery to obtain direct readings. (Other investigators mentioned in this section obtained indirect BP readings, i.e., without entering an artery.) Patel attributed the beneficial effects to the control of SNS activity through yogic relaxation and through BFT influence over SCL (an activity controlled by the SNS). The patients participated in ½-hour sessions, three times a week, over a period of 3 months.

Elder et al. (1973) studied a group of 18 hypertensive patients in an experimental design which assigned 6 patients to a no-feedback (control) group, 6 to a group who were given feedback (light) for reductions in diastolic pressure, and 6 who were given verbal praise as well as the feedback. The combination of feedback plus praise produced decreases in diastolic pressure up to 25% of baseline over a period of 4 days. Both feedback groups showed decreases compared to the control group, which essentially stayed at the same level throughout the pretraining and training sessions. An interesting aspect was the decrease in systolic pressure which occurred even though feedback was provided only for decreases in diastolic pressure. A follow-up 1 week after the final session showed blood pressure at levels similar to those recorded in the last training session.

Blanchard et al. (1975) described a simple feedback system for teaching hypertensive patients to lower their pressure. The patient received feedback of systolic pressure each minute via a closed-circuit television display. The technique was found effective in reducing the pressure of four hypertensive patients. Seven hypertensive patients participated in 2-hour BFT sessions over a 9-week period in a study conducted by Goldman et al. (1975). Feedback, contingent upon beat-by-beat decreases in systolic pressure, was provided by an automated blood pressure monitoring system. Four control subjects had three weekly sessions in which blood pressure was monitored without feedback. Significant decreases in both systolic and diastolic pressure were reported for the patients but not for the control group.

A number of hypertensive patients were taught to control and reduce their level of systolic blood pressure in a study conducted by Kristt and Engel (1975). Pre-BFT blood pressure readings were first compiled at home over a 7-week period. Then the patients were trained to raise, to lower, and to alternately raise and lower their systolic pressure. Finally, blood pressure readings were taken at home during a 3-month follow-up period. Reductions in blood pressure between 10% to 15% occurred between the pretraining period and at the time of follow-up. Changes in diastolic as well as systolic blood pressure were observed. The lowered pressures occurred in patients suffering from a variety of ailments, including heart arrhythmias and cardiomegaly (enlarged heart).

Elder and Eustis (1975) used BFT of diastolic pressure in 22 hypertensive outpatients. A reduction of blood pressure was observed for these patients, but it was not as dramatic as for a group of hospitalized persons studied earlier by Elder et al. (1973). Thus, regulation of hypertension with BFT appears to be more effective with hospitalized patients than with those living in their usual environment. Perhaps the lack of careful control over eating, sleeping, and medication in the nonhospitalized hypertensives contributed to the decreased effectiveness of BFT.

This abbreviated review of BFT with hypertensives indicates that the approach may have clinical value. However, Shapiro et al. (1977) caution that the total number of patients studied with regard to BFT approaches to the reduction of blood pressure is still small, and large-scale clinical studies along with medical, physiological, and psychological evaluations are needed before BFT can be applied on a routine basis to treat high blood pressure. Engel (1977) further notes that the potential clinical usefulness of BFT in hypertension is less clear than it is for patients with cardiac arrhythmias. With these sobering commentaries regarding the state of the art, both experimental and clinical investigators will realize the difficult task ahead with respect to establishing the clinical utility of BFT in this particular application.

Applications of Skin Temperature and Blood Volume BFT

Skin temperature has been found to be related to blood flow in the skin tissue as measured by plethysmography (Sargent et al., 1972). Thus, increases or decreases in skin temperature would be related to vasodilation and vasoconstriction, respectively. Since the continuous measurement of skin temperature involves low cost and portable instrumentation and can be applied to numerous body areas, it is especially attractive as a monitoring device in ailments that involve changes in skin temperature.

The BFT of skin temperature has been described in the treatment of patients suffering from Raynaud's disease by Surwit et al. (1977) and Taub (1977). The symptoms of Raynaud's disease include intermittent constriction of arteries or arterioles of the hands and feet. During an episode of this ailment the affected extremities (fingers or toes) undergo sequential color changes, that is, from white to deep blue to bright red. The symptoms are elicited by cold and/or emotional stress and may be alleviated by heat.

Surwit et al. (1977) trained 30 female patients with Raynaud's disease to control finger skin temperature with either autogenic training or a combination of autogenic training and feedback of skin temperature. Autogenic training involves regulation of mental and body functions through concentration on preselected words. For example, one of the phrases repeated every 15 seconds in the Surwit et al. study was, "My hands feel heavy and relaxed." Patients were trained either at home or in the laboratory. All trained subjects were able to maintain finger skin temperature in a cold environment (exposure to temperatures down to 63°F for a period of 1 hour). In addition, the patients reported significant reductions in both frequency and intensity of attacks. There was no difference between the performance of autogenic training alone as compared to autogenic training plus skin temperature feedback. These researchers suggested that other forms of relaxation, including meditation, progressive relaxation or various forms of yoga, be investigated as possible aids in the treatment of Raynaud's disease.

Taub (1977) reported the training of three Raynaud's disease patients to self-regulate increases in hand temperature. At times, patients began sessions with hand temperatures at or only slightly above room temperature. For example, at a room temperature of 70°F, a patient might have a hand skin temperature of only 70° to 72°. At the same room temperature a normal person would have a skin temperature of about 85° to 90°F. With training, the patients were able to increase hand temperature into the normal range. After 20 training sessions, two patients reported decreases in the number and severity of attacks and the ability to prevent them by using, without feedback, techniques learned in the laboratory. The third patient, also trained in the winter, avoided the cold, and training effects could not be evaluated. Taub (1977) writes that several other investigators have reported success in treating Raynaud's disease with BFT, augmented by other techniques. While preliminary results appear to be encouraging, the data available are still insufficient to establish the effectiveness of BFT or other behavioral techniques in treating Raynaud's disease.

Sargent and his colleagues have used a combination of skin temperature BFT and autogenic training to treat migraine headaches (1972, 1973). Migraine is a severe form of headache often accompanied by nausea and blurring of vision. It is believed to be due to dilation in superficial cranial arteries (Dalessio, 1972). Sargent et al. (1972) treated 62 migraine patients with skin temperature BFT (handwarming) and autogenic procedures. Clinical ratings indicated that 74% of the migraine sufferers were improved. Sargent et al. (1973) reported that the combined handwarming training and autogenic procedures produced improvement in 81% of 42 migraine patients who were followed for more than 150 days. These investigators believe that one mechanism operative in their approach is the voluntary relaxation of the portion of the SNS serving the hand, resulting in the increased flow of blood to that area. Presumably, the effects of SNS relaxation spread to other body areas, including superficial (head) arteries. However, the researchers did not investigate this possible spread of relaxing effects to other body parts, thus leaving the reasons for the generalized effect rather uncertain. The use of hand skin temperature in treating migraine headache requires a great deal of additional clinical work.

The more direct cephalic vasomotor response (CVMR) was used by Feuerstein et al. (1976) and Friar and Beatty (1976) with migraine patients. Both sets of investigators used BFT to train self-regulation of vasconstriction in superficial temporal arteries, that is, those located in the scalp area above the ears. They reported success in treating migraine with BFT employing the CVMR.

Price and Tursky (1976) measured changes in temporal artery blood volume and finger blood volume in 40 migraine sufferers and 40 matched controls. The objective was to train vasodilation by providing feedback about increases in hand temperature. Ten subjects from each group were assigned to one of four treatments: (1) feedback, (2) false feedback, (3) relaxation induced by taped instructions, and (4) a neutral-tape control. Responses of migraine sufferers were very different from those of the controls. Normal subjects produced vasodilation in accordance with experimental demands, but the migraine subjects tended to show constriction, or no change, of blood vessels. There were no significant differences in vasodilation between the BFT and relaxation conditions. Both of these latter procedures were better than the irrelevant listening task in producing vasodilation. Price and

Tursky suggested that migraine sufferers be studied to determine whether stressful stimuli produce temporal artery vasoconstriction, which in turn results in headaches. A further suggestion was that if this is the case, then migraine patients might be trained not to respond to such stimuli with vasoconstriction. Feuerstein et al. (1977) investigated the use of CVMR and EMG (frontalis) BFT in two migraine and two tension headache patients. Training consisted of six sessions of CVMR and six EMG biofeedback sessions for all patients. The CVMR training helped migraine patients and EMG training helped tension headache patients to reduce the frequency and duration of headaches.

In summary, recent results with CVMR feedback with migraine sufferers seem promising with respect to alleviating symptoms and understanding more about the origins of migraine. However, as with the other measures, the CVMR requires further testing.

In conclusion, there is suggestive evidence that BFT can improve the symptoms of certain disorders. The treatment of tension headache with frontalis muscle BFT seems to be one of the more successful applications. However, the questions raised at the beginning of this chapter have not been adequately answered to date, and the process of investigating these and other questions related to BFT will keep applied and basic researchers busy for years to come. Hence, it will be a while before the necessary data are available to give an appropriate evaluation of the clinical benefits of BFT and knowledge of the underlying mechanisms involved.

We have seen by now that a tremendous amount of information has been gathered by psychophysiologists. What has been presented thus far represents only a small portion of the basic and applied research accomplished to date. The next chapter considers some of the major conceptual formulations that have been developed and used in attempts to integrate and explain some of the diverse findings in psychophysiology.

Concepts in Psychophysiology

The field of psychophysiology does not have an all-inclusive conceptual framework within which most of the collected data may be tested, integrated, and interpreted. Instead, there are a number of concepts, some old and some new, which have relevance for the interpretation of experimental findings. Some of these concepts, at least in part, contradict one another. Perhaps one day the various concepts may be reconciled and subsumed within one theoretical framework that will account for most of the existing data. This is probably an overly optimistic goal, but one for which scientists in diverse areas including psychophysiology, constantly strive.

Scientific concepts and theories enable isolated findings and information to be bound together in a meaningful pattern. They provide a basis for the interpretation of past and present information and act as stimulators for future investigations. The very experiments that are suggested by a given scientific concept may be responsible for the modification or elimination of the concept. The development of concepts includes the sharpening of predictive value and modifications to accommodate an increasing number of facts. The development of these kinds of concepts is one sign of a maturing science. The concepts that are discussed in this chapter are the law of initial values, autonomic balance, activation, stimulus response specificity, individual response specificity, cardiac-somatic coupling, adaptation and rebound, and orienting and defensive responses.

The Law of Initial Values

The law of initial values (LIV) states that a particular physiological response to a given stimulus or situation depends on the prestimulus level of the system being measured (e.g., see Wilder, 1931, 1957, 1967). More specifically, the law states that the higher the level, the smaller will be the increase in physiological responding to a given stimulus. On the other hand, the higher the level, the larger will be the decrease in response produced by stimuli normally capable of producing decreases. How might the LIV predict a change in HR in a given situation? It has been found that subjects who are fearful of mutilation show an acceleration in HR to slides of accident victims (Klorman et al., 1975). The LIV would predict that if HR is higher than usual for these persons, HR acceleration would not be as pronounced as it would be for a lower prestimulus rate. Thus, a "ceiling effect" of sorts would operate for HR increases. Suppose, further, that the prestimulus rate was also higher than usual for individuals who customarily show HR deceleration to mutilation slides. The LIV would then predict a larger HR decrease than usual in response to these slides. In effect, these subjects would now have more room for a downward shift in HR. While this test has not actually been carried out, it is an example of a procedure which could be used to test the predictive power of the LIV.

Wilder (1967) considered the LIV to apply to all responses under the control of the autonomic nervous system. However, experimental results indicate that not all physiological responses are subject to effects of prestimulus level. For example, Hord et al. (1964) found that the LIV operated as predicted for HR and respiration rate responses, but not for skin conductance or skin temperature. The experimental paradigm they used tested the LIV with respect to the part that predicts smaller upward changes in a given function with higher prestimulus levels of that activity. The physiological responses of 105 persons were measured to experimental stimuli which included sounds, lights, and mental arithmetic. When the prestimulus level of each physiological function was compared with poststimulus levels, the results led Hord et al. to conclude that the LIV does not hold for skin conductance or skin temperature.

Libby et al. (1973) predicted that pupil dilation and HR deceleration would occur as a characteristic response of subjects to interesting pictorial stimuli. Their predictions were confirmed based on the analyses of responses of 34 male subjects. Incidental to their main analysis was the observation that the magnitude of change in the two physiological variables was related to prestimulus level in both, thus supporting the LIV. They caution, however, that their repeated experience revealed wide variations in the relationship between prestimulus levels and responsivity, depending on the experimental conditions, the stimulus situation and even the subjects used. Thus, further restrictions are imposed on the applicability of the LIV and a need to delineate the extent of its limitations is emphasized.

Lovallo and Zeiner (1975) obtained results for finger blood volume which were consistent with the LIV. The cold pressor (CP) test was used as the stimulus. The CP is a procedure that involves the immersion of an extremity, in this case the left foot, in a bucket of ice water. It is often used to test degree of vasoconstriction upon stimulation. The researchers predicted that when vasoconstriction was maximal the CP would produce vasodilation, and when vasodilation was high, vasoconstriction would result. Room temperature was used to manipulate the prestimulus state of the peripheral vasculature, that is, a room at a temperature of $12°C$ ($54°F$) produced prestimulus vasoconstriction and a temperature of $32°C$ ($90°F$) resulted in vasodilation. The subjects were also tested at a room temperature of $22°C$ ($72°F$). The results of the CP were in line with their predictions since the response magnitude was not only dependent on the stimulus, but was related to the initial level of vascular tonus (i.e., vasoconstriction or vasodilation). Figure 15-1 depicts a portion of the results from the study of Lovallo and Zeiner.

White (1977) reviewed a number of studies, using salivation as a measure, to determine whether response magnitude was related to prestimulus level. The studies used different methods, subjects, and stimuli. White concluded that, in general, the LIV did not hold for salivation.

In summary, the LIV is a concept that focuses on the level of prestimulus activity for a physiological measure in determining magnitude of response. Experimental investigations suggest that certain physiological variables change in a way predicted by the

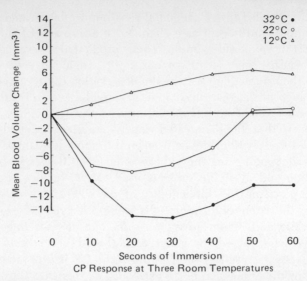

Figure 15-1. Three curves showing an increase in blood volume to cold pressor for subjects tested under 12° C room temperature and increasingly large decreases in blood volume for subjects tested at 22° C and 32° C.

law (e.g., respiration, HR, and vascular tonus). Other measures, for example, skin conductance and salivation, show changes that do not appear to be consistent with the LIV. Libby et al. (1973) urged further investigations to establish the conditions under which the concept holds true. The LIV has alerted investigators to the possible influence of prestimulus physiological activity upon reactions to stimuli.

Autonomic Balance

The concept of autonomic balance examines human performance and behavior in the context of autonomic nervous system imbalance, that is, the extent to which sympathetic nervous system or parasympathetic nervous system is dominant in an individual. The name most prominently associated with this concept is that of Wenger and his associates (Wenger, 1941, 1948, 1966; Wenger & Cullen, 1972). Wenger and co-workers have proposed that in a given individual either the SNS or the PNS may be dominant. The degree to which one or the other is dominant may be estimated by an empirically determined weighted score called Ā (autonomic balance). The person's Ā is derived from a number of autonomically innervated functions which include palmar skin conductance, respiration rate, heart period, salivation, forearm skin conductance, pulse pressure, and red dermographia (persistence of red skin after stroking with a stimulator). High Ā scores indicate PNS dominance, while low Ā scores reflect relative SNS dominance. The predominance of this autonomic factor for an individual remains constant from year to year but may show phasic changes to external or internal stimuli. The central tendency of these estimates of the autonomic factor are what Wenger means by autonomic balance (Wenger & Cullen, 1972).

Wenger (1941) has proposed that the distribution of Ā scores should be approximately normal (i.e., bell shaped, see Fig. 15-2)

Figure 15-2. The frequency distribution of the mean Ā scores (estimates of autonomic balance) for 87 children, ages 6 to 12.

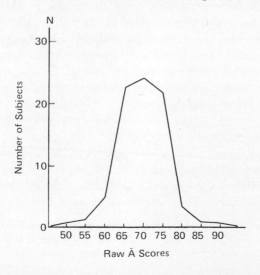

for a large random sample of individuals. In fact, Wenger has found such a distribution for samples of children (1941) and adults (1948). The curve plotted in Figure 15-2 depicts an average $\bar{A}$ of 70. Thus, individuals who score below this value would be SNS dominant and those above reflect PNS dominance, in relation to other persons in the sample. The amount by which the $\bar{A}$ score differs from the central value would indicate increasing degrees of imbalance. The procedure to obtain $\bar{A}$ scores is described by Wenger and Cullen (1972).

Wenger and his associates have conducted many large-scale studies to determine the nature of the $\bar{A}$ scores in different samples of individuals. For example, Wenger (1948) studied autonomic balance in 225 military persons hospitalized for "operational fatigue" and 98 Air Force personnel diagnosed as "psychoneurosis-anxiety state." An example of their findings was that neurotic individuals had faster respiration, higher blood pressure, and lower finger temperature than persons suffering from fatigue. This trend would indicate greater SNS activity for anxiety[1] neurotics. A sample of 488 Air Force cadets produced a normal distribution of $\bar{A}$ scores with an average at 69, very similar to that of the sample of children tested in 1941. Wenger and colleagues (1957) concluded that autonomic factor scores are related to certain personality patterns and certain diagnostic categories such as anxiety psychoneurosis, battle fatigue, and asthma. They also hypothesized in 1957 that differences in autonomic response patterns, supplemented by differences in autonomic balance, could be used to predict which persons will not react favorably to physical or psychological stress and those who might develop psychosomatic disorders. In a study designed to test the hypothesis that patients with different psychosomatic disorders would show different response patterns for variables under ANS control, Wenger et al. (1962) tested the responses of 100 hospitalized males under controlled resting states and with the CP test. The patients included 31 with stomach ulcers, 36 with gastritis, and 33 with skin disorders (including 17 with neurodermatitis). The variables measured included HR, respira-

[1] Wenger et al. (1956) have defined anxiety as a generalized excessive reaction of the SNS. Smith and Wenger (1965) found low autonomic factor scores for subjects experiencing phasic anxiety.

tion rate, skin conductance, finger pulse volume, blood pressure, and skin temperature. One finding was that the resting Ā score of each patient group indicated greater SNS activity than a group of 93 normal subjects. There was no significant difference in reactivity to CP among the patient groups. Patients with gastritis, however, seemed more different from normals than other patient groups. In general, the results did not support the hypothesis but did show differences in Ā score for patients and nonpatients.

Smith and Wenger (1965) estimated Ā for 11 graduate students under phasic anxiety (immediately before taking an oral examination for the Ph.D. degree) and under relatively relaxed conditions, either 1 month later (eight persons) or 1 month earlier. The hypothesis that Ā would significantly decrease during anxiety, thus indicating SNS dominance, was confirmed. For example, on the day of the examination the subjects had less salivary output, higher blood pressure, shorter heart period, and higher sublingual (under tongue) temperature. In another study, Wineman (1971) investigated changes in Ā during the menstrual cycle of five young women. The autonomic variables studied were sublingual temperature, heart period, diastolic blood pressure, salivary output, and skin conductance. During menses, the follicular and ovulatory phases, Ā scores were higher, indicating PNS dominance. However, during the luteal phase (which is accompanied by decreased estrogen levels and increased progesterone levels) the Ā scores were lowest. Thus, Wineman concluded that the decreased estrogen levels were accompanied by a relative increase in SNS dominance.

Lovallo (1975) has reviewed a number of studies in which the CP test was used to determine patterns of physiological responsivity. He views the results of these studies as useful in understanding homeostatic[2] mechanisms, especially in relation to the concepts of LIV and autonomic balance. Lovallo provides support for the use of LIV in understanding the magnitude and direction of responses to stimuli, as well as interactions between base levels of activity and task performance under stress. He

[2] Homeostasis is the term coined by W. B. Cannon to describe the tendency of the body to maintain a state of equilibrium in the face of internal and external changes.

also emphasizes the interaction between initial values and autonomic balance in determining an individual's response to a
given stimulus. Thus, we see a possible complementarity between LIV and autonomic balance in understanding physiological responsivity.

In summary, the concept of autonomic balance, and the Ā
score, appears to provide a useful mechanism through which the
relative dominance of the PNS or SNS of an individual may be
established. However, relatively few studies to test and expand
this concept have been performed despite the fact that it has existed for some time. Most of the studies conducted to date have
been performed by Wenger and his associates. Its value as a
conceptual model would be enhanced if further studies testing
its applicability, for example, in understanding psychosomatic
disorders, were performed by a larger number of investigators.

Activation

The concept of activation attempts to explain the relationship
between variations in level of physiological activity and changes
in behavior. According to Duffy (1972) the description of behavior at any particular instant requires consideration of the goal
toward which it is directed and the intensity of the behavior.
The intensity of behavior is most commonly called "activation"
(sometimes arousal) and can be reflected in the level of responsivity in a number of physiological variables. For example, increasing levels of HR, blood pressure, muscle potentials, skin
conductance, and EEG[3] asynchrony are related to increased activation, while decreased levels of these same variables would
indicate lowered activation. Various formulations of this concept are found in the writings of Duffy (1934, 1957, 1962, 1972),
Hebb (1955), Lindsley (1951), and Malmo (1959, 1962). A
consistent idea in the writings of those who support the activation concept is that level of performance rises with increases in
physiological activity of an organism up to a point that is optimal for a given task, and beyond this point, further increases

[3] In the case of EEG, a change from slow, synchronized activity (alpha) to
fast, desynchronized records (beta) would reflect "activation."

cause a drop in performance. Thus, one basic proposition of this concept is that performance is optimal at some intermediate level of physiological activation, and the relation between the two can be described by an inverted-U-shaped curve (see Fig. 15-3). The function plotted in Figure 15-3 is based on a discussion by Malmo (1962). An important role is given to the ascending reticular activation system (ARAS) by Malmo in regulating level of cortical excitability and, hence, performance.

Let us examine how "activation" might operate in an everyday situation. Suppose that a person is very sleepy or drowsy early in the morning. The level of activation as reflected in various physiological measures would be low and performance, for ex-

Figure 15-3. The hypothetical inverted-U relationship indicates that performance is best at some moderate level of physiological activation. Malmo (1962) ascribes the upturn in the curve to effects of nonspecific stimuli that influence the cortex through the ARAS. Activity in a circulating chain of neurons is said to be facilitated by impulses arriving at the cortex. Overstimulation, on the other hand, causes neurons in the chain to be less excitable and produces the downturn in the curve observed at high activation levels.

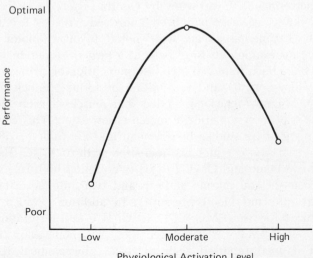

ample, in a RT task, would be poor. Later on in the day, when
the physiological variables register at some intermediate level
for this individual, performance would be best. If, then, the individual's performance and physiological responses are measured
when he or she is in a state of panic, or very high excitement, efficiency would be low while activation would be high. This last
situation would produce the downturn in the curve, thus producing the inverted-U-shaped function.

Empirical support for the activation concept is derived mainly
from studies in which level of physiological activity is manipulated and performance measures are taken and from neurophysiological findings regarding the arousal functions of the reticular
formation of the brain. In the first category of studies which offer empirical support for an inverted-U-shaped relation between
activation and performance are the many studies of induced
muscle tension (IMT) effects on task efficiency. An early example is a study by Courts (1939), who investigated the effects of
six IMT levels on verbal learning. He found that an IMT level
of one-fourth of maximum was optimal for learning. Higher degrees of tension were also superior to the no tension condition.
However, at a level of three-fourths maximum IMT learning efficiency fell below the no tension condition, thus yielding an
inverted-U-shaped relationship between level of muscle tension
and performance. In a review by Courts (1942) he noted that a
wide variety of tasks had been improved with IMT. Tasks for
which detrimental effects were noted involved motor adjustments, for example, tossing balls at a target. Moderate levels of
IMT have been found to facilitate perception of strings of numbers (Shaw, 1956) and recognition of forms (Smock & Small,
1962). Malmo (1959) contended that muscle tension induction
is one way to systematically increase activation. This contention
is supported by studies of Freeman and Simpson (1938), who
found that skin conductance increased with increased IMT, and
those of Malmo and Davis (1956), who found high relationships
between skeletal muscle activity and two autonomic measures
(heart rate and blood pressure). In addition, Pinneo (1961)
measured forearm EMG, SCL, EEG, HR, and respiration while
six levels of IMT were produced by a dynamometer in the right
hand. Pinneo reported that all these physiological responses

showed regular and continuous rises as a function of IMT level. Thus, there is good evidence that IMT is related to changes in activation.

One study frequently cited in support of the activation concept is that of Freeman (1940). This investigator measured skin conductance and RT of a single subject over a series of 100 experimental sessions. The observations were made at various times of day, over a number of days, when the subject varied widely in levels of alertness. Freeman found a curvilinear, inverted-U-shaped relation between skin conductance and RT, in which RTs were slower at high and low conductance levels and fastest at the middle levels. Stennett (1957) manipulated activation level through the use of incentive and found an inverted-U relation between tracking performance and two measures of physiological arousal (skin conductance and EMG). However, an inverted-U was not found by Schlosberg and Kling (1959), who attempted to repeat the Freeman (1940) study with a larger number of subjects. Nor was it indicated in a study by Kennedy and Travis (1948), who investigated the relationship between frontalis muscular tension, reaction time and level of performance in a continuous tracking task. Kennedy and Travis found a linear relationship between EMG level and performance, that is, tracking and RT were poor at low EMG levels and better at the higher levels of muscle tension. A similar finding was reported by Andreassi (1966) for the relationship between skin conductance and RT in a continuous monitoring task in which subjects had to respond to infrequent random signals. Andreassi found that RT was fast when SCL was high and slow when SCL was low. Intermediate SCL was not associated with best RT performance. It was suggested that perhaps an inverted-U-shaped function will be observed only when levels of activation are purposely manipulated to produce very high and low levels of physiological activity.

The neurophysiological bases for the activation concept are found in studies of the reticular formation. Moruzzi and Magoun (1949) discovered that electrical stimulation of the brain stem reticular formation (BSRF) of anesthetized cats shifted the EEG recorded at the cortex from high-voltage slow waves to low-voltage fast waves. The cat's EEG showed the signs of a nor-

mal arousal from sleep. The excitable area included the central
core of the brain stem extending from the medulla up to the hypothalamus (see Fig. 15-4). Moruzzi and Magoun concluded
that the reticular formation acted as a general alarm mechanism
that aroused the cortex, and they referred to it as the reticular
activating system (RAS). Further work by these investigators
and others who studied the behavioral and physiological effects
of stimulation and lesions in the RAS led to the recognition of
this system's importance in maintaining wakefulness and producing arousal of cortical areas under appropriate stimulus conditions. Lindsley (1951) reviewed evidence that lesions in the
ARAS (ascending reticular activating system) abolished the activation pattern of the EEG and produced a behavioral picture
of apathy and somnolence. Lindsley (1956) noted that the ARAS
projects fibers to, and receives projections from, the cerebral cortex, indicating mechanisms for interaction between these two
areas of the brain. Thus the central location and connections to
and from the ARAS point to its potential as a mechanism for
regulating and integrating input to other levels of the CNS. Fuster (1958) has provided evidence that moderate electrical stimulation of the ARAS can facilitate visual perception and RT in
monkeys. High-intensity stimulation of the ARAS led to a decrement in performance, as would be predicted by proponents of
the activation concept.

Duffy (1972) reviewed many studies that lend support to the
activation concept. One criticism of the concept (Lacey, 1967)
is that different types of activation pertain to autonomic, central
(electrocortical), and behavioral measures. Eason and Dudley
(1970) performed a study that appears to partially answer this
criticism. Three levels of activation were produced by manipu-
lating experimental conditions as follows: (1) subjects were told
that they would be shocked if they did not respond quickly to
light flashes ("high activation"), or (2) they were merely instructed to react as quickly as possible to the flashes ("moderate
activation"), or (3) they were told to observe the light flashes
without responding ("low activation"). All the physiological
variables measured (HR, SCL, EMG, and visual cortical evoked
potentials) increased with higher levels of activation. Although
HR deceleration was observed just prior to the response signal,

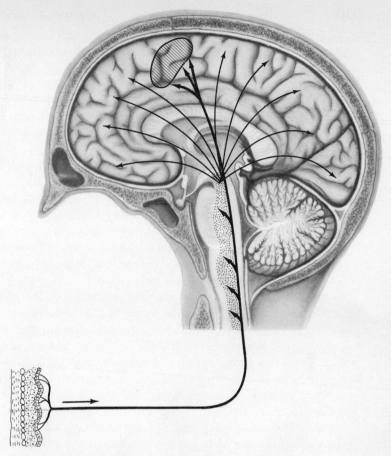

Figure 15-4. The reticular formation is the area stippled in this cross section of the brain. A sense organ (lower left) is connected to a sensory area in the brain by a pathway extending up the spinal cord. This pathway branches into the reticular formation. When a stimulus travels along the pathway, the reticular formation may "awaken" the entire brain (arrows).

at all levels of activation, the major trend showed a generalized activation which was similar for cortical, somatic and autonomic variables.

Sjoberg (1975) manipulated level of physiological activation in 25 subjects by having them work at five different loads on a bicycle ergometer. The relation between the index of activation (HR) and RT was described as an inverted-U, that is, performance was better at a medium activation level than at high and low levels. Maclean et al. (1975) stressed quick responses, provided feedback of performance under a "high activation" condition, and instructed subjects to merely count stimuli in a "low activation" condition. Measures of auditory ERPs and SCL were affected by the activation manipulations in a consistent way, that is, high activation led to higher amplitude evoked potentials and SCL. They concluded that different physiological measures co-vary when level of activation is manipulated.

In summary, it may be said that there is a good deal of empirical support for an activation concept that relates level of physiological activity to behavioral intensity. The support stems mainly from studies in which the level of physiological activity is experimentally manipulated and from neurophysiological evidence regarding the importance of the reticular formation in regulating levels of alertness. One weakness of the concept has been its lack of precision in specifying an a priori optimal physiological level for a given group of individuals performing a task under conditions in which level of activation has not been purposely manipulated. Another has been the failure of its proponents to relate it to other concepts, for example, those of LIV and autonomic balance. However, the concept has stimulated a great deal of research and appears to be able to predict changes in physiological activity and performance under conditions of physical manipulation (e.g., IMT) and some psychological manipulations (e.g., Eason & Dudley, 1970).

Stimulus Response (SR) Specificity

The concept of stimulus response specificity refers to a patterning of physiological responses according to the particular stimulus situation. It has been discussed in the writings of Ax (1953), Lacey et al. (1953, 1963), and Engel (1972), among others. The concept states that an individual's pattern of physiological activity (e.g., HR, EMG, SCL, respiration, and blood pressure) will be similar in a given situation and that the pattern may vary when the situation is different. One basic question here is whether the pattern of physiological response will indicate the kind of emotion being experienced. Or, to put it another way, what is the pattern of response in happiness versus sadness, or in anger versus fear, or in disgust versus surprise? One of the first investigators to study this experimentally was Ax (1953), who induced fear in his 43 subjects by pretending to "accidentally" shock them. Anger was produced in the same persons through insults and criticism. Ax found greater increases in respiration rate and SCL in fear than in anger. However, greater increases in EMG, diastolic blood pressure, and greater decreases in HR were observed in anger as compared to fear.

Engel (1959) compared physiological responses when subjects were hungry and when a limb was submerged in ice water (CP test). A different pattern of responding was noted under these two conditions. Responses to the CP test included increases in HR and blood pressure and a decrease in finger pulse volume. On the other hand, hunger produced decreases in blood pressure and respiration rate and an increase in skin temperature.

Variations in the stimulus situation produced different patterns in physiological responding as reported by Lacey (1959). He gave examples of situations in which HR showed a decrease while SCL increased, and instances in which they changed in the same direction (see Fig. 15-5). The divergent response of these two measures was referred to by Lacey as "directional fractionation of response." This term describes stimulus situations in which direction of change in physiological activity is contrary to the view that ANS responses must co-vary, that is, either up or down, in a given stimulus situation.

Lacey (1959) also presented evidence that tasks involving cognitive functioning (e.g., mental arithmetic) are accompanied by increases in HR while those emphasizing perceptual activities (e.g., attention to visual stimuli) led to HR deceleration. He suggested that cardiac deceleration facilitated "intake" of envi-

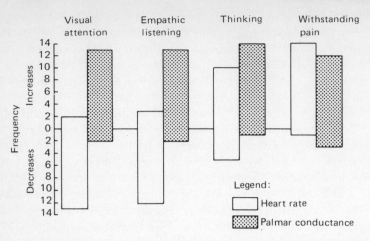

Figure 15-5. The "directional fractionation of response" according to the nature of subjects' tasks. For the 15 subjects whose responses are shown here, all four stimulus conditions produced increases in palmar conductance, but visual and auditory attending resulted in heart rate decreases, while the other tasks involving "rejection" of input resulted in heart rate increases.

ronmental stimuli, while acceleration was associated with attempts to exclude or "reject" those stimuli that would be disruptive to the performance of some cognitive function. Lacey et al. (1963) observed that cognitive activities were accompanied by HR increases, while primarily perceptual functions led to cardiac deceleration.

Directional fractionation of response has also been reported by Andreassi et al. (1969) and Hare et al. (1972). Andreassi et al. found HR to be significantly higher when subjects were required to respond to an irregular pattern of signals than with a fixed interval. In contrast, SCL and SCRs were elevated for the fixed intervals as compared to the variable presentations. The variable pattern was likened to a cognitive task, since it required more mental effort to anticipate signals when they occurred at irregular intervals. Thus, HR acceleration occurred, as would be predicted by Lacey et al. (1963) for simple cognitive tasks.

On the other hand, relatively lower HR levels were observed with regular signals, presumably because simple attention was involved in performing the task. Hare (1972) measured HR, SCL, and vasomotor activity (finger and cephalic vasoconstriction) while subjects viewed slides of homicide victims. One group was instructed to rate the slides on a 7-point scale of unpleasantness (raters), while the other group merely viewed the slides (nonraters). The nonraters showed directional fractionation which included cardiac deceleration, increased SCL, digital vasoconstriction, and cephalic vasodilation. However, the raters did not display fractionation, since they showed HR acceleration, an increase in SCL, and both digital and cephalic vasoconstriction. The results for raters were interpreted as being consistent with Lacey's (1967) hypothesis that HR increases are associated with cognitive activity. The rise in SCL was attributed to the fact that increased requirements for evaluation caused the subjects to notice more disturbing aspects of the slides.

Libby et al. (1973) found that pupil dilation was greater to unpleasant stimuli while cardiac slowing was related to pleasantness, that is, pictures rated as pleasant produced greater deceleration than those rated unpleasant. These results are a further example of directional fractionation and stimulus response specificity. A different method was used to obtain directional fractionation in an experiment by Gatchel (1976). He trained a group of subjects to produce HR deceleration while SCL was simultaneously measured and found that slowing of HR was accompanied by increases in SCL.

Cardiac deceleration has been assigned an important role in the regulation of brain function and performance in later refinements of the "intake-rejection" hypothesis. For example, Lacey (1967) argued that changes in HR and blood pressure can influence cortical activity and thereby affect sensitivity to stimuli. A decrease in HR would be sensed by baroreceptors in the carotid and aortic arteries, resulting in decreased visceral afferent[4] feedback to cortical areas, thus causing increased cortical

[4] The term "afferent" refers to impulses that flow toward a center (e.g., the brain) from a peripheral area (e.g., the blood vessels). The term "efferent" refers to impulses that flow out from a center to peripheral areas (e.g., the heart).

activity. This is partially based on neurophysiological evidence from animal studies which have shown that level of cardiovascular activity can affect EEG frequency (Bonvallet et al., 1954). Cardiovascular feedback has been shown to inhibit rage responses in cats (Bartorelli et al., 1960; Baccelli et al., 1965). In addition, Galin and Lacey (1972) recorded HR, respiration, EEG, and RT in cats under conditions in which the midbrain reticular formation was either stimulated or not stimulated. They reported that HR deceleration sometimes accompanied reticular stimulation, indicating that HR slowing and CNS arousal could occur simultaneously.

Lacey and Lacey (1974) again emphasized role of increased blood pressure and HR on afferent feedback from baroreceptors in affecting cortical activity. They point out that elevated cardiovascular activity is inhibitory, since increased baroreceptor feedback has been implicated in a slowing of EEG and decreased muscle tone, among other effects. Decreased cardiovascular activity would have opposite results in this chain of events, that is, the end result would be increased cortical activity and sensitivity to stimuli. This latter effect would also improve sensorimotor performance.

Lacey and Lacey (1978) discuss some neurophysiological findings that strongly support the notion that sensory and motor functions can be inhibited by increases in baroreceptor activity (Coleridge et al., 1976; Gahery & Vigier, 1974). For example, Coleridge et al. (1976) found that stimulation of carotid baroreceptors inhibited the activity of single neurons in the motor cortex. Lacey and Lacey point out that, by inference, sensory and motor functions may be facilitated by decreased baroreceptor afferent activity. A relation between a measure of brain activity (CNV), HR deceleration, and RT efficiency has been reported by Lacey and Lacey (1970). They found that the greater the HR deceleration during the foreperiod of a RT task, the greater was the CNV, and both of these were related to efficient RT, for example, higher CNV amplitudes and greater HR decelerations were accompanied by fast RTs. More recently, Lacey and Lacey (1977) reported that magnitude of HR deceleration was differentially affected during a single cardiac cycle, depending on when a signal to respond occurred within that cycle. This latter study was more fully discussed in chapter 11. The Laceys' hypothesis concerning cardiovascular feedback effects on attention has been criticized by Elliott (1972) and Hahn (1973). The criticisms generally called for clarification of terms such as "attention," and less reliance on HR alone as a dependent measure of cortical effects.

In summary, the studies of the Laceys and others have indicated support for stimulus or situational response specificity. That is, a consistent pattern of physiological responses will occur in a given situation. In addition, "directional fractionation," in which different physiological variables show different directions of response, has been reported in a number of investigations, particularly those that require subjects to note and detect environmental events. The "intake-rejection" hypothesis has developed into a concept concerning interactions between cardiovascular activity and the brain and its effects on behavior, especially sensorimotor performance. Available neurophysiological and psychophysiological data have prompted the Laceys to propose that decreases in cardiovascular activity facilitate sensorimotor performance and attentional processes by increasing brain activity. According to their formulation, the increased brain activity is produced by afferent feedback from baroreceptors. Conversely, increased cardiovascular activity (e.g., HR and blood pressure) decreases efficiency in the same types of activities, because increased afferent feedback from the same baroreceptors inhibits cortical and subcortical activity. It is likely that the hypotheses advanced by the Laceys and their colleagues will stimulate a great deal of additional research, and further refinements of their concepts will undoubtedly be forthcoming.

Individual Response (IR) Specificity

In the previous section, we saw that the concept of stimulus response specificity referred to the characteristics of the stimulus situation which produced a typical response from most subjects. In contrast, the concept of individual response specificity says that a particular subject has characteristic responses to most stimuli. These two concepts may seem to be contradictory at first glance, but they are not (Engel, 1972; Sternbach, 1966). The concept of SR specificity refers to response tendencies of a number of persons to a single stimulus situation, while IR specificity involves consistency of an individual's response hierarchy in a variety of stimulus situations.

The concept of IR specificity has had an interesting historical development (see Sternbach, 1966). Briefly, it had been reported by Malmo and Shagass (1949) that psychiatric patients with a history of cardiovascular problems and those with head and neck complaints responded differently to pain stimuli. For example, those with the cardiovascular symptoms showed elevated HR, while those with headaches and neck pains had higher EMG in response to pain. Malmo and associates proposed the principle of "symptom specificity" to describe situations in which psychiatric patients respond to stressful stimuli according to the physiological mechanism underlying the symptom. This principle was applied to normals by Lacey and associates (1953) and formulated as "autonomic response specificity" or what is now called "individual response specificity." The notion that individuals would respond maximally with a certain physiological response was confirmed in the 1953 study (Lacey et al.). They measured SCL, HR, and HR variability under four "stressful" conditions: cold pressor, mental arithmetic, letter association, and hyperventilation. Evidence was found for maximal response in the same physiological variable under different stress conditions. Further, they concluded that some people responded to different stimuli with a fixed pattern, for example, the greatest response change might be HR, followed by SCL and then HR variability. An example of this response patterning to various stimulating conditions was provided by Lacey (1959). He obtained results that indicated similar response patterns to the CP test, mental arithmetic, and word fluency within a given subject. For example, diastolic blood pressure decreased for one subject, while it consistently increased for a different subject under the conditions just mentioned. Engel (1960) measured a number of physiological variables in a group of young women while they were presented with a variety of stimulus conditions. The data indicated the simultaneous occurrence of IR specificity and SR specificity for these subjects. Moos and Engel (1962) reported that hypertensive subjects showed more blood pressure changes in reacting to stressors than did arthritic patients. However, those with arthritis showed more EMG increases in muscles overlying the arthritic joints than did hypertensives. More recently, Hodapp et al. (1975) reported that 20 hypertensives responded to landscape slides with a greater rise in systolic blood pressure than did a group of 31 matched normal control subjects. Thus the concept of IR specificity may have implications for studying certain psychosomatic reactions, as initially suggested by the work of Malmo and Shagass (1949).

Schnore (1959) obtained findings that have relevance to the concepts of IR specificity and activation. A group of male subjects had a number of physiological measures taken (including forearm EMG, HR, systolic blood pressure, and respiration rate) while they performed tracking or arithmetic tasks under conditions designed to produce low or high arousal. For example, under high-arousal conditions for tracking, subjects performed under the threat of an electric shock, while in the low-arousal condition, tracking trials were presented as though they were not part of the experiment proper. The results indicated that during the different stimulus situations subjects showed highly individual response patterns (both somatic and autonomic) even when variations produced increases in the overall level of activation. These findings were interpreted in support of Lacey et al. (1953) and Lacey and Lacey (1958) with regard to IR specificity for autonomic variables. Further, Schnore reported that four of the measures (HR, blood pressure, respiration rate, and right forearm EMG) consistently differentiated between high- and low-arousal conditions. Schnore observed that despite individual patterns of response, persons placed in an arousing situation showed an increase in most physiological functions. The increases were relative, since, for example, while an individual might have shown increases in HR and EMG under arousal, the level of HR may have been high and EMG low in comparison with others.

There are limitations to the IR specificity concept. Lacey and Lacey (1958) point out that while most persons may have some tendency for IR specificity, quantitative differences exist. This point is illustrated in a study of Wenger et al. (1961), who found that only 8 of 30 male subjects (27%) showed complete IR specificity. A tendency toward a stable hierarchy in autonomic response pattern to different stimuli was found in 22 of the subjects (73%). Sternbach (1966) presents several studies which indicate that IR specificity is unstable over time, especially as the number of stimulus and physiological response variables are increased. The possible role of explicit (e.g., instructions) and implicit sets (e.g., preconceived ideas) of subjects as possible factors affecting IR specificity have also been discussed by Sternbach (1966).

Cardiac-Somatic Hypothesis

According to the cardiac-somatic hypothesis, cardiac response changes are seen as facilitating the preparation for, and performance of, a behavioral response. For example, there is an association between cardiac response (e.g., HR deceleration) and the inhibition of ongoing somatic activity not relevant to performance of the task (Obrist et al., 1970). Reductions in somatic and cardiac activity are viewed as biological manifestations of changes in attention (Obrist et al., 1974). Further, HR deceleration is considered to reflect a central (brain) mechanism which adjusts cardiac activity to metabolic requirements. The major proponents of this view have been Obrist and his associates, who emphasize that the "coupling" between cardiac-somatic responses occurs because both are reflections of brain processes concerned with preparatory activities.

Support for the hypothesis is derived from a variety of studies by Obrist and colleagues (Obrist et al., 1969; Webb & Obrist, 1970; Obrist et al., 1970). For example, Obrist et al. (1970) measured somatic activity (chin EMG and eye blinks) and HR while subjects performed a simple RT task in which various foreperiods were used. In one group of 31 subjects, HR decelerations were blocked by intravenous administrations of atropine, which inhibits the vagus nerve. Another 31 persons performed without the drug. When cardiac deceleration was not blocked, faster reaction times were associated with greater decreases in both heart and muscle activity. The cessation of eye movements and blinks was the most pronounced effect. Blocking cardiac deceleration, however, did not influence performance. The HR deceleration observed in the RT task was explained in terms of efferent processes initiated in the brain which had effects on both cardiac and somatic responses. In another study, Obrist (1968) found that increases in somatic activity paralleled increases in HR. A classical aversive conditioning situation was employed in which EMG increases from the chin and jaw were accompanied by cardiac acceleration. This was interpreted as evidence for cardiac-somatic linkage.

Obrist et al. (1973) studied the relationship between RT, HR, and measures of task-irrelevant somatic activity (eye movements and blinks, chin EMG, general bodily activity, and respiration). The subjects were four groups of children (4, 5, 8, and 10 years old) and an adult reference population. It was reported, for all groups, that a decrease in HR and a drop in task-irrelevant somatic activities were coincident with making the relevant response.

Obrist et al. (1974) suggested that HR may be uncoupled for somatic activity under conditions of intense stress brought about by a subject's uncertainties and which involve sympathetic nervous system influences. Thus, they proposed that HR is coupled to somatic activity in behavioral situations which involve minimal sympathetic influences on the heart, that is, are not stressful. To test this proposal Lawler et al. (1976) measured HR and somatic activity of 25 male college students and 25 fifth-grade boys while they performed a choice RT task. Attention was manipulated by varying uncertainty (probability of a warning signal occurring) and motivation (money and feedback vs. no money and no feedback). With respect to the cardiac-somatic relationship, variations in uncertainty produced systematic effects only on HR during the foreperiod, that is, HR accelerations increased as uncertainty increased. Variations in motivation were differentiated only by forearm EMG during the foreperiod, that is, it increased with increases in motivation. However, increases in motivation increased the average level of both HR and forearm EMG. Thus the variable of stimulus uncertainty seemed to result in cardiac-somatic uncoupling. Further, forearm EMG increases during the foreperiod were considered as relevant somatic activity and were contrasted to decreases in chin EMG.

Obrist (1976) argues that situations in which the individual is minimally involved, or relatively passive (e.g., simple RT), are those in which cardiac-somatic coupling is evident. That is, the emotional involvement is such that the cardiovascular system is mobilized for a metabolic state which is not demanding. However, emotional states that evoke active coping mechanisms mobilize the cardiovascular system for dealing with high metabolic requirements. Lacey and Lacey (1974) do not agree that the metabolic relationship between HR and somatic activity explains decreased HR during the preparatory interval of a RT trial. They believe that the somatic changes reported by Obrist and associates for the RT paradigm are small and not too significant metabolically.

Some support for the idea that emotional involvement may mobilize the cardiovascular system comes from a recent study by Obrist et al. (1978). Obrist and his associates studied the effects of varying the subject's opportunity to cope with stressors upon tonic levels of HR, carotid pulse wave, and BP (diastolic and systolic). In a first experiment, persons who believed they could control an aversive stimulus (shock) maintained elevated levels of HR, carotid pulse wave, and systolic BP as compared to those who believed they could not control the shock. In a second experiment, three stressors were used. The subjects had no control over two of these (CP and a sexually arousing pornographic movie) but did have control over a third one, that is, they could avoid a shock by good performance. The subjects had significantly elevated levels of HR, carotid pulse, and systolic BP during the portion of the experiment where they could control the stressor. The effects of sympathetic innervation on responsivity during coping and no-coping conditions was examined in a third experiment. Sympathetic innervations were blocked with a beta-adrenergic blocking agent (propranolol, 4 mg intravenously). The results showed that when SNS influence on the heart and vasculature were blocked the physiological response differences between coping and no-coping situations were abolished. The authors interpret the results as evidence that providing a subject with an opportunity to cope with stressful events produces more appreciable sympathetic influences on the cardiovascular system than conditions where control is minimal or not possible. Obrist and colleagues call for additional studies to determine how various behavioral stressors might influence cardiovascular responsivity.

The cardiac-somatic hypothesis has been fruitful with regard to suggesting experiments. It is the newest of the concepts discussed in this chapter and appears to be in a developmental stage. Current and future research will determine its eventual form. In this context, it should be noted that none of the concepts presented here are completely fixed, and their forms may change as additional research findings foster new interpretations.

Adaptation and Rebound

Adaptation describes the decrease in physiological responsivity that occurs with repeated presentation of the same stimulus. For example, a change in skin conductance may be produced when a person's name is called out while the response is being measured. But as the name is repeated over and over again, the novelty or unexpectedness wears off and the SCR may diminish until it is nonexistent. The psychological effect may be likened to boredom produced by the repetition of the same stimulus. Sternbach (1966) observed that while we do not know why adaptation occurs it might be considered in terms of survival value for the species. More specifically, it would be a waste of energy if a number of similar stimuli, occurring in rapid succession, produced the same magnitude of response as the initial one.

The phenomenon of rebound may be observed when physiological variables return to values below those of prestimulus levels. If the SNS response to an intense stimulus, such as an electric shock or a pistol shot, is large in magnitude, then we may observe a poststimulus return of physiological variables to values below that of prestimulus levels. This overshooting of prestimulus levels in a direction opposite to that produced by an intense stimulus is called "rebound." Lang et al. (1972) point out that rebound is not due exclusively to antagonistic functions of the SNS and PNS, because it is observed to occur in responses mediated solely by the SNS (e.g., SCL). Sternbach (1966) notes that although we do not know why rebound occurs, it must be taken into account in the conduct of experimental investigations.

Orienting and Defensive Responses

Pavlov (1927) described a reflex that apparently enables animals to attend to novel and possibly biologically important stimuli. He noticed that a conditioned response failed to occur in a dog if an unusual stimulus was attended to by the dog who had previously evidenced conditioning. The response was termed the "orienting" or "what is it?" reflex. Lynn (1966) has described some of the physiological changes observed to occur when a novel stimulus is presented to humans. They include increased SCL, EMG, and pupil dilation; activation of the EEG pattern; a decrease in HR; vasoconstriction in the limbs; and vasodilation in the blood vessels of the head. These physiological changes are said to be directed at facilitating a possible response to the new stimulus.

Sokolov (1963) distinguished between the orienting response and the defensive response. While the OR occurred to novel stimuli, the DR was indicated as an accompaniment of intense, potentially painful, stimuli. As an example, it was proposed that cephalic vasoconstriction signals the DR, while vasoconstriction of blood vessels in the limbs is related to the OR. Graham and Clifton (1966) suggested that the OR would be accompanied by HR deceleration, while HR acceleration would most likely represent a DR to stimuli of prepain intensity. This suggestion was confirmed in a study by Raskin et al. (1969), in which HR deceleration (OR) was observed to occur with an 80-db (moderate) sound, while an increase in HR (DR) was produced by a 120-db (intense) sound. However, the dominant cephalic response was vasoconstriction. Hence, the cephalic vasomotor responses did not differentiate between ORs and DRs as predicted by Sokolov.

Hare (1973) recorded HR of 10 persons who feared spiders and compared them to 10 others who were not fearful. The 20 subjects viewed six spider slides and 24 slides of neutral objects, e.g., landscapes. Those individuals who feared spiders showed a DR in the form of accelerated HR, while those persons who were not afraid evidenced HR deceleration (OR), especially when they found the slides to be interesting. There seems to be a correspondence with the Lacey's "intake-rejection" hypothesis here. Namely, it appears that HR deceleration is associated with stimulus intake and the OR, while HR acceleration accompanies stimulus rejection and the DR. The OR–DR concept has obvious implications for psychophysiology. However, Lang et al. (1972) have noted several difficulties with Sokolov's conceptualization. For example, it does not explain selective attention or emotional specificity very well, and in addition, it has proven difficult to obtain measures of the DR.

The concepts that we have discussed in this chapter have been advanced by a relatively small number of workers in the field of psychophysiology. Still required is a broad theoretical framework which can perhaps help to integrate the various conceptual approaches. The concepts presented here have had the effect of stimulating much research. Data collection in the field is currently proceeding at a rapid pace, and we may look forward to the confirmation and refinement of present concepts and the development of new ones.

Appendix I
Environmental Influences on
Physiological Responses

There are a number of environmental factors, both internal and external, that can affect physiological measures. Among these factors are drugs, hormones, body temperature, air temperature, and oxygen. Some of the studies to be presented here may not be strictly psychophysiological in that they fail to use a behavioral measure. However, the influence of environmental factors must be considered because of the effects they may produce on both behavioral and physiological responses. Our discussion of environmental effects will start with the EEG and continue in the same order in which the various physiological measures are presented in the main body of this book. The material presented in the EEG section covers, for the most part, research performed subsequent to a review by Shagass (1972). In another very comprehensive review, Stroebel (1972) discussed the behavioral and physiological effects of drugs and included sections on EEG and autonomic response patterns.

Internal and External Environmental Factors and the Electroencephalogram

Drugs

The EEG is a valuable technique for an objective assessment of psychoactive drugs, that is, drugs having either a psychologically depressing or stimulating effect. This usefulness is further enhanced when behavioral or performance tests, as well as blood samples to determine the amount of the drug in the bloodstream, are conducted. In addition, the use of drugs in EEG studies may help to understand some of the biochemical factors in the brain that are involved in the production of the EEG.

Table A-1 is taken from Brown (1976) and provides a useful classification of some familiar drugs and their psychological effects. We shall examine effects on EEG of psychoactive drugs in the hallucinogen, opiate, and depressant categories.

The effects of drugs on behavior are by no means always clearcut and understandable. There are many factors operating including the "placebo effect." The placebo effect refers to the fact that the mere taking of a pill may have powerful suggestive effects so as to influence either some physiological response or behavior. A placebo is an inert substance, such as lactose, which can be made into pill form and may be administered in experiments to separate real effects of an active drug from suggestion effects of pill taking. Brown (1976) advises that correlations be-

Table A-1   Drugs Commonly Employed for Mind Alteration

	Type	Examples
Experience expanding	Hallucinogens	LSD
		Mescaline
		Marijuana
	Stimulants	Amphetamines
		Cocaine
		Caffeine
Experience restricting	Opiates (narcotics)	Heroin
		Morphine
		Methadone
	Depressants	Barbiturates
		Alcohol
		Nicotine
		Tranquilizers
		Solvents
		Methaqualone

Source: From H. Brown, *Brain and Behavior*, Oxford University Press, 1976, p. 296.

tween drug actions and their consequences must be treated with caution. For example, alcohol may alter emotionality by depressing cortical inhibitory systems, while amphetamines produce a similar effect by stimulating subcortical facilitory areas. Let us now examine some studies of drugs and their effects on the EEG.

LSD

Lysergic acid diethylamide (LSD) is a known "psychotomimetic" drug; that is, it produces some symptoms of mental illness such as hallucination and changes in mood and behavior. Investigators who have measured brain activity after administration of LSD generally agree that EEG amplitude decreases, alpha rhythms disappear, and the tracings become low in voltage and high in frequency (Rodin & Luby, 1966). The LSD effects increase progressively over a period of 1 to 2 hours following intravenous administration. Thus the psychological effects may be related to faster brain activity, indicating a more aroused nervous system. The effects of LSD and several other psychoactive agents were studied by Fink et al. (1967). Their computer analyses of the EEG spectrum indicated that beta activity was enhanced by LSD.

Marijuana

The effects of marijuana on EEG and psychological test performance were studied by Dornbush et al. (1971). The subjects were 10 male medical students who smoked cigarettes containing a high amount of marijuana (22.5 mg), a low amount (7.5 mg), or a placebo (the placebo was oregano, a spice that supposedly looks, smells, and tastes like "pot"). Measures of EEG, reaction time, short-term memory, and time estimation were taken under the different conditions. An increase in the percentage of time spent in alpha (8 to 13.5 Hz) activity and decreases in beta (18.5 to 24.5 Hz) and theta (4 to 7.5 Hz) activity occurred with the high dose but not with the low dose or the placebo. In addition, RT was reliably slowed, and performance on a short-term memory task was inhibited by the high dose. Accuracy of time estimation was not affected at any of the dose levels used. A similar result was obtained by Roth et al. (1973), who tested the effects of smoking cigarettes containing marijuana or synthetic trans-tetrahydrocannabinol (THC) on EEGs of 12 young male chronic users. The amount of EEG alpha activity increased with the marijuana but not with a placebo. The THC showed EEG effects that were in between the marijuana and the placebo, although both the THC and marijuana cigarettes contained 10 mg of the drugs. Thus the amount of alpha activity, the brain wave associated with a relaxed waking state, increased with marijuana use in these two experiments.

Heroin and Methadone

The short-term effects of heroin upon the EEG and other physiological measures was investigated by Volavka et al. (1974). Nineteen detoxified male postaddicts received 25 mg of heroin intravenously, on two occasions, and a placebo, also intravenously, on two other occasions. Heroin produced a significant decrease in EEG frequency within the first 5 minutes after injection. The decrease peaked at 15 minutes postinjection and remained at peak level when the 30-minute observation period ended. Respiration rate decreased from a mean of 18.5 cycles per minute before the injection to 7.6 cycles within 5 minutes after the administration of heroin. The authors suggest the possibility that some portion of the EEG decrease may have been caused by changes of blood chemistry resulting from decreased ventilation. A RT test indicated that reactions of the 19 subjects were significantly slower within 15 to 20 minutes after heroin injection than after the placebo.

The drug methadone is an analgesic that has widespread use as a detoxifying agent for narcotic addicts. Kay (1975) described the effects of methadone administration and withdrawal on the EEG of six volunteer prisoners. The procedure involved the oral administration of 100 mg of methadone daily during a stabilization phase lasting 51 to 56 days. Then an abstinence phase was instituted which entailed a complete, abrupt withdrawal of methadone for a 5-month period. During the stabilization phase, significantly increased amounts of delta and theta activity and a slowing of alpha activity in the EEGs of the waking subjects were observed. The EEG activity returned to the normal control level after 10 weeks of the withdrawal period. The author points out that chronic administration of narcotic analgesics, such as methadone, may produce persistent functional changes in the nervous system. The appearance of delta waves in the EEG records of awake subjects is considered to be abnormal. The alpha changes (slowing) produced by the administration of methadone over a long period of time were similar to those obtained by Volavka et al. (1974) with the administration of a single dose of heroin. Both drugs had obvious CNS effects as indicated by the records of brain activity.

Hypnotics and Tranquilizers

Single doses of hypnotic drugs (nitrazepam and amylobarbitone) produced EEG changes in 10 normal subjects which were still observable 18 hours after administration (Malpas et al., 1970). In a follow-up study (Malpas et al., 1974) with 10 anxious patients, the EEG showed changes with administration of hypnotic drugs (slow waves indicative of drowsiness and sleep), but the changes were not so pronounced as those noted in the earlier study with normal subjects. The authors suggest that the minor EEG changes in the 1974 study might have been due, in part, to the development of drug tolerance, since the hypnotics were taken for seven consecutive nights rather than in a single dose as in the 1970 study. West and Driver (1974) concluded that the EEG can be of value in diagnosing barbiturate intoxication in heroin-methadone addicts who deny taking barbiturates. They reported an investigation of 15 young addicts in which a greater amount of rhythmic fast components of the EEG was found in the records of those patients who admitted taking barbiturates than in those who denied it and had negative urines.

Nakra et al. (1975) examined the tranquilizing effects of metoclopramide (Maxolon) and prochlorperazine on EEGs and motor performance of 10 volunteers. The EEG was recorded from the left temporal area and from the vertex. The two drugs were given at .15 mg/kg of body weight, over a period of weeks. Both drugs increased the amount of slow wave activity (2 to 4 Hz) and feelings of lethargy and sedation. However, neither had significant effects on the measure of motor performance used (e.g., RT and key tapping rate).

Alcohol

Murphree (1973) noted that 1 minute after injection of a barbiturate (thiopental) fast frequency activity of 21 to 25 cps appeared in the EEG record. This curious phenomenon, in which activation of the EEG is produced by a substance that is supposed to be a depressant, is known as the "barbiturate buzz" and appears after relatively small doses of intravenously injected barbiturates (e.g., 1.5 mg/kg of thiopental). The question which Murphree asked was whether such effects could be found after drinking an alcoholic beverage. The EEG of a male subject was recorded for 10 minutes after drinking bourbon whiskey (1.00 ml/kg pure alcohol). This is the equivalent to about 6 oz of 80 proof whiskey for a 150-lb person. The EEG record showed a mixture of high-amplitude alpha with a "buzz" in the beta range. The subject acted giddy and "high" before and after the recording. Results from this and other subjects led Murphree to conclude that alcohol can produce stimulant effects as well as being a depressant in other instances. He suggests that the fast EEG activity observed after ingestion of alcohol may be due in part to disinhibition in the CNS and in part to catecholamine release. Catecholamines have a sympathomimetic action; that is, they mimic the stimulating effects of the SNS.

The effects of "experimental hangover" on the EEG were investigated by Sainio et al. (1976). The EEGs of 27 healthy male volunteers were recorded 14 to 16 hours after they drank an amount of pure alcohol equivalent to drinking about 11 oz of 80 proof whiskey, for a 150-lb individual. (Individuals who weighed more or less were given proportionate amounts, based on body weight.) At the 14 to 16 hour interval, when hangover is supposed to peak, 5 of the subjects reported severe hangover, 21 mild hangover, and 1 reported no hangover at all. Analyses of the EEG at this time showed a decrease and slowing of alpha activity and an increase in theta activity (4 to 7 Hz). A significant increase in the amount of 7 to 8 Hz activity was noted, as compared to the control condition in which subjects drank water. The researchers ruled out blood alcohol level, acidosis, hypoglycemia, or fatigue as a cause of the EEG change and concluded that the slowing of EEG during hangover was caused by the depressant action of alcohol, or its metabolites, on cortical function. Thus the long-term effects of alcohol seem to be different in terms of EEG activity than short-term effects. No "barbiturate buzz" was reported by Sainio et al., but it must be noted that they recorded 14 to 16 hours after alcohol ingestion, while Murphree recorded EEG immediately afterward.

Nicotine (Smoking)

Ulett and Itil (1969) tested the effects of cessation and resumption of cigarette smoking (nicotine) on the EEGs of eight males who were heavy smokers (more than one pack of cigarettes a day). Individuals tested were deprived of cigarettes for 24 hours, during which time the EEG showed a slowing of activity. This slowing was reversed when two cigarettes were smoked after the deprivation period. A similar result was obtained by Philips (1971). Six moderate smokers were tested after smoking for 5 minutes or engaging in conversation for 5 minutes. After smoking, the EEG showed an "activation pattern" in the form of decreased amplitude and a desynchronized EEG record. Thus, nicotine seems to speed EEG activity of smokers. Knott and Venables (1977) measured EEG alpha of 10 nonsmokers, 17 deprived smokers, and 13 nondeprived smokers before and after they smoked two cigarettes. The deprived smokers had a slower dominant alpha frequency than nonsmokers before the two groups smoked. The two cigarettes brought their EEG frequency up to the level of nonsmokers. Knott and Venables discuss the possibility that smoking is an attempt by smokers to achieve the psychological state associated with higher alpha frequencies, that is, one of increased efficiency and attention. They indicate that their results support the hypothesis that deprived smokers, as compared to nonsmokers, are characterized by a state of cortical underactivity, and smoking increases their activity to a level comparable to that which nonsmokers are at naturally.

In summary, the studies reviewed in this section indicate that marijuana and heroin both have depressant effects on brain activity and performance (methadone has effects similar to heroin). Two tranquilizers (Nakra et al., 1975) increased EEG slow wave activity but had no performance effects. Hypnotic drugs produced slowing of EEG, while LSD resulted in low-amplitude, high-frequency brain waves. Alcohol was seen to have short-term activating effects, but produced depressant effects after a longer period of time. Nicotine (cigarette smoking) appears to speed the EEG frequency of smokers and bring it up to the level of nonsmokers.

Hormones

The endocrine system consists of ductless glands that secrete their chemicals (called hormones) directly into the bloodstream. These hormones have profound influence over many body functions, and in addition, their undersecretion or oversecretion may have behavioral effects. The endocrine system is regulated by the nervous system (primarily through connections between the hypothalamus and pituitary gland) and, therefore, the EEG may be able to reflect interactions between these systems. EEG activity has been found to be increased in cases of hyperthyroidism (excessive secretion of the hormone thyroxin) and decreased in hypothyroidism (Thiebaut et al., 1958; Hermann & Quarton, 1964). A lack of adrenal cortical hormones has been related to slow brain activity, which can be speeded up through administration of the hormone cortisone (Engel & Margolin, 1942).

Vogel et al. (1971) conducted two studies to examine the effects of gonadal (sex) hormones on EEG responses. The EEG response measured was the "driving" response, defined as the production of EEG waves at the same frequency as a flashing light for two consecutive seconds. Thus, for example, if a flashing light was presented to a subject 15 times a second, the driving response would be evidenced if EEG waves occurred at a rate of 15 cycles per second for at least a 2-second period. Vogel et al. found that EEG driving was significantly less when blood estrogen levels were high. The first study was done with 14 normally menstruating women and significantly less EEG driving was observed during the preovulatory phase of the menstrual cycle, when blood estrogen levels are rising, than in the postovulatory phase when both estrogen and progesterone levels are high. In a second study, the EEG driving response was manipulated by administering estrogen and progesterone to six women who required hormone therapy for secondary amenorrhea; that is, their menstrual cycle had stopped completely some time after it had started at puberty. For these women, EEG driving was decreased significantly after administration of estrogen compared to the EEG response which occurred after combined administration of estrogen and progesterone. It was hypothesized that estrogen inhibited the EEG driving response through the steroid's known ability to inhibit monoamine oxidase (MAO). The MAO reduces supplies of monoamines in the brain, such as norepinephrine, which facilitate neural transmission. Thus, if MAO activity in the brain is depressed, EEG driving should be diminished, since substances that enhance transmission block the driving response to light. Since progesterone is an antagonist to estrogen, their combined administration should allow EEG driving to occur, as was found in the Vogel et al. study.

A later experiment by Vogel et al. (1974) provides further support for the hypothesis regarding the relationship between MAO activity and the EEG driving response. This time 10 male subjects were given the drug isocarboxazid (Marplan) which is known to inhibit MAO. A reduced level of MAO in blood samples, several days after the administration of Marplan, was significantly related to decreases in the EEG driving response. They interpreted these results as reflecting the disruptive effect of central adrenergic processes upon EEG driving responses to photic stimulation.

In a related study, Creutzfeldt et al. (1976) studied EEG changes during the menstrual cycle of 32 normal women, aged 20 to 28. The EEGs, blood hormone levels, and psychological test performances were measured for 16 spontaneously menstruating women and 16 women taking oral contraceptives. A significant increase in alpha frequency occurred in the spontaneous group during the luteal phase of the cycle, and this increase in alpha was significantly correlated with an improvement in RT, simple arithmetic, and spatial orientation. (The luteal phase is one in which the hormone progesterone reaches a peak level, and it occurs shortly after ovulation.) No such acceleration of alpha frequency nor performance improvement was observed in the oral contraceptive group. As a possible physiological mechanism for the increase in alpha frequency, the authors postulate a shortening of inhibitory postsynaptic potentials (IPSPs) in the thalamus during the luteal phase. They speculate that this decreased inhibition might also cause the improvement in RT and other tests. Another interesting suggestion by these authors is that the increased alpha frequency might be the physiological basis of premenstrual tension, that is, the increased CNS activation may be the basis of the increased feelings of irritability noticed by women at the end of the luteal phase, just prior to menstruation. The several studies reviewed indicate that hormones can affect EEG activity. However, these internal events may be difficult to control in the usual experimental situation.

Oxygen

The CNS is critically dependent upon oxygen supply for its functioning. Hence, it would be logical to expect changes in the oxygen supply, or factors that influence it, to be reflected in brain activity. Past studies have indicated that a lack of oxygen caused a slower frequency and higher amplitude EEG, while oxygen excess increased EEG frequency (Gibbs et al., 1940; Engel, 1945). Several recent investigations have examined oxygen effects somewhat indirectly, that is, through studies of elderly persons, whose cerebral blood flow and oxygen are usually reduced, and through alterations in the usual breathing mixture as encountered in deep sea diving habitats and at high altitudes.

The relationship between cerebral blood flow and EEG frequency has been clearly demonstrated by Ingvar et al. (1976). They found a high positive correlation between EEG frequency and a measure of cerebral blood flow and oxygen consumption; that is, EEG frequency decreased with decreased blood flow and oxygen consumption.

A number of studies cited by Cole et al. (1975) indicate that EEG activity in elderly persons sometimes shows a slowing, for example, a decrease in alpha frequency. Papaverine HCL (Pavabid) is a vasodilator (a drug that dilates blood vessels and increases blood flow). Cole et al. administered Papaverine (300 mg) to 10 healthy elderly persons (mean age of 68) over a 2-week period. They reported that Papaverine altered EEG activity by increasing the percentage of time spent in alpha, without affecting mood or psychological test performance. The psychological tests included one of short-term memory (digit span), problem solving (Block Design), attention (continuous performance test), and self- and machine-paced digit symbol substitutions. The authors suggested that the lack of effect upon psychological test performance may have been due to the fact that the subjects were already functioning at high levels.

The EEGs of 10 centenarians (persons 100 years of age or older) were examined by Hubbard et al. (1976). Seven of the 10 subjects were considered "healthy," since they were living in the community and had been examined for evidence of CNS or psychiatric disorder. The EEGs of the three persons with CNS disease were abnormal. The average EEG frequency of the seven healthy subjects was 8.62 Hz, or 1 to 2 Hz slower than the alpha rhythm reported for normal middle-aged and young adults, respectively. Three of these seven subjects showed one EEG abnormality, a presence of slow waves in the delta range. The authors note that from these results it would appear that the fall in alpha frequency becomes negligible after 80 to 90 years of age. Hubbard et al. (1976) concluded that results for centenarians are compatible with the notion of a causal relationship between atherosclerosis, a drop in cerebral blood flow, increased incidence of slow waves, and a decrease in alpha frequency.

Rostain and Charpy (1976) investigated the effects on EEG of two simulated deep dives, in which subjects breathed a helium-oxygen mixture. Previous research by Rostain and Naquet (1974) had established that deep diving to a simulated depth of 300 m (about 990 ft) resulted in increased theta rhythm, a decrease of alpha and beta, and a lowering of the level of vigilance. The Rostain and Charpy (1976) experiment took place in two stages: in the first part, two subjects stayed at 500 m (about 1650 ft) for 100 hours, and in the second, two subjects stayed at 610 m (about 2000 ft) for 80 minutes. EEG changes, relative to "surface" recordings were similar to the previous study in that theta activity increased, fast activity was depressed, and an EEG resembling Stage 1 sleep appeared. The authors concluded that the EEG changes could be due either to deficits in cerebral oxygenation, decreased blood flow, or to alterations in metabolic processes caused by hyperbaric (high air pressure) conditions.

The effects of sleep at high altitude on the EEG as compared to sea level sleep was investigated by Reite et al. (1975). All-night sleep EEG was recorded from six male army recruits, first during two nights at sea level (160 ft) and then during four nights while sleeping at the Pikes Peak research station (14,110 ft). Sleep at high altitude was initially characterized by decreases in Stage 3 and 4 sleep (see Table 4-1) and an increase in number of awakenings. This was accompanied by subjective complaints of sleeplessness. The authors were unsure whether the results were due to less oxygen intake (hypoxemia) at the high altitude or to alkalosis (increase in blood pH levels) often present after arrival at high altitude. Both hypoxemia and alkalosis decreased during continuous exposure to altitude, and the authors related this to improvement in the objective and subjective quality of sleep as the experiment progressed in time.

In summary, studies in which oxygen deficit is indicated provide evidence for a slowing of EEG activity associated with such decreased supply.

Body Temperature

An early study of body temperature effects on the EEG indicated that alpha wave frequency increased with temperature increases (Hoagland, 1936). Essentially the same conclusion was reached by O'Hanlon et al. (1974), who increased body core temperature (to 102.2°F) by diathermy while EEG and perceptual acuity was measured. In this study, "body core" referred to temperature measured at the subject's tympanic membrane (eardrum) by a thermistor. Previous experimentation had shown that tympanic temperature approximates brain temperature. The results of the O'Hanlon study showed that mean alpha frequency increased with increases in body core temperature. The reason for the increase in synchronous brain activity with increases in body temperature and increases in the amount of unsynchronized (beta) activity with decreases in body temperature still remains unknown, but may be related to the role of metabolic factors in the production of EEG activity.

Effects of Environmental Factors on Event-related Potentials (ERPs)

This section examines some studies dealing with the effects of drugs, hormones, and oxygen level upon ERPs.

Drugs

There are numerous studies of the effects of pharmacologic agents upon ERPs. Many of these were reviewed by Shagass (1972), who noted that various changes in ERPs occur as the result of drug action. For example, diazepam has been found to reduce the amplitude of the visual ERP (VEP) and somatosensory ERP (SEP). This would imply that beneficial effects with a psychiatric population are related to decreased cortical responsivity. Lithium carbonate seems to restrict the range of cortical responsivity to sensory stimuli, and Shagass suggests that it may improve the functioning of central mechanisms by improving the balance between excitatory and inhibitory processes. Lithium has been frequently used in the treatment of manic-depressive patients in recent years. Manic-depressives show tremendously exaggerated mood swings, ranging from extreme excitement to immobilizing depression.

Tranquilizers and Barbiturates

The commonly used tranquilizer Valium (diazepam) has been found to decrease the amplitude of human VEPs (Bergamasco, 1966). The effects of 7.5 to 10 mg of intravenously administered Valium on the VEPs and SEPs of nine normal persons was investigated by Ebe et al. (1969). The amplitudes of both VEPs and SEPs was reduced.

Saletu et al. (1972) investigated the effects of chlorpromazine and diazepam on the SEPs of healthy male subjects. Chlorpromazine is a widely used antipsychotic drug. While the placebo did not affect the SEP, 50 mg of chlorpromazine prolonged latencies of all components 2 hours after administration. In addition, chlorpromazine resulted in decreased amplitudes of the late components of the SEP (those occurring at 150 msec or later). Diazepam (5 mg) resulted in a decrease in SEP amplitude. Thus, it appears that both drugs suppressed brain activity, with the chlorpromazine having more potent effects since it produced both latency and amplitude changes.

Tecce et al. (1975) measured CNV and RT of 28 normal women after they were given 50 mg of chlorpromazine or a placebo. The experimental paradigm was that of a constant foreperiod RT situation in which S1 was a light flash and S2 was a tone which occurred 1.5 seconds after the light and was terminated by a key press. They found that this relatively small dose of chlorpromazine significantly reduced electrical brain activity (CNV) and lowered alertness (slower RTs) in the third hour after administration of the drug. Tecce et al. concluded that CNV amplitude appears to be an accurate indicator of drug-produced changes in alertness. In summary, the general pattern of results for diazepam and chlorpromazine is one in which brain activity is suppressed.

The effects of a barbiturate on the VEP were illustrated by Bergamini and Bergamasco (1967). Thiopental was administered intravenously and was found to modify the VEP by decreasing its amplitude during initial stages of anesthesia. When barbiturate anesthesia was deeper (and delta waves were present in the EEG) the early components of the VEP completely disappeared, that is, those that normally occurred before 60 msec.

The effects of two barbiturates on CNV and attention performance was tested by Tecce et al. (1977). Thirty male subjects were randomly assigned to either pentobarbital (100 mg), phenobarbital (100 mg), or placebo groups (10 subjects per group). Pentobarbital has short duration effects, while those of phenobarbital are relatively long-lasting. The CNV was recorded from frontal (F_z), central (C_z), and parietal (P_z) scalp areas. The measure of attention was time to respond to a target letter in a series of letters. The only significant drug effect was a decrease in CNV amplitude recorded from P_z 2 hours after administration of phenobarbital. This was accompanied by a decrement in attention performance.

Amphetamine is a CNS stimulant and has been used as an antidepressant in psychiatric patients. Amphetamine had an unexpected effect on the CNV in the first hour after administration in a number of normal individuals (Tecce & Cole, 1974). Thirteen of 20 adults who were given 10 mg of dextroamphetamine evidenced lower CNV amplitudes and drowsiness during the first hour following administration of the drug. The other seven showed alertness and increased CNV amplitude. All subjects showed increased alertness and CNV amplitudes 2 and 3 hours following the drug. Tecce and Cole concluded that amphetamine is not a simple CNS stimulant but can produce an early, transient depression in brain activity, accompanied by feelings of lethargy in some persons. Thus, results with barbiturates indicate suppression of brain activity, while one suggestive study with amphetamine indicated that early effects may be stimulating or depressing, depending on the individual.

Effects of Marijuana on ERP

Lewis et al. (1973) tested the effects of known oral doses of tetrahydrocannabinol (THC), the active ingredient in marijuana, on the VEPs and SEPs of 10 male and 10 female subjects. The subjects were equally divided into two groups: frequent smokers (three times a week) and infrequent smokers (two times a month). Three dosage levels (.2, .4, and .6 mg/kg of body weight) were administered to each subject on flavored sugar cubes. (These dosage levels are equivalent to about 10 mg, 20 mg, and 40 mg of THC for a 150-lb subject.) The highest dose (.6 mg/kg) produced delays in the appearance of the various wave components of the VEP. There was little effect on amplitude. All dose levels produced subjective "highs." The finding was interpreted in terms of increased thresholds of cortical and subcortical neurons by the action of THC; that is, it took longer for responses to visual stimulation to occur.

Roth et al. (1973) studied the effects of smoking a marijuana cigarette (10 mg endogenous THC) on the auditory ERPs

(AEPs) of 12 chronic users. A placebo cigarette (containing .5 mg of THC) and another cigarette containing synthetic THC (10 mg) were also smoked. Roth and colleagues found no latency effects, but decreased AEP amplitudes were noted with the real marijuana cigarette. The reduced effect of synthetic THC may be related to the fact that purified THC undergoes greater destruction during smoking than THC contained endogenously in the marijuana leaf.

Low et al. (1973) measured visual and auditory ERPs and the CNV 45 minutes before and 45 minutes after smoking a marijuana cigarette containing high (9.1), low (4.8), or less than .01 mg of $\triangle^9$ THC. Performance in a complex auditory discrimination task was simultaneously measured. High doses of marijuana resulted in longer auditory ERP latencies, and interfered with the discrimination task. The CNV increased in amplitude as a consequence of marijuana smoking. Kopell et al. (1972) also found enhancement of CNV with THC. Thus, marijuana appears to slow, and in one instance to reduce in amplitude, sensory ERPs. However, the evidence suggests an enhancement of CNV with marijuana. The enhancement has been interpreted by Kopell et al. as indicating that subjects who are intoxicated can better attend to relevant, simple stimuli as required in the CNV paradigm. These interesting marijuana effects on ERPs require further investigation.

Alcohol

The effects of alcohol on ERPs have been studied by a number of investigators. For example, Gross et al. (1966) measured auditory ERPs of 10 subjects after they drank either 100 cc of water with ice or 100 cc of 90 proof whiskey (about 3 oz) with ice. All components of the AEP were reduced after ingestion of alcohol, with maximal effect noted 15 to 30 minutes after consumption. Similar results were found by Lewis et al. (1970), who administered alcohol doses equivalent to about 1 and 3 oz for a 150-lb subject. Somatosensory and visual ERPs were measured after administration of either alcohol condition or a water placebo. The higher alcohol dose reduced amplitudes of VEP and SEP late components. The smaller dose and placebo had no effect. Rhodes et al. (1975) reported that alcohol reduced the amplitude of VEPs recorded from the central scalp. Similar to earlier studies it was the later components (60 to 200 msec) which were affected most by the alcohol. Salamy and Williams (1973) demonstrated that as the blood alcohol concentration (BAC) level of subjects increased, amplitude of the SEP decreased. Again, the major effects were on later components of ERPs. Salamy (1973) also found the SEP amplitude to decrease with BAC. An illustration from Salamy (1973) is reproduced in Figure A-1 and shows a clear decrease in the SEP for one subject from Condition A (placebo) to B (low dose) to C (high dose). Thus, it is clear that alcohol has an effect on the neural processes reflected by ERPs. The results of Lewis et al. (1970) led them to conclude that alcohol exerts a depressant effect on subcortical areas first (e.g., the reticular formation) and later on the cortex. It had previously been hypothesized that cortical effects appeared before subcortical ones.

Nicotine

Hall et al. (1973) investigated the effects of smoking withdrawal and resumption upon the VEP. They measured VEPs of nine smokers (three-quarters to three packs per day) to four intensities of light. The VEPs were taken during different baseline periods: before abstinence from smoking, after 12 and 36 hours of abstinence, and finally after resumption of smoking (one cigarette). The results showed a decrease in VEP amplitude during the no-smoking period and an increase in VEP amplitude when smoking was resumed. Hall and his associates suggested that the increased VEP amplitude may indicate that the processing of sensory stimuli by the brain is changed when smokers use tobacco. Perhaps the withdrawal of nicotine for smokers is distracting, in which case it might result in lower VEPs. Distracting stimuli have been shown to reduce CNV amplitude (e.g., see Tecce, 1972).

In summary, the drug studies reviewed here indicate that tranquilizers have depressant effects upon ERPs. Alcohol, marijuana, and barbiturates have depressant effects, but the effects of marijuana are different from the other two, since they are sometimes

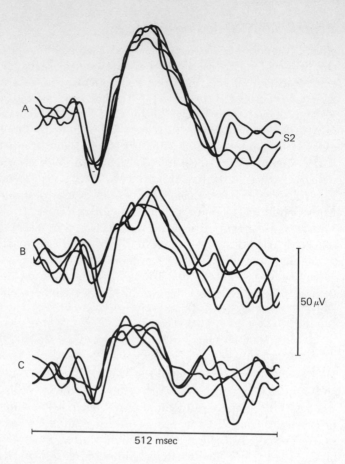

Figure A-1. Dose-response relationship between evoked potential amplitude and blood alcohol concentration (BAC). Four superimposed single EPs recorded from one subject under three alcohol treatments: A, placebo (BAC of o mg %); B, low dose (BAC of 50–65 mg %); C, high dose (BAC of 95–110 mg %).

manifested as delays in ERP components, rather than as decreases in amplitude. There is nothing in the results of ERP studies to contradict the generally accepted notion that the effects of depressant drugs are mainly upon the ARAS. Abstinence from cigarette smoking seems to depress the VEPs of regular smokers, while resumption restores the VEPs to original levels. This finding could be important in terms of the possible physiological mechanisms that cause certain individuals to become heavy smokers, or it may only reflect a distracting effect of nicotine withdrawal for these persons. More work is needed to settle this question.

Oxygen and Breathing Mixture Effects

When divers breathe compressed air at a depth of 100 feet or more, they may suffer from compressed air intoxication, sometimes referred to as nitrogen narcosis. Approximately 80% of the air we breathe at sea level is nitrogen. At sea level pressure the nitrogen has no effects, but at high pressures, it can cause varying degrees of narcosis.[1] After an hour or more of breathing air at high pressures, some of the symptoms of alcohol intoxication are observed, including giddiness and drowsiness. Nitrogen narcosis has been referred to as "raptures of the depths" because it sometimes occurred in deep sea divers.

Bennett et al. (1969) showed that hyperbaric nitrogen and oxygen both depressed the amplitude of the auditory ERP. They concluded that these results supported the hypothesis that breathing these gases at high pressures affected such subcortical systems as the ARAS of the brain stem. The effects of inhaling 10%, 20%, and 30% nitrous oxide in oxygen were compared with those of pure oxygen in 12 normal individuals (Jarvis & Lader, 1971). Reaction time was also measured under each of these drug conditions. All components of the AEP were reduced according to dose level of nitrous oxide, that is, the higher the dose the greater the decrease in amplitude. RT was also prolonged in a dose-related manner.

[1] Oxygen is also toxic at high pressures. It has detrimental effects on the CNS and may cause convulsions and coma if breathed at high pressures for a prolonged period of time.

Bevan (1971) recorded the AEP and CNV from 13 experienced divers before, during and following an exposure to an increased air pressure simulating a depth of 300 ft in sea water. The AEP was significantly reduced, but the CNV was not. These results were interpreted as indicating the generation of the AEP and CNV by different CNS mechanisms. It was also suggested that the AEP was attenuated because of inhibition effects on the ARAS, while the CNV was considered to be a self-propagating phenomenon, initiated by the interaction between specific and nonspecific and associational thalamic nuclei. However, two other investigators questioned Bevan's assumption that the CNV and AEP are generated by independent mechanisms (Smith & Strawbridge, 1974). They point out that the AEP is more complex (has more components) than the CNV, and a reduction in amplitude could reflect an actual change in amplitude of individual potentials, latency variations, or changes in cortical area acting in synchrony. In their own study, Smith and Strawbridge measured AEP, VEP, and CNV while subjects breathed air and 100% pure oxygen at sea level. No effect of hyperoxia was found on the AEP, VEP, or CNV. They suggested that further studies be done on the effects of breathing pure oxygen at pressures greater than one atmosphere.

In summary, hyperbaric conditions seem to have depressant effects on sensory ERPs but not on the CNV. Preliminary interpretations would suggest a different generating mechanism for ERPs and CNVs, an implication contained in the classificatory system of Vaughan (1969) in which sensory ERPs and CNVs were separately categorized.

Effects of Hormones on ERP

The undersecretion of the hormone thyroxin by the thyroid gland can have serious psychological effects in both infants and adults. A condition known as myxedema develops in adults with thyroxin deficiency (hypothyroidism) and is characterized by apathy and mental sluggishness, among other effects. The ERPs of patients with hypothyroidism were studied before and after administration of thyroid hormone (Nishitani & Kooi, 1968). The hormone resulted in decreased latencies and increased amplitudes of the ERP, that is, the nervous system showed greater responsivity to stimuli.

An excess of thyroxin, or hyperthyroidism, results in extreme nervousness, insomnia, and tremor owing to stimulating effects of this hormone on the nervous system. Hyperthyroidism was produced experimentally by administering 300 mg of the thyroid hormone triiodothyronine (T3) to normal persons (Kopell et al. 1970). The T3 was found to increase the amplitude of VEPs when subjects were not selectively attending to visual stimuli but had no effect when they were selectively attending. The researchers interpreted this as a reduction in selective attention, as measured by VEP amplitude, caused by T3, that is, the hormone appeared to increase cortical response to nonsignificant information, while not affecting response to significant stimuli.

The somatosensory and visual ERPs of 14 persons suffering from hyperthyroidism were compared with the ERPs of 45 normal control individuals in an experiment conducted by Takahashi and Fujitani (1970). They found that amplitudes of each component of the SEP and VEP were greater in hyperthyroid than in normal persons. No significant latency differences were noted between the patient and normal groups. Straumanis and Shagass (1977) administered T3 to 12 normal subjects and found increased SEP amplitudes during the first 100 msec following the stimulus. Thus the general results for the thyroid hormone seem to correlate an excess with greater ERP amplitudes and deficiencies with lower amplitudes, possibly reflecting differential sensitivity of the CNS to stimuli when levels of this hormone are either high or low.

A number of investigators have reported that women have larger amplitude ERPs than men (e.g., see Shagass, 1972). Buchsbaum et al. (1974) conducted an experiment to determine possible reasons for the noted sex differences. Visual and auditory ERPs of 166 normal males and females, aged 6 to 60, and 10 females with gonadal dysgenesis (lacking in estrogen or progesterone production) were measured. The 10 female patients were compared with normal women. The role of gonadal hormones in producing the sex differences in amplitude seemed to be ruled out on two counts: (1) females had larger ERPs than males at all ages (prepuberty and postmenopause), and (2) ERPs of female patients did not differ from those of normals. Another finding of interest in this study was that no correlation between skull thickness and AEP was found, suggesting that anatomical differences in the skulls of men and women do not explain the observed sex differences in ERP amplitudes.

Environmental Factors and the Electromyogram (EMG)

Drugs

Girke et al. (1975) noted complaints of muscular weakness in manic-depressive patients undergoing long-term lithium treatment. To test the hypothesis that this was due to a disturbance in peripheral neuromuscular function, they measured EMGs of seven healthy volunteers before, during, and after lithium administration. The EMG was recorded from the extensor digitorum brevis muscle of the right foot. They found that the duration of potentials was increased and nerve conduction velocity was decreased after 1 week of lithium intake. Both muscle potential duration and nerve conduction returned to near prelithium levels 1 week after the administration of lithium sulfate was discontinued. The authors hypothesized that lithium may exert its effects by influencing magnesium metabolism, which in turn may affect the regulation of enzymes such as ATP.

Exercise

Milner-Brown et al. (1975) reported that the degree to which firing of motor units in one muscle are synchronized is affected by the use of the muscle in physical exercise. That is, the impulses from two or more motor units coincide in time more frequently than would be expected for unrelated firings. Recordings from the first dorsal interosseus muscle of the hand in seven weightlifters showed significantly more synchronization than in seven control subjects. Further, records from four additional subjects before and after 6 weeks of exercise involving the same hand muscle showed a significant increase in the level of motor unit synchronization. The authors suggested that the different firing patterns of exercised versus nonexercised muscles may be due to enhancement of connections from motor cortex to spinal motoneurons to produce synchronization of motor units during steady, voluntary contractions. One may wonder whether this type of synchronization of motor units occurs in the development of a skilled motor performance.

Environmental Factors and Electrodermal Activity (EDA)

Hormones and Drugs

Venables and Christie (1973) discuss the possibility of hormonal influences upon EDA. For example, they point out that progesterone has been found to decrease eccrine gland sweat output and that ACTH has similar effects. Presumably, then, these hormones have the potential to affect EDA. In fact, a decrease in resting SCL was found during the luteal phase in the menstrual cycle of 12 female subjects (Little & Zahn, 1974). Progesterone level reaches its peak during the luteal phase. Further, Little and Zahn found significant increases in SCR during the ovulatory portion of the menstrual cycle, the time when estrogen reaches peak levels in the body.

The effects of preanesthetic doses of diazepam on SCRs obtained under thiopental sodium induction was investigated by Williams et al. (1975). The subjects were physiologically normal young female patients about to undergo operations. One half received 10 mg of diazepam or 10 mg of a placebo intravenously. The diazepam subjects required significantly less thiopental sodium (44%) to reach the point at which spontaneous SCRs abruptly ceased than did the placebo group. Corsico et al. (1976) compared the effects of two psychoactive drugs, etifoxine (300 mg) and dextroamphetamine (5 mg) on SCRs and pursuit-rotor performance of six undergraduates. All persons received a placebo and the two drugs in a double-blind procedure over a 3-week period. The subjects were tested before, 2 hours after, and 6 hours after drug administration. At the 2-hour period, both drugs led to significant reductions in SCR magnitude and improved pursuit-rotor performance as compared to the placebo condition. These differences disappeared 6 hours after the administration of the three treatments.

In summary, although the amount of data is scanty, it would appear that both hormones and drugs can affect EDA. Thus, investigators of electrodermal phenomena should be aware of these possible influences and gather appropriate information from subjects so that these factors may be accounted for in the design of their experiments.

Racial and Experimenter Effects

Johnson and Corah (1963) found that black subjects had lower SCL than whites. A number of other researchers have obtained similar findings (e.g., Bernstein, 1965; Johnson & Landon, 1965; Juniper & Dykman, 1967; Malmo, 1965). Johnson and Corah (1963) hypothesized that the difference might be due to either a thicker stratum corneum in blacks or a difference in the number of active eccrine sweat glands. This latter hypothesis was tested in a study by Johnson and Landon (1965) in which they used 30 black and 29 white subjects. No difference in the number of active sweat glands was found. However, Malmo (1965) found less finger sweating for his 7 dark-skinned as compared to 52 light-skinned subjects. Bernstein (1965) found lower SCL for blacks as compared to whites and also reported a significant examiner effect. That is, subjects tested by one experimenter showed higher SCL than those seen by a second experimenter. However, the white and black subjects did not respond differentially to the two experimenters. Juniper and Dykman (1967) reported that 29 white males had a higher sweat gland count than did 13 blacks in a similar age range (20 to 60 years). In addition, SCL of blacks was lower. The effects of race and experimenter's race were studied by Fisher and Kotses (1973). The SCL and SCR frequency and magnitude of 12 white and 12 black subjects were measured under two conditions. Two black and two white experimental assistants (naive as to the purpose of the study) obtained the measurements. Blacks had lower SCLs, as previously reported. The race of the experimenter did have an effect on SCR amplitude and frequency. For example, the size of the SCR was greater in magnitude and took longer to habituate for white subjects who were tested by black experimenters. Fisher and Kotses concluded that novelty was a factor in the result, since the presence of black experimenters was a relatively infrequent occurrence.

One common denominator in these studies seems to be skin color, that is, darker skin being related to lower SCLs. A device to objectively measure intensity of skin color (in reflectance units) was developed by Korol et al. (1975). These investigators measured skin color of 25 whites and 25 blacks with their "pigmentometer" and correlated these with SCL. They reported that degree of skin pigmentation was related to SCL, that is, the darker the skin color the lower the SCL. It is still not clear whether the racial differences found are due to genetic elements other than skin color, for example, number of sweat glands or some other factor. Perhaps studies comparing other racial groups would be of value in answering this basic question. In the meantime, skin color is a possible variable that investigators must be aware of in conducting studies.

Another variable is that of the experimenter's sex. For example, Fisher and Kotses (1974) found that male subjects had higher SCL and a greater number of SCRs when a female served as experimenter than when the experimenter was a male. These experimenters also suggest a stimulus novelty explanation. That is, the female experimenter is a relatively novel situation in the psychological laboratory, and stimulus novelty has been related to EDA in past experimentation. However, arousal is also a possibility, especially when there is mutual attraction between female experimenters and male subjects.

Experimental Situation and EDA

When a subject enters a novel experimental situation, his SCL is likely to be elevated. When he settles down and relaxes, SCL will drop, and when the actual experiment is about to start, it will again show an increase. This appears to reflect activity of the SNS in a new situation where the individual observes a large amount of electronic equipment in a strange laboratory and does not know what to expect. As has been pointed out by Woodworth and Schlosberg (1954), the changes in SCL and number of SCRs during the performance of an experimental task are affected by apprehension, relief, the work itself, and habituation. Since EDA is so sensitive to a variety of stimulus variables, it may be best to test subjects in more than one experimental session to enable situational effects to dissipate. Similarly, it may be desirable to use persons who have served in previous experiments, as long as this does not interfere with the nature of the study, to reduce these extraneous effects. These same observations would hold true in the use of other physiological measures but are perhaps most critical in the measurement of the very sensitive EDA.

Environmental Factors and Pupil Size

Drugs

The narcotic analgesic, morphine, produces pupillary constriction through its CNS effects (Goth, 1964). Pupillography was used by Robinson et al. (1974) to study pupil size of 10 heroin users during the first 6 days of withdrawal. Five control subjects were used for comparison purposes. In the acute heroin intoxication state, the pupils of patients were significantly constricted relative to controls, that is, the average diameters were 3.5 mm and 5.0 mm, respectively. Ten hours after the last dose of heroin, there was no difference between patients and controls. As withdrawal progressed the pupils of patients continued to dilate until at the end of the 6-day period the patients had significantly larger pupils than controls. The authors concluded that pupil diameter is a good differential indicator of heroin intoxication and withdrawal.

Another drug that produces pupillary constriction is pilocarpine. It can produce this action if applied to the surface of the eye in a 1% solution. Pupillary dilation is produced by the drug atropine. In ophthalmologic and research settings it is applied to the eye as a 0.5% to 1.5% solution. Homatropine is preferable to atropine because it is much shorter in duration of action (Goth, 1964). Pupillary dilation can also be caused by neosynephrine (Hansmann et al., 1974).

Ambient Illumination

Ambient illumination has an effect upon pupil diameter such that intensity increases result in pupillary constriction and decreases produce dilation (e.g., see Young & Biersdorf, 1954). Woodhouse and Campbell (1975) examined the interesting hypothesis that the pupil constricts in bright light in order to lower retinal illumination and prepares the eye, in advance, for the return to dimmer illumination. To test this suggestion, they measured sensitivity of the eye when the pupil was dilated with a 2% homatropine solution and under natural (mobile) conditions. The eye was considerably more sensitive to stimuli with a mobile pupil than with a continually dilated pupil. Thus the authors argue that the natural pupil reduces the level of light adaptation by lowering retinal illumination and this ensures more rapid dark adaptation upon the return to low light levels.

Effects of Drugs on Eye Movements

Holzman et al. (1975) measured the effects of three different drugs on the pursuit eye movements of five normal adult males. The subjects were asked to follow a moving pendulum with their eyes for a 30-second period while horizontal eye movements were measured binocularly. Deviations from smooth pursuit movements were quantified as velocity arrests, that is, the number of times pursuit was interrupted when the eyes should have been tracking. The drugs diazepam (Valium) and chlorpromazine had no significant effects on pursuit movements. However, sodium secobarbital (Seconal, 100 mg) affected the ability to follow the moving target with smooth-pursuit eye movements. Prolonged testing of Seconal effects (130 mg) with one subject showed that this barbiturate produced eye-tracking and eye movement disruptions that persisted for 24 hours.

The effects of Valium on the reading eye movements of 18 male college students was studied by Stern et al. (1974). The administration of Valium, as compared to a placebo, produced an increased frequency of long fixation pauses, an increased duration of fixations, and a decreased velocity of saccadic eye movements during line shifts. These changes were correlated with a decrease in the amount of material read.

Environmental Factors and Heart Activity

Drugs

A number of drugs are known to affect heart activity. Among
them are ones used for therapeutic purposes. For example, one
effect of the drug digitalis is to increase the contractility of cardiac muscle, or its capacity to do work. Nitroglycerin acts to
increase blood flow to the heart by producing vasodilation (Goth,
1964).

Nicotine

The effects of cigarette smoking on heart rate were studied by
Elliott and Thysell (1968). The HR of 18 habitual smokers (one
to two packs per day) were measured under three conditions:

1. Dragging on an unlit cigarette every 30 seconds for 5 minutes
   (sham smoking)
2. Deep breathing every 30 seconds for 5 minutes
3. Inhaling cigarette smoke every 30 seconds for 5 minutes

The investigators found that neither sham smoking (unlit cigarette) nor deep breathing influenced HR. However, actual
smoking raised HR 20 bpm, on the average, over resting levels.
Fifteen minutes after actual smoking ceased the HR was still
11 bpm over resting levels. The authors interpreted the increased
HR in terms of the increased heart activity required to overcome the vasoconstrictive effects of smoking, that is, HR
speeded up to compensate for reduced blood flow.

The effects of rapid and normal cigarette smoking on HR, as
compared to sham smoking, were investigated by Danaher et al.
(1976). The rapid smoking condition consisted of inhaling every
6 seconds on a cigarette, while regular smoking involved inhaling
a cigarette at normal rate. The sham smoking condition was accomplished by inhaling on an unlit cigarette every 6 seconds.
Rapid smoking of cigarettes produced significantly higher HR
than regular smoking, and regular smoking resulted in HR
which was significantly elevated over the sham smoking condition.

The effects of smoking nicotine cigarettes upon HR seem to be rather consistent, that is, a significant elevation occurs.

Marijuana

Clark et al. (1974) tested the effects of marijuana upon heart activity of 28 subjects, half of whom were experienced users. The drug was inhaled through a filtered breathing apparatus. The most consistent effect was an increase in HR. Clark (1975) reviewed a number of studies of marijuana effects upon heart rate. Increases in HR from 18% to 51% over control levels have been reported with administration of synthetic (Δ^9 THC) or real marijuana. Some researchers suggest that marijuana produces its effects on heart activity through increased SNS activity mediated by epinephrine release. Others propose that marijuana may have its effects on HR by inhibiting vagus nerve activity, thus allowing HR to increase. The exact mechanisms of the effect still remain to be elucidated.

Cocaine

Fischman et al. (1976) administered cocaine intravenously, in doses ranging from 4 to 32 mg, to nine adult males. Mean HR was 74 bpm predrug, 100 bpm after 16 mg of cocaine, and 112 bpm after 32 mg. In general, HR peaked at 10 minutes, regardless of dose level, and returned to predrug baseline after 46 minutes. Control injection of saline solution had no effects on HR.

In summary, both marijuana and cocaine act to accelerate HR. The mechanism by which this increase is produced remains obscure.

Water Submersion

Psychologists and physiologists have used soundproof chambers and water immersion to study the effects of reduced sensory input (isolation) upon humans. The water immersion technique has been less commonly employed since subjects generally seemed to spend less time (voluntarily) in water immersion than in quiet room situations. Forgays and McClure (1974) conducted a study to compare tolerance to these two environments. The main dependent variables were time voluntarily spent in the two environments, subjective time estimates, and HR. The subjects were 10 healthy individuals (5 male and 5 female). The investigators reported that 7 of 10 subjects tolerated the maximum time (6 hours) in the soundproofed cubicle, while only 2 remained submerged in a 7-ft tank of water for 6 hours. The water in the tank was at a very comfortable temperature (94°F), and subjects breathed through a face mask while suspended vertically by a harness. The average time spent in the room was 5¼ hours compared to 4½ hours in the water tank. The subjects underestimated the time they spent in the room by 1 hour, whereas they overestimated tank time by ¼ hour. The average HR was 67 bpm in the room and 81 bpm while submerged in a virtually weightless condition. The authors concluded that water immersion is a more stressful isolation condition, with subjects being more aroused than in the quiet room condition.

Gooden et al. (1975) measured the HR of freely swimming scuba divers using ultrasonic telemetry. The HR data were obtained from six divers (three professional and three amateur) during a mission designed to perform a biological survey of a coral reef. The dives did not require strenuous physical effort, according to the researchers, and ranged in depth from 21 to 23 m. All the divers showed elevated HR on the reef (106 bpm) as compared to measures taken just before entering the water (95 bpm). The highest HR on the reef was recorded from an amateur diver (153 bpm) and the lowest from an experienced diver (87 bpm). The individual differences in HR were quite large among the six divers, with the professional divers showing lower rates during dives than the amateurs. The results of the two experiments just described indicate that HR is higher during water submersion than under dry conditions.

Environmental Factors and Blood Pressure

Drugs

A number of drugs are known to affect blood pressure levels. For example, reserpine and pentobarbital sodium are known to lower blood pressure, while epinephrine increases it (Goth, 1964). The blood pressure of 79 healthy male students was measured 2 months before and on the day before final examinations (Ruttkay-Nedecky & Cagan, 1969). Subjects were administered either a barbiturate (10 mg of phenobarbital) or a placebo (double blind) on both occasions. Both the placebo and the barbiturate produced significant decreases in systolic and diastolic blood pressure measures.

The effects of two drugs (imipramine and methylphenidate) and a placebo on the blood pressure and pulse rate of 47 hyperactive children was studied by Greenberg and Yellin (1975). The children ranged in age from 6 to 13 years and completed an 8-week double-blind study in which half of the patients received one of the drugs followed by a placebo, while the other half received the placebo first. Imipramine was found to produce significant increases in blood pressure (both systolic and diastolic) and pulse rate. Methylphenidate did not affect either of these variables. The authors recommend caution in using imipramine to treat hyperactive children.

Exercise and Blood Pressure

Buccola and Stone (1974) studied a number of physiological variables of 36 elderly men before and after they participated in a 14-week exercise program. The men ranged in age from 60 to 79 and participated in either a cycling program (20 subjects) or in a walk-jog program (16 subjects). The two groups trained for 25 to 50 minutes a day, 3 days a week. Both groups showed significant reductions in blood pressure and weight. Systolic pressure dropped from an average of 147 mm Hg to 141 mm Hg (4.1%) and diastolic decreased from 79 mm Hg to 72 mm Hg (8.9%). Thus, elderly persons appear to benefit physiologically from regular light exercise.

To summarize, various drugs can result in the lowering or raising of blood pressure. Regulated physical exercise appears to have beneficial effects on blood pressure measures in elderly persons.

Appendix II
EEG Recording System

For EEG research, a good recorder should have the following specifications. The first stage of amplification (or gain) should allow for multiplication of the signal by a factor of at least 1000. Additional amplification by a factor of 1000 will raise it to a level suitable for data transmission or recording, that is, an amplification of 10^6 or 1,000,000. Variable filtering[1] should be provided to eliminate unwanted signals from the record. A high input impedance[2] of 1 to 10 million Ω is desirable, since it can reduce error caused by changes in electrode-scalp resistance. The sensitivity of the recorder should allow readings of 1, 2, 5, 10, 50, and 100 μV per each millimeter (mm) of pen deflection. The ink-writing system should be flexible enough to follow a signal faster than the highest frequencies you may be interested in (e.g., 50 cps). If not, connection of the recording system to an oscilloscope should be easy to accomplish in order to view the highest frequencies. Variable paper speeds should be available. A desirable paper speed for EEG recording is about 50 mm per second. Slower or faster speeds may be used depending on the application. A calibrating device should enable the determination of signal amplitude on the ink writer.

An ohm meter built into the physiological recorder measures

[1] The main purpose of a filter is to prevent unwanted frequency components from being recorded. Thus, if you are not interested in frequencies above 100 Hz, you would set your filter to screen these out. Variable filtering enables you to eliminate more than one frequency band.

[2] Impedance is the opposition to current flow in a circuit.

resistance of the skin to a small electric current. If skin resistance is too high, the recording will not be clear. The equipment should be adequately grounded to prevent accidental shocking of the subject. Grounding also eliminates unwanted electrical signals from the recording by sending them to a neutral location. The third, or ground, lead of the plug is generally connected to a water pipe and from there reaches the earth surrounding the building.

When the EEG is recorded for clinical purposes, the patient may lie on his back, and the leads are attached to a terminal which then leads, by way of a large shielded cable, to the EEG recorder. In most research situations, except perhaps those studying EEG during sleep, the subject sits upright, since the investigator usually requires the person to engage in some type of activity, whether it be learning, problem solving, or signal detection. The laboratory should be quiet and free from auditory or visual distractions. A well-lit, air-conditioned environment will help to make the subject comfortable in performing his task. Many EEG researchers use sound-attenuated, electrically shielded chambers for the conduct of their experiments. The subject is usually provided with a comfortable chair or bed in the experimental chamber. These chambers are commonly equipped with one-way viewing windows so that the subject can be observed from the outside or visual stimulus materials can be conveniently presented. A well-equipped laboratory will also contain a multichannel FM tape system for permanent recordings of the EEG or other physiological measures. These data can later be played back for additional or off-line analysis. The use of computers in the control of experiments and analysis of data is becoming more common among investigators in the area of psychophysiology.

Appendix III
Laboratory Safety

Laboratories that use physiological recorders should take proper precautions to protect human subjects or patients from possible electric shocks or burns. If an accidentally high electric current passes through the skin it can produce pain or tissue damage. If it is very high and flows across the body, it could interfere with heart activity. Ventricular fibrillation of the heart is the most frequent cause of death in fatal electrical accidents.

Protection Against Electric Shock

Modern physiological recorders use various techniques to protect subjects from shock. For example, many of them use transistor circuits (in the first stage amplifiers connected to the electrodes) to isolate the subject from high-voltage circuits. However, even though the probability of shock is very low, additional precautions must be taken. One approach is to fuse each electrode lead to prevent shocks through inadvertent shorts between the electrodes and associated circuitry. A 5-mA fuse would limit electric current flow to a safe level in the advent of a malfunction. This would be especially important when making recordings that require the placement of electrodes on either side of the body, as is commonly done in measuring heart activity, for example, electrodes placed on the right and left arms. Another approach would be to connect each electrode to ground

through voltage-limiting diodes. (A diode is a device that limits
current flow to one direction.)

Since electric current passed across the body is more dangerous than current limited to one side, the use of one-sided measurement is preferred where feasible. For example, skin conductance measures should be made from the same hand rather than
using two hands. Similarly, ground electrodes should be placed
on the same side of the body as active electrodes whenever
possible.

Methods of Accident Prevention

A number of techniques to prevent or minimize the probability
of occurrence of an electrical accident have been outlined by
Cromwell et al. (1976).

Grounding

Grounding may be achieved by connecting the metal case of a
piece of equipment to ground by a wire or by using three-pronged
plugs in which the ground connection is established by the
round contact in the plug. In the event of an electrical short, the
current will flow through the case and be shunted off to ground.

Use of Low Voltage

The use of low voltage calls for operating equipment at lower
voltages than that provided by electrical outlets (they commonly provide 115 V). One way of doing this is to operate equipment from batteries. Another method is to use a small trans-
former which reduces the power requirement for operating the
equipment (e.g., from 115 to 6 V).

Isolation of Subject-connected Parts

Isolation requires the use of amplifiers that are completely isolated from ground.

Ground-fault Interrupter

Interrupters involve the use of a circuit that is designed to automatically interrupt power, like a circuit breaker, when a person touches a defective piece of equipment and current returns to ground through his body.

Dos and Don'ts

In their book, Cromwell et al. (1976) provide a list of "dos and don'ts" with respect to making the operation of electrical equipment as safe as possible. These lists are summarized here:

Dos

1. Familiarize yourself with the equipment by studying its proper usage as explained in the operating manuals.
2. Always follow correct operating procedures.
3. Report any irregularities of equipment function to appropriate personnel. For example, intermittent operation, slight electric shocks, or loose controls should be brought to the attention of an electronics technician or engineer or maintenance personnel employed by the equipment manufacturer.

Don'ts

1. Don't remove plugs from outlets by pulling the line cord. This can break or loosen the ground wire.
2. Don't use "adapter" plugs, that is, two-pronged plugs that enable you to plug a three-pronged piece of equipment into an ungrounded outlet. The wiring should be redone to accommodate three-prong plugs; otherwise, grounding is not possible.
3. Don't use extension cords. If absolutely necessary, use heavy-duty, three-wire cords that provide for ground connections.
4. Don't run carts over, or step on, electrical cables or connectors. This can cause breaks in the ground wire.
5. Don't operate any piece of electrical equipment without being thoroughly familiar with its operation and possible shock hazards.

References

Chapter 1

Boring, E. G. *A history of experimental psychology* (2nd ed.). New York: Appleton-Century-Crofts, 1950.

Coleman, J. C. *Abnormal psychology and modern life*. Dallas: Scott, Foresman, 1976.

Feuerstein, M., & Schwartz, G. E. Training in clinical psychophysiology: Present trends and future goals. *American Psychologist*, 1977, *32*, 560-567.

Gardner, E. *Fundamentals of neurology* (6th ed.). Philadelphia: Saunders, 1975.

Gray, H. *Anatomy—descriptive and surgical*. Pick, T. P. & Howden, R. (Eds.), New York: Bounty Books, 1977.

Guyton, A. C. *Basic human physiology: Normal function and mechanisms of disease*. Philadelphia: Saunders, 1977.

Johnson, H. J. & May, J. R. The educational process in psychophysiology. *Psychophysiology*, 1973, *10*, 215-217.

Penfield, W., & Roberts, L. *Speech and brain mechanisms*. Princeton: Princeton University Press, 1959.

Pick, J. *The autonomic nervous system*. Philadelphia: Lippincott, 1970.

Sternbach, R. A. *Principles of psychophysiology*. New York: Academic Press, 1966.

Venables, P. H. & Martin, I. *Manual of psychophysiological methods*. Amsterdam: North-Holland, 1967.

Chapter 2

Beatty, J., Greenberg, A., Deibler, W. P., & O'Hanlon, J. F. Operant control of theta rhythm affects performance in a radar monitoring task. *Science*, 1974, *183*, 871-873.

Brown, B. *New mind, new body, biofeedback: New directions for the mind.* New York: Harper & Row, 1974.

Callaway, E. *Brain electrical potentials and individual psychological differences.* New York: Grune & Stratton, 1975.

Elul, R. Randomness and synchrony in the generation of the electroencephalogram. In H. Petsche & M. A. B. Brazier (Eds.), *Synchronization of EEG activity in epilepsies.* New York: Springer-Verlag, 1972, pp. 59-77.

Evans, C. C. Comments on: "Occipital sharp waves responsive to visual stimuli." *Electroencephalography and Clinical Neurophysiology,* 1952, *4,* 111.

Gardner, E. *Fundamentals of neurology.* Philadelphia: Saunders, 1975.

Gastaut, H. Etude electrocorticographique de la reactivite des rythmes rolandiques. *Revue Neurologique,* 1952, *87,* 176-182.

Gastaut, Y. Un signe electroencephalographique peu connu: Les pointes occipitales survenant pendant 1 ouverture des yeux. *Revue Neurologique,* 1951, *84,* 640-643.

Grossman, S. P. *Essentials of physiological psychology.* New York: Wiley, 1973.

Jasper, H. H. Report of the committee on methods of clinical examination in electroencephalography. *Electroencephalography and Clinical Neurophysiology,* 1958,*10,* 370-375.

Kennedy, J. L., Gottsdanker, R. M., Armington, J. C., & Gray, F. E. A new electroencephalogram associated with thinking. *Science,* 1948, *108,* 527-529.

Koshino, Y., & Niedermeyer, E. Enhancement of rolandic mu rhythm by pattern vision. *Electroencephalography and Clinical Neurophysiology,* 1976, *38,* 535-538.

Maulsby, R. L. An illustration of emotionally evoked theta rhythm in infancy: Hedonic hypersynchrony. *Electroencephalography and Clinical Neurophysiology,* 1971, *31,* 157-165.

Noback, C. R., & Demarest, R. J. *The human nervous system.* New York: McGraw-Hill, 1975.

Walter, W. G. *The living brain.* New York: Norton, 1953.

Chapter 3

Andreassi, J. L. Alpha and problem solving: A demonstration. *Perceptual and Motor Skills,* 1973, *36,* 905-906.

Beatty, J., & Kornfeld, C. Relative independence of conditioned EEG changes from cardiac and respiratory activity. *Physiology and Behavior,* 1972, *9,* 733-736.

Busk, J., & Galbraith, G. C. Electroencephalography of visual-motor practice in man. *Electroencephalography & Clinical Neurophysiology*, 1975, *38*, 415-422.

Davidson, R. J., & Schwartz, G. E. The influence of musical training on patterns of EEG asymmetry during musical and non-musical self-generation tasks. *Psychophysiology*, 1977, *14*, 58-63.

Dement, W. C., & Kleitman, N. Cyclic variations in EEG during sleep and their relation to eye movements, body motility, and dreaming. *Electroencephalography and Clinical Neurophysiology*, 1957, *9*, 673-680. (a)

Dement, W. C., & Kleitman, N. The relation of eye movements during sleep to dream activity: An objective method for the study of dreaming. *Journal of Experimental Psychology*, 1957, *53*, 339-346. (b)

Ellingson, R. J. Brain waves and problems of psychology. *Psychological Bulletin*, 1956, *53*, 1-34.

Elson, B. D., Hauri, P., & Cunis, D. Physiological changes in yoga meditation. *Psychophysiology*, 1977, *14*, 52-57.

Fink, M., Itil, T., & Shapiro, D. Digital computer analysis of the human EEG in psychiatric research. *Comprehensive Psychiatry*, 1967, *8*, 521-538.

Galbraith, G. C., London, P., Leibovitz, M. P., Cooper, L. M., & Hart, J. T. Electroencephalography and hypnotic susceptibility. *Journal of Comparative and Physiological Psychology*, 1970, *72*, 125-131.

Gale, A., Morris, P., Lucas, B., & Richardson, A. Types of imagery and imagery types: An EEG study. *British Journal of Psychology*, 1972, *63*, 523-531.

Galin, D., & Ellis, R. R. Asymmetry in evoked potentials as an index of lateralized cognitive processes: Relation to EEG alpha asymmetry. *Neuropsychologia*, 1975, *13*, 45-50.

Galin, D., & Ornstein, R. Lateral specialization of cognitive mode: An EEG study. *Psychophysiology*, 1972, *9*, 412-418.

Giannitrapani, D. Electroencephalographic differences between resting and mental multiplication. *Perceptual and Motor Skills*, 1966, *22*, 399-405.

Giannitrapani, D. EEG average frequency and intelligence. *Electroencephalography & Clinical Neurophysiology*, 1969, *27*, 480-486.

Griesel, R. D. A study of cognitive test performance in relation to measures of speed in the electroencephalogram. *Psychologia Africana*, 1973, *15* 41-52.

Hayes, R. W., & Venables, P. H. EEG measures of arousal during RFT performance in "Noise". *Perceptual and Motor Skills*, 1970, *31*, 594.

Khrizman, T. P. Characteristics of interventral relationships in electrical processes of the brain in 2 to 3 year old children during voluntary motor acts. *Voprosy Psikhologii*, 1973, *19*, 107-117.

Lansing, R. W., Schwartz, E., & Lindsley, D. B. Reaction time and EEG activation under alerted and nonalerted conditions. *Journal of Experimental Psychology*, 1959, *58*, 1-7.

Leavitt, F. EEG activation and reaction time. *Journal of Experimental Psychology*, 1968, *77*, 194-199.

Lindsley, D. B. Electroencephalography. In J. McV Hunt (Ed.), *Personality and the behavior disorders*. New York: Ronald Press, 1944.

London, P., Hart, J. T., & Leibovitz, M. P. EEG alpha rhythms and susceptibility to hypnosis. *Nature*, 1968, *219*, 71-72.

Maxwell, A. E., Fenwick, P. B., Fenton, G. W., & Dollimore, J. Reading ability and brain function: A simple statistical model. *Psychological Medicine*, 1974, *4*, 274-280.

McKee, G., Humphrey, B., & McAdam, D. W. Scaled lateralization of alpha activity during linguistic and musical tasks. *Psychophysiology*, 1973, *10*, 441-443.

Morgan, A. H., MacDonald, H., & Hilgard, E. R. EEG alpha: Lateral asymmetry related to task, and hypnotizability. *Psychophysiology*, 1974, *11*, 275-282.

Rostain, J. C., & Naquet, R. Le syndrome nerveux des hautes pressions: Caracteristiques of evolution en fonction de divers moddes de compression. *Review of EEG and Neurophysiology*, 1974, *4*, 107-124.

Satterfield, J. H., Cantwell, D. P., Saul, R. E., & Usin, A. Intelligence, academic achievement and electroencephalography abnormalities in hyperactive children. *American Journal of Psychiatry*, 1974, *131*, 391-395.

Shagass, C. Electrical activity of the brain. In N. S. Greenfield & R. A. Sternbach (Eds.), *Handbook of psychophysiology*. New York: Holt, Rinehart & Winston, 1972, pp. 263-328.

Surwillo, W. W. Timing of behavior in senescence and the role of the central nervous system. In G. A. Talland (Ed.), *Human aging and behavior*. New York, Academic Press, 1968.

Surwillo, W. W. Human reaction time and period of the EEG in relation to development. *Psychophysiology*, 1971, *8*, 468-482. (a)

Surwillo, W. W. Interhemispheric EEG differences in relation to short-term memory. *Cortex*, 1971, *7*, 246-253. (b)

Surwillo, W. W. Latency of EEG attenuation ("blocking") in relation to age and reaction time in normal children. *Developmental Psychobiology*, 1972, *5*, 223-230.

Surwillo, W. W. Speed of movement in relation to period of the EEG in normal children. *Psychophysiology*, 1974, *11*, 491-496.

Surwillo, W. W. The EEG in the prediction of human reaction time during growth and development. *Biological Psychology*, 1975, *3*, 79-90.

Thompson, L., & Botwinick, J. The role of the preparatory interval in the relationship between EEG, alpha-blocking and reaction time. *Psychophysiology*, 1966, *3*, 131-142.

Thompson, L. & Botwinick, J. Age differences in the relationship between EEG arousal and reaction time. *The Journal of Psychology*, 1968, *68*, 167-172.

Vogel, W., & Broverman, D. M. Relationship between EEG and test intelligence: A critical review. *Psychological Bulletin*, 1964, *62*, 132-144.

Warren, L. R., & Harris, L. J. Arousal and memory: Phasic measures of arousal in a free recall task. *Acta Psychologica*, 1975, *39*, 303-310.

Warren, L. R., Peltz, L., & Haueter, E. S. Patterns of EEG alpha during word processing and relations to recall. *Brain and Language*, 1976, *3*, 283-291.

Woodworth, R. S., & Schlosberg, H. *Experimental psychology*, New York: Holt, 1954.

Chapter 4

Aarons, L. Sleep-assisted instruction. *Psychological Bulletin*, 1976, *83*, 1-40.

Ali, M. R. Pattern of EEG recovery under photic stimulation by light of different colors. *Electroencephalography & Clinical Neurophysiology*, 1972, *33*, 332-335.

Ali, M. R. Cortical habituation response to coloured lights and its relation to perception of stimulus duration, *Electroencephalography & Clinical Neurophysiology*, 1973, *35*, 550-552.

Aserinsky, E., & Kleitman, N. Regularly occurring periods of eye motility, and concomitant phenomena, during sleep. *Science*, 1953, *118*, 273-274.

Beatty, J. Similar effects of feedback signals and instructional information on EEG activity. *Physiology and Behavior*, 1972, *9*, 151-154.

Beatty, J. Greenberg, A., Deibler, W. P., & O'Hanlon, J. F. Operant control of occipital theta rhythm affects performance in a radar monitoring task. *Science*, 1974, *183*, 871-873.

Berlyne, D. E. Attention as a problem in behavior therapy. In D. I.

Mostofsky (Ed.), *Attention: Contemporary theory and analysis.* New York: Appleton-Century-Crofts, 1970, pp. 25-49.

Berlyne, D. E., & McDonnell, P. Effects of stimulus complexity and incongruity on duration of EEG desynchronization. *Electroencephalography & Clinical Neurophysiology,* 1965, *18*, 156-161.

Brownman, C. P., & Tepas, D. I. The effects of pre-sleep activity on all-night sleep. *Psychophysiology,* 1976, *13*, 536-540.

Brown, B. Recognition of aspects of consciousness through association with EEG alpha activity represented by a light signal. *Psychophysiology,* 1970, *6*, 442-452.

Bryden, G., & Holdstock, T. L. Effects of night duty on sleep patterns of nurses. *Psychophysiology,* 1973, *10*, 36-42.

Christie, B., Delafield, G., Lucas, B., Winwood, M., & Gale, A. Stimulus complexity and the electroencephalogram: Differential effects of the number and the variety of display elements. *Canadian Journal of Psychology,* 1972, *26*, 155-170.

Claridge, G. S., & Harrington, R. N. An EEG correlate of the Archimedes spiral aftereffect and its relationship with personality. *Behavior Research and Therapy,* 1963, *1*, 217-229.

Clarke, A. M., Michie, P. T., Andreassen, A. G., Viney, L. L., & Rosenthal, R. Expectancy effects in a psychophysiological experiment. *Physiological Psychology,* 1976, *4*, 137-144.

Dement, W. C. & Kleitman, N. Cyclic variations in EEG during sleep and their relation to eye movements, body motility, and dreaming. *Electroencephalography & Clinical Neurophysiology,* 1957, *9*, 673-690.

Eberlin, P. & Mulholland, T. Bilateral differences in parietal-occipital EEG induced by contingent visual feedback. *Psychophysiology,* 1976, *13*, 212-218.

Estes, W. K. (Ed.). *Attention and memory.* New York: Halstead Press, 1976.

Fath, S. J., Wallace, L. A., & Worsham, R. W. The effect of intermittent auditory stimulation on the occipital alpha rhythm. *Physiological Psychology,* 1976, *4*, 185-188.

Firth, H. Habituation during sleep. *Psychophysiology,* 1973, *10*, 43-51.

Foulkes, W. D. Dream reports from different stages of sleep. *Journal of Abnormal and Social Psychology,* 1962, *65*, 14-25.

Gale, A. Some EEG correlates of sustained attention. In R. R. Mackie (Ed.), *Vigilance.* New York: Plenum Press, 1977, pp. 263-283.

Giannitrapani, D. Scanning mechanisms and the EEG. *Electroencephalography & Clinical Neurophysiology,* 1971, *30*, 139-146.

Hebb, D. O. *A textbook of psychology.* Philadelphia: Saunders, 1958.

Horne, J. A., & Porter, J. M. Exercise and human sleep. *Nature*, 1975, *256*, 573-575.

Johnson, L. C. Learned control of brain wave activity. In J. Beatty & H. Legewie (Eds.), *Biofeedback and behavior*. New York: Plenum, 1977, pp. 73-93.

Johnson, L. C., Townsend, R. E., & Wilson, M. R. Habituation during sleeping and waking. *Psychophysiology*, 1975, *12*, 574-584.

Kahneman, D. *Attention and effort*. Englewood Cliffs, N. J.: Prentice-Hall, 1973.

Kamiya, J. Operant control of the EEG alpha rhythm and some of its reported effects on consciousness. In C. T. Tart (Ed.), *Altered states of consciousness*. New York: Wiley, 1969, pp. 507-515.

Kripke, D. F., Cook, B., & Lewis, O. F. Sleep of night workers: Electroencephalography recordings. *Psychophysiology*, 1970, *7*, 377-384.

Langford, G. W., Meddis, R., & Pearson, A. J. D. Awakening latency from sleep for meaningful and non-meaningful stimuli. *Psychophysiology*, 1974, *11*, 1-5.

Lehmann, D., & Koukkou, M. Computer analysis of EEG wakefulness— Sleep patterns during learning of novel and familiar sentences. *Electroencephalography & Clinical Neurophysiology*, 1974, *37*, 73-84.

Levere, T. E., Bartus, R. T., Morlock, G. W., & Hart, F. D. Arousal from sleep: Responsiveness to different auditory frequencies equated for loudness. *Physiology & Behavior*, 1973, *10*, 53-57.

Levere, T. E., Davis, N., Mills, J., & Berger, E. H. Arousal from sleep: The effects of cognitive value of auditory stimuli. *Physiological Psychology*, 1976, *4*, 376-382.

Levere, T. E., Morlock, G. W., & Hart, F. D. Arousal from sleep: The differential effect of frequencies equated for loudness. *Physiology & Behavior*, 1974, *12*, 573-582.

Loomis, A. L., Harvey, E. N., & Hobart, G. Distribution of disturbance patterns in the human electroencephalogram, with special reference to sleep. *Journal of Neurophysiology*, 1938, *1*, 413-430.

Lubin, A., Moses, J. M., Johnson, L. D., & Naitoh, P. The recuperative effects of REM sleep and Stage 4 sleep on human performance after complete sleep loss: Experiment 1. *Psychophysiology*, 1974, *11*, 133-146.

Mackworth, N. H. Researches on the measurement of human performance. Medical Research Council Special Report No. 268. London: H. M. Stationary Office, 1950.

McDonald, D. G., Schicht, W. W. Frazier, R. E., Shallenberger, H. D.,

& Edwards, D. J. Studies of information processing in sleep. *Psychophysiology*, 1975, *12*, 624-629.

Meddis, R., Pearson, A. J., & Langford, G. An extreme case of healthy insomnia. *Electroencephalography & Clinical Neurophysiology*, 1973, *3*, 181-186.

Moses, J. M., Johnson, L. C., Naitoh, P., & Lubin, A. Sleep stage deprivation and total sleep loss: Effects on sleep behavior. *Psychophysiology*, 1975, *12*, 141-146.

Mostofsky, D. I. (Ed.). *Attention: Contemporary theory and analysis.* New York: Appleton, Century-Crofts, 1970.

Mulholland, T. Training visual attention. *Academic Therapy*, Fall 1974, *10*.

Naitoh, P. Sleep deprivation in humans. In P. H. Venables & M. J. Christie (Eds.), *Research in psychophysiology*, New York: Wiley, 1975, ch. 7.

Nowlis, D. P., & Kamiya, J. The control of electroencephalographic alpha rhythms through auditory feedback and the associated mental activity. *Psychophysiology*, 1970, *6*, 476-484.

Oswald, I., Taylor, A. M., & Treisman, M. Discriminative responses to stimulation during human sleep. *Brain*, 1960, *83*, 440-453.

Pavlov, I. P. *Conditioned reflexes.* Oxford: Clarendon Press, 1927.

Rechtschaffen, A. The psychophysiology of mental activity during sleep. In F. J. McGuigan & R. A. Schoonover (Eds.), *The psychophysiology of thinking.* New York: Academic Press, 1973, pp. 153-205.

Shagass, C. Electrical activity of the brain. In N. S. Greenfield & R. A. Sternbach (Eds.) *Handbook of psychophysiology.* New York: Holt, Rinehart & Winston, 1972, pp. 263-328.

Simon, C. W., & Emmons, W. H. Responses to material presented during various levels of sleep. *Journal of Experimental Psychology*, 1956, *51*, 89-97.

Snyder, F., & Scott, J. The psychophysiology of sleep. In N. S. Greenfield & R. A. Sternbach. *Handbook of psychophysiology.* New York: Holt, Rinehart & Winston, 1972, pp. 645-708.

Sokolov, E. N. *Perception and the conditioned reflex.* Oxford: Pergamon Press, 1963.

Tecce, J. J. Contingent negative variation (CNV) and psychological processes in man. *Psychological Bulletin*, 1972, *77*, 73-108.

Valle, R. S., & Levine, J. M. Expectation effects in alpha wave control. *Psychophysiology*, 1975, *12*, 306-309.

Vignaendra, V. Positive occipital sharp transients of sleep: Relationships to nocturnal sleep cycle in man. *Electroencephalography & Clinical Neurophysiology*, 1974, *37*, 239-246.

Wang, C. C., Marple, H. D., & Carlson, H. EEG desynchronization during pitch discrimination. *Journal of Auditory Research,* 1975, *15,* 140-145.

Webb, W. B., & Agnew, H. W. The effects of a chronic limitation of sleep length. *Psychophysiology,* 1974, *11,* 265-274.

Williams, H. L., Hammack, J. T., Daly, R. L., Dement, W. C., & Lubin, A. Responses to auditory stimulation, sleep loss and the EEG stages of sleep. *Electroencephalography & Clinical Neurophysiology,* 1964, *16,* 269-279.

Williams, H. L., Morlock, H. C., & Morlock, J. V. Instrumental behavior during sleep. *Psychophysiology,* 1966, *2,* 208-216.

Williams, H. L., & Williams, C. L. Nocturnal EEG profiles and performance. *Psychophysiology,* 1966, *3,* 164-175.

Woodward, D. P., & Nelson, P. D. A user oriented review of the literature on the effects of sleep loss, work-rest schedules, and recovery on performance. *Technical Report ARC-206,* Office of Naval Research, Arlington, Va. 1974.

Zhirmunskaya, E. A., Beyn, E. S., Volkov, V. N., Voitenko, G. A., & Konyukhova, G. R. Correlation analysis of EEG changes during recognition of images of objects. *Electroencephalography & Clinical Neurophysiology,* 1975, *39,* 255-259.

Chapter 5

Amadeo, M., & Shagass, C. Brief latency click-evoked potentials during waking and sleep in man. *Psychophysiology,* 1973, *10,* 244-250.

Andreassi, J. L., DeSimone, J. J., Friend, M. A., & Grota, P. A. Hemispheric amplitude asymmetries in the auditory evoked potential with monaural and binaural stimulation. *Physiological Psychology,* 1975, *3,* 169-171.

Andreassi, J. L., & Greco, J. R. Effects of bisensory stimulation on reaction time and the evoked cortical potential. *Physiological Phychology,* 1975, *3,* 189-194.

Andreassi, J. L., Mayzner, M. S., Beyda, D. R., & Davidovics, S. Effects of induced muscle tension upon the visual evoked potential and motor potential. *Psychonomic Science,* 1970, *20,* 245-247.

Arezzo, J., & Vaughan, H. G., Jr. Cortical potentials associated with voluntary movements in the monkey. *Brain Research,* 1975, *88,* 99-104.

Beck, E. C. Electrophysiology and behavior. *Annual Review of Psychology,* 1975, *26,* 233-262.

Becker, W., Iwase, R., Jurgens, R., & Kornhuber, H. H. Bereitschaftspotential preceding voluntary slow and rapid hand movements. In W. C. McCallum & J. R. Knott (Eds.), *The responsive brain*. Bristol: John Wright & Sons, 1976, pp. 99-102.

Bergamini, L., & Bergamasco, B. *Cortical evoked potentials in man*. Springfield: C. C Thomas, 1967.

Brown, W. S., Marsh, J. T., & Smith, J. C. Contextual meaning effects on speech-evoked potentials. *Behavioral Biology*, 1973, 9, 755-761.

Buchsbaum, M. Average evoked response and stimulus intensity in identical and fraternal twins. *Physiological Psychology*, 1974, 2, 365-370.

Buchsbaum, M., and Fedio, P. Visual information and evoked responses from the left and right hemispheres. *Electroencephalography and Clinical Neurophysiology*, 1969, 26, 266-272.

Buchsbaum, M., & Fedio, P. Hemispheric differences in evoked potentials to verbal and nonverbal stimuli in the left and right visual fields. *Physiology and Behavior*, 1970, 5, 207-210.

Buchsbaum, M., Gillin, J. C., & Pfefferbaum, A. Effect of sleep stage and stimulus intensity on auditory average evoked responses. *Psychophysiology*, 1975, 12, 707-712.

Butler, R. A., Keidel, W. D., & Spreng, M. An investigation of the human cortical evoked potential under conditions of monaural and binaural stimulation. *Acta Otolaryngologica*, 1969, 68, 317-326.

Callaway, E. *Brain electrical potentials and individual psychological differences*. New York: Grune & Stratton, 1975.

Cohen, J. Very slow brain potentials relating to expectancy: The CNV. In E. Donchin & D. B. Lindsley (Eds.), *Average evoked potentials: methods, results, evaluations*. NASA, Washington, D.C.: U.S. Gov't. Printing Office, 1969.

Cooper, R. Methodology of slow potential changes. In W. C. McCallum & J. R. Knott (Eds.), *The responsive brain*. Bristol: John Wright & Sons, 1976, pp. 1-4.

Cooper, R., McCallum, W. C., Newton, P., Papakostopoulos, D., Pocock, P. V., & Warren, W. J. Cortical potentials associated with the detection of visual events. *Science*, 1977, 196, 74-77.

Courchesne, E., Hillyard, S. A., & Galambos, R. Stimulus novelty, task relevance and the visual evoked potential in man. *Electroencephalography & Clinical Neurophysiology*, 1975, 39, 131-143.

Davis, A. E., & Wada, J. A. Hemispheric asymmetry: Frequency analysis of visual and auditory evoked responses to non-verbal stimuli. *Electroencephalography & Clinical Neurophysiology*, 1974, 37, 1-9.

Deecke, L. Potential changes associated with motor action, reflex responses and readiness (Chairman's opening remarks). In W. C. McCallum & J. R. Knott (Eds.), *The responsive brain*. Bristol: John Wright & Sons, 1976, pp. 91-93.

Donchin, E., & Lindsley, D. B. Average evoked potentials and reaction times to visual stimuli. *Electroencephalography & Clinical Neurophysiology*, 1966, *20*, 217-223.

Eason, R. G., Aiken, L. R., White, C. T., & Lichtenstein, M. Activation and behavior: II. Visually evoked cortical potentials in man as indicants of activation level. *Perceptual and Motor Skills*, 1964, *19*, 875-895.

Eason, R. G., & Dudley, L. M. Effect of stimulus size and retinal locus of stimulation on visually evoked cortical responses and reaction in man. *Psychonomic Science*, 1971, *23*, 345-347.

Eason, R. G., Oden, D., & White, C. T. Visually evoked cortical potentials and reaction time in relation to site of retinal stimulation. *Electroencephalography & Clinical Neurophysiology*, 1967, *22*, 313-324.

Eason, R. G., & White, C. T. Averaged occipital responses to stimulation of sites in the nasal and temporal halves of the retina. *Psychonomic Science*, 1967, *7*, 309-310.

Galambos, R., Benson, P., Smith, T. S., Schulman-Galambos, C., & Osier, H. On hemispheric differences in evoked potentials to speech stimuli. *Electroencephalography & Clinical Neurophysiology*, 1975, *39*, 279-283.

Galin, D., & Ellis, R. Asymmetry in evoked potentials as an index of lateralized cognitive processes: Relation to EEG alpha asymmetry. *Neuropsychologia*, 1975, *13*, 45-50.

Geddes, L. A. The measurement of physiological phenomena. In C. C. Brown (Ed.), *Methods in psychophysiology*. Baltimore, Williams & Wilkins, 1967, pp. 369-452.

Goff, W. R., Allison, T., & Vaughan, H. G. Jr. The functional neuroanatomy of event-related potentials. In E. Callaway, P. Teuting, & S. H. Koslow (Eds.), *Event-related potentials in man*. New York: Academic Press, 1978, pp. 1-80.

Grabow, J., & Elliott, F. W. The electrophysiologic assessment of hemispheric asymmetries during speech. *Journal of Speech and Hearing Research*, 1974, *17*, 64-72.

Jewett, D. L., Romano, M. N., & Williston, J. S. Human auditory evoked potentials: Possible brain stem components detected on the scalp. *Science*, 1970, *167*, 1517-1518.

Jewett, D. L., & Williston, J. S. Auditory evoked far fields averaged for the scalp of humans. *Brain*, 1971, *94*, 681-696.

Karlin, L., Martz, M. J., Brauth, S. E., & Mordkoff, A. M. Auditory evoked potentials, motor potentials and reaction time. *Electroencephalography & Clinical Neurophysiology*, 1971, *31*, 129-136.

Kimura, D. Cerebral dominance and the perception of verbal stimuli. *Canadian Journal of Psychology*, 1961, *15*, 166-171.

Kimura, D. Functional asymmetry of the brain in dichotic listening. *Cortex*, 1967, *3*, 163-178.

Kornhüber, H. H., & Deecke, L. Cerebral potential changes in voluntary and passive movements in man: Readiness potential and reafferent potential. *Pflügers Arch. ges. Physiol.*, 1965, *284*, 1-17.

Landau, S. G., & Buchsbaum, M. Average evoked response and muscle tension. *Physiological Psychology*, 1973, *1*, 56-60.

Majkowski, J., Bochenek, Z., Bochenek, W., Knapik-Fijalkowska, D., & Kopec, J. Latency of averaged evoked potentials to contralateral and ipsilateral auditory stimulation in normal subjects. *Brain Research*, 1971, *24*, 416-419.

Matsumiya, Y., Tagliasco, V., & Lombroso, C. T. Auditory evoked response: Meaningfulness of stimuli and interhemispheric asymmetry. *Science*, 1972, *175*, 790-792.

McCallum, W. C., Papakostopoulos, D., & Griffith, H. B. Distribution of CNV and other slow potential changes in human brainstem structures. In W. C. McCallum & J. R. Knott (Eds.), *The responsive brain*. Bristol: John Wright & Sons, 1976, pp. 205-210.

Mendel, M. I., Hosick, E. C., Windman, T. R., Davis, H., Hirsh, S. K., & Dinges, D. F. Audiometric comparison of the middle and late components of the adult auditory evoked potentials awake and asleep. *Electroencephalography & Clinical Neurophysiology*, 1975, *38*, 27-33.

Mendel, M. I., & Kupperman, G. L. Early components of the averaged electroencephalic response to constant level clicks during rapid eye movement sleep. *Audiology*, 1974, *13*, 23-32.

Morrell, L. K., & Morrell, F. Evoked potentials and reaction times: A study of intraindividual variability. *Electroencephalography & Clinical Neurophysiology*, 1966, *20*, 567-575.

Morrell, L. K., & Salamy, J. G. Hemispheric asymmetry of electrocortical responses to speech stimuli. *Science*, 1971, *174*, 164-166.

Morris, C. J. Electroencephalographic and evoked potential correlates of reaction time and visual discrimination performance. *Psychonomic Science*, 1971, *23*, 193-195.

Näätänen, R. Selective attention and evoked potentials in humans: A critical review. *Biological Psychology*, 1975, *2*, 237-307.

Peters, J. F., & Mendel, M. I. Early components of the averaged electroencephalic response to monaural and binaural stimulation. *Audiology*, 1974, *13*, 195-204.

Picton, T. W., Hillyard, S. A., Krausz, H. I., & Galambos, R. Human auditory evoked potentials. I. Evaluation of components. *Electroencephalography & Clinical Neurophysiology*, 1974, *36*, 179-190.

Price, L. L., Rosenblut, B., Goldstein, R., & Shepherd, D. C. The averaged evoked response to auditory stimulation. *Journal of Speech and Hearing Research*, 1966, 9, 361-370.

Regan, D. *Evoked potentials in psychology, sensory physiology and clinical medicine*. New York: Wiley, 1972.

Rhodes, L. E., Dustman, R. E., & Beck, E. C. The visual evoked response: A comparison of bright and dull children. *Electroencephalography & Clinical Neurophysiology*, 1969, *27*, 364-372.

Richlin, M., Weisinger, M., Weinstein, S., Giannini, M., & Morganstern, M. Interhemispheric asymmetries of evoked cortical responses in retarded and normal children. *Cortex*, 1971, 7, 98-105.

Ritter, W. Intracranial sources of event-related potentials. In D. Otto (Ed.), *Multidisciplinary perspectives in event-related brain potential research*. Washington, D.C.: Gov't. Printing Office (in press).

Ritter, W., Simson, R., & Vaughan, H. G. Association cortex potentials and reaction time in auditory discrimination. *Electroencephalography & Clinical Neurophysiology*, 1972, *33*, 547-555.

Ritter, W., Vaughan, H. G., Jr., & Costa, L. D. Orienting and habituation to auditory stimuli: A study of short term changes in average evoked responses. *Electroencephalography & Clinical Neurophysiology*, 1968, *25*, 550-556.

Samuels, I. Reticular mechanisms and behavior. *Psychological Bulletin*, 1959, *56*, 1-25.

Scheibel, M. E., & Scheibel, A. B. Anatomical basis of attention mechanisms in vertebrate brains. In G. L. Quarton, T. Melnechuk, & F. O. Schmitt (Eds.), *The neurosciences: A study program*. New York: The Rockefeller University Press, 1967.

Shagass, C. Elecrical activity of the brain. In N. S. Greenfield & R. A. Sternbach (Eds.), *Handbook of psychophysiology*. New York: Holt, Rinehart & Winston, 1972, pp. 263-328. (a)

Shagass, C. *Evoked brain potentials in psychiatry*. New York: Plenum, 1972. (b)

Shagass, C., & Trusty, D. Somatosensory and visual cerebral evoked response changes during sleep. In J. Wortis (Ed.), *Recent advances in biological psychiatry*. Vol. VIII. New York: Plenum Press, 1966, pp. 321-334.

Simson, R. C., Vaughan, H. G., Jr., & Ritter, W. The scalp topography of potentials in auditory and visual go–no go tasks. *Electroencephalography & Clinical Neurophysiology,* (in press).

Squires, N. K., Squires, K. C., & Hillyard, S. A. Two varieties of long-latency positive waves evoked by unpredictable auditory stimuli in man. *Electroencephalography & Clinical Neurophysiology,* 1975, *38,* 387-401.

Sutton, S., Braren, M., & Zubin, J. Evoked-potential correlates of stimulus uncertainty. *Science,* 1965, *150,* 1187-1188.

Sutton, S., Teuting, P., Zubin, J., and John, E. R. Evoked potential correlates of stimulus uncertainty. *Science,* 1967, *155,* 1436-1439.

Tecce, J. J. Contingent negative variation (CNV) and psychological processes in man. *Psychological Bulletin,* 1972, *77,* 73-108.

Teyler, T. J., Roemer, R. A., & Harrison, T. F. Human scalp-recorded evoked potential correlates of linguistic stimuli. *Bulletin of the Psychonomic Society,* 1973, *1,* 333-334.

Townsend, R. E., House, J. F., & Johnson, L. C. Auditory evoked potential in Stage 2 and REM sleep during a 30-day exposure to tone pulses. *Psychophysiology,* 1976, *13,* 54-57.

Vaughan, H. G., Jr. The relationship of brain activity to scalp recordings of event-related potentials. In E. Donchin & D. B. Lindsley (Eds.), *Average evoked potentials.* Washington, D.C.: NASA, 1969, pp. 45-94.

Vaughan, H. G., Costa, L. D., & Gilden, L. The functional relation of visual evoked response and reaction time to stimulus intensity. *Vision Research,* 1966, *6,* 645-656.

Vaughan, H. G., Costa, L. D., & Ritter, W. Topography of the human motor potential. *Electroencephalography & Clinical Neurophysiology,* 1968, *25,* 1-10.

Vaughan, H. G., & Hull, R. C. Functional relation between stimulus intensity and photically evoked cerebral responses in man. *Nature,* 1965, *206,* 720-722.

Vaughan, H. G., & Ritter, W. The sources of auditory evoked responses recorded from the human scalp. *Electroencephalography & Clinical Neurophysiology,* 1970, *28,* 360-367.

Walter, W. G., Cooper, R., Aldridge, V. J., McCallum, W. C., & Winter, A. L. Contingent negative variation: An electrical sign of sensory motor association and expectancy in the human brain. *Nature,* 1964, *203,* 380-384.

Weitzman, E. D., & Kremen, H. Auditory evoked responses during different stages of sleep in man. *Electroencephalography & Clinical Neurophysiology,* 1965, *18,* 65-70.

Wood, C., Goff, W. R., & Day, R. S. Auditory evoked potentials during speech perception. *Science,* 1971, *173,* 1248-1251.

Chapter 6

Andreassi, J. L., Balinsky, B., Gallichio, J. A., DeSimone, J. J., & Mellers, B. W. Hypnotic suggestion of stimulus change and visual cortical evoked potential. *Perceptual and Motor Skills,* 1976, *42,* 371-378. (a)

Andreassi, J. L., De Simone, J. J., Gallichio, J. A., & Young, N. E. *Evoked cortical potentials and information processing.* Fourth Annual Report, Contract N00014-72-A-0406-0006, Office of Naval Research, December, 1976. (b)

Andreassi, J. L., DeSimone, J. J., & Mellers, B. W. Amplitude changes in the visual evoked cortical potential with backward masking. *Electroencephalography & Clinical Neurophysiology,* 1976, *41,* 387-398. (c)

Andreassi, J. L., Mayzner, M. S., Beyda, D. R., & Davidovics, S. Visual cortical evoked potentials under conditions of sequential blanking. *Perception & Psychophysics,* 1971, *10,* 164-168.

Andreassi, J. L., Mayzner, M. S., Stern, M., & Okamura, H. Visual cortical evoked potentials under conditions of apparent motion. *Physiological Psychology,* 1973, *1,* 118-120.

Andreassi, J. L., Stern, M., & Okamura, H. Visual cortical evoked potentials as a function of intensity variations in sequential blanking. *Psychophysiology,* 1974, *11,* 336-345.

Armington, J. C., Corwin, T. R., and Marsetta, R. Simultaneously recorded retinal and cortical responses to patterned stimuli. *Journal of the Optical Society of America,* 1971, *61,* 1514-1521.

Barlow, J. S. Evoked responses in relation to visual perception and oculomotor reaction times in man. *Annals of the New York Academy of Sciences,* 1964, *112,* 432-467.

Beck, E. C. The variability of potentials evoked by light in man; the effect of hypnotic suggestion. *Proceedings of Utah Academy of Sciences, Arts, and Letters,* 1963, *40,* 202-204.

Beck, E. C., Dustman, R. E., & Beier, E. G. Hypnotic suggestions and visually evoked potentials. *Electroencephalography & Clinical Neurophysiology,* 1966, *20,* 397-400.

Begleiter, H., & Platz, A. Cortical evoked potentials to semantic stimuli. *Psychophysiology,* 1969, *6,* 91-100. (a)

Begleiter, H., & Platz, A. Evoked potentials: Modifications by classical conditioning. *Science*, 1969, *166*, 769-711. (b)

Begleiter, H., Porjesz, B., Yerre, C., & Kissin, B. Evoked potential correlates of expected stimulus intensity. *Science*, 1973, *179*, 814-816.

Begleiter, H., Gross, M. M., & Kissin, B. Evoked cortical responses to affective visual stimuli. *Psychophysiology*, 1967, *3*, 336-344.

Brown, W. S., Marsh, J. T., & Smith, J. C. Contextual meaning effects on speech-evoked potentials. *Behavioral Biology*, 1973, *9*, 755-761.

Brown, W. S., Marsh, J. T., & Smith, J. C. Evoked potential waveform differences produced by the perception of different meanings of an ambiguous phrase. *Electroencephalography & Clinical Neurophysiology*, 1976, *41*, 113-123.

Bull, K., & Lang, P. J. Intensity judgments and physiological response amplitude. *Psychophysiology*, 1972, *9*, 428-436.

Butler, R. A. The cumulative effects of different stimulus repetition rates on the auditory evoked response in man. *Electroencephalography & Clinical Neurophysiology*, 1973, *35*, 337-345.

Callaway, E. *Brain electrical potentials and individual psychological differences*. New York: Grune & Stratton, 1975.

Chalke, F. C. R., & Ertl, J. Evoked potentials and intelligence. *Life Sciences*, 1965, *4*, 1319-1322.

Chapman, R. M., & Bragdon, H. R. Evoked responses to numerical and nonnumerical visual stimuli while problem solving. *Nature*, 1964, *203*, 1155-1157.

Chatrian, G. E., Canfield, R. C., Knauss, T. A., & Lettich, E. Cerebral responses to electrical tooth pulp stimulation in man: An objective correlate of acute experimental pain. *Neurology*, 1975, *25*, 745-757.

Clarke, P. G. Are visual evoked potentials to motion-reversal produced by direction-sensitive brain mechanisms? *Vision Research*, 1974, *14*, 1281-1284.

Clynes, M., Kohn, M., & Lifshitz, K. Dynamics and spatial behavior of light evoked potentials, their modification under hypnosis, and on-line correlation in relation to rhythmic components. *Annals of New York Academy of Science*, 1964, *112*, 468-509.

Clynes, M., & Kohn, M. Spatial visual evoked potentials as physiologic language elements for color and field structure. In W. Cobb & C. Morocutti (Eds.), *The evoked potentials*. New York: Elsevier, 1967. Pp. 82-96.

Cooper, R., McCallum, W. C., Newton, P., Papakostopoulos, D., Pocock, P. V., & Warren, W. J. Cortical potentials associated with the detection of visual events. *Science*, 1977, *196*, 74-77.

Davis, F. B. The measurement of mental capability through evoked potential recordings. (*Educational Records Research Bulletin* No. 1.), Greenwich, Conn.: Educational Records Bureau, 1971.

Donchin, E., & Lindsley, D. B. Visually evoked response correlates of perceptual masking and enhancement. *Electroencephalography & Clinical Neurophysiology*, 1965, *19*, 325-335.

Donchin, E., Wicke, J., & Lindsley, D. B. Cortical evoked potentials and perception of paired flashes. *Science*, 1963, *141*, 1285-1286.

Eason, R. G., Harter, M. R., & White, C. T. Effects of attention and arousal on visually evoked cortical potentials and reaction time in man. *Physiology and Behavior*, 1969, *4*, 283-289.

Eason, R. G., White, C. T., and Bartlett, N. Effects of checkerboard pattern stimulation on evoked cortical responses in relation to check size and visual field. *Psychonomic Science*, 1970, *21*, 113-115.

Engel, R., & Henderson, N. B. Visual evoked responses and IQ scores at school age. *Developmental Medicine and Child Neurology*, 1973, *15*, 136-145.

Ertl, J. P., & Schaffer, W. W. P. Brain response correlates of psychometric intelligence. *Nature*, 1969, *223*, 421-422.

Friedman, D., Simson, R., Ritter, W., & Rapin, I. Cortical evoked potentials elicited by real speech words and human sounds. *Electroencephalography & Clinical Neurophysiology*, 1975, *38*, 13-19. (a)

Friedman, D., Simson, R., Ritter, W., & Rapin, I. The late positive component (P 300) and information processing in sentences. *Electroencephalography & Clinical Neurophysiology*, 1975, *38*, 255-262. (b)

Fruhstorfer, H., Soveri, P., & Järvilehto, T. Short-term habituation of the auditory evoked response in man. *Electroencephalography & Clinical Neurophysiology*, 1970, *28*, 153-161.

Funakoshi, M., & Kawamura, Y. Summated cerebral evoked responses to taste stimuli in man. *Electroencephalography & Clinical Neurophysiology*, 1971, *30*, 205-209.

Galbraith, G. C., Cooper, L. M., & London, P. Hypnotic susceptibility and the sensory evoked response. *Journal of Comparative & Physiological Psychology*, 1972, *80*, 509-514.

Galbraith, G. C., Gliddon, J. B., & Busk, J. Visual evoked responses in mentally retarded and non retarded subjects. *American Journal of Mental Deficiency*, 1970, *75*, 341-348.

Groves, P. M., & Eason, R. G. Effects of attention and activation on the visual evoked cortical potential and reaction time. *Psychophysiology*, 1969, *5*, 394-398.

Gucker, D. K. Correlating visual evoked potentials with psychometric intelligence variation in technique. *Perceptual and Motor Skills,* 1973, 37, 189-190.

Guerrero-Figueroa, R., & Heath, R. G. Evoked responses and changes during attentive factors in man. *Archives of Neurology,* 1964, 10, 74-84.

Haider, M., Spong, P., & Lindsley, D. B. Attention, vigilance, and cortical evoked potentials in humans. *Science,* 1964, 145, 180-182.

Halliday, A. M., & Mason, A. A. The effect of hypnotic anaesthesia on cortical responses. *Journal of Neurology, Neurosurgery & Psychiatry,* 1964, 27, 300-312.

Harter, M. R. Evoked cortical responses to checkerboard patterns: Effect of check-size as a function of retinal eccentricity. *Vision Research,* 1970, 10, 1365-1376.

Harter, M. R., & Salmon, L. E. Intra-modality selective attention and evoked cortical potentials to randomly presented patterns. *Electroencephalography & Clinical Neurophysiology,* 1972, 32, 605-613.

Harter, M. R., & White, C. T. Effects of contour sharpness and check-size on visually evoked cortical potentials. *Vision Research,* 1968, 8, 701-711.

Hernandez-Peon, R., & Donoso M. Influence of attention and suggestion upon subcortical evoked electrical activity in the human brain. In L. vanBogaert & J. Radermacker (Eds.) *First international on neurological sciences,* Vol. 3. New York: Pergamon Press. 1959, pp. 385-396.

Honda, H. Visually evoked potentials during pattern discrimination tasks. *Tohoku Psychologica Folia,* 1973, 32, 45-54.

Honda, H. Visually evoked potentials during pattern discrimination tasks (II): Further evidence. *Tohoku Psychologica Folia,* 1974, 33, 119-133.

Jenness, D. Auditory evoked response differentiation with discrimination learning in humans. *Journal of Comparative & Physiological Psychology,* 1972, 80, 75-90.

John, E. R., Harrington, R. N., & Sutton, S. Effects of visual form on the evoked response. *Science,* 1967, 155, 1439-1442.

Karlin, L. Cognition, preparation and sensory-evoked potentials. *Psychological Bulletin,* 1970, 73, 122-136.

Kinney, J. A. S., McKay, C. L. Test of color-defective vision using the visual evoked response. *Journal of the Optical Society of America,* 1974, 64, 1244-1250.

Kinney, J. S. McKay, C. L., Mensch, A. J., & Luria, S. M. Techniques for analysing differences in VERs: Colored and patterned stimuli. *Vision Research,* 1972, 12, 1733-1747.

Lelord, G., Laffont F., & Jusseaume, P. H. Conditioning of evoked potentials in children of differing intelligence. *Psychophysiology*, 1976, *13*, 81-85.

Mackay, D. M. Evoked brain potentials as indicators of sensory information processing. *Neurosciences Research Program Bulletin*, 1969, *7* (3).

Mackay, D. M., & Rietveld, W. J. Electroencephalogram potentials evoked by accelerated visual motion. *Nature*, 1968, *677*, 678.

Maffei, L., & Campbell, F. W. Neurophysiological localization of the vertical and horizontal visual coordinates in man. *Science*, 1970, *167*, 386-387.

Morrell, L., & Salamy, J. G. Hemispheric asymmetry of electrocortical responses to speech stimuli. *Science*, 1971, *174*, 164-166.

Moskowitz, A. F., Armington, J. C., & Timberlake, G. Corners, receptive fields, and visually evoked potentials. *Perception and Psychophysics*, 1974, *15*, 325-330.

Näätänen, R. Selective attention and evoked potentials. *Annales Academie Scientiarum Fennica*, 1967, *151*, 1-226.

Osborne, R. T. Psychometric correlates of the visual evoked potential. *Acta Psychologica*, 1969, *29*, 303-308.

Perry, N. W., Childers, D. G., & Falgout, J. C. Chromatic specificity of the visual evoked response. *Science*, 1972, *177*, 813-815.

Perry, N. W., McCoy, J. G., Cunningham, W. R., Falgout, J. C., & Street, W. J. Multivariate visual evoked response correlates of intelligence. *Psychophysiology*, 1976, *13*, 323-329.

Picton, T. W., Goodman, W. S., & Bryce, D. P. Amplitude of evoked responses to tones of high intensity. *Acta Oto-Laryngologica*, 1970, *70*, 77-82.

Porjesz, B., & Begleiter, H. The effects of stimulus expectancy on evoked brain potentials. *Psychophysiology*, 1975, *12*, 152-157.

Regan, D. *Evoked potentials in psychology, sensory physiology and clinical medicine*. New York: Wiley, 1972.

Regan, D., & Spekreijse, H. Evoked potential indications of colour blindness. *Vision Research*, 1974, *14*, 89-95.

Rhodes, L. E., Dustman, R. E., Beck, E. C. The visual evoked response: A comparison of bright and dull children. *Electroencephalography and Clinical Neurophysiology*, 1967, *27*, 364-372.

Rietveld, W. J., Tordoir, W.E.M., Hagenouw, J.R.B., Lubbers, J. A., & Spoor, Th. Visual evoked responses to blank and to checkerboard patterned flashes. *Acta Physiol. Pharmacol. Neerl.*, 1967, *14*, 259-285.

Ritter, W., Vaughan, H. G., Jr., & Costa, L. D. Orienting and habituation to auditory stimuli: A study of short term changes in average evoked responses. *Electroencephalography & Clinical Neurophysiology*, 1968, *25*, 550-556.

Ruch, T. C., Patton, H. D., Woodbury, J. W., & Towe, D. L. (Eds.). *Neurophysiology*. Philadelphia: Saunders, 1965.

Ruchkin, D. S., & Sutton, S. Visual evoked and emitted potentials and stimulus significance. *Bulletin of the Psychonomic Society*, 1973, *2*, 144-146.

Rust, J. Cortical evoked potential, personality and intelligence. *Journal of Comparative and Physiological Psychology*, 1975, *89*, 1220-1226.

Salamy, J., Potvin, A., Jones, K., & Landreth, J. Cortical evoked responses to labyrinthine stimulation in man. *Psychophysiology*, 1975, *12*, 55-61.

Sandler, L. S., & Schwartz, M. Evoked responses and perception: Stimulus content versus stimulus structure. *Psychophysiology*, 1971, *8*, 727-739.

Satterfield, J. H. Evoked cortical response enhancement and attention in man: A study of responses to auditory and shock stimuli. *Electroencephalography & Clinical Neurophysiology*, 1965, *19*, 470-475.

Schiller, P. H. Behavioral and electrophysiological studies of visual masking. In K. N. Leibovic (Ed.), *Information processing in the nervous system*. New York: Springer-Verlag, 1969, pp. 141-165.

Schiller, P. H., & Chorover, S. L. Metacontrast: Its relation to evoked potentials. *Science*, 1966, *153*, 1398-1400.

Schweitzer, P. K., & Tepas, D. I. Intensity effects of the auditory evoked brain response to stimulus onset and cessation. *Perception and Psychophysics*, 1974, *16*, 396-400.

Shagass, C. *Evoked brain potentials in psychiatry*. New York: Plenum Press, 1972.

Shagass, C., & Schwartz, M. Cerebral responsiveness in psychiatric patients. *Archives of General Psychiatry*, 1963, *8*, 177-189.

Shagass, C., & Schwartz, M. Recovery functions of somato-sensory peripheral nerve and cerebral evoked responses in man. *Electroencephalography & Clinical Neurophysiology*, 1964, *17*, 126-135.

Shipley, T., Jones, R. W., & Fry, A. Intensity and the evoked occipitogram in man. *Vision Research*, 1966, *6*, 657-667.

Shucard, D. W., & Horn, J. L. Evoked cortical potentials and measurement of human abilities. *Journal of Comparative & Physiological Psychology*, 1972, *78*, 59-68.

Siegfried, J. B. The effects of checkerboard pattern check size on the VECP. *Bulletin of the Psychonomic Society*, 1975, *6*, 306-308.

Smith, D. B., Allison, T., Goff, W. R., & Principato, J. J. Human odorant evoked responses: Effects of trigeminal or olfactory deficit. *Electroencephalography & Clinical Neurophysiology*, 1971, *30*, 313-317.

Spehlmann, R. The averaged electrical responses to diffuse and patterned light in the human. *Electroencephalography & Clinical Neurophysiology*, 1965, *19*, 560-569.

Tecce, J. J. Attention and evoked potentials in man. In D. I. Mostofsky (Ed.), *Attention: Contemporary theory and analysis*. New York: Appleton-Century-Crofts, 1970, pp. 331-365.

Vaughan, H. G., Jr., Costa, L. D., & Gilden, L. The functional relation of visual evoked response and reaction time to stimulus intensity. *Vision Research*, 1966, *6*, 645-656.

Vaughan, H. G., & Hull, R. C. Functional relation between stimulus intensity and photically evoked cerebral responses in man. *Nature*, 1965, *206*, 720-722.

Vaughan, H. G., & Silverstein, L. Metacontrast and evoked potentials: A reappraisal. *Science*, 1968, *160*, 207-208.

Walsh, J. K., & Tepas, D. I. Human evoked brain responses following loud pure tones. *Bulletin of the Psychonomic Society*, 1975, *5*, 375-377.

Weinberg, H., Walter, W. G., & Crow, H. J. Intra-cerebral events in humans related to real and imaginary stimuli. *Electroencephalography & Clinical Neurophysiology*, 1970, *29*, 1-9.

Werner, H. Studies on contour. I. Qualitative analyses. *American Journal of Psychology*, 1935, *47*, 40-64.

White, C. T. Evoked cortical responses and patterned stimuli. *American Psychologist*, 1969, *24*, 211-214.

White, C. T., & Eason, R. G. Evoked cortical potentials in relation to certain aspects of visual perception. *Psychological Monographs: General & Applied*, 1966, *80*, 1-14.

Wood, C. C., Goff, W. R., & Day, R. S. Auditory evoked potentials during speech perception. *Science*, 1971, *173*, 1248-1251.

Yoshida, S., Iwahara, S., & Nagamura, N. The effect of stimulus orientation on the visual evoked potential in human subjects. *Electroencephalography & Clinical Neurophysiology*, 1975, *39*, 53-57.

Chapter 7

Beck, E. C. Electrophysiology and behavior. *Annual Review of Psychology*, 1975, *26*, 233-262.

Becker, W., Iwase, R., Jurgens, R., & Kornhuber, H. H. Bereitschaftspotential preceding voluntary slow and rapid hand movements. In

W. C. McCallum & J. R. Knott (Eds.), *The responsive brain.* Bristol: John Wright & Sons, 1976, pp. 99-102.

Begleiter, H., & Porjesz, B. Evoked brain potentials as indicators of decision making. *Science*, 1975, *187*, 754-755.

Borda, R. P. Drive and performance related aspects of the CNV in rhesus monkeys. *Electroencephalography & Clinical Neurophysiology*, 1970, *29*, 173-180.

Callaway, E. *Brain electrical potentials and individual differences.* New York: Grune & Stratton, 1975.

Cant, B. R., & Bickford, R. G. The effect of motivation on the contingent negative variation (CNV). *Electroencephalography & Clinical Neurophysiology*, 1967, *23*, 594. (Abstract)

Cohen, J., & Walter, W. G. The interaction of responses in the brain to semantic stimuli. *Psychophysiology*, 1966, *2*, 187-196.

Costell, R. M., Lunde, D. T., Kopell, B. S., & Wittner, W. K. Contingent negative variation as an indicator of sexual object preference. *Science*, 1972, *177*, 718-720.

Courchesne, E., Hillyard, S. A., & Galambos, R. Stimulus novelty, task relevance and the visual evoked potential in man. *Electroencephalography & Clinical Neurophysiology*, 1975, *39*, 131-143.

Deecke, L. Potential changes associated with motor action, reflex responses and readiness (Chairman's opening remarks). In W. C. McCallum & J. R. Knott (Eds.), *The responsive brain.* Bristol: John Wright & Sons, 1976, pp. 91-93.

Donald, M. W., & Goff, W. R. Attention related increases in cortical responsivity dissociated from the contingent negative variation. *Science*, 1971, *172*, 1163-1166.

Donchin, E. On evoked potentials, cognition, and memory. *Science*, 1975, *190*, 1004-1005.

Donchin, E., Kubovy, M., Kutas, M., Johnson, R. Jr., & Herning, R. I. Graded changes in evoked response (P300) amplitude as a function of cognitive activity. *Perception & Psychophysics*, 1973, *14*, 319-324.

Donchin, E., Tueting, P., Ritter, W., Kutas, M., & Heffley, E. On the independence of the CNV and P300 components of the human averaged evoked potential. *Electroencephalography & Clinical Neurophysiology*, 1975, *38*, 449-461.

Ford, J. M., Roth, W. T., Dirks, S. J., & Kopell, B. S. Evoked potential correlates of signal recognition between and within modalities. *Science*, 1973, *181*, 465-466.

Ford, J. M., Roth, W. T., & Kopell, B. S. Attention effects on auditory evoked potentials to infrequent events. *Biological Psychology*, 1976, *4*, 65-77.

Friedman, D., Hakerem, G., Sutton, S., & Fleiss, J. L. Effect of stimulus uncertainty on the pupillary dilation response and the vertex evoked potential. *Electroencephalography & Clinical Neurophysiology*, 1973, *34*, 475-484.

Gaillard, A. W. Effects of warning signal modality on the contingent negative variation (CNV). *Biological Psychology*, 1976, *4*, 139-154.

Hillyard, S. A. Relationships between the contingent negative variation (CNV) and reaction time. *Physiology & Behavior*, 1969, *4*, 351-357.

Hillyard, S. A. Relationships between the contingent negative variation signs of selective attention in the human brain. *Science*, 1973, *182*, 177-179.

Hillyard, S. A., Squires, K. C., Bauer, J. W., & Lindsay, P. H. Evoked potential correlates of auditory signal detection. *Science*, 1971, *172*, 1357-1360.

Hirsh, S. K. Vertex potentials associated with an auditory discrimination. *Psychonomic Science*, 1971, *22*, 173-175.

Irwin, D. A., Knott, J. R., McAdam, D. W., & Rebert, C. S. Motivational determinants of the "contingent negative variation." *Electroencephalography & Clinical Neurophysiology*, 1966, *21*, 538-543.

Karlin, L. Cognition, preparation, and sensory-evoked potentials. *Psychological Bulletin*, 1970, *73*, 122-136.

Kornhuber, H. H., & Deecke, L. Hirnpotentialanderungen bei Willkurbewegungen und passiven Berwegungen des Menschen: Bereitschaftspotential und reafferente Potentiale. *Pflügers Archiv fur die gesamte Physiologie des Menschen und der Tiere*, 1965, *284*, 1-17.

Loveless, N. E., & Sanford, A. J. Slow potential correlates of preparatory set. *Biological Psychology*, 1974, *1*, 303-314.

Low, M. D., Borda, R. P., Frost, J. D., Jr., & Kellaway, P. Surface negative slow potential shift associated with conditioning in man. *Neurology*, 1966, *16*, 771-782.

Low, M. D., Coats, A. C., Rettig, G. M., & McSherry, J. W. Anxiety, attentiveness-alertness: A phenomenological study of the CNV. *Neuropsychologia*, 1967, *5*, 379-384.

Low, M. D., & McSherry, J. W. Further observations of psychological factors involved in CNV genesis. *Electroencephalography & Clinical Neurophysiology*, 1968, *25*, 203-207.

McAdam, D. W., & Seales, D. M. Bereitschaftspotential enhancement with increased level of motivation. *Electroencephalography & Clinical Neurophysiology*, 1969, *27*, 73-75.

McCallum, C. The contingent negative variation as a cortical sign of

416　　　　　　　　　　　　　　　　　　REFERENCES

attention in man. In C. R. Evans & T. B. Mulholland (Eds.), *Attention in neurophysiology*. London: Butterworths, 1969, pp. 40-63.

McCallum, W. C., Papakostopoulos, D., & Griffith, H. B. Distribution of CNV and other slow potential changes in human brainstem structures. In W. C. McCallum & J. R. Knott (Eds.), *The responsive brain*. Bristol: John Wright & Sons, 1976, pp. 205-210.

McCallum, W. C., & Walter, W. G. The effects of attention and distraction on the contingent negative variation in normal and neurotic subjects. *Electroencephalography & Clinical Neurophysiology*, 1968, *25*, 319-329.

Musicant, R. Evoked potentials and attention. *Biological Psychology Bulletin*, 1975, *4*, 1-9.

Näätänen, R. Evoked potential, EEG, and slow potential correlates of selective attention. *Acta Psychological Supplement*, 1970, *33*, 178-192.

Näätänen, R. Selective attention and evoked potentials in humans: A critical review. *Biological Psychology*, 1975, *2*, 237-307.

Naitoh, P., Johnson, L. C., & Lubin, A. Modification of surface negative slow potential (CNV) in the human brain after total sleep loss. *Electroencephalography & Clinical Neurophysiology*, 1971, *30*, 17-22.

Okita, T., & Ohtani, A. The effects of active attention switching between the ears on averaged evoked potentials. *Electroencephalography & Clinical Neurophysiology*, 1977, *42*, 198-204.

Peters, J. F., Billinger, T. W., & Knott, J. R. Event related potentials of brain (CNV and P300) in a paired associate learning paradigm. *Psychophysiology*, 1977, *14*, 579-585.

Picton, T. W., & Hillyard, S. A. Human auditory evoked potentials: II. Effects of attention. *Electroencephalography & Clinical Neurophysiology*, 1974, *36*, 191-200.

Poon, L. W., Thompson, L. W., & Marsh, G. R. Average evoked potential changes as a function of processing complexity. *Psychophysiology*, 1976, *13*, 43-49.

Rebert, C. S. The effect of reaction time feedback on reaction time and contingent negative variation. *Psychophysiology*, 1972, *9*, 334-339.

Rebert, C. S., & Tecce, J. J. A summary of CNV and reaction time. In: W. C. McCallum & J. R. Knott (Eds.), *Event-related slow potentials of the brain: Their relations to behavior*. Amsterdam: Elsevier, 1973, pp. 173-178.

Ritter, W., & Vaughan, H. G. Averaged evoked responses in vigilance and discrimination: A reassessment. *Science*, 1969, *164*, 326-328.

Ritter, W., Vaughan, H. G., Jr., & Costa, L. D. Orienting and habituation to auditory stimuli: A study of short term changes in average evoked responses. *Electroencephalography & Clinical Neurophysiology,* 1968, *25,* 550-556.

Rohrbaugh, J. W., Donchin, E. & Ericksen, C. W. Decision making and the P300 component of the cortical evoked response. *Perception and Psychophysics,* 1974, *15,* 368-374.

Roth, W. T., & Kopell, B. S. P300: An orienting reaction in the human auditory evoked response. *Perceptual & Motor Skills,* 1973, *36,* 219-225.

Ruchkin, D. S., & Sutton, S. Visual evoked and emitted potentials and stimulus significance. *Bulletin of the Psychonomic Society,* 1973, *2,* 144-146.

Ruchkin, D. S., & Sutton, S. Latency characteristics and trial by trial variation of emitted potentials. In J. E. Desmedt (Ed.), *Cerebral evoked potentials in man.* In press.

Ruchkin, D. S., Sutton, S., & Tueting, P. Emitted and evoked P300 potentials and variation in stimulus probability. *Psychophysiology,* 1975, *12,* 591-595.

Schwent, V. L., Hillyard, S. A., & Galambos, R. Selective attention and the auditory vertex potential: I. Effects of stimulus delivery rate. *Electroencephalography & Clinical Neurophysiology,* 1976, *40,* 604-614.

Smith, D., Donchin, E., Cohen, L., & Starr, A. Auditory evoked potentials in man during selective binaural listening. *Electroencephalography & Clinical Neurophysiology,* 1970, *78,* 146-152.

Squires, K. C., Donchin, E., Herning, R. I., & McCarthy, G. On the influence of task relevance and stimulus probability on event related potential components. *Electroencephalography & Clinical Neurophysiology,* 1977, *42,* 1-14.

Squires, K. C., Hillyard, S., & Lindsay, P. Vertex potentials evoked during auditory signal detection: Relation to decision criteria. *Perception & Psychophysics,* 1973, *14,* 265-272.

Squires, K. C., Squires, N. K., & Hillyard, S. A. Decision related cortical potentials during an auditory signal detection task with cued observation intervals. *Journal of Experimental Psychology: Human Perception & Performance,* 1975, *104,* 268-279.

Squires, N. K., Squires, K. C., & Hillyard, S. A. Two varieties of long-latency positive waves evoked by unpredictable auditory stimuli in man. *Electroencephalography & Clinical Neurophysiology,* 1975, *38,* 387-401.

Sutton, S. The sensitivity of the evoked potential to psychological variables. Paper presented at the meetings of the EEG Society, Washington, D.C., 1970.

Sutton, S., Braren, M., & Zubin, J. Evoked potential correlates of stimulus uncertainty. *Science*, 1965, *150*, 1187-1188.

Sutton, S., Teuting, P., Zubin, J., & John, E. R. Evoked potential correlates of stimulus uncertainty. *Science*, 1967, *155*, 1436-1439.

Tecce, J. J. Contingent negative variation and individual differences. *Archives of General Psychiatry*, 1971, *24*, 1-16.

Tecce, J. J. Contingent negative variation (CNV) and psychological processes in man. *Psychological Bulletin*, 1972, *77*, 73-108.

Tecce, J. J., & Hamilton, B. T. CNV reduction by sustained cognitive activity (distraction). In W. C. McCallum & J. R. Knott (Eds.), *Event-related slow potentials of the brain: Their relations to behavior*. Amsterdam: Elsevier, 1973, Supplement 33, pp. 229-237.

Tecce, J. J., Savignano-Bowman, J., & Meinbresse, D. Contingent negative variation and the distraction-arousal hypothesis. *Electroencephalography & Clinical Neurophysiology*, 1976, *41*, 227-286.

Tecce, J. J., & Scheff, N. M. Attention reduction and suppressed direct-current potentials in the human brain. *Science*, 1969, *164*, 331-333.

Tueting, P., Sutton, S., & Zubin, J. Quantitative evoked potential correlates of the probability of events. *Psychophysiology*, 1970, *7*, 385-394.

Vaughan, H. G., Jr. The relationship of brain activity to scalp recordings of event-related potentials. In E. Donchin & D. B. Lindsley (Eds.), *Average evoked potentials*. Washington, D.C.: NASA, 1969, pp. 45-94.

Walter, W. G., Cooper, R., Aldridge, V. J., McCallum, W. C., & Winter, A. L. Contingent negative variation: An electrical sign of sensory-motor association and expectancy in the human brain. *Nature*, 1964, *203*, 380-384.

Weerts, T. C., & Lang, P. J. The effects of eye fixation and stimulus and response location on the contingent negative variation (CNV). *Biological Psychology*, 1973, *1*, 1-19.

Weinberg, H., Walter, W. G., Cooper, R., & Aldridge, V. J. Emitted cerebral events. *Electroencephalography & Clinical Neurophysiology*, 1974, *36*, 449-456.

Weinberg, H., Walter, W. G., & Crow, H. J. Intracerebral events in humans related to real and imaginary stimuli. *Electroencephalography & Clinical Neurophysiology*, 1970, *29*, 1-9.

Wilkinson, R. T., & Spence, M. T. Determinants of the post-stimulus resolution of contingent negative variation. *Electroencephalography & Clinical Neurophysiology*, 1973, *35*, 503-509.

Chapter 8

Alexander, A. B. An experimental test of assumptions relating to the use of electromyographic biofeedback as a general relaxation technique. *Psychophysiology*, 1975, *12*, 656-662.

Andreassi, J. L., Rapisardi, S., & Whalen, P. M. Autonomic responsivity and reaction time under fixed and variable signal schedules. *Psychophysiology*, 1969, *6*, 58-69.

Bartoshuk, A. K. Electromyographic gradients as indicants of motivation. *Canadian Journal of Psychology*, 1955, *9*, 215-230.

Bartoshuk, A. K. EMG gradients and EEG amplitudes during motivated listening. *Canadian Journal of Psychology*, 1956, *10*, 156-163.

Basmajian, J. V. Control and training of individual motor units. *Science*, 1963, *20*, 662-664.

Basmajian, J. V. Learned control of single motor units. In G. E. Schwartz & J. Beatty (Eds.), *Biofeedback, theory and research*. New York: Academic Press, 1977, pp. 415-431.

Basmajian, J. V., & Newton, W. J. Feedback training of parts of buccinator muscle in man. *Psychophysiology*, 1974, *11*, 92.

Bliwise, D., Coleman, R., Bergmann, B., Wincor, M. S., Pivik, R. T., & Rechtschaffen, A. Facial muscle tonus during REM and NREM sleep. *Psychophysiology*, 1974, *11*, 497-508.

Chapman, A. J. An electromyographic study of social facilitation: A test of the "Mere Presence" hypothesis. *British Journal of Psychology*, 1974, *65*, 123-128.

Clites, M. S. Certain somatic activities in relation to successful and unsuccessful problem solving: III. *Journal of Experimental Psychology*, 1936, *19*, 172-192.

Cohen, M. J. The relation between heart rate and electromyographic activity in a discriminated escape-avoidance paradigm. *Psychophysiology*, 1973, *10*, 8-20.

Davis, J. F. *Manual of surface electromyography*. WADC Technical Report 59-184, 1959.

Davis, R. C. The relation of muscle action potentials to difficulty and frustration. *Journal of Experimental Psychology*, 1938, *23*, 141-158.

Davis, R. C. Set and muscular tension. *Indiana University Publications*, Science Series, 1940, No. 10.

Diggory, J. C., Klein, S. J., & Cohen, M. Muscle-action potentials and

420

estimated probability of success. *Journal of Experimental Psychology*, 1964, *68*, 449-455.

Duffy, E. *Activation and behavior*, New York: Wiley, 1962.

Duffy, E. Activation. In N. S. Greenfield & R. A. Sternbach (Eds.), *Handbook of psychophysiology*. New York: Holt, Rinehart & Winston, 1972, pp. 577-622.

Eason, R. G. Relation between effort, tension level, skill, and performance efficiency in a perceptual-motor task. *Perceptual & Motor Skills*, 1963, *16*, 297-317.

Eason, R. G., & Branks, J. Effect of level of activation on the quality and efficiency of verbal and motor tasks. *Perceptual & Motor Skills*, 1963, *16*, 525-543.

Eason, R. G., & White, C. T. Relationship between muscular tension and performance during rotary pursuit. *Perceptual & Motor Skills*, 1960, *10*, 199-210.

Eason, R. G., & White, C. T. Muscular tension, effort and tracking difficulty: Studies of parameters which affect tension level and performance efficiency. *Perceptual & Motor Skills*, 1961, *12*, 331-372.

Eastman, M. C., & Kamon, E. Posture and subjective evaluation at flat and slanted desks. *Human Factors*, 1976, *18*, 15-26.

Gardner, E. *Fundamentals of neurology*. Philadelphia: Saunders, 1975.

Goldstein, I. B. Electromyography: A measure of skeletal muscle response. In N. S. Greenfield & R. A. Sternbach (Eds.), *Handbook of psychophysiology*. New York: Holt, Rinehart & Winston, 1972, pp. 329-365.

Guyton, A. C. *Basic human physiology*. Philadelphia: Saunders, 1977.

Hardyck, D. C., & Petrinovich, L. F. Treatment of subvocal speech during reading. *Journal of Reading*, 1969, *12*, 1-11.

Hardyck, D. C., Petrinovich, L. F., & Ellsworth, D. W. Feedback of speech muscle activity during silent reading: Rapid extinction. *Science*, 1966, *154*, 1467.

Haynes, J., Mosely, D., & McGowan, W. T. Relaxation training and biofeedback in the reduction of frontalis muscle tension. *Psychophysiology*, 1975, *12*, 547-552.

Holloway, F. A., & Parsons, O. A. Physiological concomitants of reaction time performance in normal and brain-damaged subjects. *Psychophysiology*, 1972, *9*, 189-198.

Jacob, S. W., & Francone, C. A. *Structure and function in man*. Philadelphia: Saunders, 1970.

Kennedy, J. L., & Travis, R. C. Prediction of speed of performance by muscle action potentials. *Science*, 1947, *105*, 410-411.

Kennedy, J. L., & Travis, R. C. Prediction and control of alertness: II.

Continuous tracking. *Journal of Comparative & Physiological Psychology*, 1948, *41*, 203-210.

Kennedy, J. L., & Travis, R. C. Prediction and control of alertness: III. Calibration of the alertness indicator and further results. *Journal of Comparative & Physiological Psychology*, 1949, *42*, 45-57.

Kinsman, R. A., O'Banion, K., Robinson, S., & Staudemnayer, H. Continuous biofeedback and discrete posttrial verbal feedback in frontalis muscle relaxation training. *Psychophysiology*, 1975, *12*, 30-35.

Lansing, R. W., Schwartz, E., & Lindsley, D. B. Reaction time and EEG activation under alerted and non-alerted conditions. *Journal of Experimental Psychology*, 1959, *58*, 1-7.

Lippold, O.C.J. Electromyography. In P. H. Venables & I. Martin (Eds.), *Manual of psycho-physiological methods*. Amsterdam: North-Holland, 1967, pp. 245-297.

Malmo, R. B. *On emotions, needs, and our archaic brain*. New York: Holt, Rinehart, & Winston, 1975.

McCormick, E. J. *Human factors in engineering and design*. New York: McGraw-Hill, 1976.

McGuigan, F. J. Electrical measurement of covert processes as an explication of "higher mental events." In F. J. McGuigan & R. A. Schoonover (Eds.), *The psychophysiology of thinking*. New York: Academic Press, 1973, pp. 343-385.

McGuigan, F. J., & Bailey, S. C. Covert response patterns during the processing of language stimuli. *Interamerican Journal of Psychology*, 1969, *3*, 289-299.

McGuigan, F. J., Keller, B., & Stanton, E. Covert language responses during silent reading. *Journal of Educational Psychology*, 1964, *55*, 339-343.

McGuigan, F. J., & Rodier, W. I., III. Effects of auditory stimulation on covert oral behavior during silent reading. *Journal of Experimental Psychology*, 1968, *76*, 649-655.

Obrist, P. A. Heart rate and somatic-motor coupling during classical aversive conditioning in humans. *Journal of Experimental Psychology*, 1968, *77*, 180-183.

Obrist, P. A., Webb, R. A., & Sutterer, J. R. Heart rate and somatic changes during aversive conditioning and a simple reaction time task. *Psychophysiology*, 1969, *5*, 696-723.

Obrist, P. A., Webb, R. A., Sutterer, J. R., & Howard, J. L. Cardiac deceleration and reaction time: An evaluation of two hypotheses. *Psychophysiology*, 1970, *6*, 695-706.

Ortengren, R., Andersson, G., Broman, M., Magnusson, R., & Petersen, I. Vocational electromyography: Studies of localized muscle fatigue at the assembly line. *Ergonomics*, 1975, *18*, 157-174.

Pishkin, V. Electromyography in cognitive performance by schizophrenics and normals. *Perceptual & Motor Skills*, 1973, *37*, 382.

Pishkin, V., & Shurley, J. T. Electrodermal and electromyographic parameters in concept identification. *Psychophysiology*, 1968, *5*, 112-118.

Pishkin, V., & Wolfgang, A. Electromyographic gradients in concept identification with numbers of irrelevant dimensions. *Journal of Clinical Psychology*, 1964, *20*, 61-67.

Surwillo, W. W. Psychological factors in muscle-action potentials: EMG gradients. *Journal of Experimental Psychology*, 1956, *52*, 263-272.

Thompson, R. F., Lindsley, D. B., & Eason, R. G. Physiological psychology. In J. B. Sidowski (Ed.), *Experimental methods and instrumentation in psychology*. New York: McGraw-Hill, 1966.

Travis, R. C., & Kennedy, J. L. Prediction and control of alertness. III. Calibration of the alertness indicator and further results. *Journal of Comparative & Physiological Psychology*, 1949, *40*, 457-461.

Van Liere, D. W. Characteristics of the muscle tension response to paired tones. *Journal of Experimental Psychology*, 1953, *46*, 319-324.

Wallerstein, H. An electromyographic study of attentive listening. *Canadian Journal of Psychology*, 1954, *8*, 228-238.

Wilcott, R. C., & Beenken, M. G. Relation of integrated surface electromyography and muscle tension. *Perceptual & Motor Skills*, 1957, *7*, 295-298.

Wilkinson, R. T. Muscle tension during mental work under sleep deprivation. *Journal of Experimental Psychology*, 1962, *64*, 565-571.

Zucchi, M., & Galeazzi, A. Preliminary research concerning modifications of muscular tension (EMG gradient) during a graphic-motor task in subjects from 7 to 14 years of age. *Archivo di Psicologia, Neurologia e Psichiatria*, 1971, *32*, 94-102.

Chapter 9

Andreassi, J. L. Some physiological correlates of verbal learning task difficulty. *Psychonomic Science*, 1966, *6*, 69-70. (a)

Andreassi, J. L. Skin-conductance and reaction-time in a continuous auditory monitoring task. *The American Journal of Psychology*, 1966, *79*, 470-474. (b)

Andreassi, J. L., & Whalen, P. M. Some physiological correlates of learning and overlearning. *Psychophysiology,* 1967, *3,* 406-413.

Andreassi, J. L., Rapisardi, S. C., & Whalen, P. M. Autonomic responsivity and reaction time under fixed and variable signal schedules. *Psychophysiology,* 1969, *6,* 58-69.

Baugher, D. M. An examination of the nonspecific skin resistance response. *Bulletin of the Psychonomic Society,* 1975, *6,* 254-256.

Berlyne, D. E. *Conflict, arousal and curiosity.* New York: McGraw-Hill, 1960.

Bernstein, A. S. The orienting response and direction of stimulus change. *Psychonomic Science,* 1969, *12,* 127-128.

Bernstein, A. S., Taylor, K., Austen, B. G., Nathanson, M., & Scarpelli, A. Orienting response and apparent movement toward or away from the observer. *Journal of Experimental Psychology,* 1971, *87,* 37-45.

Berry, R. N. Skin conductance levels and verbal recall. *Journal of Experimental Psychology,* 1962, *63,* 275-277.

Brown, C. H. The relation of magnitude of galvanic skin responses and resistance levels to the rate of learning. *Journal of Experimental Psychology,* 1937, *20,* 262-278.

Cowles, M. P. The latency of the skin resistance response and reaction time. *Psychophysiology,* 1973, *10,* 177-183.

Darrow, C. W. The functional significance of the galvanic skin reflex and perspiration on the backs and palms of the hands. *Psychological Bulletin,* 1933, *30,* 712.

Eason, R. G., Beardshall, A., & Jaffee, S. Performance and physiological indicants of activation in a vigilance situation. *Perceptual & Motor Skills,* 1965, *20,* 3-13.

Edelberg, R. Electrical properties of the skin. In C. C. Brown (Ed.), *Methods in psychophysiology.* Baltimore: Williams & Wilkins, 1967, pp. 1-53.

Edelberg, R. The information content of the recovery limb of the electrodermal response. *Psychophysiology,* 1970, *6,* 527-539.

Edelberg, R. Electrical activity of the skin. In N. S. Greenfield & R. A. Sternbach (Eds.), *Handbook of psychophysiology.* New York: Holt, Rinehart & Winston, 1972, pp. 367-418. (a)

Edelberg, R. Electrodermal recovery rate, goal-orientation and aversion. *Psychophysiology,* 1972, *9,* 512-520. (b)

Edelberg, R., & Wright, D. J. Two GSR effector organs and their stimulus specificity. Paper read at the Society for Psychophysiological Research, Denver, 1962.

Freeman, G. L. The relationship between performance level and bodily activity level. *Journal of Experimental Psychology*, 1940, *26*, 602-608.

Freeman, G. L., & Simpson, R. M. The effect of experimentally induced muscular tension upon palmar skin resistance. *Journal of General Psychology*, 1938, *18*, 319-326.

Geen, R. G., & Rakosky, J. J. Interpretations of observed aggression and their effect on GSR. *Journal of Experimental Research in Personality*, 1973, *6*, 280-292.

Gringes, W. W., & Dawson, M. E. Complex variables in conditioning. In W. F. Prokasy & D. C. Raskin (Eds.), *Electrodermal activity in psychological research*. New York: Academic Press, 1973, pp. 203-254.

Hamrick, N. D. Physiological and verbal responses to erotic visual stimuli in a female population. *Behavioral Engineering*, 1974, *2*, 9-16.

Jacob, S. W., & Francone, C. A. *Structure and function in man*. Philadelphia: Saunders, 1970.

Juniper, K. J., Jr., Blanton, D. E., & Dykman, R. A. Palmar skin resistance and sweat-gland counts in drug and non-drug states. *Psychophysiology*, 1967, *4*, 231-243.

Juniper, K. J., Jr., & Dykman, R. A. Skin resistance, sweat-gland counts, salivary flow, and gastric secretion: Age, race, and sex differences, and intercorrelations. *Psychophysiology*, 1967, *4*, 216-222.

Kimmel, H. D. Instrumental conditioning. In W. F. Prokasy & D. C. Raskin (Eds.), *Electrodermal activity in psychological research*. New York: Academic Press, 1973, pp. 255-282.

Kimmel, H. D., & Gurucharri, F. W. Operant GSR conditioning with cool air reinforcement. *Pavlovian Journal of Biological Science*, 1975, *10*, 239-245.

Krupski, A., Raskin, D. C., & Bakan, P. Physiological and personality correlates of commission errors in an auditory vigilance task. *Psychophysiology*, 1971, *8*, 304-311.

Lacey, J. I., Kagan, J., Lacey, B. C., & Moss, H. A. The visceral level: Situational determinants and behavioral correlates of autonomic response patterns. In P. H. Knapp (Ed.), *Expression of the emotions in man*. New York: International University Press, 1963, pp. 161-196.

Lacey, J. I., & Lacey, B. C. The relationship of resting autonomic activity to motor impulsivity. In *The brain aond human behavior*. Baltimore: Williams & Wilkins, 1958, 144-209.

Lanzetta, J. T., Cartwright-Smith, J., & Kleck, R. E. Effects of non-verbal dissimulation on emotional experience and autonomic arousal. *Journal of Personality and Social Psychology,* 1976, *33,* 354-370.

Little, B. C., & Zahn, T. P. Changes in mood and autonomic functioning during the menstrual cycle. *Psychophysiology,* 1974, *11,* 579-590.

Lykken, D. T., & Venables, P. H. Direct measurement of skin conductance: A proposal for standardization. *Psychophysiology,* 1971, *8,* 656-671.

Lynn, R. *Attention, arousal and the orientation reaction.* Oxford: Pergamon Press, 1966.

Maltzman, I., Harris, L., Ingram, E., & Wolff, C. A primacy effect in the orienting reflex to stimulus change. *Journal of Experimental Psychology,* 1971, *87,* 202-206.

Maltzman, I., Kantor, W., & Langdon, B. Immediate and delayed retention, arousal, and the orienting and defensive reflexes. *Psychonomic Science,* 1966, *6,* 445-446.

Manning, S. K., & Melchiori, M. P. Words that upset urban college students: Measured with GSRs and rating scales. *Journal of Social Psychology,* 1974, *94,* 305-306.

O'Gorman, J. G. Change in stimulus conditions and the orienting response. *Psychophysiology,* 1973, *10,* 465-470.

Pavlov, I. P. *Conditioned reflexes* (G. V. Anrep, trans.). London: Oxford University Press, 1927.

Prokasy, W. F., & Kumpfer, K. L. Classical conditioning. In W. F. Prokasy & D. C. Raskin (Eds.), *Electrodermal activity in psychological research.* New York: Academic Press, 1973, pp. 157-202.

Prokasy, W. F., Williams, W. C., & Clark, L. G. Skin conductance response conditioning with CS intensities equal to and greater than UCS intensity. *Memory & Cognition,* 1975, *3,* 277-281.

Pugh, L. A., Oldroyd, C. R., Ray, T. S., & Clark, M. L. Muscular effort and electrodermal responses. *Journal of Experimental Psychology,* 1966, *71,* 241-248.

Ross, S., Dardano, J., & Hackman, R. Conductance levels during vigilance task performance. *Journal of Applied Psychology,* 1959, *43,* 65-69.

Schlosberg, H. Three dimensions of emotion. *Psychological Review,* 1954, *61,* 81-88.

Schlosberg, H., & Kling, J. W. The relationship between "tension" and efficiency. *Perceptual & Motor Skills,* 1959, *9,* 395-397.

Shackel, B. Skin drilling: A method of diminishing galvanic skin potentials. *American Journal of Psychology,* 1959, *72,* 114-121.

Shean, G. D. Instrumental modification of the galvanic skin response:

Conditioning or control? *Journal of Psychosomatic Research,* 1970, *14,* 155-160.

Siddle, D. A., & Heron, P. A. Effects of length of training and amount of tone frequency change on amplitude of autonomic components of the orienting response. *Psychophysiology,* 1976, *13,* 281-287.

Sokolov, E. N. *Perception and the conditioned reflex.* New York: Pergamon Press, 1963.

Stern, R. M. Operant modification of electrodermal responses and/or voluntary control of GSR. Paper presented at the meeting of the Society for Psychophysiological Research, 1970.

Stern, R. M., & Kaplan, B. E. Galvanic skin response: Voluntary control and externalization. *Journal of Psychosomatic Research,* 1967, *10,* 349-353.

Surwillo, W. W., & Quilter, R. E. The relation of frequency of spontaneous skin potential responses to vigilance and age. *Psychophysiology,* 1965, *1,* 272-276.

Venables, P. H., & Christie, M. J. Mechanism, instrumentation, recording techniques, and quantification of responses. In W. F. Prokasy & D. C. Raskin (Eds.), *Electrodermal activity in psychological research.* New York: Academic Press, 1973, pp. 1-124.

Venables, P. H., & Martin, I. Skin resistance and skin potential. In P. H. Venables & I. Martin (Eds.), *Manual of psycho-physiological methods.* Amsterdam: North-Holland, 1967, pp. 53-102.

Waid, W. M. Degree of goal orientation, level of cognitive activity and electrodermal recovery rate. *Perceptual & Motor Skills,* 1974, *38,* 103-109.

Waters, W. F., McDonald, D. G., & Koresko, R. L. Habituation of the orienting response: A gating mechanism subserving selective attention. *Psychophysiology,* 1977, *14,* 228-236.

Wilcott, R. C. Effects of local blood removal on skin resistance and potential. *Journal of Comparative & Physiological Psychology,* 1958, *51,* 295-300.

Wilcott, R. C. On the role of the epidermis in the production of skin resistance and potential. *Journal of Comparative & Physiological Psychology,* 1959, *52,* 642-649.

Wilcott, R. C. Arousal sweating and electrodermal phenomena. *Psychological Bulletin,* 1967, *67,* 58-72.

Woodburne, R. T. *Essentials of human anatomy.* New York: Oxford University Press, 1978.

Woodworth, R. S., & Schlosberg, H. *Experimental psychology.* New York: Holt, 1954.

Yaremko, R. M., Blair, M. W., & Leckart, B. T. The orienting reflex to

changes in a conceptual stimulus dimension. *Psychonomic Science,*
1970, *2,* 115-116.

Yaremko, R. M., & Butler, M. C. Imaginal experience and attenuation of the galvanic skin response to shock. *Bulletin of the Psychonomic Society,* 1975, *5,* 317-318.

Yaremko, R. M., Glanville, B. B., & Leckart, B. T. Imagery-mediated habituation of the orienting reflex. *Psychonomic Science,* 1972, *27,* 204-206.

Zimny, G. H., & Weidenfeller, E. W. Effects of music upon GSR and heart-rate. *The American Journal of Psychology,* 1963, *76,* 311-314.

Chapter 10

Antes, J. R. The time course of picture viewing. *Journal of Experimental Psychology,* 1974, *103,* 62-70.

Bakan, P. Hypnotizability, laterality of eye movement and functional brain asymmetry. *Perceptual & Motor Skills,* 1969, *28,* 927-932.

Barlow, J. D. Pupillary size as an index of preference in political candidates. *Perceptual & Motor Skills,* 1969, *28,* 587-590.

Beatty, J. Prediction of detection of weak acoustic signals from patterns of pupillary activity preceding behavioral response. *UCLA Technical Report,* May 1975.

Beatty, J., & Kahneman, D. Pupillary changes in two memory tasks. *Psychonomic Science,* 1966, *5,* 371-372.

Bernick, N., Kling, A., & Borowitz, G. Physiologic differentiation of sexual arousal and anxiety. *Psychosomatic Medicine,* 1971, *33,* 341-352.

Bortel, F. J. Van. Commercial applications of pupillometrics. In F. M. Bass, C. W. King, & E. A. Pessemier (Eds.), *Applications of the sciences in marketing management.* New York: Wiley, 1968, pp. 439-453.

Carver, R. P. Pupil dilation and its relationship to information processing during reading and listening. *Journal of Applied Psychology,* 1971, *55,* 126-134.

Coren, S., & Hoenig, P. Effect of non-target stimuli upon length of voluntary saccades. *Perceptual & Motor Skills,* 1972, *34,* 499-508. (a)

Coren, S., & Hoenig, P. Eye movements and decrement in the Oppel-Kundt illusion. *Perception & Psychophysics,* 1972, *12,* 224-225. (b)

Colman, F., & Paivio, A. Pupillary dilation and mediation processes during paired-associate learning. *Canadian Journal of Psychology*, 1970, *24*, 261-270.

Day, M. E. An eye-movement phenomenon relating to attention, thought and anxiety. *Perceptual & Motor Skills*, 1964, *19*, 443-446.

Festinger, L., White, C. W., & Allyn, M. R. Eye movements and decrement in the Muller-Lyer illusion. *Perception & Psychophysics*, 1968, *3*, 376-382.

Ford, A., White, C. T., & Lichtenstein, M. Analysis of eye movements during free search. *Journal of the Optical Society of America*, 1959, *49*, 287-292.

Geacintov, T., & Peavler, W. Pupillography in industrial fatigue assessment. *Journal of Applied Psychology*, 1974, *59*, 213-216.

Goldwater, B. C. Psychological significance of pupillary movements. *Psychological Bulletin*, 1972, *77*, 340-355.

Gould, J. D. Eye movements during visual search. *IBM Research Report* (RC 2680) Yorktown Heights, N.Y., 1969.

Gould, J. D. Looking at pictures. *IBM Research Report* (RC 4991), Yorktown Heights, N.Y., 1974.

Gould, J. D., & Peeples, D. R. Eye movements during visual search and discrimination of meaningless, symbol and object patterns. *Journal of Experimental Psychology*, 1970, *85*, 51-55.

Gould, J. D., & Schaffer, A. Eye movement patterns during visual information processing. *Psychonomic Science*, 1965, *3*, 317-318.

Gould, J. D., & Schaffer, A. Eye-movement parameters in pattern recognition. *Journal of Experimental Psychology*, 1967, *74*, 225-229.

Gur, R. E. Conjugate lateral eye movements as an index of hemispheric activation. *Journal of Personality & Social Psychology*, 1975, *31*, 751-757.

Gur, R. E., Gur, R. C., & Harris, L. J. Cerebral activation, as measured by subjects' lateral eye movements, is influenced by experimenter location. *Neuropsychologia*, 1975, *13*, 35-44.

Guyton, A. C. *Basic human physiology: Normal function and mechanisms of disease*. Philadelphia: Saunders, 1974.

Hakerem, G. Pupillography. In P. H. Venables & I. Martin (Eds.), *Manual of psychophysiological methods*. Amsterdam: North-Holland, 1967, pp. 335-349.

Hakerem, G., & Sutton, S. Pupillary response at visual threshold. *Nature*, 1966, *212*, 485-486.

Haltrecht, E. J., & McCormack, P. D. Monitoring eye movements of slow and fast learners. *Psychonomic Science*, 1966, *6*, 461-462.

Hess, E. H. Attitude and pupil size. *Scientific American,* 1965, *212,* 46-54.

Hess, E. H. Pupillometrics. In N. S. Greenfield & R. A. Sternbach (Eds.), *Handbook of psychophysiology.* New York: Holt, Rinehart & Winston, 1972, pp. 491-531.

Hess, E. H. *The tell-tale eye.* New York: Van Nostrand Reinhold, 1975.

Hess, E. H., Beaver, P. W., & Shrout, P. E. Brightness contrast effects in a pupillometric experiment. *Perception & Psychophysics,* 1975, *18,* 125-127.

Hess, E. H., & Polt, J. M. Pupil size as related to interest value of visual stimuli. *Science,* 1960, *132,* 349-350.

Hess, E. H., & Polt, J. M. Pupil size in relation to mental activity during simple problem solving. *Science,* 1964, *143,* 1190-1192.

Hess, E. H., Seltzer, A. L., & Shlien, J. M. Pupil responses of hetero- and homosexual males to pictures of men and women: A pilot study. *Journal of Abnormal Psychology,* 1965, *70,* 165-168.

Jacob, S. W., & Francone, C. A. *Structure and function in man.* Philadelphia: Saunders, 1970.

Janisse, M. P. (Ed.). *Pupillary dynamics and behavior.* New York: Plenum, 1974. (a)

Janisse, M. P. Pupil size, affect and exposure frequency. *Social Behavior & Personality,* 1974, *2,* 125-146. (b)

Kahneman, D., & Beatty, J. Pupil diameter and load on memory. *Science,* 1966, *154,* 1583-1585.

Kahneman, D., & Beatty, J. Pupillary responses in a pitch-discrimination task. *Perception & Psychophysics,* 1967, *2,* 101-105.

Kahneman, D., & Peavler, W. S. Incentive effects and pupillary changes in association learning. *Journal of Experimental Psychology,* 1969, *79,* 312-318.

Kahneman, D., & Wright, P. Changes of pupil size and rehearsal strategies in a short-term memory task. *Quarterly Journal of Experimental Psychology,* 1971, *23,* 187-196.

Kinsbourne, M. Eye and headturning indicates cerebral lateralization. *Science,* 1972, *176,* 539-541.

Kocel, K., Galen, D., Ornstein, R., & Merrin, E. L. Lateral eye movement and cognitive mode. *Psychonomic Science,* 1972, *27,* 223-224.

Krugman, H. E. Some applications of pupil measurement. *Journal of Marketing Research,* 1964, *1,* 15-19.

Lacey, J. I., Kagan, J., Lacey, B. C., & Moss, H. A. The visceral level: Situational determinants and behavioral correlates of autonomic response patterns. In P. Knapp (Ed.), *Expression of the emotions in man.* New York: International Universities, 1963, pp. 161-196.

Libby, W. L., Lacey, B. C., & Lacey, J. I. Pupillary and cardiac activity during visual attention. *Psychophysiology*, 1973, *10*, 270-294.

Loftus, G. R. Eye fixations and recognition memory for pictures. *Cognitive Psychology*, 1972, *3*, 525-551.

Lowenfeld, I. E. Pupil size. *Survey of Ophthalmology*, 1966, *11*, 291-294.

Lowenstein, O., & Lowenfeld, I. E. The pupil. In H. Davson (Ed.), *The eye*. Vol. 3 *Muscular mechanisms*. New York: Academic Press, 1962.

Lowenstein, O., & Lowenfeld, I. E. The sleep-waking cycle and pupillary activity. *Annals of the New York Academy of Sciences*, 1964, *117*, 142-156.

Mack, A., Fendrich, R., & Sirigatti, S. A rebound illusion in visual tracking. *American Journal of Psychology*, 1973, *86*, 425-433.

Mackworth, N. H., Kaplan, I. T., & Metlay, W. Eye movements during vigilance. *Perceptual & Motor Skills*, 1964, *18*, 397-402.

Mackworth, N. H., & Morandi, A. J. The gaze selects informative details within pictures. *Perception & Psychophysics*, 1967, *2*, 547-552.

McCormack, P. D., Haltrecht, E. J., & Hannah, T. E. Monitoring eye movements during the learning of successive paired-associate lists. *Journal of Verbal Learning and Verbal Behavior*, 1967, *6*, 950-953. (a)

McCormack, P. D., Hannah, T. E., Bradley, W. J., & Moore, T. E. Monitoring eye movements under conditions of high and low intralist response (meaningful) similarity. *Psychonomic Science*, 1967, *8*, 517-518. (b)

Nakano, A. Eye movements in relation to mental activity of problem-solving. *Psychologia: An International Journal of Psychology in the Orient*, 1971, *14*, 200-207.

Noton, D., & Stark, L. Scanpaths in saccadic eye movements while viewing and recognizing patterns. *Vision Research*, 1971, *11*, 929-942. (a)

Noton, D., & Stark, L. Eye movements and visual perception. *Scientific American*, 1971, *224*, 34-43. (b)

Paivio, A. Psychophysiological correlates of imagery. In F. J. McGuigan & R. A. Schoonover (Eds.), *The psychophysiology of thinking*. New York: Academic Press, 1973, 263-295.

Paivio, A., & Simpson, H. M. The effect of word abstractness and pleasantness on pupil size during an imaginery task. *Psychonomic Science*, 1966, *5*, 55-56.

Peavler, W. S. Pupil size, information overload, and performance differences. *Psychophysiology*, 1974, *11*, 559-566.

Peavler, W. S., & McLaughlin, J. P. The question of stimulus content and pupil size. *Psychonomic Science,* 1967, *8,* 505-506.
Polt, J. M. Effect of threat of shock on pupillary response in a problem-solving situation. *Perceptual & Motor Skills,* 1970, *31,* 587-593.
Poock, G. K. Information processing vs. pupil diameter. *Perceptual & Motor Skills,* 1973, *37,* 1000-1002.
Shackel, B. Eye movement recordings by electrooculography. In P. H. Venables & I. Martin (Eds.), *Manual of psycho-physiological methods.* Amsterdam: North-Holland, 1967, pp. 299-334.
Shackel, B., & Davis, J. R. A second survey with electro-oculography. *British Journal of Ophthalmology,* 1960, *44,* 337-346.
Simms, T. M. Pupillary response of male and female subjects to pupillary difference in male and female picture stimuli. *Perception & Psychophysics,* 1967, *2,* 553-555.
Simpson, H. M., & Hale, S. M. Pupillary changes during a decision-making task. *Perceptual & Motor Skills,* 1969, *29,* 495-498.
Stanners, R. F., Headley, D. B., & Clark, W. R. The pupillary response to sentences: Influences of listening set and deep structure. *Journal of Verbal Learning and Verbal Behavior,* 1972, *11,* 257-263.
Stelmack, R. M., & Mandelzys, N. Extraversion and pupillary response to affective and taboo words. *Psychophysiology,* 1975, *12,* 536-540.
Teitelbaum, H. A. Spontaneous rhythmic ocular movements: Their possible relationship to mental activity. *Neurology,* 1954, *4,* 350-354.
Tinker, M. A. The study of eye movements in reading. *Psychological Bulletin,* 1946, *43,* 93-120.
Tryon, W. W. Pupillometry: A survey of sources of variation. *Psychophysiology,* 1975, *12,* 90-93.
Uttal, W. R., & Smith, P. Recognition of alphabetic characters during voluntary eye movements. *Perception & Psychophysics,* 1968, *3,* 257-264.
Venezky, R. L. Research on reading processes: A historical perspective. *American Psychologist,* 1977, *32,* 339-345.
Volkmann, F. C., & Volkmann, J. Eye fixations and latency in a simplified search situation. *Perceptual & Motor Skills,* 1971, *33,* 971-979.
White, C. T., & Ford, A. Eye movements during simulated radar search. *Journal of The Optical Society of America,* 1960, *50,* 909-913.
Williams, L. G. The effects of target specification on objects fixated during visual search. *Acta Psychologica,* 1967, *27,* 335-360.
Williams, L. G. Studies of extrafoveal discrimination and detection. In *Visual search.* Washington, D.C.: National Academy of Sciences, 1973, pp. 77-92.

Woodhouse, J. M., & Campbell, F. W. The role of the pupil light reflex in aiding adaptation to the dark. *Vision Research,* 1975, *15,* 649-653.

Woodmansee, J. J. The pupil reaction as an index of positive and negative affect. Paper presented at the convention of The American Psychological Association, Washington, D.C. 1967.

Woodworth, R. S. *Experimental psychology.* New York: Holt, 1938.

Woodworth, R. S. & Schlosberg, H. *Experimental psychology.* New York: Holt, 1954.

Wright, P. & Kahneman, D. Evidence for alternative strategies of sentence retention. *Quarterly Journal of Experimental Psychology,* 1971, *23,* 197-213.

Yarbus, A. L. *Eye movements and vision.* New York: Plenum Press, 1967.

Young, F. A. & Biersdorf, W. R. Pupillary contraction and dilation in light and darkness. *Journal of Comparative & Physiological Psychology,* 1954, *47,* 264-268.

Chapter 11

Andreassi, J. L. Some physiological correlates of verbal learning task difficulty. *Psychonomic Science,* 1966, *6,* 69-70.

Andreassi, J. L. & Whalen, P. M. Some physiological correlates of learning and overlearning. *Psychophysiology,* 1967, *3,* 406-413.

Ax, A. R. The physiological differentiation between fear and anger in humans. *Psychosomatic Medicine,* 1953, *15,* 147-150.

Bankart, C. P., & Elliott, R. Heart rate and skin conductance in anticipation of shocks with varying probability of occurrence. *Psychophysiology,* 1974, *11,* 160-174.

Bergman, J. S., & Johnson, H. J. Sources of information which affect training and raising of heart rate. *Psychophysiology,* 1972, *9,* 30-39.

Blanchard, E. B., & Young, L. D. Self-control and cardiac functioning: A promise yet unfulfilled. *Psychological Bulletin,* 1973, *79,* 145-163.

Botwinick, J., & Thompson, L. W. Cardiac functioning and reaction time in relation to age. *Journal of Genetic Psychology,* 1971, *119,* 127-132.

Brener, J. Heart rate. In P. H. Venables & I. Martin (Eds.), *Manual of psychophysiological methods.* Amsterdam: North-Holland, 1967, pp. 103-131.

Brown, C. S. Instruments in psychophysiology. In N. S. Greenfield & R. A. Sternbach (Eds.), *Handbook of psychophysiology*. New York: Holt, 1972, pp. 159-195.

Carriero, N. J., & Fite, J. Cardiac deceleration as an indicator of correct performance. *Perceptual & Motor Skills*, 1977, *44*, 275-282.

Cohen, D. H., & McDonald, R. L. A selective review of central neural pathways involved in cardiovascular control. In P. A. Obrist, A. H. Black, J. Brener, & L. V. DiCara (Eds.), *Cardiovascular psychophysiology*. Chicago: Aldine, 1974, pp. 33-59.

Deane, G. E. Cardiac activity during experimentally induced anxiety. *Psychophysiology*, 1969, *6*, 17-30.

Edwards, D. C., & Alsip, J. E. Stimulus detection during periods of high and low heart rate. *Psychophysiology*, 1969, *5*, 431-434.

Elliott, R. Tonic heart rate: Experiments on the effects of collative variables lead to a hypothesis about its motivational significance. *Journal of Personality and Social Psychology*, 1969, *12*, 211-288.

Elliott, R. The motivational significance of heart rate. In P. A. Obrist, A. H. Black, J. Brener, & L. V. DiCara (Eds.), *Cardiovascular psychophysiology*. Chicago: Aldine, 1974, pp. 505-537.

Elliott, R. Heart rate in anticipation of shocks which have different probabilities of occurrences. *Psychological Reports*, 1975, *36*, 923-931.

Elliott, R., Bankart, B., & Light, T. Differences in the motivational significance of heart rate and palmar conductance: Two tests of a hypothesis. *Journal of Personality and Social Psychology*, 1970, *14*, 166-172.

Elliott, R., & Graf, V. Visual sensitivity as a function of phase of cardiac cycle. *Psychophysiology*, 1972, *9*, 357-361.

Evans, J. F. Social facilitation in a competitive situation. *Canadian Journal of Behavioural Science*, 1971, *3*, 276-281.

Evans, J. F. Resting heart rate and the effects of an incentive. *Psychonomic Science*, 1972, *26*, 99-100.

Evans, J. F. Motivational effects of being promised an opportunity to engage in social comparison. *Psychological Reports*, 1974, *34*, 175-181.

Frankenhaeuser, M., & Johansson, G. Task demand as reflected in catecholamine excretion and heart rate. *Journal of Human Stress*, 1976, *2*, 15-23.

Furedy, J. J., & Poulos, C. X. Heart-rate decelerative Pavlovian conditioning with tilt as UCS: Towards behavioural control of cardiac dysfunction. *Biological Psychology*, 1976, *4*, 93-106.

Gang, M. J., & Teft, L. Individual differences in heart rate responses to affective sound. *Psychophysiology*, 1975, *12*, 423-426.

Germana, J., & Klein, S. B. The cardiac component of the orienting response. *Psychophysiology*, 1968, *4*, 324-328.

Goldstein, J. H., Harman, J., McGhee, P. E., & Karasik, R. Test of an information-processing model of humor: Physiological response changes during problem- and riddle-solving. *Journal of General Psychology*, 1975, *92*, 59-68.

Graham, F. K., & Clifton, R. K. Heart-rate change as a component of the orienting response. *Psychological Bulletin*, 1966, *65*, 305-320.

Graham, F. K., Slaby, D. A. Differential heart rate changes to equally intense white noise and tone. *Psychophysiology*, 1973, *10*, 347-362.

Gunn, C. G., Wolf, S., Block, R. T. & Person, R. J. Psychophysiology of the cardiovascular system. In N. S. Greenfield & R. A. Sternbach, (Eds.), *Handbook of psychophysiology*. New York: Holt, 1972, pp. 457-489.

Guyton, A. C. *Basic human physiology: Normal function and mechanisms of disease*. Philadelphia: Saunders, 1977.

Hare, R. D. Cardiovascular components of orienting and defensive responses. *Psychophysiology*, 1972, 9, 606-614.

Hare, R. D. Orienting and defensive responses to visual stimuli. *Psychophysiology*, 1973, *10*, 453-464.

Hare, R. D., & Blevings, G. Defensive responses to phobic stimuli. *Biological Psychology*, 1975, *3*, 1-13.

Hatton, H. M., Berg, W. K., & Graham, F. K. Effects of acoustic rise time on heart rate response. *Psychonomic Science*, 1970, *19*, 101-103.

Headrick, M. W., & Graham, F. K. Multiple component heart rate responses conditioned under paced respiration. *Journal of Experimental Psychology*, 1969, *79*, 486-494.

Hnatiow, M., & Lang, P. J. Learned stabilization of cardiac rate. *Psychophysiology*, 1965, *1*, 330-336.

Ira, G. H., Whalen, R. E., & Bogdonoff, M. D. Heart rate changes in physicians during daily "stressful" tasks. *Journal of Psychosomatic Research*, 1963, 7, 147-150.

Jacob, S. W., & Francone, C. A. *Structure and function in man*. Philadelphia: Saunders, 1970.

Jennings, J. R., & Wood, C. C. Cardiac cycle time effects on performance, phasic cardiac responses and their intercorrelation in choice reaction time. *Psychophysiology*, 1977, *14*, 297-307.

Katkin, E. S., & Murray, E. N. Instrumental conditioning of autonomically mediated behavior: Theoretical and methodological issues. *Psychological Bulletin*, 1968, *70*, 52-68.

Keffe, F. B., & Johnson, L. C. Cardiovascular responses to auditory stimuli. *Psychonomic Science*, 1970, 19, 335-337.

Kimble, G. A. *Hilgard and Marquis' conditioning and learning*. New York: Appleton-Century-Crofts, 1961.

Kimmel, H. D. Instrumental conditioning. In W. F. Prokasy & D. C. Raskin (Eds.), *Electrodermal activity in psychological research*. New York: Academic Press, 1973, pp. 255-282.

Klinger, E., Gregoire, K. C., & Barta, S. G. Physiological correlates of mental activity: Eye movements, alpha, and heart rate during imagining, suppression, concentration, search, and choice. *Psychophysiology*, 1973, 10, 471-477.

Klorman, R. Habituation of fear: Effects of intensity and stimulus order. *Psychophysiology*, 1974, 11, 15-26.

Klorman, R. Contingent negative variation and cardiac deceleration in a long preparatory interval: A developmental study. *Psychophysiology*, 1975, 12, 609-617.

Klorman, R., Wiesenfeld, A. R., & Austin, M. L. Autonomic responses to affective visual stimuli. *Psychophysiology*, 1975, 12, 553-560.

Klorman, R., Weissberg, R. P., & Wiesenfeld, A. R. Individual differences in fear and autonomic reactions to affective stimulation. Paper presented at the meeting of the Society for Psychophysiological Research, October 1976, San Diego, California.

Lacey, B. C., & Lacey, J. I. Studies of heart rate and other bodily processes in sensorimotor behavior. In P. A. Obrist, A. H. Black, J. Brener, & L. V. DiCara (Eds.), *Cardiovascular psychophysiology*. Chicago: Aldine, 1974, pp. 538-564.

Lacey, B. C., & Lacey, J. I. Change in heart period: A function of sensorimotor event timing within the cardiac cycle. *Physiological Psychology*, 1977, 5, 383-393.

Lacey, J. I. Somatic response patterning and stress: Some revisions of activation theory. In M. H. Appley & R. Trumbull (Eds.), *Psychological stress: Issues in research*. New York: Appleton-Century-Crofts, 1967, pp. 14-42.

Lacey, J. I., Kagan, J., Lacey, B. C., & Moss, H. A. The visceral level: Situational determinants and behavioral correlates of autonomic response patterns. In P. H. Knapp (Ed.), *Expression of the emotions in man*. New York: International Universities Press, 1963, pp. 161-196.

Lang, P. J. Learned control of human heart rate in a computer directed environment. In P. A. Obrist, A. H. Black, J. Brener, & L. V. Dicara (Eds.), *Cardiovascular psychophysiology*, Chicago: Aldine, 1974, pp. 392-405.

Lang, P. J. Presidential address. Annual meeting of the Society for Psychophysiological Research, 1977.

Lang, P. J., & Twentyman, C. T. Learning to control heart rate: Effects of varying incentive and criterion of success on task performance. *Psychophysiology*, 1976, *13*, 378-385.

Laurell, H., & Lisper, H. O. Changes in subsidiary reaction time and heart-rate during car driving, passenger travel and stationary conditions. *Ergonomics*, 1976, *19*, 149-156.

Malmo, R. B. Physiological gradients and behavior. *Psychological Bulletin*, 1965, *64*, 225-234.

McCanne, T. R., & Sandman, C. A. Human operant heart rate conditioning: The importance of individual differences. *Psychological Bulletin*, 1976, *83*, 587-601.

Notterman, J. M., Schoenfeld, W. N., & Bersh, P. J. A comparison of three extinction procedures following heart rate conditioning. *Journal of Abnormal and Social Psychology*, 1952, *47*, 674-677.

Nowlin, J. B., Eisdorfer, C., Whalen, R., & Troyer, W. G. The effect of exogenous changes in heart rate and rhythm upon reaction time performance. *Psychophysiology*, 1970, *7*, 186-193.

Obrist, P. A. The cardiovascular-behavioral interaction as it appears today. *Psychophysiology*, 1976, *13*, 95-107.

Obrist, P. A., Howard, J. L., Sutterer, J. R., Hennis, R. S., & Murrell, D. J. Cardiac-somatic changes during a simple reaction time task: A developmental study. *Journal of Experimental Child Psychology*, 1973, *16*, 346-362.

Obrist, P. A., Webb, R. A., & Sutterer, J. R. Heart rate and somatic changes during aversive conditioning and a simple reaction time task. *Psychophysiology*, 1969, *5*, 696-723.

Ohkubo, T., & Hamley, E. J. Assessment of human performance in learning a skill involved in driving. *Journal of Human Ergology*, 1972, *1*, 95-110.

Raskin, D. C., Kotses, H., & Bever, J. Cephalic vasomotor and heart rate measures of orienting and defensive reflexes. *Psychophysiology*, 1969, *6*, 149-159.

Roman, J., Older, H., & Jones, W. L. Flight research program: VII. Medical monitoring of Navy carrier pilots in combat. *Aerospace Medicine*, 1967, *38*, 133-139.

Rule, B. G., & Hewitt, L. S. Effects of thwarting on cardiac response and physical aggression. *Journal of Personality and Social Psychology*, 1971, *19*, 181-187.

Saxon, S. A., & Dahle, A. J. Auditory threshold variations during periods of induced high and low heart rates. *Psychophysiology*, 1971, *8*, 23-29.

Schell, A. M., & Catania, J. The relationship between cardiac activity and sensory acuity. *Psychophysiology*, 1975, *12*, 147-151.
Schwartz, G. E. Cardiac responses to self-induced thoughts. *Psychophysiology*, 1971, *8*, 462-467.
Shapiro, A. H. Behavior of Kibbutz and urban children receiving an injection. *Psychophysiology*, 1975, *12*, 79-82.
Shearn, D. N. Operant conditioning of heart rate. *Science*, 1962, *137*, 530-531.
Sokolov, E. *Perception and the conditioned reflex*. New York: MacMillan, 1963.
Spence, D. P., Lugo, M., & Youdin, R. Cardiac change as a function of attention to and awareness of continuous verbal text. *Science*, 1972, *176*, 1344-1346.
Steele, W. G., & Lewis, M. A longitudinal study of the cardiac response during a problem-solving task and its relationship to general cognitive function. *Psychonomic Science*, 1968, *11*, 275-276.
Surwillo, W. W. Human reaction time and endogneous heart rate changes in normal subjects. *Psychophysiology*, 1971, *8*, 680-682.
Thackray, R. I., Touchstone, R. M., & Jones, K. M. Effects of simulated conic booms on tracking performance and autonomic response. *Aerospace Medicine*, 1972, *43*, 13-21.
Van Egeren, L. F., Headrick, M. N., & Hein, P. L. Individual differences in autonomic responses: Illustration of a possible solution. *Psychophysiology*, 1972, *9*, 626-633.
Velden, M., & Juris, M. Perceptual performance as a function of intracycle cardiac activity. *Psychophysiology*, 1975, *12*, 685-692.
Wallace, R. K., & Benson, H. The physiology of meditation. *Scientific American*, 1972, *226*, 84-90.
Webb, R. A., & Obrist, P. A. The physiological concomitants of reaction time performance as a function of preparatory interval and preparatory interval series. *Psychophysiology*, 1970, *6*, 389-403.
Wells, D. T. Large magnitude voluntary heart rate changes. *Psychophysiology*, 1973, *10*, 260-269.

Chapter 12

Blanchard, E. B., & Young, L. D. Self-control of cardiac functioning: A promise as yet unfulfilled. *Psychological Bulletin*, 1973, *79*, 145-163.
Brown, C. C. The techniques of plethysmography. In C. C. Brown (Ed.), *Methods in psychophysiology*. Baltimore: Williams & Wilkins, 1967.

Christie, D. J., & Kotses, H. Bidirectional operant conditioning of the cephalic vasomotor response. *Journal of Psychosomatic Research,* 1973, *17,* 167-170.

Cook, M. R. Psychophysiology of peripheral vascular changes. In P. A. Obrist, A. H. Black, J. Brener, & L. V. Dicara (Eds.), *Cardiovascular psychophysiology.* Chicago: Aldine, 1974, pp. 60-84.

Cromwell, L., Arditti, M., Weibell, F. J., Pfeiffer, E. A., Steele, B. & Labok, J. A. *Medical instrumentation for health care.* Englewood Cliffs, N.J.: Prentice-Hall, 1976.

DiCara, L. V., & Miller, N. E. Instrumental learning of systolic blood pressure responses by curarized rats: Dissociation of cardiac and vascular changes. *Psychosomatic Medicine,* 1968, *30,* 489-494.

Doob, A. N., & Kirshenbaum, H. M. The effects on arousal of frustration and aggressive films. *Journal of Experimental Social Psychology,* 1973, *9,* 57-64.

Ettema, J. H., & Zielhuis, R. L. Physiological parameters of mental load. *Ergonomics,* 1971, *14,* 137-144.

Fey, S. G., & Lindholm, E. Systolic blood pressure and heart rate changes during three sessions involving biofeedback or no feedback. *Psychophysiology,* 1975, *12,* 513-519.

Gardner, E. *Fundamentals of neurology* (6th ed.). Philadelphia: Saunders, 1975.

Geen, R. G. The meaning of observed violence: Real vs. fictional violence and consequent effects on aggression and emotional arousal. *Journal of Research in Personality,* 1975, *9,* 270-281.

Geen, R. G., & Stonner, D. The meaning of observed violence: Effects on arousal and aggressive behavior. *Journal of Research in Personality,* 1974, *8,* 55-63.

Geer, J. H. Cognitive factors in sexual arousal: Toward an amalgram of research strategies. Paper delivered at the annual convention of the American Psychological Association, New Orleans, 1974.

Geer, J. H. Sexual functioning—Some data and speculations on psychophysiological assessment. Paper presented at the Behavior Assessment Conference: West Virginia University, October 1975.

Geer, J. H., Morokoff, P., & Greenwood, P. Sexual arousal in women: The development of a measurement device for vaginal blood volume. *Archives of Sexual Behavior,* 1974, *3,* 559-564.

Geer, J. H., & Quartararo, J. D. Vaginal blood volume responses during masturbation and resultant orgasm. *Archives of Sexual Behavior,* 1976, *5,* 1-42.

Gentry, W. D. Sex differences in the effects of frustration and attack on emotion and vascular processes. *Psychological Reports,* 1970, *27,* 383-390.

Ginsberg, S., & Furedy, J. J. Stimulus repetition, change, and assessments of sensitivities of and relationships among an electrodermal and two plethysmographic components of the orienting reaction. *Psychophysiology*, 1974, *11*, 35-43.

Grollman, S. *The human body*. New York: Macmillan, 1964.

Gunn, C. G., Wolf, S., Block, R. T., & Person, R. J. Psychophysiology of the cardiovascular system. In N. S. Greenfield & R. A. Sternbach (Eds.), *Handbook of psychophysiology*. New York: Holt, Rinehart, & Winston, 1972, pp. 457-489.

Guyton, A. C. *Basic human physiology*. Philadelphia: Saunders, 1977.

Hare, R. D. Orienting and defensive responses to visual stimuli. *Psychophysiology*, 1973, *10*, 453-464.

Heiman, J. R. A psychophysiological exploration of sexual arousal patterns in females and males. *Psychophysiology*, 1977, *14*, 266-274.

Jacob, S. W., & Francone, C. A. *Structure and function in man* (2nd ed.). Philadelphia: Saunders, 1970.

Laws, D. R., & Bow, R. A. An improved mechanical strain gauge for recording penile circumference change. *Psychophysiology*, 1976, *13*, 596-599.

Lee, A. L., Tahmoush, A. J., & Jennings, J. R. An LED-transistor photoplethysmograph. *IEEE Transactions on Biomedical Engineering*, 1975, *22*, 248-250.

Levander, S. E., Lidberg, L., & Schalling, D. Habituation of the digital vasoconstrictive orienting response. *Journal of Experimental Psychology*, 1974, *102*, 700-705.

McConaghy, N. Penile volume responses to moving and still pictures of male and female nudes. *Archives of Sexual Behavior*, 1974, *3*, 565-570.

Oster, P. J., Stern, J. A., & Figar, S. Cephalic and digital vasomotor orienting responses: The effect of stimulus intensity and rise time. *Psychophysiology*, 1975, *12*, 642-648.

Ruttkay-Nedecky, I. & Cagán, S. Blood pressure of students the day before examination: A double-blind study of the effects of barbiturate and placebo. *Psychotherapy and Psychosomatics*, 1969, *17*, 196-200.

Shapiro, D., Schwartz, G. E., & Tursky, B. Control of diastolic blood pressure in man by feedback and reinforcement. *Psychophysiology*, 1972, 9, 296-304.

Shapiro, D., Tursky, B., Gershon, E., & Stern, M. Effects of feedback and reinforcement on the control of human systolic blood pressure. *Science*, 1969, *163*, 588-590.

Shapiro, D., Tursky, B., & Schwartz, G. E. Differentiation of heart rate and systolic blood pressure in man by conditioning. *Psychosomatic Medicine*, 1970, *32*, 417-423.

Shean, G. D. Vasomotor conditioning and awareness. *Psychophysiology*, 1968, *5*, 22-30.

Sintchak, G., & Geer, J. H. A vaginal plethysmograph system. *Psychophysiology*, 1975, *12*, 113-145.

Sokolov, E. N. *Perception and the conditioned reflex*. New York: Macmillan, 1963.

Steptoe, A., Smulyan, H., & Gribbon, B. Pulse wave velocity and blood pressure change: Calibration and applications. *Psychophysiology*, 1976, *13*, 488-493.

Tahmoush, A. J., Jennings, J. R., Lee, A. L., Camp, S., & Weber, F. Characteristics of a light emitting diode-transistor photo-plethysmograph. *Psychophysiology*, 1976, *13*, 357-362.

Tursky, B. The indirect recording of human blood pressure. In P. A. Obrist, A. H. Black, J. Brener, & L. V. DiCara (Eds.), *Cardiovascular psychophysiology*. Chicago: Aldine, pp. 93-105.

Tursky, B., & Greenblatt, D. J. Local vascular and thermal changes that accompany electric shock. *Psychophysiology*, 1967, *3*, 371-380.

Tursky, B., Shapiro, D., & Schwartz, G. E. Automated constant cuff-pressure system to measure average systolic and diastolic blood pressure in man. *IEEE Transactions on Biomedical Engineering*, 1972, *19*, 271-276.

Wilkie, F., & Eisdorfer, C. Intelligence and blood pressure in the aged. *Science*, 1971, *172*, 959-962.

Zuckerman, M. Physiological measures of sexual arousal in the human. In N. S. Greenfield & R. A. Sternbach (Eds.), *Handbook of psychophysiology*. New York: Holt, Rinehart & Winston, 1972, pp. 709-740.

Chapter 13

Arthur, R. O. The GSR Unit. *Journal of Polygraph Studies*, 1971, *5*, 1-4.

Barland, G. H., & Raskin, D. C. Detection of deception. In W. F. Prokasy & D. C. Raskin (Eds.), *Electrodermal activity in psychological research*. New York: Academic Press, 1973, pp. 417-477.

Barland, G. H., & Raskin, D. C. An evaluation of field techniques in detection of deception. *Psychophysiology*, 1975, *12*, 321-330.

Barnet, A. B., Ohlrich, E. S., & Shanks, B. L. EEG evoked responses to repetitive auditory stimulation in normal and Down's Syndrome infants. *Developmental Medicine and Child Neurology*, 1971, *13*, 321-329.

Beck, E. C., Dustman, R. E., & Lewis, E. G. The use of the Averaged Evoked Potential in the evaluation of central nervous system disorders. *International Journal of Neurology*, 1975, 9, 211-232.

Bersh, P. J. A validation of polygraph examiner judgments. *Journal of Applied Psychology*, 1969, 53, 399-403.

Bigum, H. B., Dustman, R. E., & Beck, E. C. Visual and somato-sensory evoked responses from Mongoloid and normal children. *Electroencephalography and Clinical Neurophysiology*, 1970, 28, 576-585.

Callaway, E. *Brain electrical potentials and individual psychological differences.* New York: Grune & Stratton, 1975.

Callaway, E., Jones, R. T., & Donchin, E. Auditory evoked potential variability in schizophrenia. *Electroencephalography & Neurophysiology*, 1970, 29, 421-428.

Callaway, E., Jones, R. T., & Layne, R. S. Evoked responses and segmental set of schizophrenia. *Archives of General Psychiatry*, 1965, 12, 83-89.

Cutrow, J., Parks, A., Lucas, N., & Thomas, K. The objective use of multiple physiological indices in detection of deception. *Psychophysiology*, 1972, 9, 578-588.

Dustman, R. E., & Beck, E. C. The evoked response: Its use in evaluating brain function of children and young adults. *Mental Health in Children*, 1976, II.

Hare, R. D. Psychopathy, autonomic functioning and the orienting response. *Journal of Abnormal Psychology*, Monograph Supplement, 1968, 73, 1-24.

Hare, R. D. Psychopathy. In P. H. Venables & M. J. Christie (Eds.), *Research in psychophysiology.* New York: Wiley, 1975, pp. 325-348.

Harter, M. R., & White, C. T. Effects of contour sharpness and checksize on visually evoked cortical potentials. *Vision Research*, 1968, 8, 701-711.

Itil, T. M. Qualitative and quantitave EEG findings in schizophrenia. In L. R. Mosher (Ed.), *Schizophrenia.* Rockville: National Institute of Mental Health, 1977, pp. 61-79.

Itil, T. M., Hsu, W., Klingberg, H., Saletu, B., & Gannon, P. Digital-computer-analyzed all-night sleep EEG patterns (Sleep patterns) in schizophrenics. *Biological Psychiatry*, 1972, 4, 3-16.

Jewett, D. L., & Williston, J. S. Auditory evoked far-fields averaged from the scalp of humans. *Brain*, 1971, 94, 681-696.

Jewett, E. L., Romano, M. N., & Williston, J. S. Human auditory potentials: Possible brainstem components detected on the scalp. *Science*, 1970, 167, 1517-1518.

John, E. R., Karmel, B. Z., Corning, W. C., Easton, P., Brown, D., Ahn, H., John, M., Harmony, T., Prichep L., Toro, A., Gerson, I., Bartlett, F., Thatcher, R., Kaye, H., Valdes, P., & Schwartz, E. Neurometrics, numerical taxonomy identifies different profiles of brain functions within groups of behaviorally similar people. *Science*, 1977, *196*, 1393-1410.

Kercher, G. A., & Walker, C. E. Reactions of convicted rapists to sexually explicit stimuli. *Journal of Abnormal Psychology*, 1973, *81*, 46-50.

Kinney, J.A.S., & McKay, C. Test of color-defective vision using the visual evoked response. *Journal of the Optical Society of America*, 1974, *64*, 1244-1250.

Kubis, J. F. *Comparison of voice analysis and polygraph as lie detection procedures*. Contract DAADO5-72-C-0217, U.S. Army Land Warfare Laboratory, Aberdeen Proving Ground, Maryland, 1973.

Lacey, J. I. Somatic response patterning and stress: Some revisions of activation. In M. H. Appley & R. Trumbell (Eds.), *Psychological stress: Issues in research*. New York: Appleton-Century-Crofts, 1967, pp. 14-44.

Lader, M., & Noble, P. The affective disorders. In P. H. Venables & M. J. Christie (Eds.), *Research in psychophysiology*. New York: Wiley, 1975, pp. 259-281.

Lieblich, I., Shakhar, G. B., & Kugelmass, S. Validity of the guilty knowledge technique in a prisoner's sample. *Journal of Applied Psychology*, 1976, *61*, 89-93.

Lombroso, C. T., Duffy, F. H., & Robb, R. M. Selective suppression of cerebral evoked potentials to patterned light in amblyopia ex anopsia. *Electroencephalography & Clinical Neurophysiology*, 1969, *27*, 238-247.

Lykken, D. T. Psychology and the lie detector industry. *American Psychologist*, 1974, *29*, 725-739.

Mackie, R. R. *Vigilance: Theory, operational performance and physiological correlates*. New York: Plenum Press, 1977.

Mackworth, N. H. *Researches on the measurement of human performance*. (MRC Spec. Rep. 268). London: H. M. Stationary Office, Medical Research Council, 1950.

McCallum, W. C. The CNV and conditionability in psychopaths. *Electroencephalography & Clinical Neurophysiology*, 1973, *33*, 337-343.

McCallum, W. C., & Abraham, P. The contingent negative variation in psychosis. *Electroencephalography & Clinical Neurophysiology*, 1973, *33*, 329-335.

McCallum, W. C., & Walter, W. G. The effects of attention and distraction on the contingent negative variation in normal and neurotic subjects. *Electroencephalography & Clinical Neurophysiology,* 1968, 25, 319-329.

Munsterberg, H. *On the witness stand.* New York: Doubleday, Page and Co., 1908.

Noble, P., & Lader, M. Depressive illness, pulse rate and forearm blood flow. *The British Journal of Psychiatry,* 1971, 119, 261-266.

Noel, P., & Desmedt, J. E. Somatosensory cerebral evoked potentials after vascular lesions of the brainstem and diencephalon. *Brain,* 1975, 98, 113-128.

O'Hanlon, J. F., & Kelly, G. R. Comparison of performance and physiological changes between drivers who perform well and poorly during prolonged vehicular operation. In R. R. Mackie (Ed.), *Vigilance: Theory, operational performance and physiological correlates.* New York: Plenum Press, 1977, pp. 87-109.

Orne, M. T., Thackray, R. I., & Paskewitz, D. A. On the detection of deception. In N. S. Greenfield & R. A. Sternbach (Eds.), *Handbook of psychophysiology.* New York: Holt, Rinehart & Winston, 1972, pp. 743-785.

Podlesny, J. A., & Raskin, D. C. Physiological measures and the detection of deception. *Psychological Bulletin,* 1977, 84, 782-799.

Rapin, I. Testing for hearing loss with auditory evoked responses—successes and failures. *Journal of Communication Disorders,* 1974, 7, 3-10.

Rapin, I., Graziani, L. J., & Lyttle, M. Summated auditory evoked responses for audiometry: Experience in 51 children with congenital rubella. *International Journal of Audiology,* 1969, 8, 371-376.

Raskin, D. C., Barland, G. H., & Podlesny, J. A. Validity and reliability of detection of deception. *Polygraph,* 1977, 6, 1-39.

Raskin, D. C., & Hare, R. D. Psychopathy and detection of deception in a prison population. *Psychophysiology,* 1978, in press.

Regan, D. *Evoked potentials in psychology, sensory physiology and clinical medicine.* London: Chapman and Hall, 1972.

Rhodes, L. E., Dustman, R. E., & Beck, E. C. The visual evoked response: A comparison of bright and dull children. *Electroencephalography & Clinical Neurophysiology,* 1969, 27, 364-372.

Richlin, M., Weisinger, M., Weinstein, S., Giannini, M., & Morganstern, M. Interhemispheric asymmetries of evoked cortical responses in retarded and normal children. *Cortex,* 1971, 1, 98-105.

Rose, D. E., Keating, L. W., Hedgecock, L. D., Miller, K. E., & Schreurs, K. K. A comparison of evoked responses audiometry and routine clinical audiometry. *Audiology,* 1972, 11, 238-243.

Roth, W. T., & Cannon, E. H. Some features of the auditory evoked response in schizophrenics. *Archives of General Psychiatry*, 1972, 27, 466-471.

Schalling, D., Lidberg, L., Levander, S. E., & Dahlin, Y. Spontaneous autonomic activity as related to psychopathy. *Biological Psychology*, 1973, 1, 83-97.

Shagass, C. *Evoked potentials in psychiatry.* New York: Plenum Press, 1972.

Shagass, C. Early evoked potentials. In L. R. Mosher (Ed.), *Schizophrenia.* Rockville: National Institute of Mental Health, 1977, pp. 80-92.

Shagass, C., & Schwartz, M. Evoked potential studies in psychiatric patients. *Annals of New York Academy of Science*, 1964, 112, 526-542.

Shimizu, H. Evoked response in eighth nerve lesions. *Laryngoscope*, 1968, 78, 2140-2152.

Spohn, H. E., Thetford, P. E., & Cancro, R. The effects of phenothiazine medication on skin conductance and heart rate in schizophrenic patients. *Journal of Nervous and Mental Disease*, 1971, 152, 129-139.

Starr, A., Achor, L. J. Auditory brainstem responses in neurological disease. *Archives of Neurology*, 1975, 32, 761-768.

Starr, A., & Hamilton, A. E. Correlation between confirmed sites of neurological lesions and abnormalities of far-field brainstem responses. *Electroencephalography & Clinical Neurophysiology*, 1976, 41, 595-608.

Straumanis, J. J., Jr., Shagass, C., & Overton, D. A. Auditory evoked responses in young adults with Down's Syndrome and idiopathic mental retardation. *Biological Psychiatry*, 1973, 6, 75-79.

Vaughan, H. G., & Katzman, R. Evoked response in visual disorders. *Annals of The New York Academy of Sciences*, 1964, 112, 305-319.

Vaughan, H. G., Katzman, R., & Taylor, J. Alterations of visual evoked response in the presence of homonymous visual defects. *Electroencephalography & Clinical Neurophysiology*, 1963, 15, 737-746.

Venables, P. H. Psychophysiological studies of schizophrenic pathology. In P. H. Venables & M. J. Christie (Eds.), *Research in psychophysiology.* New York: Wiley, 1975, pp. 282-324.

Woodworth, R. S., & Schlosberg, H. *Experimental psychology.* New York: Holt, 1954.

White, C. T., & Bonelli, L. Binocular summation in the evoked potential as a function of image quality. *American Journal of Optometry and Archives of the American Academy of Optometry*, 1970, 47, 304-309.

White, C. T., & Hansen, D. Complex binocular interaction and other effects in the visual evoked response. *American Journal of Optometry and Physiological Optics*, 1975, 52, 674-678.

Chapter 14

Basmajian, J. V., Kukulka, C. G., Narayan, M. G., & Takebe, K. Biofeedback treatment of foot-drop after stroke compared with standard rehabilitation technique: Effects on voluntary control and strength. *Archives of Physical Medicine and Rehabilitation*, 1975, 56, 231-236.

Bates, D. B., Macklem, P. T., & Christie, R. V. *Respiratory function in diseases*. Philadelphia: Saunders, 1971.

Benson, H., Shapiro, D., Tursky, B., & Schwartz, G. E. Decreased systolic blood pressure through operant conditioning techniques in patients with essential hypertension. *Science*, 1971, 173, 740-741.

Black, A. H. & Cott, A. A perspective on biofeedback. In J. Beatty, & H. Legewie, (Eds.), *Biofeedback and behavior*. New York: Plenum Press, 1977, pp. 7-19.

Blanchard, E. B., Young, L. D., & Haynes, M. R. A simple feedback system for the treatment of elevated blood pressure. *Behavior Therapy*, 1975, 6, 241-245.

Bleecker, E. R., & Engel, B. T. Learned control of cardiac rate and cardiac conduction in the Wolff-Parkinson-White syndrome. *New England Journal of Medicine*, 1973, 288, 560-562.

Braud, L. W., Lupin, M. N., & Braud, W. G. The use of electromyographic biofeedback in the control of hyperactivity. *Journal of Learning Disabilities*, 1975, 8, 420-425.

Brown, B. B. *New mind new body*. New York: Harper & Row, 1974.

Budzynski, T. H. Clinical implications of electromyographic training. In G. E. Schwartz, & J. Beatty (Eds.), *Biofeedback: Theory and research*. New York: Academic Press, 1977, pp. 433-448.

Budzynski, T., Stoyva, J., & Adler, C. Feed-back-induced muscle relaxation: Application to tension headache. *Journal of Behavior Therapy & Experimental Psychiatry*, 1970, 1, 205-211.

Budzynski, T., Stoyva, J., Adler, C. S., & Mullaney, D. J. EMG biofeedback and tension headache: A controlled outcome study. *Psychosomatic Medicine*, 1973, 35, 484-496.

Cleeland, C. S. Behavioral techniques in the modification of spasmodic torticollis. *Neurology*, 1973, 23, 1241-1247.

Coleman, J. C. *Abnormal psychology and modern life*. Dallas: Scott, Foresman, 1976.

Cox, D. J., Freundlich, A., & Meyer, R. G. Differential effectiveness of electromyograph feedback, verbal relaxation instructions, and medication placebo with tension headaches. *Journal of Consulting & Clinical Psychology*, 1975, *43*, 892-898.

Dalessio, D. *Wolff's headache and other head pain*. (3rd ed.). New York: Oxford University Press, 1972.

Elder, S. T., & Eustis, N. K. Instrumental blood pressure conditioning in out-patient hypertensives. *Behavioral Research and Therapy*, 1975, *13*, 185-188.

Elder, S. T., Ruiz, Z. R., Deabler, H. L., & Dillendoffer, R. L. Instrumental conditioning of diastolic blood pressure in essential hypertensive patients. *Journal of Applied Behavior Analysis*, 1973, *6*, 377-382.

Engel, B. T. Biofeedback as treatment for cardiovascular disorders: A critical review. In J. Beatty, & H. Legewie (Eds.), *Biofeedback and behavior*. New York: Plenum Press, 1977, pp. 395-401.

Engel, B. T., Nikoomanesh, P., & Schuster, M. M. Operant conditioning of rectosphincteric responses in the treatment of fecal incontinence. *The New England Journal of Medicine*, 1974, *290*, 646-649.

Engel-Sittenfeld, P. Biofeedback in the treatment of neuromuscular disorders. In J. Beatty, & H. Legewie (Eds.), *Biofeedback and behavior*. New York: Plenum Press, 1977, pp. 427-438.

Feuerstein, M., & Adams, H. E. Cephalic vasomotor feedback in the modification of migraine headache. *Biofeedback and Self-Regulation*, 1977, *2*, 241-254.

Feuerstein, M., Adams, H. E., & Beiman, I. Cephalic vasomotor and electromyographic feedback in the treatment of combined muscle contraction and migraine headaches in a geriatric case. *Headache*, 1976, *16*, 232-237.

Finley, W. W. Effects of sham feedback following successful SMR training in an epileptic. *Biofeedback and Self-Regulation*, 1976, *1*, 227-235.

Finley, W. W. Operant conditioning of the EEG in two patients with epilepsy: Methodological and clinical considerations. *Pavlovian Journal of Biological Science*, in press.

Friar, R., & Beatty, J. Migraine: Management by trainer control of vasoconstriction. *Journal of Consulting & Clinical Psychology*, 1976, *44*, 46-53.

Fried, J. J. Biofeedback: Teaching your body to heal itself. *Family Health*, 1974, *6*, 18-21.

Friedman, A. P., & Merritt, H. H. *Headache: diagnosis and treatment*. Philadelphia: Davis, 1959.

Gastaut, H. Comments on "Biofeedback in Epileptics: Equivocal relationship of reinforced EEG frequency to seizure reduction" by Bonnie J. Kaplan, *Epilepsia*, 1975, *16*, 487-490.

Goldman, H., Kleinman, K. M., Snow, M. Y., Bidus, D. R., & Korol, B. Relationship between essential hypertension and cognitive functioning: Effects of biofeedback. *Psychophysiology*, 1975, *12*, 569-573.

Guitar, B. Reduction of stuttering frequency using analog electromyographic feedback. *Journal of Speech & Hearing Research*, 1975, *18*, 672-685.

Haynes, S. N., Griffin, P., Mooney, D., & Parise, M. Electromyographic biofeedback and relaxation instructions in the treatment of muscle contraction headaches. *Behavior Therapy*, 1975, *6*, 672-678.

Johnson, L. C. Learned control of brain wave activity. In J. Beatty & H. Legewie (Eds.), *Biofeedback and behavior*. New York: Plenum Press, 1977, pp. 73-93.

Johnson, R. K., & Meyer, R. G. Phased biofeedback approach for epileptic seizure control. *Journal of Behavior Therapy & Experimental Psychiatry*, 1974, *5*, 185-187.

Kaplan, B. J. Biofeedback in epileptics: Equivocal relationship of reinforced EEG frequency to seizure reduction. *Epilepsia*, 1975, *6*, 477-485.

Kotses, H., Glaus, K. D., Crawford, P. L., Edwards, J. E., & Scherr, M. S. Operant reduction of frontalis EMG activity in the treatment of asthma in children. *Journal of Psychosomatic Research*, 1976, *20*, 453-459.

Kristt, D. A., & Engel, B. T. Learned control of blood pressure in patients with high blood pressure. *Circulation*, 1975, *51*, 370-378.

Kuhlman, W. N., & Allison, T. EEG feedback training in the treatment of epilepsy: Some questions and some answers. *Pavlovian Journal of Biological Science*, in press.

Lamontagne, Y., Hand, I., Annable, L., & Gagnon, M. Physiological and psychological effects of alpha and EMG feedback training with college drug users. *Canadian Psychiatric Association Journal*, 1975, *20*, 337-349.

Lang, P. J., Troyer, W. G., Twentyman, C. T., & Gatchel, R. J. Differential effects of heart rate modification training on college students, older males, and patients with ischemic heart disease. *Psychosomatic Medicine*, 1975, *37*, 429-446.

Lanyon, R. I. Effect of biofeedback-based relaxation on stuttering during reading and spontaneous speech. *Journal of Consulting and Clinical Psychology*, 1977, *45*, 860-866.

Lanyon, R. I., Barrington, C. C., & Newman, A. C. Modification of stuttering through EMG biofeedback: A preliminary study. *Behavior Therapy*, 1976, 7, 96-103.

Legewie, H., Cleary, P., & Aackensperger, W. EMG-recording and biofeedback in the diagnosis and therapy of stuttering: A case study. *European Journal of Behavioral Analysis & Modification*, 1975, 1, 137-143.

Lubar, J. F., & Bahler, W. W. Behavioral management of epileptic seizures following EEG biofeedback training of the sensorimotor rhythm. *Biofeedback and Self-Regulation*, 1976, 1, 77-104.

Melzack, R., & Perry, C. Self-regulation of pain: The use of alphafeedback and hypnotic training for the control of chronic pain. *Experimental Neurology*, 1975, 46, 452-469.

Middaugh, S. Comparison of voluntary muscle contractions with and without EMG feedback in persons with neuromuscular dysfunction. Paper presented at the 17th annual meeting of the Society for Psychophysiological Research, 1977.

Miller, N. E. Introduction. In N. E. Miller, T. X. Barber, L. V. DiCara, J. Kamiya, D. Shapiro, & J. Stoyva (Eds.), *Biofeedback and self-control 1973: An Aldine annual on the regulation of bodily processes and consciousness*. Chicago: Aldine, 1974, pp. 11-20.

Patel, C. H. Yoga and biofeedback in the management of hypertension. *Lancet*, November 10, 1973, 1053-1055.

Price, K. P., & Tursky, B. Vascular reactivity of migraineurs and nonmigraineurs: A comparison of responses to self-control procedures. *Headache*, 1976, 16, 210-217.

Raskin, M., Johnson, G., & Rondestvedt, J. W. Chronic anxiety treated by feedback-induced muscle relaxation. *Archives of General Psychiatry*, 1973, 28, 263-267.

Reeves, J. L., & Mealiea, W. L. Biofeedback-assisted cue-controlled relaxation for the treatment of flight phobias. *Journal of Behavior Therapy & Experimental Psychiatry*, 1975, 6, 105-109.

Sargent, J. D., Green, E. E., & Walters, E. D. The use of autogenic feedback training in a pilot study of migraine and tension headaches. *Headache*, 1972, 12, 120-124.

Sargent, J. D., Walters, E. D., & Green, E. E. Psychosomatic self-regulation of migraine headaches. *Seminars in Psychiatry*, 1973, 5, 415-428.

Schwartz, G. E., & Shapiro, D. Biofeedback and essential hypertension: Current findings and theoretical concerns. *Seminars in Psychiatry*, 1973, 5, 493-503.

Schwitzgebel, R. L., & Rugh, J. D. Of bread, circuses, and alpha machines. *American Psychologist*, 1975, 30, 363-370.

Seifert, A. R., & Lubar, J. F. Reduction of epileptic seizures through

EEG biofeedback training. *Biological Psychology*, 1975, *3*, 157-184.

Shapiro, D. A monologue on biofeedback and psychophysiology. *Psychophysiology*, 1977, *14*, 213-227.

Shapiro, D., Mainardi, J. A., & Surwit, R. S. Biofeedback and self-regulation in essential hypertension. In G. E. Schwartz & J. Beatty (Eds.), *Biofeedback: Theory and research*. New York: Academic Press, 1977, pp. 313-347.

Sterman, M. B. Neurophysiologic and clinical studies of sensorimotor EEG biofeedback training: Some effects on epilepsy. *Seminars in Psychiatry*, 1973, *5*, 507-524.

Sterman, M. B., & Friar, L. Suppression of seizures in an epileptic following EEG feedback training. *Electroencephalography & Clinical Neurophysiology*, 1972, *33*, 89-95.

Sterman, M. B., MacDonald, L. R., & Stone, R. K. Biofeedback training of the sensorimotor EEG rhythm in man: Effects on epilepsy. *Epilepsia*, 1974, *15*, 395-416.

Stoyva, J. Why should muscular relaxation be clinically useful? Some data and 2½ models. In J. Beatty & H. Legewie (Eds.), *Biofeedback and behavior*. New York: Plenum Press, 1977, pp. 449-472.

Stroebel, C. F., & Glueck, B. C. Biofeedback treatment in medicine and psychiatry: An ultimate placebo? *Seminars in Psychiatry*, 1973, *5*, 379-393.

Surwit, R. S., Pilon, R. N., & Fenton, C. H. Behavioral treatment of Raynaud's Disease. Paper presented at Seventeenth Annual Meeting of the Society for Psychophysiological Research, October 19-22, 1977, Philadelphia.

Takebe, K., & Basmajian, J. V. Gait analysis in stroke patients to assess treatments of footdrop. *Archives of Physical Medicine and Rehabilitation*, 1976, *57*, 305-310.

Taub, E. Self-regulation of human tissue temperature. In G. E. Schwartz & J. Beatty (Eds.), *Biofeedback: Theory and research*. New York: Academic Press, 1977, pp. 265-300.

Weiss, T., & Engel, B. T. Operant conditioning of heart rate in patients with premature ventricular contractions. *Psychosomatic Medicine*, 1971, *33*, 301-322.

Weiss, T., & Engel, B. T. Evaluation of an intra-cardiac limit of learned heart rate control. *Psychophysiology*, 1975, *12*, 310-312.

Chapter 15

Andreassi, J. L. Skin-conductance and reaction-time in a continuous auditory monitoring task. *The American Journal of Psychology*, 1966, 79, 470-474.

Andreassi, J. L., Rapisardi, S. C., & Whalen, P. M. Autonomic responsivity and reaction time under fixed and variable signal schedules. *Psychophysiology*, 1969, 6, 58-69.

Ax, A. The physiological differentiation between fear and anger in humans. *Psychosomatic Medicine*, 1953, 15, 433-442.

Baccelli, G., Guazzi, M., Libretti, A., & Zanchetta, A. Pressoceptive and chemoceptive aortic reflexes in decorticate and decerebrate cats. *American Journal of Physiology*, 1965, 208, 708-714.

Bartorelli, C., Bizzi, E., Libretti, A., & Zanchetta, A. Inhibitory control of sinocarotid pressoceptive afferents on hypothalamic autonomic activity and sham rage behavior. *Archives Italiennes de Biologie*, 1960, 98, 309-326.

Bonvallet, M., Dell, P., & Hiebel, G. Tonus sympathique et activite electrique corticale. *Electroencephalography & Clinical Neurophysiology*, 1954, 6, 119-144.

Coleridge, H. M., Coleridge, J.C.G., & Rosenthal, R. Prolonged inactivation of cortical pyramidal tract neurons in cats by distension of the carotid sinus. *Journal of Physiology*, 1976, 256, 635-649.

Courts, F. A. Relation between experimentally induced muscle tension and memorization. *Journal of Experimental Psychology*, 1939, 25, 235-256.

Duffy, E. Emotion: An example of the need for reorientation in psychology. *Psychological Review*, 1934, 41, 184-198.

Duffy, E. The psychological significance of the concept of "arousal" or "activation." *Psychological Review*, 1957, 64, 265-275.

Duffy, E. Activation. In N. S. Greenfield & R. A. Sternbach (Eds.), *Handbook of psychophysiology*. New York: Holt, Rinehart, & Winston, 1972, pp. 577-622.

Eason, R. G., & Dudley, L. M. Physiological and behavioral indicants of activation. *Psychophysiology*, 1971, 7, 223-232.

Elliott, R. The significance of heart rate for behavior: A critique of Lacey's hypothesis. *Journal of Personality & Social Psychology*, 1972, 22, 398-409.

Engel, B. T. Some physiological correlates of hunger and pain. *Journal of Experimental Psychology*, 1959, 57, 389-396.

Engel, B. T. Stimulus-response and individual-response specificity. *Archives of General Psychiatry*, 1960, *2*, 305-313.

Engel, B. T. Response specificity. In N. S. Greenfield & R. A. Sternbach (Eds.), *Handbook of psychophysiology*. New York: Holt, Rinehart, & Winston, 1972, pp. 571-576.

Freeman, G. L. The relationship between performance level and bodily activity level. *Journal of Experimental Psychology*, 1940, *26*, 602-608.

Freeman, G. L., & Simpson, R. M. The effect of experimentally induced muscular tension upon palmar skin resistance. *Journal of General Psychology*, 1938, *18*, 319-326.

French, J. D. The reticular formation. *Scientific American*, 1957, *196*, 54-60.

Fuster, J. M. Effects of stimulation of brain stem on tachistoscopic perception. *Science*, 1958, *127*, 150.

Gahery, Y., & Vigier, D. Inhibitory effects in the cuneate nucleus produced by vago-aortic afferent fibers. *Brain Research*, 1974, *75*, 241-246.

Galin, D., & Lacey, J. I. Reaction time and heart rate response pattern: Effects of mesencephalic reticular formation stimulation in cats. *Physiology & Behavior*, 1972, *8*, 729-739.

Gatchel, R. J. The effect of voluntary control of heart rate deceleration on skin conductance level: An example of response fractionation. *Biological Psychology*, 1976, *4*, 241-248.

Graham, F. K., & Clifton, R. K. Heart-rate change as a component of the orienting response. *Psychological Bulletin*, 1966, *65*, 305-320.

Hahn, W. W. Attention and heart rate: A critical appraisal of the hypothesis of Lacey and Lacey. *Psychological Bulletin*, 1973, *79*, 59-70.

Hare, R. D. Response requirements and directional fractionation of autonomic response. *Psychophysiology*, 1972, *9*, 419-427.

Hare, R. D. Orienting and defensive responses to visual stimuli. *Psychophysiology*, 1973, *10*, 453-464.

Hebb, D. O. Drives and the C.N.S. (conceptual nervous system). *Psychological Review*, 1955, *62*, 243-254.

Hodapp, V., Weyer, G., & Becker, J. Situational stereotypy in essential hypertension patients. *Journal of Psychosomatic Research*, 1975, *19*, 113-121.

Hord, D. J., Johnson, L. C., & Lubin, A. Differential effect of the law of initial value (LIV) on autonomic variables. *Psychophysiology*, 1964, *1*, 79-87.

Kennedy, J. L., & Travis, R. C. Prediction and control of alertness. II:

Continuous tracking. *Journal of Comparative & Physiological Psychology*, 1948, *41*, 203-210.

Klorman, R., Weisenfeld, A. R., & Austin, M. L. Autonomic responses to affective visual stimuli. *Psychophysiology*, 1975, *12*, 553-560.

Lacey, B. C., & Lacey, J. I. Change in heart period: A function of sensorimotor event timing within the cardiac cycle. *Physiological Psychology*, 1977, *5*, 383-393.

Lacey, B. C., & Lacey, J. I. Studies of heartrate and other bodily processes in sensorimotor behavior. In P. A. Obrist, A. H. Black, J. Brener, & L. V. DiCara (Eds.), *Cardiovascular psychophysiology*. Chicago: Aldine, 1974, pp. 538-564.

Lacey, B. C., & Lacey, J. I. Two-way communication between the heart and the brain: Significance of time within the cardiac cycle. *American Psychologist*, 1978, *33*, 99-113.

Lacey, J. I. Psychophysiological approaches to the evaluation of psychotherapeutic process and outcome. In E. A. Rubinstein & M. B. Parloff (Eds.), *Research in psychotherapy*. Washington, D.C.: American Psychological Association, 1959.

Lacey, J. I. Somatic response patterning and stress: Some revisions of activation theory. In M. H. Appley & R. Trumbull (Eds.), *Psychological stress: Issues in research*. New York: Appleton-Century-Crofts, 1967, pp. 14-42.

Lacey, J. I., Bateman, D. E., & Van Lehn, R. Autonomic response specificity: An experimental study. *Psychosomatic Medicine*, 1953, *15*, 8-21.

Lacey, J. I., Kagan, J., Lacey, B. C., & Moss, H. A. The visceral level: Situational determinant and behavioral correlates of autonomic response patterns. In P. H. Knapp (Eds.), *Expression of the emotions in man*. New York: International Universities Press, 1963.

Lacey, J. I., & Lacey, B. C. Verification and extension of the principle of autonomic response stereotypy. *American Journal of Psychology*, 1958, *71*, 50-73.

Lacey, J. I., & Lacey, B. C. Some autonomic-central nervous system interrelationships. In P. Black (Ed.), *Physiological correlates of emotion*. New York: Academic Press, 1970.

Lang, P. J., Rice, D. G., & Sternbach, R. A. The psychophysiology of emotion. In N. S. Greenfield & R. A. Sternbach (Eds.), *Handbook of psychophysiology*, New York: Holt, Rinehart, & Winston, 1972, pp. 623-643.

Lawler, K. A., Obrist, P. A., & Lawler, J. E. Cardiac and somatic response patterns during reaction time task in children and adults. *Psychophysiology*, 1976, *13*, 448-455.

Libby, W. L., Lacey, B. C., & Lacey, J. I. Pupillary and cardiac activity during visual attention. *Psychophysiology*, 1973, 10, 270-294.

Lindsley, D. B. Emotion. In S. S. Stevens (Ed.). *Handbook of experimental psychology*. New York: Wiley, 1951, pp. 473-516.

Lindsley, D. B. Physiological psychology. *Annual Review of Psychology*, 1956, 7, 323-348.

Lovallo, W., & Zeiner, A. R. Some factors influencing the vasomotor response to cold pressor stimulation. *Psychophysiology*, 1975, 12, 499-505.

Lynn, R. *Attention, arousal and the orientation reaction*. Oxford: Pergamon Press, 1966.

Maclean, V., Ohman, A., & Lader, M. Effects of attention, activation and stimulus regularity on short-term "habituation" of the averaged evoked response. *Biological Psychology*, 1975, 3, 57-69.

Malmo, R. B. Activation. In A. J. Bachrach (Ed.), *Experimental foundations of clinical psychology*. New York: Basic Books, 1962, pp. 386-422.

Malmo, R. B., & Davis, J. F. Physiological gradients as indicants of "arousal" in mirror tracing. *Canadian Journal of Psychology*, 1956, 10, 231-238.

Malmo, R. B., & Shagass, C. Physiologic study of symptom mechanisms in psychiatric patients under stress. *Psychosomatic Medicine*, 1949, 11, 25-29.

Moos, R. H., & Engel, B. T. Psychophysiological reactions in hypertensive and arthritic patients. *Journal of Psychosomatic Research*, 1962, 6, 227-241.

Moruzzi, G., & Magoun, H. W. Brain stem reticular formation and activation of the EEG. *Electroencephalography & Clinical Neurophysiology*, 1949, 1, 455-473.

Obrist, P. A. Heart rate and somatic-motor coupling during classical aversive conditioning in humans. *Journal of Experimental Psychology*, 1968, 77, 180-193.

Obrist, P. A. The cardiovascular-behavioral interaction as it appears today. *Psychophysiology*, 1976, 13, 95-107.

Obrist, P. A., Gaebelein, C. J., Teller, E. S., Langer, A. W., Grignolo, A., Light, K. C., & McCubbin, J. A. The relationship among heart rate, carotid dP/dt and blood pressure in humans as a function of the type of stress. *Psychophysiology*, 1978, 15, 102-115.

Obrist, P. A., Howard, J. L., Lawler, J. E., Galosy, R. A., Meyers, K. A., & Gaebelein, C. J. The cardiac somatic interaction. In P. A. Obrist, A. H. Black, J. Brener, & L. V. DiCara (Eds.), *Cardiovascular psychophysiology*. Chicago: Aldine, 1974, pp. 136-162.

454

Obrist, P. A., Howard, J. L., Sutterer, J. R., Hennis, R. S., & Murrell, D. J. Cardiac-somatic changes during a simple reaction time task: A developmental study. *Journal of Experimental Child Psychology,* 1973, *16*, 346-362.

Obrist, P. A., Webb, R. A., & Sutterer, J. R. Heart rate and somatic changes during aversive conditioning and a simple reaction time task. *Psychophysiology,* 1969, *5,* 696-723.

Obrist, P. A., Webb, R. A., Sutterer, J. R., & Howard, J. L. Cardiac deceleration and reaction time: An evaluation of two hypotheses. *Psychophysiology,* 1970, *6,* 695-706.

Pavlov, I. P. *Conditioned reflexes: An investigation of the physiological activity of the cerebral cortex.* London: Oxford University Press, 1927.

Pinneo, L. R. The effects of induced muscle tension during tracking on level of activation and on performance. *Journal of Experimental Psychology,* 1961, *62,* 523-531.

Raskin, D. C., Kotses, H., & Bever, J. Cephalic vasomotor and heart rate measures of orienting and defensive reflexes. *Psychophysiology,* 1969, *6,* 149-159.

Schlosberg, H., & Kling, J. W. The relationship between "tension" and efficiency. *Perceptual & Motor Skills,* 1959, *9,* 395-397.

Schnore, M. M. Individual patterns of physiological activity as a function of task differences and degree of arousal. *Journal of Experimental Psychology,* 1959, *58,* 117-128.

Shaw, W. A. Facilitating effects of induced tension upon the perception span for digits. *Journal of Experimental Psychology,* 1956, *51,* 113-117.

Sjoberg, H. Relations between heart rate, reaction speed, and subjective effort at different work loads on a bicycle ergometer. *Journal of Human Stress,* 1975, *1,* 21-27.

Smith, D. B., & Wenger, M. A. Changes in autonomic balance during phasic anxiety. *Psychophysiology,* 1965, *1,* 267-271.

Smock, C. D., & Small, V. H. Efficiency of utilization of visual information as a function of induced muscular tension. *Perceptual & Motor Skills,* 1962, *14,* 39-44.

Sokolov, E. N. *Perception and the conditioned reflex.* New York: Mac-Millan, 1963.

Stennett, R. G. The relationship of performance level to level of arousal. *Journal of Experimental Psychology,* 1957, *54,* 54-61.

Sternbach, R. A. *Principles of psychophysiology.* New York: Academic Press, 1966.

Webb, R. A., & Obrist, P. A. The physiological concomitants of reaction time performance as a function of preparatory interval and preparatory interval series. *Psychophysiology*, 1970, *6*, 389-403.

Wenger, M. 'A. The measurement of individual differences in autonomic balance. *Psychosomatic Medicine*, 1941, *3*, 427-434.

Wenger, M. A. Studies of autonomic balance in Army Air Force personnel. *Comparative Psychology Monographs*, 1948, *19*.

Wenger, M. A. Studies of autonomic balance: A summary. *Psychophysiology*, 1966, *2*, 173-186.

Wenger, M. A., Clemens, T. L., Coleman, D. R., Cullen, T. D., & Engel, B. T. Autonomic response specificity. *Psychosomatic Medicine*, 1961, *23*, 185-193.

Wenger, M. A., Clemens, T. L., & Cullen, T. D. Autonomic functions in patients with gastrointestinal and dermatological disorders. *Psychosomatic Medicine*, 1962, *24*, 268-273.

Wenger, M. A., & Cullen, T. D. Studies of autonomic balance in children and adults. In N. S. Greenfield & R. A. Sternbach (Eds.) *Handbook of psychophysiology*. New York: Holt, Rinehart, & Winston, 1972, pp. 535-569.

Wenger, M. A., Engel, B. T., & Clemens, T. L. Studies of autonomic response patterns: Rationale and methods. *Behavioral Science*, 1957, *2*, 216-221.

Wenger, M. A., Jones, F. N., & Jones, M. H. *Physiological psychology*, New York: Holt, 1956.

White, K. D. Salivation and the law of initial value. *Psychophysiology*, 1977, *14*, 560-562.

Wilder, J. The law of initial values in neurology and psychiatry. *Journal of Nervous & Mental Disease*, 1957, *125*, 73-86.

Wilder, J. *Stimulus and response: The law of initial value*. Bristol: J. Wright, 1967.

Wilder, J. The "law of initial values," a neglected biological law and its significance for research and practice (1931). In S. W. Porges & M. G. H. Coles (Eds.), *Psychophysiology*. Stroudsberg: Dowden, Hutchinson & Row, 1976, pp. 38-46.

Wineman, E. W. Autonomic balance changes during the human menstrual cycle. *Psychophysiology*, 1971, *8*, 1-6.

Appendix I

Bennett, P. B., Ackles, K. N., & Cripps, V. J. Effects of hyperbaric nitrogen and oxygen on auditory evoked responses in man. *Aerospace Medicine*, 1969, *40*, 521-525.

Bergamasco, B. Studio delle modificazioni della responsivita corticale nell' uomo indotte de farmaci ad azione sul SNC. *Sistema Nervoso,* 1966, *18,* 155-164.

Bergamini, L., & Bergamasco, B. *Cortical evoked potentials in man.* Springfield: C. C Thomas, 1967.

Bernstein, A. S. Race and examiner as significant influence on basal skin impedance. *Journal of Personality and Social Psychology,* 1965, *1,* 346-349.

Bevan, J. The human auditory evoked response and CNV in hyperbaric air. *Electroencephalography & Clinical Neurophysiology,* 1971, *30,* 198-204.

Brown, H. *Brain and behavior,* New York: Oxford, 1976.

Buccola, V. A., & Stone, W. J. Effects of jogging and cycling programs on physiological and personality variables in aged men. *The Research Quarterly,* 1974, *46,* 134-139.

Buchsbaum, M. S., Henkin, R. I., & Christiansen, R. L. Age and sex differences in averaged evoked responses in a normal population, with observations on patients with gonadal sysgenesis. *Electroencephalography & Clinical Neurophysiology,* 1974, *37,* 137-144.

Clark, S. C., Marijuana and the cardiovascular system. *Pharmacology, Biochemistry & Behavior,* 1975, *3,* 299-306.

Clark, S. C., Greene, C., Karr, G. W., MacCannell, K. L., & Milstein, S. L. Cardiovascular effects of marijuana in man. *Canadian Journal of Physiology, and Pharmacology,* 1974, *52,* 706-719.

Cole, J. O., Branconnier, R. J., & Martin, G. F. Electroencephalographic and behavioral changes associated with papaverine administration in healthy geriatric subjects. *Journal of the American Geriatrics Society,* 1975, *23,* 295-300.

Corsico, R., Moiziszowica, J., Bursuck, L., & Rovaro, E. Evaluation of the psychotropic effect of etifoxine through pursuit rotor performance and GSR. *Psychopharmacologia,* 1976, *45,* 301-303.

Creutzfeldt, O. D., Arnold, P. M., Becker, D., Langenstein, S., Tirsch, W., Wilhelm, H., & Wuttke, W. EEG changes during spontaneous and controlled menstrual cycles and their correlation with psychological performance. *Electroencephalography & Clinical Neurophysiology,* 1976, *40,* 113-131.

Danaher, B. G., Lichtenstein, E., & Sullivan, J. M. Comparative effects of rapid and normal smoking on heart rate and carboxyhemoglobin. *Journal of Consulting & Clinical Psychology,* 1976, *44,* 556-563.

Dornbush, R. L., Fink, M., & Freedman, A. M. Marijuana, memory and perception. *American Journal of Psychiatry,* 1971, *128,* 194-197.

Ebe, M., Meier-Ewert, K., & Broughton, R. Effects of intravenous diazepam (valium) upon evoked potentials of photosensitive epileptic and normal subjects. *Electroencephalography & Clinical Neurophysiology*, 1969, *27*, 429-435.

Elliott, R., & Thysell, R. A note on smoking and heart rate. *Psychophysiology*, 1968, *5*, 280-283.

Engel, G. L. Mechanisms of fainting. *Journal of Mt. Sinai Hospital, New York*, 1945, *12*, 170-190.

Engel, G. L., & Margolin, S. G. Neuropsychiatric disturbances in internal disease: Metabolic factors and electroencephalographic correlations. *Archives of Internal Medicine*, 1942, *70*, 236-259.

Fischman, M. W., Schuster, C. R., Resnekov, L., Shick, J. F. E., Krasnesor, N. A., Fennell, W., & Freedman, D. X. Cardiovascular and subjective effects of intravenous cocaine administration in humans. *Archives of General Psychiatry*, 1976, *33*, 983-989.

Fisher, L. E., & Kotses, H. Race difference and experimenter race effect in galvanic skin response. *Psychophysiology*, 1973, *10*, 578-582.

Fisher, L. E., & Kotses, H. Experimenter and subject sex effects in the skin conductance response. *Psychophysiology*, 1974, *11*, 191-196.

Forgays, D. G., & McClure, G. N. A direct comparison of the effects of the quiet room and water immersion isolation techniques. *Psychophysiology*, 1974, *11*, 346-349.

Gibbs, F. A., Williams, D., & Gibbs, E. L. Modification of the cortical frequency by spectrum by changes in CO_2, blood sugar and O_2. *Journal of Neurophysiology*, 1940, *3*, 49-58.

Girke, W., Krebs, F. A., & Muller-Oerlinghausen, B. Effects of lithium on electromyographic recordings in man. *International Pharmacopsychiatry*, 1975, *10*, 24-36.

Gooden, B. A., Feinstein, R., & Skutt, H. R. Heart rate responses of scuba divers via ultrasonic telemetry. *Undersea Biomedical Research*, 1975, *2*, 11-19.

Goth, A. *Medical pharmacology*. St. Louis: C. V. Mosby, 1964.

Greenberg, L. M., & Yellin, A. M. Blood pressure and pulse changes in hyperactive children treated with imipramine and methylphenidate. *American Journal of Psychiatry*, 1975, *132*, 1325-1326.

Gross, M. M., Begleiter, H., Tobin, M., & Kissin, B. Changes in auditory evoked response induced by alcohol. *The Journal of Nervous and Mental Disease*, 1966, *143*, 152-156.

Hall, R. A., Rappaport, M., Hopkins, H. K., & Griffin, R. Tobacco and evoked potential. *Science*, 1973, *180*, 212-214.

Hermann, H. T., & Quarton, C. G. Changes in alpha frequency with change in thyroid hormone level. *Electroencephalography & Clinical Neurophysiology*, 1964, *16*, 515-518.

Hoagland, H. Electrical brain waves and temperature. *Science*, 1936, *84*, 139-140.

Hubbard, O., Sunde, D., & Goldensohn, E. S. The EEG in centenarians. *Electroencephalography & Clinical Neurophysiology*, 1976, *40*, 407-417.

Ingvar, D. H., Sjolund, B., & Ardo, A. Correlation between dominant EEG frequency cerebral oxygen uptake and blood flow. *Electroencephalography & Clinical Neurophysiology*, 1976, *41*, 268-276.

Jarvis, M. J., & Lader, M. H. The effects of nitrous oxide on the auditory evoked response in a reaction time task. *Psychopharmacologia*, 1971, *20*, 201-212.

Johnson, L. C., & Corah, N. L. Racial differences in skin resistance, *Science*, 1963, *139*, 766-767.

Johnson, L. C., & Landon, M. M. Eccrine sweat gland activity and racial differences in resting skin conductance. *Psychophysiology*, 1965, *1*, 322-329.

Kay, D. C. Human sleep and EEG through a cycle of methadone dependence. *Electroencephalography & Clinical Neurophysiology*, 1975, *38*, 35-44.

Knott, V. J., & Venables, P. H. EEG alpha correlates of non-smokers, smokers, smoking, and smoking deprivation. *Psychophysiology*, 1977, *14*, 150-156.

Koppell, B. S., Tinklenberg, J. R., & Hollister, L. E. Contingent Negative Variation amplitudes, marijuana and ethanol. *Archives of General Psychiatry*, 1972, *27*, 809-811.

Kopell, B. S., Wittmer, W. K., Lunde, D., Warrick, G., & Edwards, D. Influence of triiodothyronine on selective attention in man as measured by the visual averaged evoked potential. *Psychosomatic Medicine*, *32*, 1970, 495-502.

Korol, B., Bergfeld, G. R., & McLaughlin, L. J. Skin color and autonomic nervous system measures. *Physiology and Behavior*, 1975, *14*, 575-578.

Lewis, E. G., Dustman, R. E., & Beck, E. C. The effects of alcohol on visual and somatosensory evoked responses. *Electroencephalography and Clinical Neurophysiology*, 1970, *28*, 202-205.

Lewis, E. G., Dustman, R. E., Peters, B. A., Straight, R. C., & Beck, E. C. The effects of varying doses of Δ^9–Tetrahydrocannabinol on the human visual and somatosensory evoked response. *Electroencephalography and Clinical Neurophysiology*, 1973, *35*, 347-354.

Low, M. D., Klonoff, H., & Marcus, A. The neurophysiological basis of the marijuana experience. *Canadian Medical Association Journal*, 1973, *108*, 157-164.

Malmo, R. B. Finger-sweat prints in the differentiation of low and high incentive. *Psychophysiology*, 1965, *1*, 231-240.

Malpas, A., Rowan, A. J., Joyce, C.R.B., & Scott, D. F. Persistent behavioral and electroencephalographic changes after single doses of nitrazepam and amylobarbitone sodium. *British Medical Journal,* 1970, *2,* 762-765.

Milner-Brown, H. S., Stein, R. B., & Lee, R. G. Synchronization of human motor units: Possible roles of exercise and supraspinal reflexes. *Electroencephalography & Clinical Neurophysiology,* 1975, *38,* 245-254.

Murphree, H. B. EEG and other evidence for mixed depressant and stimulant actions of alcoholic beverages. *Annals of the New York Academy of Sciences,* 1973, *215,* 325-331.

Nakra, B. R. S., Bond, A. J., & Lader, M. H. Comparative psychotropic effects of metoclopramide and prochlorperazine in normal subjects. *Journal of Clinical Pharmacology,* 1975, *15,* 449-454.

Nishitani, H., & Kooi, K. A. Cerebral evoked responses in hypothyroidism. *Electroencephalography & Clinical Neurophysiology,* 1968, *24,* 554-560.

O'Hanlon, J. F., McGrath, J. J., & McCauley, M. E. Body temperature and temporal acuity. *Journal of Experimental Psychology,* 1974, *102,* 788-794.

Philips, C. The EEG changes associated with smoking. *Psychophysiology,* 1971, *8,* 64-74.

Reite, M., Jackson, D., Cahoon, R. L., & Weil, J. V. Sleep physiology at high altitude. *Electroencephalography & Clinical Neurophysiology,* 1974, *38,* 463-471.

Rhodes, L. E., Obitz, F. W., & Creel, D. Effect of alcohol and task on hemispheric asymmetry of visually evoked potentials in man. *Electroencephalogy & Clinical Neurophysiology,* 1975, *38,* 561-568.

Rodin, E., & Luby, E. Effects of LSD-25 on the EEG and photic evoked responses. *Archives of General Psychiatry,* 1966, *14,* 435-441.

Rostain, J. C., & Charpy, J. P. Effects upon the EEG of psychometric performance during deep dives in helium-oxygen atmosphere. *Electroencephalography & Clinical Neurophysiology,* 1976, *40,* 571-584.

Roth, W. T., Galanter, M., Weingartner, H., Vaughan, T. B., & Wyatt, R. J. Marijuana and synthetic-trans-tetrahydrocannabinol: Some effects on the auditory evoked response and background EEG in humans. *Biological Psychiatry,* 1973, *6,* 221-233.

Sainio, K., Leino, T., Huttunen, M. O., & Ylikahri, R. H. EEG changes during experimental hangover. *Electroencephalography & Clinical Neurophysiology,* 1976, *40,* 535-538.

Salamy, A. The effects of alcohol on the variability of the human evoked potential. *Neuropharmacology*, 1973, *12*, 1103-1107.

Salamy, A., & Williams, H. The effects of alcohol on sensory evoked and spontaneous cerebral potentials in man. *Electroencephalography & Clinical Neurophysiology*, 1973, *35*, 3-11.

Saletu, B., Saletu, M., & Itil, T. Effect of minor and major tranquilizers on somatosensory evoked potentials. *Psychopharmacologia*, 1972, *24*, 347-358.

Smith, C. B., & Strawbridge, P. J. Auditory and visual evoked potentials during hyperoxia. *Electroencephalography & Clinical Neurophysiology*, 1974, *37*, 393-398.

Straumanis, J. J., & Shagass, C. Electrophysiological effects of triiodothyroidism and propranolol. *Psychoparmacologia*, 1976, *46*, 283-288.

Stroebel, C. F. Psychophysiological pharmacology. In N. S. Greenfield & R. A. Sternbach (Eds.), *Handbook of psychophysiology*. New York: Holt, Rinehart, & Winston, 1972, pp. 787-838.

Takahashi, K., & Fujitani, Y. Somatosensory and visual evoked potentials in hypothyroidism. *Electroencephalography & Clinical Neurophysiology*, 1970, *29*, 551-556.

Tecce, J. J. Contingent negative variation (CNV) and psychological processes in man. *Psychological Bulletin*, 1972, *77*, 73-108.

Tecce, J. J., & Cole, J. O. Amphetamine effects in man: Paradoxical drowsiness and lowered electrical brain activity (CNV). *Science*, 1974, *185*, 451-453.

Tecce, J. J., Cole, J. O., Mayer, J., & Lewis, D. C. Barbiturate effects on brain functioning (CNV) and attention performance in normal men. *Psychopharmacology Bulletin*, 1977, *13*, 64-66.

Tecce, J. J., Cole, J. O., & Savignano-Bowman, J. Chlorpromazine effects on brain activity (contingent negative variation) and reaction time in normal women. *Psychopharmacologia*, 1975, *43*, 293-295.

Thiebaut, F., Rohmer, F., & Wackenheim, A. Contribution a l'etude electroencephalographique des syndromes endocriniens. *Electroencephalography & Clinical Neurophysiology*, 1958, *10*, 1-30.

Ulett, J. A., & Itil, T. M. Quantitative EEG in smoking and smoking deprivation. *Science*, 1969, *164*, 969-970.

Vaughan, H. G. The relationship of brain activity to scalp recordings of event-related potentials. In E. Donchin & D. B. Lindsley (Eds.), *Averaged evoked potentials*. Washington, D.C.: NASA, 1969, pp. 45-94.

Vogel, W., Broverman, D. M., & Klaiber, L. EEG responses in regularly menstruating women and in amenorrheic women treated with ovarian hormones. *Science*, 1971, *172*, 388-391.

Vogel, W., Broverman, D. M., Klaiber, E. L., & Kobayasri, Y. EEG driving responses as a function of monamine oxidase. *Electroencephalography & Clinical Neurophysiology*, 1974, *36*, 205-207.

Volavka, J., Levine, R., Feldstein, S., & Fink, M. Short term effects of heroin in man: Is EEG related to behavior? *Archives of General Psychiatry*, 1974, *30*, 677-681.

West, L., & Driver, M. V. Antisocial behavior, barbiturate addiction and associated EEG changes. *British Journal of Psychiatry*, 1974, *125*, 470-471.

Williams, J. G., Jones, J. R., & Williams, B. The chemical control of preoperative anxiety. *Psychophysiology*, 1975, *12*, 46-49.

Appendix III

Cromwell, L., Arditti, M., Weibell, F. J., Pfeiffer, E. A., Steele, B., & Labok, J. A. *Medical instrumentation for health care*, Englewood Cliffs, N.J.: Prentice-Hall, 1976.

Index

Ā. *See* Autonomic balance score Ā.

Accident prevention. *See* Safety, laboratory.

Acetylcholine, 230

Actin filament. *See* Skeletal muscle anatomy.

Action potential of neuron, 19,20; negative after potential, 19, 21; positive after potential, 19, 21; spike potential, 19, 21

Activation theory, 334-340; arousal, 338, 339; ascending reticular activating system (ARAS), 26, 36, 335, 338, 339, 373; induced muscle tension (IMT), 336; inverted U-shaped curve, 335-337; manipulated activation level, 336, 340; neurophysiological bases, 337, 338; unmanipulated activation level, 337; wakefulness, 338, 339

Adenosine diphosphate (ADP), 149

Adaptation and rebound theory, 351, 352

Adenosine triphosphate (ATP), 149

ADP, 149

Affective states. *See* Pupillary response.

Afferent feedback. *See* Stimulus response specificity.

All-or-none principle of neuronal firing, 17

Alpha wave, 26, 27; biofeedback, 305-307, 315-318; definition, 26, 27

Amblyopia, 291

Anger. *See* Heart activity.

Anxiety, 313, 314, 332, 333; autonomic balance score, 332, 333; EMG biofeedback and, 313, 314

Arteries, 262-265

Ascending reticular activating system (ARAS), 25, 26. *See also* Activation theory.

Asthma. *See* Biofeedback applications.

Attention, 51, 52, 106-108, 248-251; contingent negative variation, 71, 72; orienting response, 51, 248-251; signal detection, 52; vigilance, 51, 52, 106, 107

Attitude. *See* Pupillary response.

Auditory evoked potential (AEP), 70, 71

Auditory system testing. *See* Sensory system testing, evoked potential audiometry

Autonomic balance, 330-334; anxiety, 332, 333; cold pressor (CP) test, 329, 333; homeostasis, 333; menstruation, 333; PNS dominance, 331, 332; psychosomatic disorders, 332, 333; SNS dominance, 331, 332

Autonomic balance score Ā, 331-333
Autonomic nervous system (ANS),
9-11, 199, 200, 330-332, 341
Autonomic response specificity, 346
Averaged evoked potential. See
Event-related potentials.
Axon, 14-20

Baroreceptors, 230, 231, 265, 343-
345
Behavior disorders, 296-301; anxiety neurosis and contingent negative variation, 298; anxiety neurosis and electrodermal activity,
299; psychiatric patients and
event-related potential "recovery
functions," 297, 298; psychopathy
and contingent negative variation,
298; psychopathy and electrodermal activity, 300; psychopathy
and electroencephalogram, 299;
schizophrenia and contingent
negative variation, 298; schizophrenia and electrodermal activity, 299, 300; schizophrenia and
electroencephalogram, 299;
schizophrenia and event-related
potential, 296-299
Beta wave. See Electroencephalogram.
Biofeedback, 303-326; alpha wave,
305-307, 315-318; blood pressure
(BP), 320-323; blood volume,
325, 326; compared to relaxation
procedures, 308; cephalic vasomotor response (CVMR), 325,
326; electroencelphalogram
(EEG), 315-318; electromyogram
(EMG), 308-315; equipment
schematic, 306; heart activity,
318-320; procedure, 305-307;
skin temperature, 323-325
Biofeedback applications, 308-326;
anxiety, 313, 314; asthma, 314;
epilepsy, 315-317; "foot drop,"
311, 312; hyperactivity, 315; hy-

pertension, 320-323; incontinence,
312, 313; migraine, 324-326;
neuromuscular disorder, 311-313;
pain, chronic, 317-318; premature
ventricular contraction, 318, 319;
Raynaud's disease, 323, 324; relaxation, 313, 314; stuttering, 310,
311; tachycardia, 319; tension
headache, 308-310; torticollis, 312
Bipolar recording, 33
Bite board, 215
Blood pressure, 262-276, 320-323;
aggression, 273; biofeedback,
320-323; detection of deception,
286, 287, 383; epinephrine, 385;
exercise effects, 385; frustration,
272, 273; hypertension, 320-323,
385; imipramine, 385; instrumental conditioning, 274-276; intelligence test performance, 272;
mental load, 271, 272; methylphenidate, 385; pentobarbital
sodium, 384, 385; phenobarbital,
385; regulation of, 265, 320-323;
reserpine, 384-385
Blood pressure measurement, 266-
268; constant cuff pressure, 267;
pulse wave velocity, 268; sphygmomanometer, 266, 267; ultrasonic, 268
Blood vessels, 262-265; arteries,
262, 263; arterioles, 262, 263;
capillaries, 263, 264; innervation,
263, 264; veins, 263, 264
Blood volume, 262, 276-280, 325,
326; biofeedback, 325, 326; classical conditioning, 280; defensive
response, 278, 352, 353; erotic
fantasies, 277, 278; erotic stimuli,
277, 278; genital blood volume,
276-278; habituation, 279; instrumental conditioning, 280; intensity of stimulus, 279; masturbation, 277, 278; orienting response,
278-280, 352, 353; pornographic
stimuli, 277; regulation of, 266;
rise time of stimuli, 279; romantic

stimuli, 278; sexual response, 276-278

Blood volume measurement, 268-271; electrical impedance, 269; hydraulic system, 269; penile strain gauge, 270, 271; photo-electric system, 269; plethysmo-graph, 268, 269; pneumatic system, 269; vaginal photoplethys-mograph, 270

Brain electrical activity, source of, 13, 14

Brain stem potential, 72, 294-296

Brain structures, 22-26; brain stem, 22, 23; cerebellum, 22, 23; cere-brum, 22, 23

Cannon-Bard theory, 5

Cardiac cycle. See Heart activity.

Cardiac-somatic hypothesis, 348-351; active coping, 350; classical aversive conditioning, 349; coping vs. no coping, 350; irrelevant somatic activities, 348, 349; pas-sive coping, 350; preparatory ac-tivities, 348, 349; reaction time, 348, 349; stressful events, 349-351

Cardiotachometer, 236

Cardiovascular measures, 231-236, 266-271

Cardiovascular system, 227-231, 262-266

Carotid sinus reflex. See Heart activity.

Central nervous system, 9-11, 337-340, 364, 365

Cerebrum, 22-25; fissure of Rolando (central sulcus), 22, 24; fissure of Sylvius (lateral sulcus), 22, 24; frontal lobe, 22, 24; occipital lobe, 22, 24; parietal lobe, 22, 24; post-central cortex, 22, 24; precentral cortex, 22, 24; temporal lobe, 22, 24

Chronaxy. See Neuron.

Classical conditioning. See Blood volume, Electroencephalogram,

Electromyogram, Event-related potentials, Heart activity.

CNS. See Central Nervous system.

CNV. See Contingent negative variation.

Color defects, 291-292; deutera-nopia, 292; protanopia, 292; tritanopia, 292

Conditioned response (CR), 195-197

Conditioned stimulus (CS), 195-197

Constant cuff pressure. See Blood pressure measurement.

Contingent negative variation (CNV), 71-74, 78, 79, 122-128, 344, 368-370, 374; distraction-attention hypothesis, 124, 125; effort, 125, 126; measurement, 78, 79; modality of stimulus, 126; reaction time, 124; relation to P300, 142, 143; sexual preference, 127; uncertainty, 127

Corpus callosum, 25, 26

Cortical evoked potentials. See Event-related potentials.

Deception, detection of, 281-288; card test, 283; control question test, 284; field studies, 282, 285; guilty knowledge test, 283, 285; Keeler polygraph, 283; laboratory studies, 286-288; peak of tension test, 284; physiological measures used, 281-288; psychopathy and lie detection, 285; relevant-irrelevant question test, 284; re-liability of polygraph tests, 284; validity of polygraph tests, 283, 284

Defensive response (DR). See Blood volume, Heart activity.

Delta wave. See Electroencephalo-gram.

Dendrite, 14-16

Depolarization, 19

Dermographic persistence, 331

Diastole, 230, 232, 272

Dilation of pupil, 199-202
Directional fractionation, 341-343
Down's syndrome, 292, 293
Dreaming, 60, 61, 63
Drug effects. *See* Blood pressure,
Electrodermal activity, Electro-
encephalogram, Electromyogram,
Event-related potentials, Eye
movements, Heart activity, Pupil-
lary response.

Eccrine sweat gland, 174, 175
ECG. *See* Electrocardiogram.
EDA. *See* Electrodermal activity.
EEG. *See* Electroencephalogram.
Electrocardiogram (ECG), 231-237
Electrodermal activity (EDA), 171-
198; ACTH effects, 377; affective
stimuli, 188-190; aggression, 189;
classical conditioning, 196, 197;
data analysis, 183, 184; dextroamphetamine, 377; electrodermal
recovery rate, 190, 191; emotional
expression, 190; erotic stimuli,
189, 190; etifoxine, 377; experimental situation, 379, 380; experimenter effects, 378, 379; instrumental conditioning, 197, 198;
learning, 187, 188; measurement,
179-183; motivation, 190, 191;
orienting response, 192-195; progesterone, 377; racial differences,
378, 379; reaction time, 184-186,
337, 338; schizophrenia, 299, 300;
signal detection, 185, 186, 191,
192; skin conductance level, 177-
179; skin conductance response,
177-179; skin potential level, 177,
178; skin potential response, 177,
178; skin resistance level, 177,
179; skin resistance response, 177,
178
Electroencephalogram (EEG), 26-
69; activation of EEG, 36; aftereffects of stimulus, 50; alcohol,
360, 361; alpha wave, 26, 27,
305-307; altitude effects, 366;
amylobarbitone, 359; asymmetry,
43-45; attention, 51, 52; average
alpha frequency, 38; beta wave,
28; biofeedback, 305-307, 315-
318; body temperature, 366, 367;
cerebral blood flow, 364, 365;
classical conditioning, 54, 55;
color of stimuli, 50; complexity of
stimuli, 49; cortisone, 362; delta
wave, 28, 59-61; deprivation of
sleep, 67-69; depth of sleep and
capacity to respond, 61-63; discrimination of stimuli, 53, 54;
dreaming, 60, 61, 63; EEG half
waves, 38; EEG period, 37, 38;
estrogen, 363; helium-oxygen mix-
tures, 365; hemispheric asymmetry as function of task, 43-45;
heroin, 358, 359; hypnosis, 46,
47; imagery, 46, 47; insomnia, 68,
69; intelligence, 39-43; isocarboxazid, 363; kappa wave, 28;
k-complex, 26, 47, 64; lambda
wave, 28; learning, sleep, 63-65;
lysergic acid diethylamide
(LSD), 356, 357; marijuana, 357,
358; meaningfulness of stimuli,
62, 63; measurement, 29-34, 387-
388; meditation, 47; methadone,
358, 359; metoclopromide, 359,
360; monoamine oxidase (MAO),
363; mu wave, 29; musical task,
45; nicotine, 361, 362; nitrazepam, 359; operant conditioning,
55-58; oxygen effects, 364, 365;
pre-sleep activities and sleeping
EEG, 66, 67; prochlorperazine,
359, 360; progesterone, 363; reaction time, 35-38; schizophrenia,
299; signal detection, 51, 52;
sleep stages, 61; spatial performance, 43, 44; spectral analysis,
42; structuring of stimuli, 53;
theta wave, 28, 56; thyroxin, 362;
verbal performance, 43-45; verticality, rod & frame test, 53; vigi-

lance, 51, 52; visuomotor performance, 38, 39

Electromyogram (EMG), 144-172; biofeedback, 308-315; classical conditioning, 167; concept identification, 168; exercise, 376, 377; fatigue, 163-165; grip strength and EMG, 151, 152; instrumental conditioning, 165-167; integrated EMG recordings, 153, 170; lithium, 376; measurement, 150-157; motivated performance, 169-171; muscle action potential, 157; probability success, 168; problem solving, 167, 168; reaction time, 158-160, 338; reading improvement, 162; sleep, 169, 170; subvocal speech, 161-163; tracking, 160, 161, 337, 347

EMG. See Electromyogram.

Event-related potentials (ERP), 70-143; acceleration evoked potential, 105, 196; alcohol, 370-373; amphetamine, 369; attention, 106-108; auditory evoked potential, 71; barbiturates, 368, 369; Bereitshaftspotential. See readiness potential; bisensory stimulation, 81-84; brain stem potentials, 72; chlorpromazine, 367, 368; classical conditioning, 100, 101; color perception, 117-120; contingent negative variation, 71, 74, 78, 79, 122-128, 129, 130, 344, 368-370, 374; decision making. See P300; diazepam, 367, 368; discrimination. See P300; "far-field" potential, 72; frequency of stimulation, 103, 104; hemispheric asymmetries, 84-89; hyperbaric conditions, 373, 374; hypnosis, 101, 102; intelligence, 92-95; intensity of stimulation, 103; language, 97-99; learning, 100, 101; lithium, 367; long latency potential. See P300; marijuana, 369, 370; masking (vis-

ual), 113-117; meaning, 95, 96; measurement, 72-79; motion, 120, 121; motor potentials, 72-74, 82, 83; nicotine, 371, 373; nitrous oxide, 373; origin of ERPs, 72-74; oxygen, 373, 374; pain, 105; pentobarbital, 368; perception (pattern, size, orientation), 108-111; phenobarbital, 368, 369; quantification, 77, 78; reaction time, 80-82; readiness potential (RP), 71, 74, 79, 128-130; schizophrenia, 296-299; sensory evoked potential, 70; sleep and event-related potentials, 89-91; smell evoked potential, 70, 104; somatosensory evoked potential, 71; taste evoked potential, 104, 105; thyroxin, 374, 375; visual evoked potential, 71, 75, 76

Evoked potential audiometry. See Sensory system testing.

Eye movements, 210-226, 381 chlorpromazine, 381; diazepam, 381; electrooculography (EOG), 212-215; involuntary eye movement, 211; lateral eye movement and hemispheric dominance, 218, 219; learning, 217; measurement, 212-215; Muller-Lyer illusion, 225; Oppel-Kundt illusion, 225, 226; pattern recognition and discrimination, 223, 224; pictorial examination, 223, 224; problem solving, 217-219; reading, 219, 220; rebound illusion, 226; scan paths, 223, 224; sodium secobarbital, 381; types of movement, 211, 212; vigilance, 221, 301, 302; visual search, 220- 222; voluntary eye movement, 211

Eye muscles, 210, 211; cortical control, 211; innervation, 210

Fear, 250, 253-255, 282, 352; detection of deception, 282; physiological difference from anger,

Fear (*Cont.*)
253; of snakes, 254; of spiders, 254, 352
Féré effect, 173
Fillmore, M., 386
Frontal lobe, 24
Functional localization in brain, 22-24; Brodmann numbering system, 22, 24

Galvanic skin response, 173
Guilty knowledge test. See Deception, detection of.

Heart activity, 227-261; anger, 253; atria, left and right, 227-229; atrioventricular (A-V) node, 228, 229; biofeedback, 318-320; cardiac control, 228-231; cardiac cycle, 231, 232, 239, 240, 344; carotid sinus reflex, 230, 231; classical conditioning, 256-258; cocaine, 383; competition, 255, 256; complex motor activity, 241; defensive response, 248-250; digitalis, 382; fear, 250, 253-255, frustration, 253, 254; heart period, 235, 236; imagery and thoughts, 244, 245; intake-rejection hypothesis, 242, 243; instrumental conditioning, 258-261; learning, 241, 242; marijuana, 383; measurement, 231-237; meditation, 244; motivation, 255, 256; nicotine, 382, 383; nitroglycerin, 382; orienting response, 248-250; perceptual thresholds, 245, 246; physiological cost of stress (demanding task), 352; premature ventricular contraction (PVC). See Biofeedback; problem solving, 242, 243; reaction time, 238-240; schizophrenia, 300; scuba diving, 384; stimulus significance, 246-248; stress, 251-253; tachycardia. See Biofeedback; ventricles, left and right,

227-230; water submersion, 383, 384
Hemispheric asymmetry. See Electroencephalogram, Event-related potentials.
Hypertension. See Blood pressure.
Hypnosis. See Electroencephalogram, Event-related potentials.

Individual response specificity, 345-348; autonomic response specificity, 346; consistency of physiological response hierarchy, 347, 348; symptom specificity, 346
Inion, 30-32
Instrumental conditioning. See Electroencephalogram, Electrodermal activity.
Intake-rejection hypothesis. See Stimulus response specificity.
Integrated EMG recordings. See Electromyogram.
Intelligence. See Electroencephalogram, Event-related potentials.
Inverted-U hypothesis. See Activation theory.

James-Lange theory, 5

Keeler polygraph, 283
Korotkoff sounds, 267

Lateral eye movement (LEM), 218, 219
Law of initial values, 328-330
Learning. See Electrodermal activity, Electroencephalogram, Electromyogram, Event-related potentials, Eye movement, Heart activity, Pupillary response.
Lie detection (LD). See Deception, detection of.

MAP (muscle action potential). See Electromyogram.
Marijuana. See Drug effects.

Meditation. *See* Electroencephalogram.
Menstrual cycle, 362-364
Migraine headache, 324-326
Monopolar recording, 29-33
Motor unit. *See* Skeletal muscle contraction.
Muscle, 144-150; fatigue, 150; fiber, 146, 147; hypertrophy, 150
Muscle action potential. *See* Electromyogram.
Music effects on electrodermal activity, 188, 189; effects on heart activity, 188, 189

Nasion, 30-32
Neocortex. *See* Cerebrum.
Nerve impulse, 16-21
Nervous system, 7-11; autonomic, 9-11; central, 9-11, 14-26; extrapyramidal motor system, 145; organization of, 10; peripheral, 9-11; pyramidal motor systems, 144
Nervous system disorders, 290, 294-296; brain damage and somatosensory evoked potentials, 296; brain death and event-related potentials, 294; epilepsy and visual evoked potentials, 294; neuromuscular disorders, EMG biofeedback and, 311-313
Neuron, 13-21; after potentials, 19-21; all-or-none law, 17; chronaxy of, 17; depolarization, 19; ionic mechanisms, 19, 20; neurilemma, 15, 16; refractory periods, 21; resting potential, 19; rheobase of, 17; types, 14, 15
Norepinephrine, 230

Occipital cortex, 24
Ohmmeter. *See* Recording system, Electroencephalogram.
Operant conditioning. *See* Instrumental conditioning.

Orienting and defensive response theory, 352, 353
Orienting response (OR). *See* Blood volume, Electrodermal activity, Heart activity, P300, Orienting and defensive response theory.
Oscilloscope, 306

P300, 130-143; attention, 135-139; decision making, 131-133; detection of stimuli, 140, 141; discrimination, 141, 142; emitted and evoked P300s, 140; orienting response, 139, 140; probability of stimulus occurrence, 133-135; relation to CNV, 142, 143
Parasympathetic nervous system, 9-11, 199, 331-334, 351
Parietal lobe, 24
Peak of tension test. *See* Deception, detection of.
Period analysis, 37, 38
Photic driving, 362, 363
Photoplethysmography. *See* Blood volume measurement.
Physiological pschology, discipline of, 6, 7
Placebo, 356
Plethysmograph. *See* Blood volume measurement.
PNS. *See* Parasympathetic nervous system.
Polygraph, 283-287
Psychopathy, 285, 298, 300
Psychophysiology, discipline of, 6, 7
Pulse wave velocity. *See* Blood pressure measurement.
Pupillary response, 199-210; affective states, 205-207; atropine, 380; attitude, 207; digit span and cognitive load, 204, 208, 209; fatigue effects, 202; heroin, 380; homatropine, 380, 381; imagery, 204, 205; information processing, 207-209; iris musculature, 199, 200; latency of, 200; learning, 205; long-term memory, 204;

Pupillary response (*Cont.*)
mental effort, 203-205; mental
multiplication, 203, 204; parasympathetic nervous system control, 199, 200; pilocarpine, 380;
short-term memory, 208, 209; signal detection, 209, 210; sympathetic nervous system control,
199, 200
Pupillary response measurement,
200-202; Hess technique, 201;
Lowenstein pupillograph, 201;
Whittaker pupillometer, 201, 202;

Rapid eye movement (REM), 60-63
Raynaud's disease, 323, 324
Reaction time task, 35, 36
Readiness potential (Bereitschaftspotential), 128-130; relation to
CNV, 129, 130; reward effects,
130; scalp distribution, 130; voluntary movement, 128, 129
Recording system, electroencephalogram, 387, 388; amplification,
387; filtering, 387; FM tape recording system, 388; grounding,
388; impedance, 387; ohm meter,
387, 388; paper speed, 387;
shielded chamber, 388
Retardation, mental, 292, 293
REM, 60-63
Rheobase. *See* Neuron.
R wave, electrocardiogram, 231-234

Saccadic movement, 211
Safety, laboratory, 389-391
Salivation, 281, 329; law of initial
value, 329
Schizophrenia. *See* Electrodermal
activity, Electroencephalogram,
Event-related potentials, Heart
activity.
Sensory system testing, 288-291;
AEPs to study hearing deficits,
288-290; color blindness detec-
tion, 291, 292; detection of lesions

in visual system using VEPs, 290,
291; evoked potential audiometry,
288, 289; visual acuity measurement with VEPs, 291
Sexual arousal, 190, 276-278
Sinoatrial (S-A) node, 228-230
Skeletal muscle anatomy, 146-148
actin filament, 146, 147; fasciculus, 146, 147; muscle fiber, 146;
myofibril, 146; sarcomere, 146
Skeletal muscle contraction, 145-
150; action potential, 148; motor
unit, 148, 149; myosin fibrils,
146, 147; neuromuscular junction,
149
Skin, 174, 175; stratum corneum,
174; stratum germinativum, 174;
stratum granulosum, 174; stratum
lucidum, 174; stratum spinosum,
174
Skin, anatomy of, 174-177; dermis,
174, 175; eccrine sweat gland,
174, 175
Skin conductance level (SCL). *See*
Electrodermal activity.
Skin conductance response (SCR).
See Electrodermal activity.
Skin function, 174-177; protective,
176; thermoregulatory, 176, 177
Skin potential level. *See* Electroder-
mal activity.
Skin potential response (SPR). *See*
Electrodermal activity.
Skin resistance level. *See* Electro-
dermal activity.
Skin resistance response (SRR). *See*
Electrodermal activity.
Sleep, 58-69, 89-91, 169, 170; depri-
vation, 67-69; stages, 61
Somatic nervous system, 9-11
Somatosensory cortex, 24
Somatosensory evoked potential, 71
Sphygmomanometer. *See* Blood
pressure measurement.
Stimulus response specificity, 340-
345; afferent feedback, 343-345;
attention, 341, 345; baroreceptors,

343-345; cardiac acceleration, 341, 344, 345; cardiac deceleration, 341-345; cognitive activities, 341-343; directional fractionation of response, 341-343, 345; intake-rejection hypothesis, 343-345; perceptual activities, 341; sensori-motor performance, 344, 345
Sympathetic nervous system (SNS), 9-11, 199, 230, 231, 263, 264, 325, 331-334, 349-351
Synapse, 15, 17-20
Systole, 230, 232

Tarchanoff effect, 173
Thalamus, 25, 26; projections to cortex, 25, 26
Theta wave. See Electroencephalogram.
Trephining, 4

Ultrasonic. See Blood pressure measurement.
Unconditioned stimulus (UCS), 195 196

Vagus nerve, 230
Vasoconstriction, 264, 266, 270
Vasodilation, 264, 266
Ventricles of brain, 23-25
Vigilance, 51, 52, 191, 192, 301, 302

Wechsler Adult Intelligence Scale (WAIS), 41
Wechsler Intelligence Scale for Children (WISC), 43
Wechsler Preschool and Primary Scale of Intelligence (WPPSI), 94

Copyrights and Acknowledgments

Fig. 1-1   Copyright © 1978 by Gahan Wilson. Reprinted by permission.

Fig. 2-1   From C. R. Noback and R. J. Demarest. *The Human Nervous System*. Copyright © 1975, McGraw Hill Publishing Company. Reprinted by permission.

Fig. 2-2   From C. R. Noback and R. J. Demarest. *The Human Nervous System*. Copyright © 1975, McGraw Hill Publishing Company. Reprinted by permission.

Fig. 2-3   From C. R. Noback and R. J. Demarest. *The Human Nervous System*. Copyright © 1975, McGraw Hill Publishing Company. Reprinted by permission.

Fig. 2-5   Modified from C. R. Noback and R. J. Demarest. *The Human Nervous System*. Copyright © 1975, McGraw Hill Publishing Company. Reprinted by permission.

Fig. 2-6   Modified from C. R. Noback and R. J. Demarest. *The Human Nervous System*. Copyright © 1975, McGraw Hill Publishing Company. Reprinted by permission.

Fig. 2-7   From S. P. Grossman. *Essentials of physiological psychology*. New York: Wiley, 1973, as taken from H. H. Jasper, "Electroencephalography" in W. Penfield & T. C. Erickson, *Epilepsy and Cerebral Localization*. Springfield: C. C. Thomas, 1941.

Fig. 2-9   Adapted from E. Callaway. *Brain Electrical Potentials and Individual Psychological Differences*. New York: Grune & Stratton, 1975. Reprinted by permission.

Fig. 4-1   From F. Snyder and J. Scott. "The psychophysiology of sleep" in N. S. Greenfield and R. A. Sternbach (Eds.), *Handbook of Psychophysiology*. Copyright © 1972 by Holt, Rinehart & Winston. Reprinted by permission of Holt, Rinehart & Winston.

Fig. 5-1   From H. G. Vaughan. "The relationship of brain activity to scalp recordings of event-related potentials" in E. Donchin & D. B. Lindsley (Eds.), *Average Evoked Potentials*. Washington, D.C.: NASA, 1969. Reprinted by permission.

Fig. 5-2   Left side of figure is from J. J. Teece. "Contingent negative varia-